243-66
242-308
321-325

MIDDLE ENGLISH LYRICS

AUTHORITATIVE TEXTS
CRITICAL AND HISTORICAL BACKGROUNDS
PERSPECTIVES ON SIX POEMS

➤➤ A NORTON CRITICAL EDITION ◄◄

MIDDLE ENGLISH LYRICS

AUTHORITATIVE TEXTS
CRITICAL AND HISTORICAL BACKGROUNDS
PERSPECTIVES ON SIX POEMS

➤➤◄◄

Selected and Edited by

MAXWELL S. LURIA
TEMPLE UNIVERSITY

RICHARD L. HOFFMAN
VIRGINIA POLYTECHNIC INSTITUTE
AND STATE UNIVERSITY

W · W · NORTON & COMPANY

New York · London

The Harley Lyrics, edited by G. L. Brook (Manchester University Press, 4th edition, 1968). Selections used by permission of the publisher.

English Lyrics of the Thirteenth Century, edited by Carleton Brown, 1932; *Religious Lyrics of the Fourteenth Century,* edited by Carleton Brown, 2nd edition (corrected) revised by G. V. Smithers, 1957; *Religious Lyrics of the Fifteenth Century,* edited by Carleton Brown, 1939; *Secular Lyrics of the Fourteenth and Fifteenth Centuries,* edited by R. H. Robbins, 2nd edition, 1955; *The Early English Carols,* edited by Richard Leighton Greene, 1935. Selections used by permission of The Clarendon Press, Oxford.

The Poems of William Dunbar, edited by W. Mackay Mackenzie (reprinted 1960, Faber and Faber Ltd.). Selections used by permission of the publisher.

The Works of Geoffrey Chaucer, edited by F. N. Robinson (Houghton Mifflin Company, 2nd edition, 1957). Selections used by permission of the publisher. *The Poems and Fables of Robert Henryson, Schoolmaster of Dunfermline,* edited by H. Harvey Wood (2d edition, 1958), Oliver and Boyd, Edinburgh; Barnes and Noble, New York. Selection used by permission of Oliver and Boyd.

W. W. Norton & Company, Inc., 500 Fifth Avenue, New York, N.Y. 10110

Library of Congress Cataloging in Publication Data

Luria, Maxwell, 1932–   comp.
   Middle English lyrics.

   (A Norton critical edition)
   Bibliography: p.
   1. English poetry—Middle English (1100–1500)
2. English poetry—Middle English (1100–1500)—
History and criticism. 3. Lyric poetry. I. Hoffman.
Richard Lester, joint comp. II. Title.
PR1187.L8   821'.04   73–19768
ISBN 0-393-04379-7
ISBN 0-393-09338-7 {pbk.}

PRINTED IN THE UNITED STATES OF AMERICA

7 8 9 0

In memory of our fathers

Samuel Jerome Luria
1892–1970
and
Lester Samuel Hoffman
1908–1972

Contents

Preface

The delightful treasures of Middle English lyric are still, for some reason, *terra incognita* to the general reader. More surprisingly, they are often neglected or disdained even by students of medieval literature. Although the splendid achievements of *dolce stil nuovo*, of troubadour and goliard and Minnesinger, are widely appreciated and readily accessible in excellent translations,[1] most of their admirers appear to command little more of the native tradition than the charming but overworked "Sumer is icumen in."

In fact, the Middle English lyric at its finest has a lapidary concentration of statement and a controlled richness of tone which, once apprehended, are not easily forgotten:

> All night by the rose, rose,
> All night by the rose I lay;
> Darf ich nought the rose stele,
> And yet ich bar the flour away.

In their copiousness and variety, too, these poems—songs of love and death, God and nature, the pleasures of the table and the fears of damnation, the ebullience of youth and the melancholy of old age—form one of the great bodies of lyric verse in world literature.[2]

The editorial labors of Carleton Brown, Rossell Hope Robbins, G. L. Brook, and others, over a period of forty years, have provided scholars with printed texts of most of the contents of the extant manuscripts. These editions, which are listed in our Select Bibliography (pp. 351–352), vary considerably with respect to comprehensiveness and adequacy of presentation; and a new edition, with variants, of the complete corpus of lyrics, based on modern editorial procedures, remains a *desideratum*. These volumes have, however, indispensably provided us with the texts offered here, and we are grateful for this pioneering work, as, indeed, for the small but growing body of explicatory criticism, which we have also found useful. Among the few earlier anthologies of Middle English lyric, that of

---

1. For bibliographical information, see Peter Dronke, *The Medieval Lyric* (New York, 1969), pp. 241 ff.
2. The term "lyric" in the present context is merely approximate, and in fact unhistorical: the earliest use of the word recorded in the OED is by Sidney, in 1581. Most "lyric" verse of the Middle Ages is radically unlike the poetry thus styled in more recent centuries, and criticism must develop sophisticated concepts for dealing with the differences. See D. W. Robertson, Jr., "Some Observations on Method in Literary Studies," *New Literary History*, 1 (1969–1970), 21–33; Stephen Manning, *Wisdom and Number* (Lincoln, Nebraska, 1962), Preface.

R. T. Davies (London, 1963) is the best, and we have profited from his admirable notes and glosses.

The present collection is larger, by nearly sixty poems, than any other anthology devoted exclusively to the lyric and is the only one which includes all thirty-one English lyrics in MS. Harley 2253, all the verses by Friar Herebert printed in Brown XIV, the long and justly famous debate poem called "The Thrush and the Nightingale" (no. 59), and virtually all the poems of any consequence given by Professor Robbins in his important and charming volume of *Secular Lyrics*. We have wished to offer up a literary feast as well as a scholarly anthology, and we have consequently held artistic merit rather than philological or historical significance to be our chief touchstone for inclusion. Most of the best Middle English lyric verse, as it happens, is anonymous;[3] but we have not, in any case, felt obliged to include "representative" selections by identified authors, such as Lydgate or Audelay, whose lyric production seems to us decidedly less interesting than the verse we have chosen. Such a late poet as Skelton, though arguably worthy of inclusion, was omitted to make room for less accessible authors. If the Scottish "makers" Dunbar and Henryson are represented by a thinner sheaf of poems than they deserve, it is for the same reason. Even Chaucer himself makes but a modest appearance in our pages. Fortunately, the work of these late medieval masters, unlike most of the pieces in this book, is available to the reader in adequate, and easily comprehensible, editions.[4]

Any editor of a Middle English text must wrestle with the problem of where his respect for manuscript authority ought to give way to consideration for his reader's ease. We have duly wrestled and are content, though scarcely complacent, with our solution. We have been guided in this delicate matter by our primary desire to reveal the poems *as poems* to readers who are not necessarily specialists in Middle English—to make them as "available" as possible —yet without doing violence to their original forms. We have, therefore, scrupulously respected their substantive integrity, while clearing away some of the orthographical and other impediments to appreciation. We have regularly modernized ð, þ, ȝ and ƿ; and, wherever necessary, we have sought to make our text readable by substituting genuine but recognizable Middle English spellings for unrecognizable or grotesque ones. Similar considerations have governed our treatment of punctuation, capitalization, and typography.

---

3. In this collection, wherever the author of a poem is known, we have given his name and dates after the text.
4. F. N. Robinson, ed., *The Works of Geoffrey Chaucer*, second ed. (Boston, 1957); W. M. Mackenzie, ed., *The Poems of William Dunbar* (London, 1932; reprinted 1960); H. H. Wood, ed., *The Poems of Robert Henryson* (Edinburgh and London, 1933; second ed., 1958); Philip Henderson, ed., *The Complete Poems of John Skelton*, third ed. (London, 1959).

Consistency has usually had to surrender to context, and the exigencies of rime and meaning have often helped determine our approach to word endings. The result, of course, will not satisfy those philological scholars who require diplomatic texts, and such will have recourse to the standard editions. Other readers, we hope, will not miss the chaos and caprice of medieval scribal practice, which is often as distracting as it is picturesque. We have tried, at all events, to make these poems readable without betraying their authenticity.[5]

Spanning four centuries and embodying several Middle English dialects, these poems vary widely in difficulty of language. We have attempted to gloss every unfamiliar or misleading word or phrase on its first appearance in each poem; but some words inevitably remain refractory. In particular, the poems in Harley 2253 contain language which has daunted all previous editors, and we cannot, alas, claim to have cut through every knot in these obscure texts.

A word is in order with regard to our arrangement and presentation of the poems, which (in one necessary sense) may seem as arbitrary as the selections themselves. We have sedulously, though perhaps not merely willfully, avoided the conventional classification of "religious" and "secular." In our view, this distinction, which has become commonplace since the editions of Brown and Robbins, more justly expresses modern culture than medieval; and, in fact, most of the manuscript collections embrace both sorts of poem.[6] To be sure, some poems are manifestly "religious" in theme and substance, and some are equally "unreligious," in that they lack a manifest religious content. Both sorts will be found in this collection, together with a rather larger number of poems which are both "religious" *and* "secular," or, rather, neither one nor the other, reflecting the characteristic medieval apprehension of man's life on a middle-earth shadowed by the Tower of Truth.[7] "Religious and secular," then, seems simplistic, and we have preferred to arrange the poems by subject, thus allowing the reader to discover for himself those peculiarly medieval modulations of sensibility which these poems embody.

For much the same reasons—departing again from the practice of Brown and Robbins—we have declined to contrive titles for these poems. Nearly all of them are untitled in the manuscripts, and it makes a difference whether one apprehends a short literary composition directly or through the prism of a title. We have preferred to give our readers the more characteristically medieval experience.

One of the most useful features of the volume should be the section of critical materials. Some twenty-five of the poems in the

5. We have made silently a very few textual emendations.
6. For example, Harley 2253; cf. G. L. Brook, ed., *The Harley Lyrics*, second ed. (Manchester, 1956), Introduction.

7. Cf. Professor Robertson's comment on "Mirie it is while sumer ilast" in *The Literature of Medieval England* (New York, 1970), p. 347.

collection are discussed here, at varying length, and the following chart will facilitate cross-reference:

Poem   Critical Discussion

"At a springe-well under a thorn" (192) 261–262, 324
"Brid one brere" (22) 264–265
"Erthe tok of erthe" (242) 307–308
"Foweles in the frith" (6) 263–264, 278–279, 319–321
"Gold and all this werldes win" (15) 262
"Heven it es a riche ture" (180) 290
"I sike when I singe" (228) 258
"I sing of a maiden" (181) 289, 325–349
"Ichot a burde in a bour ase beryl so
    bright" (26) 271
"Ichot a burde in boure bright" (33) 270
"If man him bithoghte" (233) 301–302
"In a frith as I con fare fremede" (30) 313–317
"It wes upon a Shere Thorsday" (203) 259–261
"Jentil butler, *bel ami*" (160) 284
"Lenten is come with love to toune" (4) 271–272
"Maiden in the mor lay" (138) 321–325
"Now goth sonne under wod" (190) 256–257, 317–319
"O mestress, why" (45) 286–287
"Sumer is icumen in" (3) 311–313
"Whanne mine eyhnen misten" (234) 303–305
"When the turuf is thy tour" (232) 261, 285, 305–307
"With longing I am lad" (28) 265
"With paciens thou hast us fedde" (146) 283
"Wrecche mon, why artou proud" (239) 282
"Yung men, I warne you everichon" (68) 284

Middle English spellings in the critical texts are not always the same as in the poems, but we have thought it best to leave them as we found them, relying upon the reader to make the appropriate identifications.

Princeton, August 1974   M.S.L.
                                                     R.L.H.

Richard Hoffman's death in 1981, at forty-four, took from us a scholar and teacher of conspicuous excellence and great promise. The surviving editor is better able than most to affirm that he was no less distinguished as a collaborator and friend. This new printing of *Middle English Lyrics*, in which some minor errors have been corrected but the content remains unchanged, may help keep in memory a little longer his fine discrimination and genuine scholarship.

Philadelphia, October 1986   M.L.

The Poems

I

Worldes bliss

I

Worldes bliss ne last no throwe.[1]
It wit° and wend° awey anon;   *departs / goes*
The lenger° that ich° it iknowe,   *longer / I*
The lasse° ic° finde pris° theron.   *less / I / value*
For all it is imeind° wid care,   *mingled*
Mid sorewe and wid evel fare;
And at the laste, pouere° and bare   *poor*
It let° mon, when it ginnet° gon.°   *abandons / begins / to go*
All the blisse this here and there
Bilouketh° at ende wop° and mon.°   *encompasses / weeping / moaning*

All shall gon that here mon° owet,°   *man / owns*
All it shall wenden to nout;°   *nought*
The mon that here no good ne sowet,°   *sows*
When other repen, he worth bikakt.[2]
Thenk, mon, forthy,° whil thu havest mikte,°   *therefore / might*
That thu thine gultes° here arikte,°   *guilts / set right*
And worche good by day and nikte,
Ar then thu be of lisse ilakt.[3]
Thu nost wanne Crist ure drikte
Thee asket that he havet bitakt.[4]

All the blisse of thisse life
Thu shalt, mon, enden in wep:°   *weeping*
Of huse and home and child and wife.
Sely° mon, tak therof kep!°   *unthinking / heed*
For thu shalt all beleven° here   *leave behind*
The eykte° whereof louerd° thu were;   *property / lord*

1. World's bliss lasts only a short time.
2. When others reap, he will be beguiled.
3. Before you are deprived of joy.
4. You do not know when Christ Our Lord/ Will ask you for that which He has entrusted to you.

"Worldes bliss ne last no throwe" (poem 1) as it appears in a thirteenth-century manuscript at Oxford University (MS. Rawl. G. 18, now Bodleian 14751, f. 105ᵇ). The text of this piece, together with its music, appears also in a manuscript in the British Museum (MS. Arundel 248). Reproduced by permission of the Bodleian Library, Oxford.

When thu list,° mon, upon bere,°   *lie / bier*
And slepest a swithe° druye° slep,   *very / dreary*
Ne shaltu° haben wit thee no fere°   *shall you / companion*
Butte thine werkes on an hep.°   *heap*

Mon, why seestu° love and herte   *do you set*
On worldes blisse that nout ne last?
Why tholestu that thee so ofte smerte[5]
For love that is so unstedefast?
Thu lickest huny° of thorn, iwis,°   *honey / indeed*
That seest° thy love on worldes bliss,   *set*
For full of bitternis it is.
Sore° thu mikt° ben ofgast,°   *grievously / may / terrified*
That despendes° here eykte° amiss,   *spend / possessions*
Werthurgh ben into helle itakt.[6]

Thenk, mon, wharof Crist thee wroukte,°   *made*
And do wey prude and fulthe mood.[7]
Thenk how dere he thee bokte°   *bought, redeemed*
On rode° mit his swete blood;   *Cross*
Himself he gaf for thee in pris,°   *price*
To buye thee bliss if thu be wis.°   *wise*
Bithenk thee,° mon, and up aris   *consider*
Of slouthe, and gin to worche good,[8]
Whil time to worchen is,
For elles thu art witless and wood.°   *mad*

All day thu mikt understonde
And thy mirour bifor thee sen,°   *see*
What is to don° and to wonden,°   *do / undertake*
And what to holden and to flen;°   *flee*
For all day thu siyst° wid thin eyen°   *see / eyes*
How this world went and how men deiet.°   *die*
That wite° well, that thu shalt dreyen°   *know / endure*
Det,° also° another det.°   *death / just as / does*
Ne helpet° nout ther non to lien,°   *helps / lie*
Ne may no mon bu det ageyn.[9]

Ne wort° ne good ther unforgulde,°   *will be / unrequited*
Ne non evel ne worth° unboukt;°   *will be / unpunished*
Whanne thu list,° mon, under molde°   *lie / ground*
Thu shalt haven° as thu havest wrokt.   *have*
Bithenk thee well, forthy, ic rede,°   *counsel*
And clanse thee of thine misdede,
That he thee helpe° at thine nede,   *may help*
That so dure° us havet iboukt,°   *dearly / redeemed*
And to hevene° blisse lede   *heaven's*
That evere lest° and failet nout.°   *lasts / not at all*

5. Why do you suffer that which so often pains you?
6. Wherefore you shall be taken into hell.
7. And put away pride and filthy heart.
8. From sloth, and begin to do good.
9. Nor may any man be against death.

2

Worldes blisse, have good day!
Now fram min herte wand° away.   turn
Him for to loven min hert is went,°   turned
That thurgh his side spere rent;
His herte° blod shadde for me,   heart's
Nailed to the harde tree.
That swete body was itend,°   made to suffer
Prened° wit nailes three.   pierced

Ah, Jesu! Thin holy hed°   head
Wit sharpe thornes was biweved,°   wrapped
Thy feire neb° was all bispet,°   face / spat upon
Wit spot° and blod meind° all biwet;°   spit / mingled / wet
Fro the crune to the to°   toe
Thy body was full of pine° and wo,   torment
    And wan° and red.   pale

Ah, Jesu! Thy smarte° ded°   painful / death
Be my sheld and my red°   counsel
    Fram develes lore.°   teaching
Ah, swete Jesu, thin ore!°   grace
For thine pines sore,
Thech min herte right love thee[1]
Whas° herte blod was shed for me.   whose

3

Sumer is icumen in,[2]
Lhude° sing, cuccu!°   loudly / cuckoo
Groweth sed° and bloweth° med°   seed / blooms / meadow
And springth the wude° nu.°   forest / now
Sing, cuccu!

Awe° bleteth after lomb,   ewe
Lhouth° after calve° cu,°   lows / calf / cow
Bulluc sterteth,° bucke ferteth.°   leaps / breaks wind
Murie° sing, cuccu!   merrily
Cuccu, cuccu,

1. Teach my heart to love you properly.   2. Spring has come in.

"Sumer is icumen in" (poem 3), the most famous of Middle English lyrics, is one of several songs at the beginning of a monks' commonplace-book compiled at Reading Abbey and now in the British Museum (MS. Harley 978, f. 11ᵇ). This poem has usually been dated about 1240, but some musicologists believe that a date seventy years later is more likely. Reproduced by permission of the Trustees of the British Museum.

Wel singes thu, cuccu.
Ne swik° thu naver° nu!   *cease / never*

Sing cuccu nu, sing cuccu!
Sing cuccu, sing cuccu nu!

4

Lenten° is come with love to toune,   *spring*
With blosmen° and with briddes° roune,°   *flowers / birds' / song*
 That all this blisse bringeth.
Dayeseyes° in this° dales,   *daisies / these*
Notes swete of nightegales—
 Uch° foul° song singeth.   *each / bird*
The threstelcok him threteth o;[1]
Away is here° winter wo   *their*
 When woderove° springeth.   *woodruff*
This foules singeth ferly° fele,°   *wonderfully / much*
And wliteth° on here winne wele,[2]   *chirp*
 That all the wode ringeth.

The rose raileth° hire° rode,°   *puts on / her / rosy hue*
The leves on the lighte° wode   *bright*
 Waxen all with wille.°   *pleasure*
The mone° mandeth° hire bleo,°   *moon / sends forth / light*
The lilie is lossom° to seo,°   *lovely / see*
 The fenil° and the fille.°   *fennel / chervil*
Wowes° this wilde drakes;   *woo*
Miles° murgeth° here makes,°   *animals / gladden / mates*
 Ase strem that striketh° stille.°   *flows / softly*
Mody° meneth,° so doth mo;°   *high-spirited man / laments / others*
Ichot° ich am one of tho,°   *I know / them*
 For love that likes° ille.   *pleases*

The mone mandeth hire light;
So doth the semly° sonne bright,   *fair*
 When briddes singeth breme.°   *clearly, loudly*
Deawes donketh the dounes;[3]
Deores° with here derne° rounes,   *animals / secret*
 Domes for to deme;[4]
Wormes woweth under cloude,°   *ground*
Wimmen waxeth wounder° proude,   *wonderfully*
 So well it wol° hem° seme.   *will / them*

---

1. The songthrush contends always.   3. Dew moistens the downs (hills).
2. "Winne wele": wealth of joys.   4. Tell their tales, or speak their opinions

If me shall wonte° wille° of on,°   *be lacking / pleasure / one*
This wunne weole⁵ I wole forgon°   *forego*
And wight° in wode be fleme.°   *quickly / fugitive*

[*Harley* 2253]

5

Mirie° it is while sumer ilast°   *merry / lasts*
With fugheles° song—   *birds'*
Oc nu necheth¹ windes blast
And weder° strong.   *weather*
Ey! ey! what this nicht is long,²
And ich° wid wel° michel° wrong   *I / very / much*
Soregh° and murne and fast.   *sorrow*

6

Foweles° in the frith,°   *birds / wood*
The fisses° in the flod,°   *fishes / river*
And I mon° waxe wod.°   *must / mad*
Mulch sorw° I walke with   *sorrow*
For beste of bon and blod.

7

All other love is like the mone°   *moon*
That wext° and wanet° as flowre in plein, *waxes / wanes*
As flowre that fairet° and fawet° sone, *blooms / fades*
As day that scowret° and endet° in rein. *passes rapidly / ends*

5. "Wunne weole": wealth of joys. 2. How long this night is.
1. But now draws nigh.

"Foweles in the frith" (poem 6) appears in Bodleian MS. Douce
139, now 21713, f. 5ᵃ, and is dated about 1270. Professor D. W.
Robertson notes that "the melody is not popular in character, and
the usual view that the text is secular is dubious" (*The Literature
of Medieval England* [New York: McGraw-Hill Book Co., 1970],
p. 348). Reproduced by permission of the Bodleian Library,
Oxford.

The music of "Foweles in the frith" in modern notation, as
printed by J. F. R. and C. Stainer in *Early Bodleian Music*
(London: Novello & Co., Ltd., 1901), II, 10. Reproduced by
permission of Novello & Co., Ltd.

All other love bigint° by° blisse,   *begins / with*
In wep° and wo mak° his° ending;   *weeping / makes / its*
No love ther nis that our alle lisse,°   *solaces*
Bot° what areste° in hevene° king, *except / rests / heaven's*

Whos love is . . . and ever grene,[1]
And ever full withoute waning;
His love sweteth° withoute tene,°   *sweetens / suffering*
His love is endless and aring.°   *unfailing*

All other love I flo° for thee;   *forsake*
Tell me, tell me, where thou list?°   *lie*
"In Marye milde and free°   *noble*
I schal be founde, ak° mor in Crist."   *but*

Crist me founde, nought I thee.[2] Hast!°   *haste*
Hald me to thee with all thy mein;°   *strength*
Help geld° that my love be stedfast,   *grant*
Lest thus sone it turne agein.

Whan now yet min hert is sor,
Iwis° hie° spilt min herte blod;   *indeed / they*
God canne° my lef,° I care na mor—   *knows / life*
Yet I hoppe° his will be god.°   *hope / good*

Allas! what wole° I a° Rome?   *will / at*
Seye I may in lore° of love: *code*
"Undo° I am by manne° dome,° *undone / man's / judgment*
Bot° he me help that sit above."   *unless*

The Levedy° Fortune is bothe frend and fo: *Lady*
Of pore she maket riche, of riche pore also.
She turneth wo all into wele,° and wele all into wo; *joy*
No triste no man[3] to this wele, the whel° it turnet so. *wheel*

1. [The line is incomplete.]   3. Let no man trust.
2. Christ found me, I did not find you.

9

A! Mercy, Fortune; have pitee on me,
And thinke that thu hast done gretely amisse
To parte asondre them whiche ought to be
Alwey in on.° Why hast thu do° thus?   one / done
Have I offended thee? I? Nay, iwisse!°   indeed
Then turne thy whele and be my frende again,
And sende me joy where I am nowe in pain.

And thinke what sorowe is the departing°   parting
Of two trewe hertes loving feithfully:
For parting is the most soroughfull thinge,
To min entent,° that ever yet knewe I.   in my opinion
Therfore, I pray to thee right hertely
To turne thy whele and be my frende again,
And sende me joy where I am nowe in pain.

For till we mete, I dare well say, for trouth,
That I shall never be in ease of herte.
Wherfor I pray you to have of me sume routh,°   pity
And release me of all my paines smerte,°   severe
Now—sith° thu woste° it is nat my deserte.   since / know
Then turne thy whele and be my frende again,
And sende me joy where I am nowe in pain.

10

Wele,° thu art a waried° thing;   prosperity / cursed
Unevene constu dele.[1]
Thu gevest a wreche° wele inogh,°   wretch / enough
Noght thurgh his hele.[2]
With freemen thu art ferly° feid°   wonderfully / joined
With saughte, and make hem sele;[3]
The poure i' londe naveth° no lot°   have (not) / fortune
With riche for to mele.°   speak

---

1. Unjustly can you distribute.
2. Not at all for his salvation.

3. In agreement, and give them joy.

II

To yow, my purse, and to noon other wight°　　　　　*creature*
Complayne I, for ye be my lady dere!
I am so sory, now that ye been lyght;
For certes,° but°ye make me hevy chere,　　　*certainly / unless*
Me were as leef¹ be layd upon my bere;
For which unto your mercy thus I crye:
Beth hevy ageyn, or elles mot° I dye!　　　　　　*must*

Now voucheth sauf° this day, or° yt be nyght,　*vouchsafe / before*
That I of yow the blisful soun° may here,　　　　*sound*
Or see your colour° lyk the sonne bryght,　　　*i.e., gold*
That of yelownesse hadde never pere.
Ye be my lyf, ye be myn hertes stere,°　　　　　*rudder*
Quene of comfort and of good companye:
Beth hevy ageyn, or elles moot I dye!

Now purse, that ben to me my lyves° lyght　　　*life's*
And saveour, as doun in this world here,
Out of this toune helpe me thurgh your myght,
Syn that ye wole nat ben my tresorere;°　　　　　*treasurer*
For I am shave as nye° as any frere.　　　　　　*close*
But yet I pray unto your curtesye:
Beth hevy agen, or elles moot I dye!

Lenvoy de Chaucer

O conquerour of Brutes Albyon,²
Which that by lyne° and free eleccion　　　　　*lineage*
Been verray° kyng, this song to yow I sende;　　*true*
And ye, that mowen° alle oure harmes amende,　*may*
Have mynde upon my supplicacion!

[*Geoffrey Chaucer, ca. 1340–1400*]

---

1. I would as soon.
2. "Brutes Albyon": Brutus's Albion, or Britain. (Brutus, the grandson of Aeneas, is the legendary founder of Britain, which is called "Albion" for its white Channel cliffs.)

12

Where beth° they biforen us weren?   *are*
Houndes ladden° and hawkes beren,°   *led / carried*
And hadden feld and wode;
The riche levedies° in here° bour,° *ladies / their / bower, chamber*
That wereden° gold in here tressour,°   *wore / head-dress*
With here brighte rode:°   *face*

Eten and drounken and maden hem° glad;   *themselves*
Here lif was all with gamen° ilad.°   *sport / spent*
Men keneleden° hem° biforen;   *kneeled / them*
They beren hem well swithe° heye°—   *very / high*
And in a twinkling of an eye
Here soules weren forloren.°   *lost*

Where is that laughing and that song,
That trailing[1] and that proude gong,°   *gait, going*
Tho° hawkes and tho houndes?   *those*
All that joye is went away,
That wele° is comen to weylaway,°   *prosperity / woe*
To manye harde stoundes.°   *times, conditions*

Here paradis hy nomen here,[2]
And now they lien° in helle ifere;°   *lie / together*
The fuir° it brennes° evere.   *fire / burns*
Long is "ah!" and long is "oh!"
Long is "wy!"° and long is "wo!"   *alas*
Thennes° ne cometh they nevere.   *thence*

Drey° here, man, thenne, if thou wilt,   *endure*
A litel pine° that me° thee bit;° *suffering / one / enjoins*
Withdraw thine eyses° ofte.   *comforts*
They° thy pine be unrede,°   *though / severe*
And° thou thenke° on thy mede,°   *if / think / reward*
It shall thee thinken° softe.   *seem*

If that fend,° that foule thing,   *fiend, the Devil*
Thorou wikke roun,° thorou fals egging,   *counsel*
Nethere° thee haveth icast,   *down*
Up and be good chaunpioun!
Stond, ne fall namore adoun
For a litel blast.

---

1. Walking, with long trailing garments. 2. Their paradise they took here.

Thou tak the rode° to° thy staf,   *Cross / as*
And thenk on him that thereonne gaf°   *gave*
His lif that wes so lef.°   *dear*
He it gaf for thee; thou yelde° it him;   *yield*
Agein° his fo that staf thou nim°   *against / take*
And wrek° him of that thef.°   *avenge / thief*

Of righte bileve° thou nim that sheld,   *belief*
The whiles that thou best° in that feld,   *are*
Thin hond to strengthen fonde;°   *endeavor*
And kep thy fo with staves ord,[3]
And do° that traitre seyen that word.   *make*
Biget° that murie° londe.   *win / happy*

Thereinne is day withouten night,
Withouten ende strengthe and might,
And wreche° of everich fo;   *punishment, vengeance*
Mid God himselven eche° lif,   *eternal*
And pes and rest withoute strif,
Wele withouten wo.

Maiden moder, hevene° quene,   *heaven's*
Thou might and const and owest° to bene°   *ought / be*
Oure sheld agein the fende;
Help us sunne° for to flen,°   *sin / flee*
That we moten° thy sone° iseen°   *may / Son / see*
In joye withouten ende.

13

Winter wakeneth all my care;
Now this° leves° waxeth bare;   *these / leaves*
Ofte I sike° and mourne sare°   *sigh / sorely*
   When it cometh in my thoght
   Of this worldes joye how it geth° all to noght.   *goes*

Now it is and now it nis,°   *is not*
Also it ner nere iwis.[1]
That° mony° mon seith, soth° it is: *what / many a / true*
   All goth bote° Godes wille;   *except*
   Alle we shule° deye thagh° us like[2] ille.   *shall / though*

3. And keep your foe at staff's point.   2. "Us like": it please us.
1. As if it never had been, indeed.

All that grein me graveth grene;[3]
Now it faleweth° all bidene;° — *withers / forthwith*
Jesu, help that it be sene,° — *plain, visible*
  And shild us from helle,
For I not° whider I shall° ne how longe her° dwelle. — *know not / shall go / here*

[*Harley* 2253]

14

While thou hast gode° and getest gode, — *good(s)*
For gode thou might be holde;° — *esteemed*
Who hath no gode, he can° no gode— — *can do*
A gode man so me tolde.
It is noght gode for no gode
Of gode for to be bolde;
But° thy gode to God be gode, — *unless*
Thy gode will fail and folde.
With an "V" and an "I" gode will come and go;[1]
But thy godes grounde° be gode, thy gode will worche° thee wo. — *foundation / work, produce*

That is gode that doth man gode
When he goth to the grave;
Other gode was never gode
But gode that will man save.
Gif thy gode while thou hast gode;
Gode than° might thou crave. — *then*
For it is gode to worche gode,
For God that doth it have.
With an "V" and an "I" gode is gode to wisse,° — *desire*
For with gode thou might be gode, and bye° hevene blisse. — *buy*

To do gode God gaf° thee gode, — *gave*
For thy gode and noght hisse;° — *his*
Do gode for thy soule gode,
And that is gode, iwisse.° — *indeed*
If thou hast gode and dost no gode,
That gode is gon amisse;
For evil gode is cleped° gode — *called*
For wham° man left his blisse. — *which*
With an "V" and an "I" gode is that gode doth;
Other gode was never gode for certein and forsoth.

3. All that seed (which) one buries un-   1. [The line is obscure.]
ripe.

A sliper° gode is erthly gode,   *slippery*
For that gode will away;
Goddes gode is ever gode,
And other gode is fay.°   *deadly*
Ken thy gode[2] and know thy gode
And do gode well alway;
For it is gode to worch gode
For gode that lasteth ay.
With an "V" and an "I" in gode is gode ende,
For all is gode which endes gode, and therto Crist us sende.

15

Gold and all this werldes win°   *joy*
Is nought but Cristes rode;°   *Cross*
I wolde ben° clad in Cristes skin   *be*
That ran so longe on blode,
And gon t' is herte and taken min in
Ther is a fulsum fode.[3]
Than gef I litel of[4] kith or kin,
For ther is alle gode.

[*From the Commonplace Book of John Grimestone, 1372*]

2. [There seems, especially in this stanza, to be word-play on "good" and "God."]
3. And go to his heart and take my abode/Where there is bountiful food.
4. Then would I care little for.

II

All for love

16

Now springes the spray.°   *slender shoots*
All for love ich° am so seeke°   *I / sick*
That slepen I ne may.[1]

Als° I me rode this endre° day   *as / recently past*
O'° my pleyinge,   *on*
Seih° I whar a litel may°   *saw / maiden*
Bigan to singe:
"The clot him clinge![2]
Wai° is him° i' louve-longinge   *woe / to him (who)*
Shall libben° ay."°   *live / ever*

Son° ich herde that mirie° note,   *as soon as / merry*
Thider I drogh;°   *went*
I fonde hire in an herber° swot°   *arbor / sweet*
Under a bogh°   *bough*
With joye inogh.°   *enough*
Son° I asked: "Thou mirie may,   *immediately*
Why singes thou ay?"

Than answerde that maiden swote
Midde wordes fewe:
"My lemman° me haves bihot°   *lover / promised*
Of louve trewe;
He chaunges anewe.
If I may, it shall him rewe[3]
By° this day."   *concerning*

1. [Refrain repeated after each stanza.]   3. If it is in my power, he will regret it.
2. May the earth cling to him!

17

All night by the rose, rose,
    All night by the rose I lay;
Darf ich nought the rose stele,[4]
    And yet ich bar the flour away.

18

My love is falle° upon a may:°   *fallen / maiden*
For love of hire° I defende° this day.   *her / make defense*
Love aunterus° no man forsaket:°   *adventurous / forsakes*
It woundet sore whan it him taket.
Love anterus may haven° no reste: *have*
Whare thought is newe, ther love is faste.°   *firm*
Love anterus with wo is bought:
Ther° love is trewe, it flitteth nought.   *where*

[*From the Commonplace Book of John Grimestone, 1372*]

19

Love is soft, love is swet, love is goed° sware.°   *good / speech*
Love is muche tene,° love is muchel care.   *grief*
Love is blissene mest, love is bot yare.[1]
Love is wondred° and wo, with for to fare.[2]   *distress*

Love is hap,° who it haveth; love is good hele.°   *good fortune / health*
Love is lecher and les, and lef for to tele.[3]

4. I dared not steal the rose.
1. **Love** is the greatest of joys, love is a quick remedy.
2. "With for to fare": to fare with.
3. Love is lecherous and false, and glad to entrap.

Love is douty° in the world, with for to dele.°   *doughty / deal*
Love maketh in the lond mony° unlele.°   *many / unfaithful*

Love is stalewarde and strong to striden° on stede.°   *stride / steed*
Love is loveliche° a thing to wommone° nede.   *lovely / women's*
Love is hardy° and hot as glowinde° glede.°   *bold / glowing / ember*
Love maketh mony° may° with teres to wede.° *many a / maiden / rage*

Love had his stiwart° by sty° and by strete.   *steward / path*
Love maketh mony may hire wonges° to wete.°   *cheeks / wet*
Love is hap, who it haveth, on for to hete.[4]
Love is wis, love is war° and wilful° and sete.°
     wary / headstrong / proper

Love is the softeste thing in herte may slepe.
Love is craft, love is goed with cares to kepe.°   *heed*
Love is les,° love is lef,° love is longinge.°   *false / dear / desire*
Love is fol,° love is fast,° love is frowringe.° *foolish / firm / comfort*
Love is sellich° an thing, whose° shall soth° singe.
     marvellous / whoever / truly

Love is wele,° love is wo, love is gleddede;°   *prosperity / gladness*
Love is lif, love is deth, love may us fede.°   *feed*

Were love also londrey as he is furst kene,
It were the wordlokste thing in werlde were, ich wene.[5]
It is isaid in an song, soth is isene,
Love comseth° with care and endeth with tene,°   *comes / grief*
Mid lavedy,° mid wive, mid maide, mid quene.   *lady*

20

Of everykune° tree,   *every kind of*
  Of everykune tree,
The hawethorn blowet° swotes°   *blossoms / sweetest*
  Of everykune tree.

My lemmon° she shall be,   *lover*
  My lemmon she shall be,
The fairest of erthkinne,°   *living creatures*
  My lemmon she shall be.

4. "On for to hete": to inflame one.
5. Were love as long-suffering as it is at first keen,/ It would be the worthiest thing there is in the world, I believe.

21

With right all my herte now I you grete,
  With hondert° syes,° my dere!   *a hundred / sighs*
Swete God, give us grace sone to mete,
  And sone to speken ifere.°   *together*
Annes, Annes, Annes, Annes, Annes!
Annes, be now stedfaste on° allewys,°   *in / every way*
And thinke on me, my swete Annes.
My faire Annes, my sothe° Annes,   *true*
I love youre . . . .[6]

22

Brid one brere,[1] brid, brid one brere!
  Kind° is come of love, love to crave.   *nature*
Blithful birid, on me thu rewe,°   *pity*
  Or greith, lef, greith thu me my grave.[2]

Ic° am so blithe, so bright, brid on brere;   *I*
  Whan I see that hende° in halle—   *gracious one*
She is whit of lime,° lovely, trewe,   *limb*
  She is fair, and flur° of alle.   *flower*

Mighte ic hire° at wille haven,°   *her/have*
  Stedefast of love, lovely, trewe,
Of my sorwe she may me saven;
  Joye and blisse were me° newe.   *for me*

23

Have good day, now, Mergerete,
With grete love I thee grete!

6. [The line is incomplete.]
1. Bird on briar.

2. Or make ready, dear one, make ready
for me my grave.

I wolde we mighten us° ofte mete   *each other*
In halle, in chaumbre, and in the strete,
Withoute blame of the contree°—   *country*
God geve° that so mighte it be!   *grant*

24

The smiling mouth, and laughing eyen gray,
The brestes rounde, and long small armes twain,
The hondes smothe, the sides streight and plaine,
Youre fetes° lite°—what shulde I ferther say?   *feet / little*
It is my craft° when ye are fer away   *occupation*
To muse theron in stinting of my paine—
The smiling mouth, and laughing eyen gray,
The brestes rounde, and long small armes twain.
So wolde I pray you, if I durste or may,
The sight to see as I have seene;
Forwhy° that craft me° is most faine,°   *wherefore / to me / pleasing*
And wol ben to the houre in which I day°—   *die*
The smiling mouth, and laughing eyen gray,
The brestes rounde, and long small armes twain.

[*From the French of Charles d'Orleans, 1394–1465*]

25

My gostly° fader, I me confesse,   *spiritual*
First to God and then to you,
That at a window (wot° ye how?)   *know*
I stale° a cosse° of gret sweetness,   *stole / kiss*
Which don was out° aviseness;°   *without / deliberation*
But it is don, not undon, now—
My gostly fader, I me confesse,
First to God and then to you.
But I restore it shall doutless
Agein, if so be that I mow;°   *may*

And that, God, I make a vow,
And elles° I axe° forgefness—   *else / ask*
My gostly fader, I me confesse,
First to God and then to you.

[*From the French of Charles d'Orleans, 1394–1465*]

26

Ichot a burde in a bour ase beryl so bright,[1]
Ase saphyr in selver semly° on sight,   *fair*
Ase jaspe° the gentil° that lemeth° with light, *jasper / gracious / gleams*
Ase gernet° in golde and ruby well right;°   *garnet / true*
Ase onycle he is on iholden on hight,[2]
Ase diamaund the dere° in day when he° is dight;°
                                                    costly / she / set, placed
He is coral° icud° with cayser° and knight; *red coral / famous / emperor*
Ase emeraude amorewen° this may° haveth might.
                                                in the morning / maiden
    The might of the margarite° haveth this may mere;°
                                                        pearl / excellent
    For charbocle ich hire ches by chin and by chere.[3]

Hire rode° is ase rose that red is on ris;°   *complexion / twig*
With lilie-white leres° lossum° he is;   *cheeks / lovely*
The primerole he passeth, the perwenke of pris,[4]
With alisaundre thareto, ache and anis.[5]
Cointe° ase columbine such hire cunde° is,   *pretty / nature*
Glad under gore in gro and in gris;[6]
He is blosme opon bleo, brightest under bis,[7]
With celydoine° and sauge,° as thou thyself sis.° *celandine / sage / see*
    That° sight° upon that semly, to bliss he is broght;   *he who / looks*
    He is solsecle:° to sauve° is forsoght.°   *marigold / heal / sought out*

He is papejay in pyn that beteth me my bale;[8]
To trewe tortle° in a tour° I telle thee my tale;   *turtle-dove / tower*

1. I know a maiden, in a bower, as bright as beryl.
2. As onyx, she is one highly esteemed.
3. By her expression, I recognized her as a precious red stone.
4. The cowslip she surpasses, the periwinkle of worth.
5. With horse-parsley besides, wild celery and anise.
6. Beautiful among women in gray fur.
7. She is a flower with regard to her face, brightest under fine linen.
8. She is the parrot who cures my pain for me when I am in torment.

He is thrustle thriven in thro that singeth in sale,[9]
The wilde laueroc° and wolc° and the wodewale;°

lark / hawk / singing bird

He is faucoun in frith,° dernest° in dale,   *wood / most discreet*
And with everuch° a gome° gladest in gale.°   *each / person / gaiety*
From Weye° he is wisest into Wyrhale;°   *the River Wye / Wirral*
Hire nome° is in a note of the nightegale.   *name*
  In Annote is hire nome; nempneth° it non?   *names*
  Whose° right redeth° roune° to Johon. *whoever / guesses / whisper*

Muge° he is and mondrake thourgh might of the mone,°

nutmeg / moon

Trewe triacle° itold° with tonges in trone;° *remedy / esteemed / heaven*
Such licoris° may leche° from Lyne° to Lone;°

licorice / heal / Lyn / Lune

Such sucre° mon secheth° that saneth° men sone;°

sugar / seeks / heals / quickly

Blithe iblessed of Crist, that baytheth° me my bone° *grants / prayer*
When derne° dedes in day derne° are done.   *secret / secretly*
Ase gromil° in greve° grene is the grone,° *gromwell / thicket / seed*
Ase quibibe° and comyn° cud is in crone,[1]   *cubeb / cummin*
  Cud comyn in court,° canel° in cofre,° *palace / cinnamon / chest*
  With gingiure° and sedewale° and the gilofre.°

ginger / setwall / clove

He is medicine° of might, mercie° of mede,°

remedy / compassion / reward

Rekene° ase Regnas[2] resoun to rede,°   *ready / advise*
Trewe ase Tegeu in tour, ase Wyrwein in wede,°   *garments*
Baldore° then Byrne that oft the bor° bede;° *bolder / boar / challenged*
Ase Wylcadoun he is wis, doghty of dede,
Feyrore then Floyres folkes to fede,°   *please*
Cud ase Cradoc in court carf° the brede,°   *carved / roast meat*
Hendore° then Hilde, that haveth me to hede.° *more gracious / care for*
  He haveth me to hede, this hendy,° anon;° *fair one / forthwith*
  Gentil ase Jonas, heo° joyeth° with Jon.   *she / rejoices*

[*Harley* 2253]

9. She is the thrush, doughty in contention, that sings in the hall.
1. "Cud is in crone": (which) is remarkable by reason of its head.
2. [The proper names in this stanza
have been traced to Germanic, Celtic,
and Romance texts, though identifications are problematic. See Brown XIII,
pp. 226–28.]

27

Bitwene Mersh and Averil
When spray° biginneth to springe,°   twig / grow
The lutel° fowl° hath hire° will   little / bird / her
On° hire lud° to singe.   in / language
Ich° libbe° in love-longinge   I / live
For semlokest° of alle thinge: fairest
He° may me blisse bringe;   she
Ich am in hire baundoun.°   power
   An hendy hap ich habbe ihent![1]
   Ichot° from hevene it is me sent;   I know
   From alle wimmen my love is lent,°   taken away
   And light° on Alisoun.   settled

On hew° hire her° is fair inogh,   color / hair
Hire browe browne, hire eye blake;
With lossum° chere° he on me logh,°   lovely / face / laughed
With middel° small and well imake.°   waist / made
Bote° he me wolle° to hire take   unless / will
For to ben° hire owen make,°   be / mate
Longe to liven ichulle° forsake,°   I will / refuse
And feye° fallen adoun.   doomed

Nightes when I wende° and wake—   turn
Forthy min wonges waxeth won[2]—
Levedy,° all for thine sake   lady
Longinge is ilent° me on.   come
In world nis non so witer° mon   wise
That all hire bounte° telle con: excellence
Hire swire° is whittore° then the swon,   neck / whiter
And feirest may° in toune.   maiden

Ich am for wowing° all forwake,[3]   love-making
Wery so° water in wore°   as / troubled pool
Lest eny reve° me my make   rob
Ich habbe iyerned yore.[4]
Betere is tholien° while° sore°   to suffer / a time / sorely
Then mournen evermore.
Geynest° under gore,°   kindest / petticoat
Herkne to my roun!°   song

[Harley 2253]

1. A fair destiny I have received. [Refrain repeated after each stanza.]
2. Therefore my cheeks become pale.
3. "Forwake": worn out with lying awake.
4. (For whom) I have yearned for a long time.

28

With longing I am lad°—   *afflicted*
On molde° I waxe mad—   *earth*
A maide marreth° me;   *injures*
I grede,° I grone, unglad,   *cry out*
For selden° I am sad°   *seldom / weary, sated*
That semly° for to see.   *fair one*
Levedy,° thou rewe° me!   *lady / pity*
To routhe° thou havest me rad.°   *sorrow / brought*
Be bote° of that I bad;°   *remedy / asked*
My lif is long on[1] thee.

Levedy of alle londe,
Les° me out of bonde.   *loose*
Broght ich° am in wo;   *I*
Have resting on honde,[2]
And send thou me thy sonde°   *message*
Sone,° er thou me slo.°   *quickly / slay*
My reste is with the ro;[3]
Thagh men to me han° onde,°   *have / enmity*
To love nuly noght wonde[4]
Ne lete for non of tho.[5]

Levedy, with all my might
My love is on thee light,°   *settled*
To menske° when I may;   *reverence*
Thou rew and red° me right,   *guide*
To dethe thou havest me dight;°   *condemned*
I deye longe er my day.
Thou leve° upon° my lay;   *believe / in*
Treuthe ich have thee plight,°   *promised*
To don° that° ich have hight°   *do / what / promised*
Whil my lif leste° may.   *last*

Lilie-whit he° is: *she*
Hire rode so rose on ris,[6]
That reveth° me my rest;   *robs*
Wimmon° war° and wis,   *woman / cautious*
Of prude° he bereth the pris,[7]   *pride, splendor*
Burde° on° of the best.   *maiden / one*
This wommon woneth° by° west,   *dwells / in the*

1. "Long on": caused by.
2. Bring about peace.
3. I am restless as a roe.
4. I will not hesitate to love.
5. Nor (will I) refrain because of any of them.
6. Her complexion like a rose on a twig.
7. "Bereth the pris": is most eminent.

Brightest under bis;°   *fine linen*
Hevene I tolde° all his,   *count*
That o° night were hire guest.   *one*

[*Harley* 2253]

29

Most I riden by Ribbesdale,¹
Wilde° wimmen for to wale,°   *wanton / choose*
  And welde whuch ich wolde,²
Founde were the feirest on°   *one*
That ever wes mad of blod and bon,
  In boure° best with bolde.°   *house / powerful ones*
Ase° sonnebem hire° bleo° is bright; *like / her / complexion*
In uche° londe heo° leometh° light,   *each / she / gleams*
  Thourgh tale as mon me tolde.
The lilie lossum° is and long,   *lovely*
With riche° rose and rode° among;°   *splendid / rosy hue / here*
  A fildor fax to folde.³   *and there*

Hire hed when ich biholde upon,
The sonnebeem aboute noon
  Me thoghte° that I seye;°   *it seemed to me / saw*
Hire eyen° aren grete and gray inogh;° *eyes / enough*
That lussom, when heo on me logh,°   *laughed*
  Ibend wax either breye.⁴
The mone° with hire muchele° maght°   *moon / great / power*
Ne leneth° non such light anaght°   *grants / at night*
  (That is in heovene heye)
Ase hire forhed doth in day,
For wham° thus muchel I mourne may,   *whom*
  For duel to deth I dreye.⁵

Heo hath browes bend° and heh,°   *arched / high, noble*
Whit bitwene and nout too neh;°   *close together*
  Lussum lif heo ledes;
Hire neose° is set as it well semeth;° *nose / befits*
I deye, for deth that me demeth;°   *condemns*
  Hire speche as spices spredes;

1. If I could ride through Ribblesdale.   4. Each eye-brow became arched.
2. And possess which (one) I desired.   5. On account of grief (which) I endure
3. A gold thread (she has) to bind (her   until death.
hair).

Hire lockes lefly° aren and longe,   *beautiful*
For sone° he° mighte hire murthes monge°   *forthwith / she / mingle*
    With blisse when it° bredes;°   *i.e., hair / spreads*
Hire chin is chosen° and either cheke   *beautiful*
Whit inogh and rode° on, eke,°   *rosy hue / also*
    Ase roser° when it redes.°   *rose-bush / reddens*

Heo hath a mury° mouth to mele,°   *pleasant / speak*
With lefly rede lippes lele,°   *true*
    Romaunce for to rede;°   *read*
Hire teth aren white ase bon of whal,°   *whale*
Evene set and atled° all,°   *arranged / wholly*
    Ase hende° mowe° taken hede;   *courteous persons / may*
Swannes swire° swithe° well isette,   *neck / very*
A sponne° lengore then I mette,°   *span / found*
    That freoly° is to fede.°   *beautiful / give pleasure*
Me were levere kepe hire come[6]
Then beon Pope and ride in Rome,
    Stithest° upon stede.   *strongest*

When I biholde upon hire hond,
The lilie-white lef° in lond   *leaf (or dear one)*
    Best° heo mighte beo;°   *best / be*
Either arm an elne° long,   *ell*
Baloigne mengeth all bimong;[7]
    Ase baum° is hire bleo;   *balsam*
Fingres heo hath feir to folde;°   *clasp*
Mighte ich hire have and holde,
    In world well were me.
Hire tittes° aren anunder° bis,°   *breasts / under / fine linen*
As apples two of parays,°   *the Garden of Eden*
    Youself° ye mowen° seo.   *yourselves / may*

Hire gurdel of bete gold is all,°   *completely*
Umben° hire middel small,   *around*
    That triketh° to the to,°   *hangs down / toe*
All with rubies on a rowe,
Withinne corven,° craft to knowe,°   *carved / reveal*
    And emeraudes mo;°   *more*
The bocle is all of whalles bon;
Ther withinne stont° a ston   *stands, is*
    That warneth° men from wo;   *protects*
The water that it wetes in[8]
Iwis° it wortheth° all to win;°   *indeed / becomes / wine*
    That seyen, seyden so.[9]

Heo hath a mete° middel small,   *well-proportioned*
Body and brest well mad all,
    Ase feines° withoute fere;°   *phoenix / peer*

6. I would rather wait for her arrival.   8. The water in which it is dipped.
7. Whalebone mingles quite among.   9. (Those who) saw that, said so.

Either side soft as silk,
Whittore° then the moren° milk,   *whiter / morning*
  With leofly lit° on lere.°   *hue / cheek*
All that ich you nempne° noght   *mention*
It is wonder well iwroght,
  And elles° wonder were.   *otherwise*
He mighte sayen that Crist him seye° *looked on with favor*
That mighte nightes negh hire leye:
  Hevene he hevede° here.   *would have*

[*Harley* 2253]

30

In a frith as I con fare fremede,[1]
I founde a well feir fenge° to fere;°   *prize / encounter*
Heo° glistnede ase° gold when it glemede;   *she / as*
Nes ner gome so gladly on gere.[2]
I wolde wite° in world who hire° kenede,° *know / her /gave birth to*
This burde° bright, if hire will° were.   *maiden / pleasure*
Heo me bed go my gates lest hire gremede;[3]
Ne kepte heo non hening here.[4]

"Ihere° thou me now, hendest° in helde,° *hear / most beautiful / favor*
Nav I thee none harmes to hethe.[5]
Casten° I wol thee from cares and kelde;° *protect / bitter sorrow*
Comeliche° I wol thee now clethe."°   *well / clothe*

"Clothes I have on for to caste,°   *wear*
Such as I may weore with winne;°   *joy*
Betere is were thunne boute laste[6]
Then side° robes and sinke into sinne.   *ample*
Have ye yor will, ye waxeth unwraste;°   *evil*
Afterward yor thonk° be thinne;°   *pleasure / slight*
Betre is make forewardes° faste°   *promises / secure*
Then afterward to mene° and minne."° *lament / remember*

"Of munning° ne munte° thou namore;   *memory / think*
Of menske° thou were wurthe,° by my might; *courtesy, honor / worthy*

1. In a wood as I did walk, unfamiliar.
2. There was never a person so beautiful
in clothes.
3. She commanded me to go away, lest
she become angry.
4. She did not wish to hear any insulting
suggestions.
5. I have no troubles about which to
scorn you.
6. It is better to wear thin (clothing)
without blame.

I take an hond to holde that I hore[7]
Of° all that I thee have bihight.°   *with regard to / promised*
Why is thee loth to leven on my lore[8]
Lengore then my love were on thee light?°   *settled*
Another mighte yerne° thee so yore°   *entreat / long*
That nolde° thee noght rede° so right."   *would (not) / advise*

"Such reed° me mighte spacliche° reowe°   *advice / quickly / rue*
When all my ro° were me atraght;°   *peace / taken away*
Sone thou woldest vachen° an newe,°   *fetch / new lover*
And take another withinne nye° naght.°   *nine / nights*
Thenne might I hongren° on heowe,°   *starve / family*
In uch° an hyrd° ben hated and forhaght,°   *each / household / despised*
And ben icaired° from all that I kneowe,   *separated*
And bede clevien ther I hade claght.[9]

Betere is taken a comeliche i' clothe,[1]
In armes to cusse° and to cluppe,°   *kiss / embrace*
Then a wrecche iwedded so wrothe°   *badly*
Thagh he me slowe, ne might I him asluppe.[2]
The beste red° that I con° to us bothe: *advice / know*
That thou me take and I thee toward[3] huppe;°   *go*
Thagh I swore[4] by treuthe and othe,
That° God hath shaped mey non atluppe.°   *that which / escape*

Mid° shupping° ne mey it me ashunche;°   *by means of / decree / frighten*

Nes° I never wicche° ne wile;°   *was (not) / witch / wizard*
Ich am a maide, that me ofthunche;°   *displeases*
Luef me were gome boute gile."[5]

[*Harley* 2253]

31

A wayle° whit as whalles° bon,   *beautiful woman / whale's*
A grein° in golde that goodly° shon,   *rosary bead / beautifully*
A tortle° that min herte is on,   *turtle-dove*
    In tounes,° trewe;   *in the world, alive*

7. I promise to be faithful until I grow gray.
8. Why are you reluctant to believe my advice?
9. And bid cling where I had embraced (i.e., beg the man whom I had embraced to remain faithful to me).
1. It is better to take a person comely in clothes.
2. (That) though he beat me, I might not escape him. [Compare Rosemary Woolf's discussion of this line on p. 316, below.]
3. "Thee toward": to you.
4. I.e., that I would not consent.
5. Dear to me would be a man without guile.

Hire gladshipe° nes° never gon,   *joy / is (not)*
  Whil I may glewe.°   *make music or song*

When heo° is glad,   *she*
Of all this world namore° I bad°   *no more / asked*
Then beo° with hire min one[1] bistad,°   *be / placed*
  Withoute strif;
The care that ich am in ibrad
  I wite a wif.[2]

A wif nis non so worly° wroght;°   *beautifully / made*
When heo is blithe° to bedde ibroght,   *happily*
Well were him that wiste° hire thoght,   *knew*
  That thriven° and thro.°   *beautiful / excellent*
Well I wot heo nul me noght;[3]
  Min herte is wo.

How shall that° lefly° sing   *that man / pleasantly*
That thus is marred° in mourning?   *afflicted*
Heo me wol° to dethe bring   *will*
  Longe er my day.
Gret° hire well, that swete thing   *greet*
  With eyen° gray.   *eyes*

Hire eye° haveth wounded me, iwisse,°   *eyes / indeed*
Hire bende° browen,° that bringeth blisse;   *arched / eye-brows*
Hire comely mouth that° mighte cusse°   *he who / kiss*
  In muche murthe° he were;   *joy*
I wolde chaunge min for his
  That is here fere.[4]

Wolde hire fere beo so freo,°   *generous*
And wurthes° were that so mighte beo,   *equivalents*
All for one I wolde give threo,°   *three*
  Withoute chep.°   *bargaining*
From helle to hevene and sonne to see,°   *sea*
  Nis non so yeep°   *prudent*
Ne half so freo.
Whose° wole of love be trewe, do listne me.   *whoever*

Herkneth me, I you telle;
In such wondring° for wo I welle;°   *distress of mind / suffer*
Nis no fur° so hot in helle   *fire*
  All to mon°   *man*
That loveth derne° and dar nout telle   *secretly*
  Whet him is on.[5]

1. "Min one": alone.
2. The sorrow which I suffer / I blame on a woman.
3. Well I know (that) she will not have me at all.
4. I would change mine (i.e., my mistress or my lot) for his / That is her companion.
5. What is the matter with him.

Ich° unne° hire well and heo me wo;   *I / wish*
Ich am hire frend and heo my fo;
Me thuncheth° min herte wol breke atwo   *it seems to me*
   For sorewe and sike.°   *sighing*
In° Godes greting° mote° heo go,   *with / welcome / may*
   That wayle white.

Ich wolde ich were a threstelcok,°   *songthrush*
A bounting° other° a lavercok,°   *bunting / or / lark*
   Swete brid!°   *bird*
Bitwene hire curtel° and hire smok   *gown*
   I wolde ben hid.

[*Harley* 2253]

32

In May it muryeth° when it dawes°   *is pleasant / dawns*
In dounes with this dueres plawes,[1]
   And lef° is light on linde;°   *leaf / lime tree*
Blosmes bredeth° on the bowes,   *grow*
All this wilde wightes wowes,[2]
   So well ich° underfinde.°   *I / perceive*

I not° non so freoly° flour   *do not know / beautiful*
As ledies that beth bright in bour,
   With love who mighte hem° binde;°   *them / fetter*
So worly° wimmen are by° west;   *splendid / in the*
One of hem ich herie° best   *praise*
   From Irlond into Inde.

Wimmen were the beste thing
That shup° oure heye hevene° king,   *created / heaven's*
   If feole° false nere;°   *many (men) / were not*
Heo beoth too rad upon here red
To love ther me hem lastes bed
   When heo shule fenge fere.[3]

Lut° in londe are to leve,°   *few / be believed*
Thagh me hem trewe trouthe geve,
   For tricherie to yere;[4]

1. In the hills, with these animals' pleasures.
2. All these wanton creatures make love.
3. They are too quick in their course of action/ To love where one offers sins/ When they must take mates.
4. Though one give them true faith,/ For fear of perfidy this year.

When trichour° hath his trouthe iplight,°   *deceiver / promised*
Biswiken° he hath that swete wight,°   *deceived / creature*
  Thagh he hire° othes swere.°   *to her / swear*

Wimmon, war° thee with the swike,°   *beware / traitor*
That feir and freoly° is to fike;°   *splendid / flatter*
  His fare is o to founde;[5]
So wide in world is here° won,°   *their / dwelling*
In uch° a toune untrewe is on°   *each / one*
  From Leicestre to Lounde.°   *Lound, perhaps London*

Of treuthe nis the trichour noght,
Bote he habbe his wille iwroght
  At stevening umbe stounde;[6]
Ah, feire levedis,° be on war,[7]   *ladies*
Too late cometh the yeynchar°   *means of escape*
  When love you hath ibounde.

Wimmen bueth° so feir on hewe,°   *are / hue*
Ne trow° I none that nere° trewe,   *know / were not*
  If trichour hem ne taghte;°   *taught*
Ah, feire thinges, freoly° bore,°   *nobly / born*
When me° you woweth,° beth war bifore   *one / woos*
  Whuch is worldes ahte.°   *peril*

All too late is send° ageyn°   *to send / back*
When the ledy lith° bileyn°   *lies / deflowered*
  And liveth by that he laghte;[8]
Ah, wolde lilie-leor° in lin°   *lily-cheeked (girl) / linen*
Ihere levely lores min,[9]
  With selthe° we weren saghte.°   *happiness / reconciled*

[Harley 2253]

33

Blow, northerne wind,
Send thou me my sweting!°   *dear one*
Blow, northerne wind,
Blow! Blow! Blow![1]

5. His behavior is always to be put to the test.
6. With regard to truth (fidelity), the deceiver is indifferent,/ Unless he has done his will/ At meetings sometimes.
7. "On war": on your guard.
8. And fares according to what she got.
9. Hear favorably my teachings.
1. [Refrain repeated after each stanza.]

Ichot° a burde° in boure° bright *I know / maiden / bower*
That sully° semly° is on sight, *exceedingly / comely*
Menskful° maiden of might,° *noble / power (over us)*
   Feir and free° to fonde.° *beautiful / enjoy*
In all this wurchliche° won° *splendid / world*
A burde of blod and of bon
Never yete I nuste° non *knew*
   Lussomore° in londe. *more lovely*

With lokkes lefliche° and longe, *beautiful*
With frount° and face feir to fonde, *forehead*
With murthes monie mote heo monge,[2]
   That brid° so breme° in boure, *damsel / excellent*
With lossom eye, grete and gode,
With browen° blisfol under hode.° *brows / hood*
He that reste° him on the rode° *rested / Cross*
   That leflich lif° honoure! *woman*

Hire° lure° lumes° light *her / complexion / shines*
As a launterne anight,° *at night*
Hire bleo° blikieth° so bright, *face / gleams*
   So feir heo is and fin.° *fine*
A swetly° swire° heo hath to holde, *lovely / neck*
With armes, shuldre as mon wolde,° *would wish*
And fingres feire for to folde.° *clasp*
   God wolde he° were min! *she*

Middel° heo hath menskful° small; *waist / gracefully*
Hire loveliche° chere° as cristal, *beautiful / face*
Theyes, legges, fet, and all
   Iwraght° wes of the beste. *made*
A lussum ledy lasteles° *faultless*
That sweting is and ever wes;
A betere burde never nes° *was (not)*
   Iheried° with the heste.° *praised / most noble*

Heo is dereworthe° in day, *excellent, beloved*
Graciouse, stout,° and gay, *stately*
Gentil, jolif° so° the jay, *lively / as*
   Worchliche° when heo waketh. *splendid*
Maiden muryest° of mouth; *most pleasing*
By est, by west, by north and south,
Ther nis fiele ne crouth[3]
   That such murthes° maketh. *joys*

Heo is coral of goodnesse,
Heo is rubie of rightfulnesse,° *integrity*
Heo is cristal of clannesse,° *purity*
   And banner of bealte;° *beauty*

2. With many pleasures may she mingle.
3. "Fiele ne crouth": stringed instruments.

Heo is lilie of largesse,°   *generosity*
Heo is parwenke° of prowesse,   *periwinkle*
Heo is solsecle° of swetnesse,   *marigold*
And ledy of lealte.°   *loyalty*

To Love, that leflich° is in londe,   *pleasant*
I tolde him, as ich° understonde,   *I*
How this hende° hath hent° in honde *fair one / taken*
   On° herte° that min wes,   *a / heart*
And hire knightes me han° so soght,° *have / attacked*
Siking,° Sorewing, and Thoght,   *Sighing*
Tho° three me han in bale° broght   *those / torment*
   Ageyn° the power of Pees.°   *against / Peace*

To Love I putte pleintes° mo,°   *complaints / more*
How Siking me hath siwed° so,   *followed*
And eke° Thoght me thrat° to slo° *also / threatened / slay*
   With maistry,° if he mighte,   *force*
And Serewe, sore° in balful° bende,° *grievous / harmful / bondage*
That he wolde for this hende
Me lede to my lives° ende,   *life's*
   Unlahfulliche in lighte.[4]

Hire love me lustnede uch word[5]
And beh° him to me over bord,°   *bent / table*
And bed° me hente° that hord° *bade / take / treasure*
   Of mine herte° hele:°   *heart's / cure*
"And bisecheth° that swete and swote,° *implore / fair one*
Er then thou falle as fen of fote,[6]
That heo with thee wolle of bote°   *remedy*
   Dereworthliche° dele."° *affectionately / deal*

For hire love I carke° and care,°   *grieve / sorrow*
For hire love I droupne° and dare,° *pine away / lie motionless*
For hire love my blisse is bare,
   And all ich waxe° won;°   *become / pale*
For hire love in slep I slake,°   *become weak*
For hire love all night ich wake,
For hire love mourning I make
   More then eny mon.

[*Harley 2253*]

4. Unlawfully (and) openly.
5. Love of her listened to my every word.
6. Before you fall as mud from a foot.

34

"My deth I love, my lif ich° hate,   *I*
For a levedy° shene;°   *lady / beautiful*
Heo° is bright so° dayes light   *she / as*
That is on me well sene.
All° I falewe° so doth the lef   *quite / wither*
In somer when it is grene.
If my thoght helpeth me noght,
To wham° shall I me mene?°   *whom / complain*

Sorewe and sike° and drery° mod°   *sighing / melancholy / mind*
Bindeth me so faste
That I wene° to walke° wod°   *expect / toss about / mad*
If it me lengore° laste;   *longer*
My serewe, my care, all with a word
He° mighte awey caste.   *she*
Whet helpeth thee, my swete lemmon,°   *lover*
My lif thus for to gaste?"°   *waste, ruin*

"Do wey,° thou clerk, thou art a fol!   *get away*
With thee bidde° I noght chide.°   *wish / to wrangle*
Shalt thou never live that day
My love that thou shalt bide.°   *obtain*
If thou in my boure° art take,°   *room / caught*
Shame thee may bitide;°   *befall*
Thee is bettere on fote gon
Then wicked hors to ride."

"Weylawey! Why seist thou so?
Thou rewe° on me, thy man!   *have pity (imperative)*
Thou art ever in my thoght
In londe wher° ich am.   *wherever*
If I deye for thy love,
It is thee mikel° sham;°   *great / shame*
Thou lete° me live and be thy lef°   *let (imperative) / love*
And thou my swete lemman."

"Be stille, thou fol—I calle thee right;°   *correctly*
Cost° thou never blinne?°   *can / cease*
Thou art waited° day and night   *spied on*
With° fader and all my kinne.   *by*
Be thou in my bour itake,
Lete they for no sinne¹
Me to holde and thee to slon,°   *slay*
The deth so thou maght° winne!"   *may, must*

---

1. They will not refrain for (fear of) any sin.

"Swete ledy, thou wend° thy mod,   *change (imperative)*
Sorewe thou wolt me° kithe.°   *to me / show, reveal*
Ich am all so° sory° mon   *as / sad*
So ich was whilen° blithe.°   *before / happy*
In a window ther° we stod   *where*
We custe° us fifty sithe;°   *kissed / times*
Feir biheste° maketh mony mon   *promise*
All his serewes mithe."°   *conceal*

"Weylaway! Why seist thou so?
My serewe thou makest newe.°   *anew*
I lovede a clerk all paramours;°   *as a lover*
Of love he wes full trewe;
He nes° nout blithe never a day   *was (not)*
Bote° he me sone° seye;°   *unless / quickly / might see*
Ich lovede him betere then my lif—
Whet bote° is it to leye?"°   *use / lie*

"Whil I wes a clerk in scole,
Well muchel I couthe° of lore;° *knew / learning, lore of love*
Ich have tholed° for thy love   *suffered*
Woundes fele° sore,   *very*
Fer from hom and eke° from men   *also*
Under the wode-gore.°   *forest*
Swete ledy, thou rewe of me;
Now may I no more!"

"Thou semest well° to ben a clerk,   *well-suited*
For thou spekest so stille;°   *softly*
Shalt thou never for my love
Woundes thole° grille;°   *suffer / terrible*
Fader, moder, and all my kun
Ne shall me holde so stille°   *firmly*
That I nam thin and thou art min,
To don all thy wille."

[Harley 2253]

35

When the nightegale singes,
The wodes waxen grene:
Lef° and grass and blosme springes   *leaf*

In Averil,° I wene;°   *April / expect*
And love is to min herte gon
With one° spere so kene:°   *a / sharp*
Night and day my blod it drinkes;
Min herte deth° me tene.°   *does / grieve*

Ich° have loved all this yer   *I*
That° I may love namore;   *so that*
Ich have siked mony sik,¹
Lemmon,° for thin ore.°   *sweetheart / favor*
Me° nis° love never the ner,° *to me / is (not) / nearer*
And that me reweth° sore.   *grieves*
Swete lemmon, thench° on me: *think*
Ich have loved thee yore.°   *a long time*

Swete lemmon, I preye thee
Of love one speche.
Whil I live in world so wide
Other nulle° I seche.°   *will not / seek*
With thy love, my swete leof,°   *dear*
My bliss thou mightest eche:°   *increase*
A swete cos° of thy mouth   *kiss*
Mighte be my leche.°   *physician*

Swete lemmon, I preye thee
Of a love-bene;°   *lover's petition*
If thou me lovest, as men says,
Lemmon, as I wene,
And if it thy wille be,
Thou loke that it be sene.°   *regarded favorably*
So muchel I thenke upon thee
That all I waxe grene.

Bitwene Lincolne and Lindeseye,°   *Lindsey*
Norhamptoun and Lounde,°   *Lound*
Ne wot° I non so fair a may°   *know / maiden*
As I go fore ibounde.²
Swete lemmon, I preye thee
Thou lovie° me a stounde.°   *love / while*
 I wole mone° my song   *moan*
 On wham that it is on ilong.³

[*Harley* 2253]

1. I have sighed many a sigh.
2. As (the one) for whom I go fettered.
3. About the one who caused it.

36

Lutel° wot° it any mon	*little / knows*
How derne° love may stonde,°	*secret / stand, exist*
Bote° it were a fre° wimmon	*unless / forward, immodest*
That much of love had fonde.°	*experienced*
The love of hire° ne lesteth° nowiht° longe;	*her / lasts / (not) at all*
Heo haveth me plight and witeth me with wronge.¹	
Ever and o for my leof ich am in grete thoghte;	
I thenche on hire that I ne seo nout ofte.²	

I wolde nemne° hire today	*name*
And° I dorste° hire munne;°	*if / dared / mention*
Heo° is that° feireste may°	*she / the / maiden*
Of uch° ende° of hire kunne;°	*each / fair one / family*
Bote heo me love, of me heo haves sunne.³	
Wo is him that loveth the love that he ne may ner° winne!	*never*

Adoun° I fell to hire anon°	*down / at once*
And crye, "Ledy, thin ore!°	*grace*
Ledy, ha mercy of thy mon!	
Lef° thou no false lore!°	*believe / advice*
If thou dost, it wol me reowe° sore.	*grieve*
Love drecheth° me that° I ne may live namore."	*afflicts / so that*

Mury° it is in hire tour°	*pleasing / castle*
With hatheles° and with heowes.°	*men, heroes / servants*
So it is in hire bour,°	*chamber*
With gomencs° and with gleowes.°	*pleasures / entertainments*
Bote heo me lovie,° sore it wol me rewe.°	*love / grieve*
Wo is him that loveth the love that ner nul° be trewe!	*will (not)*

Fairest fode° upo loft,⁴	*creature*
My gode luef,° I thee greete	*dear*
As fele° sithe° and oft	*many / times*
As dewes dropes beth° weete,°	*are / wet*
As sterres beth in welkne° and grases sour° and swete.	*sky / bitter*
Whose loveth untrewe, his herte is selde seete.⁵	

[Harley 2253]

1. She has promised me and blames me with injustice.
2. Ever and always for my dear one I am in great grief;/ I think of her whom I do not often see. [Refrain repeated after each stanza.]
3. Unless she love me, she will have sin on account of me.
4. "Upo loft": alive.
5. Whoever loves an unfaithful person, his heart is seldom content.

37

Wer° ther outher° in this toun   *were / either*
  Ale or win,°   *wine*
Isch° it wolde buye   *I*
  To° lemmon° min.   *for / lover*
Welle wo was so hardy
  For to make my lef all blody;[1]
Thaut° he were the kinges sone   *though*
  Of Normaundy,
Yet icholde awreke be[2]
  For lemman min.
Welle wo was me tho,[3]
  Wo was me tho;
The man that leset° that° he lovet,   *loses / what*
  Him is also.[4]
Ne erle ne lerde[5]
  Ne—no more I ne can!
But Crist ich hire biteche[6]
  That was my lemman.

38

Thei° I singe and murthes make,   *though*
It is not I wolde.[7]

Min owne dere lady fair and free,°   *well-born*
I pray you in herte ye ruwen° on me,   *take pity*
For all my liking is on thee
  Whan I on you beholde.

Wer we two togadere beine,°   *both*
Thou might me lisse° of my peine;   *relieve*
I am agast, it wol not geine°—   *avail*
  Min herte falleth colde.

1. Very cursed would be anyone so fool-hardy/ As to make my loved one all bloody.
2. Yet I would be avenged.
3. It was very bad for me then.
4. It is bad for him also.
5. Neither earl nor lord.
6. But I entrust her to Christ.
7. It is not as I would wish. [Refrain repeated after each stanza.]

Myself I wol min arnde° bede,°   *petition / make known*
The better, I hope, for to spede;
Non so well may do min nede—
   A womman so me tolde.

39

I must go walke the wood so wild,
   And wander here and there
   In dred and dedly fere,
For where I trusted, I am begild,
   And all for on.°   *one*

Thus am I banisshed from my blis
   By craft and false pretens,
   Fautles° without offens,   *faultless*
As of return no certen° is,   *certainty*
   And all for fere of on.

My bed schall be under the grenwod tree,
   A tuft of brakes° under my hed,   *bracken, ferns*
   As on from joye were fled;
Thus from my lif, day by day, I flee,
   And all for on.

The ronning stremes shall be my drinke,
   Acorns schall be my fode;
   Nothing may do me good,
But° when of your bewty I do think,   *except*
   And all for love of on.

40

I am as light as any roe
To preise wemen wher that I go.[1]

To onpreise wemen it were a shame,
For a woman was thy dame;°   *mother*

1. [Refrain repeated after each stanza.]

Our Blessed Lady bereth the name
Of all women wher that they go.

A woman is a worthy thing,
They do the washe and do the wringe;°   *wringing*
"Lullay, lullay," she dothe thee singe,
And yet she hath but care and wo.

A woman is a worthy wight:
She serveth a man both daye and night;
Therto she putteth all her might,
And yet she hathe but care and wo.

41

Care away, away, away,
Murning away.
I am forsake,
Another is take,°   *taken*
No more murne ic° may.[1]   *I*

I am sory for her sake,
Ic may well ete and drinke;
Whanne ic slepe° ic may not wake,   *sleep*
So muche on her ic thenke.

I am brout in suche a bale,°   *misery*
And brout in suche a pine,°   *grief*
Whanne ic rise up of° my bed   *from*
Me liste° well to dine.   *I desire*

I am brout in suche a pine,
Ibrout in suche a bale,
Whanne ic have righte good wine
Me liste drinke non ale.

42

Jesu that is most° of might,   *greatest*
And made man above all thing,

1. [Refrain repeated after each stanza.]

Save my true-love, bothe day and night,
And kepe her well and in good liking.

For she is alwey full curteisse,°   *courteous*
True and stedfast in every degree,
Swete as the rose that groeth on the risse,°   *branch*
As true turtill° that sittes on a tree.   *turtle-dove*

She is the demurest that I can see
Wheras° I walke by est and weste;   *wherever*
No peere she hase in my eye,
For of all women I love her beste.

Her lippes are like unto cherye,
With teethe as white as whales bone;
Her browes bente° as any can be,   *arched*
With eyes clere as cristal stoune.

Her fingers be bothe large and longe,
With pappes rounde as any ball;
Nothing, methinke, on her is wronge;
Her medill° is bothe gaunte° and small.   *middle / slender*

She hathe my harte and ever shall,
And never to change her for no newe,
But for to love her terrestreall,°   *in a worldly way*
And whiles I live to her be true.

For I have gone throughe Englond on every side,
Brettin,° Flanders, with many an oder° place,   *Brittany / other*
Yet founde I never non in these ways wide
Suche one as she is to my purpasse.°   *purpose*

Wherfore I love her without let,°   *hindrance*
And for no thing I can cease;
So ferventlye on her my harte is set,
But I dare not put me in preace.[1]

Wo be the while for my redress[2]
Sithen° I am borne to live in peine,   *since*
And thus to be lafte all comfortless,
To love and be not loved ageine.

Yet throughe governance° growethe grace;   *self-control*
I have harde men say in towne and strete,
How fortune cumethe into many a place—
And with good fortune I trust to mete.

---

1. "Put me in preace": press home my   2. Cursed be the time for my relief.
claims.

Adeu, dere harte that is so swete,
God grante you grace well for to do;
I most walke forthe true love to seke,
Into some place where it dothe growe.

But one branche I will leve with you:
I pray Jesu ye may it well kepe,
For hereafter ye shall knowe
Where kinde° cannot go, it will crepe.   *nature*

Wherfore as many times I grete you
As clarkes can write with paper and inke,
And as monye mo° as gresses grewe,°   *more / grow*
Or tonge can tell, or harte can thinke.

No more I write to you at this time,
But wherever ye be, on lande or water,
Cristes dere blessing and mine
I sende you in greeting of this letter.

43

O excellent sovereigne, most semely to see,
Both prudent and pure, like a perle of prise,°   *value*
Also fair of figure and oreant° of bewtye,   *brilliant*
Bothe cumlye and gentil, and goodly to advertise;°   *consider*
Your brethe is sweeter then balme, suger, or licoresse.
I am bolde on you, thoughe I be not able,
To write to your goodly person whiche is so ameable
    By reason.
    For ye be bothe fair and free,°   *well-bred*
    Therto wise and womanly,
    Trew as turtil° on a tree   *turtle-dove*
    Without any treason.

Your fair here° henging downe to your knee,   *hair*
With your rolling eyes whiche are as glasse clere,
And your strawbery lippes as swete as honye,
With rose red in your chekes—ye have no pere!
Your chere° is as comfortable as blossome on brere,° *countenance / briar*
And yourselfe as swete as is the gelyfloure,°   *gillyflower*
Or any lavender sedes strawen° in a coffer   *strewn*
    To smell.

Your necke like the lillye,
Your lippes like the strawberye,
As swete as any honye
That cumes to sell.[1]

Your throte as clere as cristal stone,
Nothing amisse after my derection,°   *arrangement*
And your neke as white as whales bone,
I submitte me, fair ladye, under your protection.
If I do you displeise, I will abide your correction;
Like as the master in the scole teches the childe,
To do your commandemente I will be meke and milde
    And still.
    For Jesus sake that bought us dere,
    And his moder, that meiden clere,°   *illustrious*
    Helpe to comforte my careful° chere,°   *sorrowful / countenance*
    And let me never spill.°   *meet with bad fortune*

Your love, fair ladye, I wolde feyne winne;
There is nothing erthely might me so well please.
Wherfore I pray God, or° that I beginne,   *before*
That my simple writing do you not displeise;
For I am not to blame that I do you prease,°   *praise*
O rubicounde° rose, o lillye most deliciouse,   *red*
Splendant in bewtye as a diamond most preciouse
    In sight.
    Your bright fulgent° face,   *shining*
    Replete full of grace,
    And your goodly pace,
    Makethe my harte light.

Your love I desire without any negation;
If I might it have, then wolde I be feyne;°   *glad*
Wherfore I pray you, without vareation,
Your whole minde ye will write to me ageine.
If it be good, then wolde I be feine,
And ever whiles I live to you be obedient
To fulfill your commandement as your humble servaunt
    Forever;
    And never to change you for no newe,
    But daily for your grace to sue—
    Therfore, swetharte, to me be trew,
    For I am at your plesure.

Thus at this time this bill° shall be concluded   *letter*
The more brefely for to make an ende,
I trust verely I shall not be ill usede
Of you to whome this simple letter I sende;
With love to continue this I entende,

1. "To sell": on sale.

And so I trust that ye will the same;
Criste kepe us bothe from bodely hurte and shame
    Alway.
  Adeu, farewell my swete,
  Till efte° that we mete,   *again*
  My harte ye have to kepe,
  By God that made this day.

44

Pite, that I have sought so yore° agoo,   *long*
With herte soore, and ful of besy peyne,
That in this world was never wight° so woo°   *creature / woeful*
Withoute deth,—and, yf I shal not feyne,°   *dissemble*
My purpos was to Pite to compleyne
Upon the crueltee and tirannye
Of Love, that for my trouthe° doth° me dye.   *fidelity / makes*

And when that I, be° lengthe of certeyne yeres,   *by*
Had evere in oon[1] a tyme sought to speke,
To Pitee ran I, al bespreynt° with teres,   *sprinkled*
To prayen hir on Cruelte me awreke.°   *to avenge*
But er° I myghte with any word outbreke,   *before*
Or tellen any of my peynes smerte,
I fond hir ded, and buried in an herte.

Adoun I fel when that I saugh the herse,°   *hearse*
Ded as a ston, while that the swogh° me laste: *swoon*
But up I roos, with colour ful dyverse,
And pitously on hir myn eyen I caste,
And ner the corps I gan to presen° faste,   *press forward*
And for the soule I shop° me for to preye.   *prepared*
I nas° but lorn;° ther was no more to seye.   *was (not) / forlorn*

Thus am I slayn, sith° that Pite is ded.   *since*
Allas, that day! that ever hyt shulde falle!°   *befall*
What maner man dar now hold up his hed?
To whom shal any sorwful herte calle?
Now Cruelte hath cast° to slee us alle,   *contrived*
In ydel hope, folk redeless of peyne,[2]—
Syth she is ded, to whom shul we compleyne?

1. "Evere in oon": continually.
2. In idle hope, people not knowing which way to turn on account of pain.

But yet encreseth me this wonder newe,
That no wight woot° that she is ded, but I—   *knows*
So many men as in her tyme hir knewe—
And yet she dyed not so sodeynly;
For I have sought hir ever ful besely
Sith first I hadde wit or mannes mynde;
But she was ded er that I koude hir fynde.

Aboute hir herse there stoden lustely,°   *happily*
Withouten any woo, as thoughte° me,   *(it) seemed to*
Bounte° parfyt,° wel armed and richely,   *Goodness / perfect*
And fresshe Beaute, Lust,° and Jolyte,   *Pleasure*
Assured Maner, Youthe, and Honeste,
Wisdom, Estaat, Drede,° and Governaunce,   *Fear*
Confedred° both by bonde and alliaunce.   *allied*

A compleynt had I, writen, in myn hond,
For to have put to Pittee as a bille;°   *letter*
But when I al this companye ther fond,
That rather wolden al my cause spille°   *destroy*
Then do me help, I held my pleynte stille;
For to that folk, withouten any fayle,
Withoute Pitee ther may no bille availe.

Then leve I al these vertues, sauf° Pite,   *except*
Kepynge the corps, as ye have herd me seyn,
Confedered alle by bond of Cruelte,
And ben assented when I shal be sleyn.
And I have put my complaynt up ageyn;
For to my foes my bille I dar not shewe,
Th'effect of which seith thus, in wordes fewe:—

The Bill of Complaint
Humblest of herte, highest of reverence,
Benygne flour, coroune° of veitues alle,   *crown*
Sheweth unto youre rial° excellence   *royal*
Youre servaunt, yf I durste me so calle,
Hys mortal harm, in which he is yfalle;
And noght al oonly for his evel fare,
But for your renoun, as he shal declare.

Hit stondeth thus: your contraire, Crueltee,
Allyed is ayenst your regalye,°   *royal rule*
Under colour of womanly Beaute,—
For men shulde not, lo, knowe hir tirannye,—
With Bounte, Gentilesse, and Curtesye,
And hath depryved yow now of your place
That hyghte° "Beaute apertenant° to Grace."   *is called / belonging*

For kyndely,° by youre herytage ryght,   *naturally*
Ye ben annexed° ever unto Bounte;   *attached*

And verrayly ye oughte do youre myght
To helpe Trouthe in his adversyte.
Ye be also the corowne of Beaute;
And certes,° yf ye wanten° in these tweyne,   *indeed / are lacking*
The world is lore;° ther is no more to seyne.   *lost*

Eke° what availeth Maner and Gentilesse   *also*
Withoute yow, benygne creature?
Shal Cruelte be your governeresse?
Allas! what herte may hyt longe endure?
Wherfore, but° ye the rather take cure°   *unless / care*
To breke that perilouse alliaunce,
Ye sleen hem that ben in your obeisaunce.°   *obedience*

And further over, yf ye suffre this,
Youre renoun ys fordoo° than in a throwe;°   *destroyed / short time*
Ther shal no man wite° well what Pite is.   *know*
Allas, that your renoun sholde be so lowe!
Ye be than fro youre heritage ythrowe
By Cruelte, that occupieth youre place;
And we despeyred, that seken to your grace.

Have mercy on me, thow Herenus° quene,   *Erinyes' (the Furies)*
That yow have sought so tendirly and yore;
Let som strem of youre lyght on me be sene
That love and drede yow, ever lenger the more.
For, sothly for to seyne, I bere the soore;°   *wound*
And, though I be not konnynge° for to pleyne,°   *skillful / plead*
For Goddis love, have mercy on my peyne!

My peyne is this, that what so I desire
That have I not, ne° nothing lyk therto;   *nor*
And ever setteth Desir myn hert on fire.
Eke on that other syde, where so I goo,
What maner thing that may encrease my woo,
That have I redy, unsoght, everywhere;
Me ne lakketh but my deth, and than my bere.°   *bier*

What nedeth to shewe parcel of my peyne?
Syth every woo that herte may bethynke
I suffre, and yet I dar not to yow pleyne;
For wel I wot, although I wake or wynke,
Ye rekke° not whether I flete° or synke.   *care / float*
But natheles,° yet my trouthe I shal sustene   *nevertheless*
Unto my deth, and that shal wel be sene.

This is to seyne, I wol be youres evere;
Though ye me slee by Crueltee, your foo,
Algathe° my spirit shal never dissevere   *nevertheless*

Fro youre servise, for any peyne or woo.
Sith ye be ded—allas, that hyt is soo!—
Thus for your deth I may wel wepe and pleyne
With herte sore, and ful of besy peyne.

[*Geoffrey Chaucer, ca. 1340–1400*]

45

O mestress, why
Outecast am I
All utterly
   From your pleasaunce?
Sithe° ye and I   *since*
Or° this, truly,   *before*
Familiarly
   Have had pastaunce.°   *recreation*

And lovingly
Ye wolde apply
Thy company
   To my comforte;
But now, truly,
Unlovingly
Ye do deny
   Me to resorte.°   *visit*

And me to see
As strange ye be
As thowe° that ye   *though*
   Shuld nowe deny,
Or else possess
That nobilness
To be dochess°   *duchess*
   Of grete Savoy.

But sithe that ye
So strange will be
As toward me,
   And will not medill,°   *associate*
I truste, percase,°   *by chance*
To finde some grace
To have free chaise,°   *hunting*
   And spede° as welle!   *prosper*

46

Gracius and gay,
  On her lieth all my thoght;
But° sche rew° on me today,   *unless / pity*
  To deth sche hath me broght.

Her feingeres bith° long and small,   *are*
  Her armes bith rown° and toght,°   *round / firm*
Her mouth as sweet as licory,°   *licorice*
  On her lieth all my thoght.

Her eyne° bith feir and gray,   *eyes*
  Her brues° bith well ibent,°   *brows / arched*
Her rode° as rede as rose in May,   *complexion*
  Her medill° is small and gent.°   *waist / slender*

Sche is sweet under schete;
  I love her and no mo.°   *more*
Sche hath mine hart to kepe,
  In londes wher sche go.

Sodenly° tell, I pray,   *without delay*
  To° thee my love is lend;°   *on / set*
Kisse me in my way,
  Ones ar I wend.¹

47

My cares comen ever anew.
  A, dere God, no bote° ther nis,°   *remedy / is (not)*
For I am halden for untrewe,²
  Withouten gilt, so han° I bliss!   *have*

To be trew wonet° I was;   *accustomed*
  In ony° thing that I might do   *any*
I thanked God his° grete gras;°   *for his / grace*
  Now it is I may noght° do.   *nothing*

1. Once before I depart.   2. For I am held to be untrue.

48

Thus I complain my grevous hevynesse°   *grief*
To you that knoweth the treuth of min entent.
Alas, why shuld ye be merseless—
So moch beutee as God hath you sent!
Ye may my pein relees.
Do as ye list°—I hold me content!   *please*

49

Go, hert,° hurt with adversitee,   *heart*
And let my lady thy wondes° see;   *wounds*
And sey hir° this, as I say thee: *to her*
Farwell my joy, and welcom peine,
Till I see my lady againe.

50

Alas, departing is ground of wo!
Other songe can I not singe.
But why part I my lady fro,
Sith° love was cause of our meeting?   *since*
The bitter teres of hir weeping
Min hert hath pershed° so mortally,   *pierced*
That to the deth it will me bring,
But if° I see hir hastily.   *unless*

51

I ne have joy, plesauns, nor comfort,
In youre absens, my verrey° hertes quene.   *true*
What other men think joy or disport,
To me it nis° but anger or tene;°   *is (not) / misery*
If that I laugh, it is but on the splene.[1]
Thus make I a gladful sorry chere,°   *countenance*
So noyth° me the absens of my verrey lady dere.   *annoys*

52

Alone, I live alone
And sore I sighe for one.[2]

No wondre thow° I murning° make,   *though / mourning*
For grevous sighes that mine harte dothe take,
And all is for my lady sake.
    Alone, I live alone.

She that is causer of my wo,
I mervel that she will do so,
Sithe° I love hir and no mo.°   *since / more*
    Alone, I live alone.

Thus am I brought into lovers daunce;
I wot° never how to flee the chaunce;   *know*
Wherefore I live in great penaunce.
    Alone, I live alone.

My minde is so it is content
With hir daily to be present,
And yet my servis is there misse-spent.
    Alone, I live alone.

Trow° ye that I wold be glade   *believe*
To seke a thing that will not be hade?
Saw I never man so sore bestad.°   *beset*
    Alone, I live alone.

---

1. "On the splene": in jest.   2. [Refrain repeated after each stanza.]

Ones° me to love if she began, *once*
No man with tong nore pen tell can
The joy in me that wold be than.
    Alone, I live alone.

Now pray we him that may purchase
To sende us better time and space,° *occasion*
That I may stond all in hir grace.
    Alone, I live alone.

53

Now wolde I faine° sum merthes mak, *gladly*
All only for my ladys sak
    When I her see;
But nowe I am so far fro her
    It will not be.

Thow° I be far out of her sight, *though*
I am her man both day and night,
    And so wol° be. *will*
Therfore wolde as I love her
    She loved me.

Whan she is mery, than am I gladde,
Whan she is sorry, than am I shadde,° *sad*
    And cause is why:[1]
For he liveth not that loved her
    So well as I.

She seith that she hath seen it write° *written*
That "selden° seen is sone forgeit."° *seldom / forgotten*
    It is not so—
For in good feith save° only her *except*
    I love no mo.° *more*

Wherfor I pray, bothe night and day,
That she may cast alle care away
    And leve° in rest, *live*
And evermore wherever she be
    To love me best;

---

1. And this is the reason.

And I to her to be so trewe,
And never to chaunge for no newe,
  Unto my ende,
And that I may in her service
  Ever to amend.°   *improve*

54

Honure, joy, helthe, and plesaunce,°   *pleasure*
Vertu, riches abundaunt with good ure°—   *fortune*
The Lord graunt you, which hath most puisshaunce,°   *power*
And many a gladsom yere° for to endure   *year*
With love and praise of every creature;
And for my love all prevaile it shall,
I give it you as be ye very seure,°   *sure*
With hert, body, my litel good and all.

And so you not displese with my desire,
This wolde I you biseche, that of youre grace
It like° you, lo, to graunt me all this yere   *please*
As in youre hert to have a dwelling place,
All be it never of so lite° a space;   *little*
For which as this the rente resceive ye shall
My love and service as in every case,
With hert, body, my litel good and all.

And sin° it is to you no prejudice,   *since*
Sum litel pratty° corner sekes° me°   *pretty / seek (imperative) /*
                                                           for me
Within your hert; for parde,° lo, justice   *by God*
If I offende it must yourselven be
To punisshe, like as ye the offenses see;
For I as name nor have no thing at all,
But it is soul° your owen in eche degree,   *only*
With hert, body, my litel good and all.

What so ye will, I will it to obey,
For paine or smert° how so that me bifall;   *hurt*
So am I youre, and shall to that I dey,[1]
With hert, body, my litel good and all.

[*From the French of Charles d'Orleans, 1394–1465*]

1. So am I yours, and shall be till I die.

55

Mittitur:°   *It is sent*

Go, litull bill,° and command° me hertely   *letter / commend*
Unto her that I call my trulove and lady,
Be° this same true tokenninge   *by*
That sho° see° me in a kirk° on a Friday in a morning,
                                                         she/ saw / church
With a sper-hawk° on my hand;   *sparrow-hawk*
And my mone° did by her stond;   *servant*
And an old womon sete her by,
That litull cold of curtesy,[1]
And oft on her sho did smile
To loke° on me for a while.   *look*
And yet be this another token—
To the kirke she comme° with a gentilwomon;   *came*
Even behind the kirk dore
Thay kneled bothe on the flore,
And fast thay did piter-pater—
I hope they said Matens togeder!
Yet ones° or twies° at the lest,°   *once / twice / least*
She did on me her eye kest;°   *cast*
Then went I forthe prevely,°   *secretly*
And hailsed° on thaim curtesly.   *greeted*
Be° alle the tokens truly,   *by*
Command me to her hertely.

56

Wolde God that it were so
As I coulde wishe bitwixt us two.[2]

The man that I loved altherbest°   *best of all*
  In all this contree, est other° west,   *or*
To me he is a strange gest;
  What wonder es't° thow° I be wo?°   *is it / though / woeful*

1. That little one, cold with regard to   2. [Refrain repeated after each stanza.]
courtesy.

When me were levest that he schold dwelle,[3]
  He maketh haste fro me to go;
He wold noght° sey ones° farewell   *not / once*
  When time was come that he most go.

In places ofte when I him mete,
  I dar noght speke, but forth I go;
With herte and eyes I him grete;
  So trewe of love I know no mo.°   *more*

As he is min hert° love,   *heart's*
  My dyrward° dyre,° iblessed he be;   *precious / darling*
I swere by God that is above,
  Non hath my love but only he.

I am icomferted in every side,
  The colures wexeth both fres° and newe;   *fresh*
When he is come and will abide,
  I wot° full well that he is trewe.   *know*

I love him trewely and no mo—
  Wolde God that he it knewe!
And ever I hope it schall be so;
  Then schall I chaunge for no new.

57

Were it undo° that is ido,°   *undone / done*
I wolde bewar.[1]

I lovede a child° of this cuntree,   *young man*
And so I wende° he had do me;   *supposed*
Now myself the sothe° I see,   *truth*
  That he is far.

He seide to me he wolde be trewe,
And change me for non other newe;
Now I sikke° and am pale of hewe,   *sigh*
  For he is far.

He seide his sawes° he wolde fulfille: *promises*
Therfore I lat him have all his wille;
Now I sikke and morne stille,°   *quietly*
  For he is far.

3. When I most want him to stay.   1. [Refrain repeated after each stanza.]

58

So well is me begone,[1]
  Troly, loly—
So well is me begone,
  Troly, loly.[2]

Of serving men I will begin,
  Troly, loly,
For they go mynon° trim,   elegantly
  Troly, loly.

Of met° and drink and feir clothing,   food
  Troly, loly.
By dere God I want none,
  Troly, loly.

His bonet is of fine scarlet,
  Troly, loly,
With heer° as black as geit,°   hair / jet
  Troly, loly.

His dublet is of fine satine,
  Troly, loly,
His shert well maid and trime,
  Troly, loly.

His coit° it is so trime and rounde,   coat
  Troly, loly,
His kisse is worth a hundred pounde,
  Troly, loly.

His hoise° is of London black,   hose
  Troly, loly,
In him ther is no lack,
  Troly, loly.

His face it is so lik a man,
  Troly, loly,
Who can but love him than,
  Troly, loly.

Whersoever he be, he hath my hert,
  Troly, loly,
And shall to° deth depart,°   till / separate (us)
  Troly, loly.

1. So fortunate am I.   2. [Refrain repeated after each stanza.]

So well is me begone,
    Troly, loly,
So well is me begone,
    Troly, loly.

59

Somer is comen° with love to toune,   *has come*
With blostme,° and with brides° roune.°   *blossom / bird's / song*
The note° of hasel° springeth,   *nut / hazel*
The dewes darkneth in the dale.
For longing of the nightegale,
Thes foweles murye singeth.[1]

Ic° herde a strif° bitweyes° two—   *I / dispute / between*
That on of wele,[2] that other of wo:
Bitwene two ifere.°   *together*
That on hereth° wimmen that hoe° beth hende,°
                                      praises / they / courteous
That other hem° wole° with mighte shende.° *them / wishes / to shame*
That strif ye mowen° ihere.°   *may / hear*

The nightingale is on° by nome°   *one / name*
That wol shilden° hem from shome,°   *shield / shame*
Of skathe° hoe° wole hem skere;°   *harm / she / free*
The threstelcok hem kepeth ay,[3]
He seith by nighte and eke° by day   *also*
That hy beth fendes ifere.[4]

For hy biswiketh° euchan° mon   *deceive / each*
That mest bileveth hem upon.[5]
They° hy ben milde of chere,°   *though / appearance*
Hoe° beth fikele and fals to fonde,[6]   *they*
Hoe wercheth° wo in euchan londe.   *work*
It were betere that hy nere.°   *were not (did not exist)*

Nightingale:
"It is shome to blame levedy,°   *lady (women)*
For hy beth hende° of corteisy;   *gracious*
Ich rede° that thou lete.°   *advise / desist*

1. These birds sing merrily.   4. That they are the Devil's companions.
2. The one (sings) of good fortune.   5. That most believes in them.
3. The thrush always lies in ambush for   6. "To fonde": when tested.
them.

Ne wes nevere bruche° so strong,   *sin*
Ibroke° with righte ne with wrong,   *committed*
That mon° ne mighte bete.°   *one / amend*

Hy gladieth° hem that beth wrothe,°   *gladden / angry*
Bothe the heye and the lowe;
Mid gome° hy cunne° hem grete.°   *pleasure / can / welcome*
This world nere nout if wimmen nere;[7]
Imaked hoe wes to mones fere;[8]
Nis° no thing all so swete."   *there is (not)*

Thrush:
"I ne may wimmen herien° nohut,°   *praise / not at all*
For hy beth swikele° and false of thohut,°   *deceitful / thought*
Also° ich am understonde.°   *as / informed*
Hy beth feire and bright on hewe;
Here° thout° is fals, and untrewe: *their / thought*
Ful yare ich have hem fonde.[9]

Alisaundre° the king meneth° of hem: *Alexander (the Great) / tells*
In the world nes non so crafty mon,[1]
Ne non so riche of londe.
I take witnesse of monye and fele[2]
That riche weren of worldes wele;
Muche wes hem° the shonde."°   *to them / disgrace*

Nightingale:
The nightingale hoe wes wroth:
"Fowel, me thinketh thou art me loth[3]
Sweche° tales for to showe.   *such*
Among a thousend levedies itolde,°   *counted*
Ther nis non wickede, I holde,
Ther° hy sitteth on rowe.°   *where / row*

Hy beth of herte meke and milde;
Hemself° hy cunne° from shome° shilde   *themselves / can / shame*
Withinne boures° wowe,°   *chamber's / wall*
And swettoust° thing in armes to wree°   *sweetest / embrace*
The mon that holdeth° hem in glee.°   *beholds / pleasure*
Fowel, why ne art thou it iknowe?"[4]

Thrush:
"Gentil fowel, seyst thou it me?°   *to me*
Ich habbe° with hem in boure ibe,°   *have / been*
I haved° all mine wille.   *had*

7. This world would be nothing if there were no women.
8. She was made to be man's companion.
9. Full long ago I put them to the test.
1. In the world there was no man so powerful.
2. "Monye and fele": many and sundry.
3. Bird, it seems to me you are hateful to me.
4. Bird, why do you not admit it?

Hy willeth° for a litel mede°   *will / reward*
Don° a senful, derne° dede,   *do / secret*
Here° soule for to spille.°   *their / destroy*

Fowel, me thinketh thou art les;°   *false*
They° thou be milde and softe of pes,°   *though / peace*
Thou seyst thine wille.
I take witnesse of Adam,
That wes oure furste man,
That fonde hem wicke and ille."

Nightingale:
"Threstelcok, thou art wood,°   *mad*
Other thou const to litel good[5]
This° wimmen for to shende.°   *these / shame*
It is the swetteste driwerie,°   *love*
And mest° hoe° cunnen° of curteisie.   *most / they / know*
Nis nothing all so hende.°   *kind, courteous*

The mest murthe that mon haveth here,
Whenne hoe° is maked° to his fere°   *he / mated / companion*
In armes for to wende.°   *enfold*
It is shome to blame levedy;°   *a lady*
For hem thou shalt gon sory°—   *wretched*
Of° londe ich wille thee sende."   *out of*

Thrush:
"Nightingale, thou havest wrong!
Wolt thou me senden of this lond
For° ich holde with the righte?   *because*
I take witnesse of Sire Gawain,
That° Jhesu Crist gaf° might and main   *to whom / gave*
And strengthe for to fighte:

So wide so he hevede igon,[6]
Trewe ne founde he nevere non
By daye ne by nighte."

Nightingale:
"Fowel, for° thy false mouth,   *because of*
Thy sawe° shall ben wide° couth;°   *saying / widely / known*
I rede° thee fle° with mighte.   *advise / to flee*

Ich habbe leve to ben here,
In orchard and in erbere,°   *arbor*
Mine songes for to singe.
Herd I nevere by° no levedy   *concerning*
Bote° hendinesse° and curteisy,   *except / politeness*
And joye hy gunnen° me bringe;   *did*

5. Or you know too little good.   6. As far and wide as he had gone.

Of muchele murthe hy telleth me.
Fere,° also° I telle thee,   *friend / just as*
Hy livieth in longinge.
Fowel, thou sittest on hasel bou;°   *bough*
Thou lastest° hem; thou havest wou[7]—   *blame*
Thy word shall wide springe."

Thrush:
"It springeth wide, well ich wot°—   *know*
Thou tell it him that it not!°   *knows not*
This° sawes ne beth nout newe.   *these*
Fowel, herkne to my sawe,
Ich wille thee telle of here° lawe°—   *their / customs*
Thou ne kepest nout hem iknowe.[8]

Thenk on Costantines quene—
Foul well hire semede fou and grene[9]—
How sore it gon hire rewe![1]
Hoe° fedde a crupel° in hire bour,   *she / cripple*
And helede° him with covertour.°   *concealed / coverlet*
Loke, whar° wimmen ben trewe!"   *whether*

Nightingale:
"Threstelcok, thou havest wrong!
Also° I saye one° my song,   *just as / in*
And that men witeth° wide,   *know*
Hy beth brightore under shawe°   *copse, grove*
Then the day whenne it dawe°   *dawns*
In longe someres tide.°   *time*

Come thou evere in here londe,
Hy shulen don° thee in prisoun stronge   *put*
And ther thou shalt abide.
The lesinges° that thou havest maked,   *lies*
Ther thou shalt hem forsake,
And shome thee shall bitide."°   *befall*

Thrush:
"Nightingale, thou seyst thine wille,°   *conviction*
Thou seyst that wimmen shulen me spille.°   *destroy*
Datheit° who it wolde!°   *a curse on / would wish*
In holy book it is ifounde,
Hy bringeth mony mon to grounde,
That proude weren and bolde.

Thenk upon Saunsum° the stronge,   *Samson*
How muchel his wif him dude to wronge![2]

7. "Havest wou": are wrong.   clothing became her.
8. You do not care to understand them.   1. How grievously she did regret it!
9. Full well her variegated fur and green   2. How much harm his wife did to him!

Ich wot° that hoe° him solde.   *know / she*
It is that worste hord of pris
That Jhesu makede in parais
In tresour for to holde."[3]

Nightingale:
Tho° seyde the nightingale: *then*
"Fowel, well redy[4] is thy tale;
Herkne to my lore!°   *teaching*
It is flour° that lasteth longe,   *flower*
And mest iherd° in every londe,   *praised*
And lovelich° under gore.° *lovely / clothing*

In the worlde nis° non so goed° leche,° *there is (not) / good / physician*
So milde of thoute, so feir of speche,
To hele monnes sore.°   *suffering*
Fowel, thou rewest all thy thohut;[5]
Thou dost evele, ne geineth° thee nohut;° *avails / not at all*
Ne do thou so namore!"

Thrush:
"Nightingale, thou art unwis
On hem to leyen° so muchel pris;° *place / value*
Thy mede° shall ben lene.   *reward*
Among on hundret ne beth five,
Nouther° of maidnes ne of wive,   *neither*
That holdeth hem° all clene;° *themselves / pure*

That hy ne wercheth wo in londe,
Other° bringeth men to shonde,° *or / disgrace*
And that is well iseene.°   *manifest*
And they° we sitten° therfore to strive, *though / may sit (perch)*
Bothe of maidnes and of wive,
Soth° ne seyst thou ene."°   *truth / once*

Nightingale:
"O fowel, thy mouth thee haveth ishend!° *shamed*
Thoru° wham° wes all this world iwend?° *through / whom / changed*
Of° a maide meke and milde;   *by*
Of hire sprong that holy bern°   *child*
That boren wes in Bedlehem,
And temeth° all that is wilde.   *tames*

Hoe° ne weste° of sunne° ne of shame; *she / knew / sin*
Marye wes hir righte name—
Crist hire ishilde![6]

3. It (the money she received for betraying Samson) is the worst hoard of value/ That Jesus made in Paradise/ To be held as treasure.
4. "Well redy": very glib.
5. Bird, you will regret all your thought (against women).
6. May Christ shield her!

Fowel, for thy false sawe
Forbed° I thee this wode shawe;°   *forbid / copse*
Thou fare into the filde!"

Thrush:
"Nightingale, I wes wood,°   *mad*
Other I couthe to litel good[7]
With thee for to strive.
I saye that ich am overcome
Thoru hire° that bar that holy sone,   *her*
That soffrede wundes five.

I swerie° by his holy name: *swear*
Ne shall I nevere seyen shame
By° maidnes ne by wive.   *concerning*
Out of this londe will I te,°   *go*
Ne rech° I never weder° I fle.   *care / whither*
Away ich wille drive."

60

Weping haveth° min wonges° wet   *has / cheeks*
For wikked werk° and wone° of wit;° *deed / lack / understanding*
Unblithe° I be til I ha° bet°   *unhappy / have / atoned for*
Bruches° broken, ase bok° bit,° *transgressions / book / commands*
Of levedis° love, that I ha let,°   *ladies' / abandoned*
That lemeth° all with luevly° lit;°   *gleams / beautiful / hue*
Ofte in song I have hem° set,°   *them / set, placed*
That is unsemly ther it sit.[1]
It sit and semeth° noght   *befits*
Ther° it is seid in song;   *where*
That I have of hem wroght,°   *written*
Iwis° it is all wrong.   *indeed*

All wrong I wroghte for° a wif°   *concerning / woman (Eve)*
That made us wo in world full wide;
Heo° rafte° us alle richesse rif,°   *she / robbed / abundant*
That durfte us nout in reines ride.[2]
A stithie stunte hire sturne strif,
That is in heovene hert in hide.[3]

---

7. Or I knew too little good.
1. That is unseemly where it applies
(i.e., it is unseemly to have written as I
have about ladies' love).
2. Who had no need to ride us in reins
(i.e., to show her mastery over us).
3. An excellent person put an end to her
violent strife,/ That (excellent person) is
in heaven's heart in concealment.

In hire light on ledeth lif,[4]
And shon° thourgh hire semly side.   *shone*
Though hire side he shon
Ase sonne doth thourgh the glass;
Wommon nes° wicked non   *was (not)*
Sethe° he ibore° was.   *since / born*

Wicked nis° non° that I wot°   *is (not) / none / know*
That durste° for werk° hire° wonges wete;   *dared / grief / their*
Alle heo liven from last of lot[5]
And are all hende° ase hawk in chete.°   *gracious / hall*
Forthy° on molde° I waxe mot°   *therefore / earth / sorry*
That I sawes° have seid unsete,°   *speeches / unbecoming*
My fikel fleish, my falsly° blod;   *false, deceptive*
On feld hem feole I falle to fete.[6]
To fet I falle hem feole
For falslek° fifty-folde,°   *falsehood / excessive*
Of alle untrewe° on tele°   *unfaithful persons / calumny*
With tonge ase I er° tolde.   *formerly*

Thagh told beon tales untoun in toune,
Such tiding mey tide, I nul nout teme[7]
Of brudes° bright° with browes broune,   *women / fair*
Or blisse heo beyen this briddes breme.[8]
In rude were ro with hem roune
That hem mighte henten ase him were heme.[9]
Nis king, cayser, ne clerk with croune
This semly serven that mene may seme.[1]
Semen him may on sonde[2]
This semly serven so,
Bothe with fet and honde,°   *hands*
For on° that us warp° from wo.   *one / rescued*

Now wo in world is went away,
And weole° is come ase we wolde,   *happiness*
Though a mighty, methful° may,°   *gentle / maid*
That us hath cast from cares colde.
Ever wimmen ich° herie° ay,   *I / praise*
And ever in hyrd with hem ich holde,[3]
And ever at neode I nickenay
That I ner nemnede that heo nolde.[4]

---

4. Alighted in her (i.e., born of her), one (Christ) lives.
5. They live free from every fault of behavior.
6. I fall to the ground at their feet (i.e., I humble myself much to them).
7. Though evil tales were told in the world,/ Such event may befall, I will not vouch.
8. Or they redeem bliss, these excellent maidens.

9. Among the violent, it would be peace to speak with them/ So that he might receive from them as were fitting to him.
1. There is no king, emperor, or tonsured clerk/ Who would seem to be humiliated by serving these seemly ones.
2. It must befit him on errand.
3. And I always defend them in the household.
4. And, when necessary, I deny/ Having said anything that they did not wish.

I nolde and nullit noght,[5]
For nothing now a nede,°   *of necessity*
Soth° is that I of hem ha° wroght,°   *true / have / written*
As Richard erst con rede.[6]

Richard, rote° of resoun right,   *root*
Rykening° of rym° and ron,°   *distinction / verse / poetry*
Of maidnes meke thou hast might;°   *power*
On molde° I holde thee muryest° mon.   *earth / most pleasing*
Cunde° comely ase a knight,   *well-born*
Clerk icud° that craftes° con,°   *famous / skills / knows*
In uch an hyrd thin athel is hight,
And uch an athel thin hap is on.[7]
Hap that hathel° hath hent°   *splendid fellow / received*
With hendelec° in halle;   *courtesy*
Selthe° be him sent   *happiness*
In londe of levedis alle!

[*Harley* 2253]

61

"Say° me, wight° in the brom,°   *tell / creature / broom-shrub*
Teche me how I shule° don°   *shall / act*
That min hosebonde
Me lovien° wolde."   *love*

"Hold thine tunge stille
And have all thine wille."

62

Of all creatures women be best:
Cuius contrarium verum est.[1]

5. I did not, and will not, (say) anything.
6. As Richard first did say.
7. In every household your excellence is mentioned/ And every man is involved in your destiny.
1. The opposite of this is true. [Refrain repeated after each stanza].

In every place ye may well see
That women be trewe as tirtil° on tree,   *turtle-dove*
Not liberal° in langage, but ever in secree,°   *licentious / secrecy*
And gret joye amonge them is for to be.

The stedfastnes of women will never be don,
So jentil,° so curtes° they be everychon,° *well-bred / courteous / everyone*
Meke as a lambe, still as a stone,
Croked° nor crabbed° find ye none!   *perverse / disagreeable*

Men be more cumbers° a thousand fold,   *troublesome*
And I mervail how they dare be so bold
Against women for to hold,
Seeing them so pacient, softe, and cold.

For tell a woman all your counsaile,
And she can kepe it wonderly well;
She had lever° go quik° to hell,   *rather / alive*
Than to her neighbour she wold it tell!

For by women men be reconsiled,
For by women was never man begiled,
For they be of the condicion of curtes Grisell,°   *Griselda*
For they be so meke and milde.

Now say well by° women or elles be still,   *about*
For they never displesed man by ther will;
To be angry or wroth they can° no skill,°   *have / ability*
For I dare say they think non ill.

Trow° ye that women list° to smater,°   *think / like / chatter*
Or against ther husbondes for to clater?
Nay, they had lever fast bred and water,
Then for to dele in suche a mater.

Though all the paciens in the world were drownd,
And non were lefte here on the ground,
Again in a woman it might be found,
Suche vertu in them dothe abound!

To the tavern they will not go,
Nor to the alehous never the mo,°   *more*
For, God wot,° ther hartes wold be wo,   *knows*
To spende ther husbondes money so.

If here were a woman or a maid,
That list for to go freshely arayed,
Or with fine kirchers° to go displayed,   *kerchiefs*
Ye wold say, "They be proude": it is ill said.

63

Whan netilles° in winter bere roses rede,   *nettles*
And thornes bere figges naturally,
And bromes° bere appilles in every mede,°   *shrubs / meadow*
And lorelles° bere cheris in the croppes° so hie,   *laurels / tree-tops*
And okes° bere dates so plentuosly,   *oaks*
And lekes° geve hony in ther superfluens°—   *leeks / superabundance*
   Than put in a woman your trust and confidence.

Whan whiting° walk in forestes, hartes for to chase,   *fish*
And heringes in parkes hornes boldly blowe,
And flounders more-hennes° in fennes enbrace,   *moor-hens*
And gornardes° shote rolions° out of a crosse bowe, *gurnards / fish*
And grengese° ride in hunting the wolf to overthrowe,   *goslings*
And sperlinges° rone° with speres in harness to defence—*smelts / run*
   Than put in a woman your trust and confidence.

Whan sparrowes bild chirches and stepulles hie,
And wrennes carry sakkes to the mille,
And curlews carry clothes,° horses for to drye,   *cloths*
And semewes° bring butter to the market to sell,   *sea-mews*
And wood-doves were° wood-knives, theves to kill,   *wear*
And griffons to goslings don obedience—
   Than put in a woman your trust and confidence.

Whan crabbes tak woodcokes in forestes and parkes,
And hares ben taken with sweetness of snailes,
And camelles with ther here° tak swallowes and perches,° *hair / fish*
And mise° mowe corn with waveing of ther tailes,   *mice*
Whan dukkes° of the dunghill seek the blood of Hailes,[1] *ducks*
Whan shrewd wives to ther husbondes do non offens—
   Than put in a woman your trust and confidence.

64

What, why didest thou wink when thou a wyf toke?
Thou haddest never more need brodde° to loke!   *with open eyes*

1. [Hailes Abbey, in Gloucestershire, to   to have been given in 1270 by Richard,
which the blood of Christ was supposed   Earl of Cornwall.]

A man that wedeth a wife whan he winketh,
But he stare afterward, wonder me thinketh![1]

65

Know er° thou knitte;° prove er thou preise it.

before / bind (in marriage)

If thou know er thou knit, than maist thou abate;°   *back out*
And if thou knit er thou knowe, than it is too late.
Therfore avise thee er thou the knot knitte,
For "Had I wist"° cometh too late for to loose° it.   *known / untie*

66

Man, bewar of thine wowing,°   *wooing*
For wedding is the longe wo.[2]

Loke er° thine herte be set;   *before*
Loke thou wowe er thou be knet;°   *united (in marriage)*
And if thou see thou mow° do bet,°   *may / better*
    Knet° up the heltre° and let her go.   *hang / halter*

Wives be bothe stoute and bolde;
Her° husbondes agens hem durn° not holde;   *their / dare*
And if he do, his herte is colde,
    Howsoevere the game go.

Wedowes be wol° fals, iwis,°   *well, very / certainly*
For they cun° bothe halse° and kis,   *can / embrace*
Till ones purs piked is,
    And they seyn, "Go, boy, go!"

Of madenes° I will seyn but litil,   *maidens*
For they be bothe fals and fekil,°   *fickle*
And under the tail they ben full tekil;°   *excitable*
    A° twenty devel name, let hem go!   *by*

1. Unless he stare (in madness) after-   2. [Refrain repeated after each stanza.]
ward, it seems to me curious.

67

A yong wyf and an harvest-gos,°   *goose*
  Moche gagil° with bothe;   *cackling*
A man that hath hem° in his clos,°   *them / yard*
  Reste schal he wrothe.°   *badly*

68

How! hey! it is non° les,°   *no / less*
I dar not sey° whan she seith "Pes!"°[1]   *speak / Peace!*

Yung men, I warne you everichon,°   *everyone*
Elde° wives tak ye non;   *old*
For I myself have one at hom—
I dar not seyn whan she seith "Pes!"

Whan I cum fro the plow at non,°   *noon*
In a reven° dish min mete° is don;°   *cracked / food / put*
I dar not asken our dame a spon°—   *spoon*
I dar not seyn whan she seith "Pes!"

If I aske our dame bred,
She taketh a staff and breketh min hed,
And doth° me rennen° under the bed—   *makes / run*
I dar not seyn whan she seith "Pes!"

If I aske our dame fleish,°   *meat*
She breketh min hed with a dish:
"Boy, thou art not worth a reish!"°   *rush*
I dar not seyn whan she seith "Pes!"

If I aske our dame chese,°   *cheese*
"Boy," she seith, all at ese,
"Thou are not worth half a pese."°   *pea*
I dar not seyn when she seith "Pes!"

1. [Refrain repeated after each stanza.]

69

Care away, away, away—
Care away for evermore![1]

All that I may swink° or swet,	*labor*
My wife it will both drink and ete;	
And° I sey ought,° she will me bete—	*if / anything*
Carfull° is my hart therfor!	*full of care*

If I sey ought of her but good,	
She loke on me as she war wood,°	*mad*
And will me clout about the hood—	
Carfull is my hart therfor!	

If she will to the gud ale ride,	
Me must trot all be° her side;	*by*
And whan she drink, I must abide—	
Carfull is my hart therfor!	

If I say, "It shall be thus,"	
She sey, "Thou liest, charl,° iwous!°	*churl / certainly*
Wenest° thou to overcome me thus?"	*expect*
Carfull is my hart therfor!	

If ony man have such a wife to lede,°	*deal with*
He schal know how *judicare*° cam in the Creed;	*judge*
Of his penans God do° him meed!°	*give / reward*
Carfull is my hart therfor!	

70

Welcome be ye when ye go,	
And farewell when ye come!	
So faire as ye ther be no mo,°	*more*
As bright as bery browne.	
I love you verrily° at my to,[2]	*truly*
None so moch in all this towne.	

1. [Refrain repeated after each stanza.]   2. "At my to": near me.

I am right glad when ye will go,
And sorry when ye will come!
And whan ye be out fare,°   *gone*
I pray for you sertayn,
That never man, horse, ne mare,
Bringe you to town ageyn.
To praise youre beutee I ne dare,
For drede that° men wille seyn.°   *what / say*
Farewelle! no more for you I care,
But pray you of my songe have no desdeyn!

71

I am olde whan age doth apele,°   *challenge me*
Having a yong thing that litel setteth me by.[1]
One such in a schire is too many, and fele°   *many*
Other than trew be; beholde a cause° why: *reason*
I may not as I might on my partye.[2]
Therefor I am forsake! age, age, wo° thou be!   *woe*
Youth is a traitoure, her experiens at eye;°   *first hand*
Oftentimes and many the blinde eteth many a flye!

72

To my trew love and able,
As the weder° cok he is stable,   *weather*
This letter to him be delivered.[3]

Unto you, most froward,° this lettre I write,   *perverse*
Which hath caused me so longe in dispaire;
The goodlinesse of your persone is esye° to endite,°   *easy / describe*
For he leveth° nat that can youre persone appaire°—   *lives / deride*
So comly,° best shapen, of feture most faire,   *comely*
Most fresch of contenaunce, even as an owle
Is best and most favored of ony oder fowle!

1. Having a young thing that sets little   2. I.e., I cannot perform sexually.
store by me.   3. [Refrain repeated after each stanza.]

Youre manly visage, shortly to declare,
Your forehed, mouth, and nose so flatte,
In short conclusion, best likened to an hare
Of alle living thinges, save living only a catte;
More wold I sey if I wist° what—   *knew*
That swete visage full ofte is beshrewed°   *cursed*
Whan I remembre of som bawd so lewd.

The proporcion of your body comende wele me aught,[4]
Fro the shuldre down, behinde and beforn;
If alle the peintours in a land togeder were soght,
A worse coude they not portrey thogh alle they had it sworn!
Kepe wele your pacience thogh I sende you a skorne.
Your garmentes upon you full gaily they hinge°   *hang*
As it were an olde goose had a broke winge.

Your thighes misgrowen, youre shankes much worse;
Whoso beholde youre knees so crooked—
As ech of hem bad oder Cristes curse,[5]
So go they outward; youre hammes° ben hooked;°   *thighs / bandy*
Such a peire° chaumbes° I never on looked!   *pair of / legs*
So ungoodly youre heles° ye lifte,   *heels*
And youre feet ben crooked, with evil thrifte.°   *fortune*

Who might have the love of so swete a wight,°   *man*
She might be right glad that ever was she born.
She that ones° wold in a dark night   *once*
Renne° for your love till she had caught a thorn,   *run*
I wolde her no more harme but hanged on the morn,
That hath two good eyen and ichese here suche a make,[6]
Or ones wold lift up here hole for youre sake!

Youre swete love with blody nailes,
Whiche fedeth° mo° lice than quailes.   *feeds / more*

73

To you, dere herte, variant and mutable,
Like to Carybdis which is unstable.[1]

4. I ought to commend well the proportions of your body.
5. As if each of them bade the other
(have) Christ's curse.

6. That has two good eyes and has chosen for herself such a mate.
1. [Refrain repeated after each stanza.]

O fresch floure, most plesant of prise,°   *value*
Fragrant as federfoy° to mannes inspeccion,   *feverfew*
Me semeth by youre contenaunce ye be wonder nice,[2]
You for to medil° with any retorucion;°   *contend / rhetorician*
To me ye have sent a lettre of derusion,°   *derision*
Endighted full freshly with many corious iclause.[3]
Wherfore I thanke you as I finde cause.

The Inglisch of Chaucere was nat in youre mind,
Ne Tullius° termes with so gret eloquence,   *Tully's (Cicero's)*
But ye, as uncurtes and crabbed of kinde,[4]
Rolled hem° on a hepe,° it semeth by the sentence;°
                    them / heap / language
And so dare I boldly withoute ony offence
Answere to your letter, as falleth to the purpose;
And thus I beginne, construe ye the glose.°   *gloss*

Crist of his goodnesse and of his gret might
Formed many a criator° to walke on the ground;   *creature*
But he that beholdeth you by day and by night
Shall never have cause in hert to be jocound,
Remembering your grete hede and your forhed round,
With staring eyen, visage large and huge,
And either of youre pappes like a water-bowge.°   *skin water-bottle*

Youre camused° nose, with nose-thrilles° brode,   *snub / nostrils*
Unto the chirch a noble instrument
To quenche tapers brenning° afore° the roode,°
                  burning / before / Cross
Is best apropred, at mine avisament;[5]
Your lewd° looking,° doble of entent,   *vulgar / appearance*
With courtly loke all of saferon hew,°   *hue*
That never wol faile—the colour is so trew!

Youre babir° lippes of colour ded and wan,   *thick*
With suche mouth like to Jacobes brother,
And yelow tethe not lik to the swan—
Set wide asonder, as eche cursed other;[6]
In all a lond, who coude finde suche another,
Of alle fetures so ungoodly° for to see,   *unsightly*
With brethe as swete as is the elder tree?

Youre body is formed all in proporcion,
With hanging shuldres waving with every winde,
Small in the belly as a wine toune,°   *barrel*

2. It seems to me by your countenance (that) you are wonderfully foolish.
3. Composed very freshly with many a beautifully fashioned clause.
4. But you, being discourteous and disagreeable of nature.
5. Is best assigned, in my judgment.
6. Set wide apart, as if each cursed the others.

With froward° fete, and crooked bak behinde;   *ugly*
He that you wold have alway in minde,
And for your love wold breke on oure reste,
I wold he were locched° with Lucifer the depeste.   *locked*

And of youre atire, shortly to devise,
Your templers° colured as the lowcray,° *forehead ornaments /*
                 striped cloth (?)
With dagged° hood, leid on pancake wise,   *slashed*
Your bolwerkes,° pectorelles,° and all your nice aray;
        breastworks / breast ornaments
Treuly me semeth ye are a lovely may!°   *maiden*
And namely on haliday, whan ye trip and daunce,
As a wilde goos keping your contenaunce!

Adew, dere herte, for now I make an ende
Unto suche time that I have better space.° *opportunity*
The pip° and the pose° to you I recomend, *catarrh / rheum*
And God of his mercy graunte you so mikel° grace *much*
In paradise ones° to have a resting place,   *once*
Up by the navel, fast by the water gate,
To loke after passage whan it cometh late.

Youre owne love, trusty and trewe,
You have forsake cause of a newe.

74

Women, women, love of women
Maketh bare purses with sum men.[1]

Sum be mery, and sum be sad,
And sum be besy, and sum be bad;
Sum be wilde, by Seint Chad;
 Yet all be not so,
For sum be lewed,°   *worthless*
And sum be shrewed;°   *shrewish*
Go, shrew, whersoever ye go.[2]

Sum be wise, and sum be fonde;°   *foolish*
Sum be tame, I understond;

1. [Refrain repeated after each stanza.]
2. [Last three lines repeated in each stanza.]

Sum will take bred at a mannes hond;
  Yet all be not so.

Sum be wroth and cannot tell wherfore;
Sum be skorning evermore,
And sum be tusked like a bore;
  Yet all be not so.

Sum will be dronken as a mouse;
Sum be crooked and will hurte a louse;
Sum be faire and good in a house;
  Yet all be not so.

Sum be snouted like an ape;
Sum can nother° play ne jape;   *neither*
Sum of them be well shape;
  Yet all be not so.

Sum can prate° without hire;   *chatter*
Sum make bate° in every shire;   *strife*
Sum can play chekmate with³ our sire;
  Yet all they do not so.

75

Robene sat on a gud grene hill
Kepand° a flok of fe;°   *keeping / sheep*
Mirry° Makyne said him till:°   *merry / to*
"Robene, thow rew° on me!   *pity*
I haif the luvit lowd and still¹
Thir° yeiris° two or thre;   *these / years*
My dule in dern bot gif thow dill,
Dowtles but dreid I de."²

Robene ansuerit:° "Be° the Rude,°   *answered / by / Cross*
Nathing of lufe I knaw,
Bot keipis my scheip under yone° wude—   *yonder*
Lo quhair thay raik on raw!³
Quhat hes marrit the in thy mude,⁴
Makyne, to me thow schaw:°   *show*

3. "Play chekmate with": be a match for.
1. I have loved you openly and in secret.
2. Unless you relieve my sorrow in secret,/ Doubtless I fear I shall die.
3. See where they wander in a row.
4. What has marred you in your mood.

Or quhat is lufe, or to be lude?°   *loved*
Fane wald° I leir° that law."   *would / learn*

"At luvis lair° gife° thow will leir,   *learning / if*
Tak thair ane ABC:
Be heynd,° courtas and fair of feir,°   *gentle / demeanor*
Wyse, hardy° and fre;°   *courageous / generous*
So that no denger° do the° deir,°   *disdain / you / hurt*
Quhat dule° in dern° thow dre,°   *sorrow / secret / endure*
Preis the with pane at all poweir[5]—
Be patient and previe."°   *secretive*

Robene ansuerit hir agane:
"I wait° nocht° quhat is luve,   *know / not*
Bot I haif mervell° in certane   *wonder*
Quhat makis the this wanrufe;°   *restless, unhappy*
The weddir° is fair and I am fane,°   *weather / happy*
My scheip gois° haill° aboif;°   *go / wholly / above*
And° we wald play us in this plane°   *if / valley*
Thay wald us bayth° reproif."°   *both / reprove*

"Robene, tak tent° unto my taill,°   *attention / tale*
And wirk all as I reid,°   *counsel*
And thow sall° haif my hairt all haill,° *shall / whole, entire*
Eik and° my madinheid: *and also*
Sen° God sendis bute° for baill° *since / comfort / sorrow*
And for murnyng remeid,°   *remedy*
I dern with the bot gif I daill,[6]
Dowtles I am bot deid."

"Makyne, tomorne° this ilka° tyde,° *tomorrow / same / time*
And° ye will meit° meit° me heir, *if / meet / properly*
Peraventure° my scheip ma gang° besyd° *perhaps / go / astray*
Quhill° we haif liggit° full neir—   *while / lain*
Bot mawgre haif I and I byd,[7]
Fra° thay begin to steir;° *from the time when / stir*
Quhat lyis on° hairt° I will nocht hyd;° *in / heart / hide*
Makyn, than mak gud cheir."

"Robene, thow reivis° me roif° and rest— *rob / rest*
I luve bot the allone."
"Makyne, adew; the sone° gois west,   *sun*
The day is neir-hand° gone."   *nearly*
"Robene, in dule° I am so drest   *sorrow*
That lufe wil be my bone."°   *bane*
"Ga lufe, Makyne, quhairever° thow list,° *wherever / please*
For lemman° I lue° none."   *lover / love*

"Robene, I stand in sic° a styll;°   *such / plight*
I sicht°—and that full sair."°   *sigh / sorely*

5. Take pains to strive with all your secret.
strength.   7. But may I have sorrow if I stay.
6. Unless I have intercourse with you in

"Makyne, I haif bene heir° this quhyle;° here / while
At hame God gif° I wair!"° grant / were
"My huny Robene, talk ane quhill,° while
Gif° thow will do na mair."° if / more
"Makyne, sum uthir man begyle,
For hamewart I will fair."

Robene on his wayis went
Als° licht as leif° of tre; as / leaf
Mawkin murnit° in hir intent mourned
And trowd° him nevir to se. believed
Robene brayd° attour° the bent;° darted / across / heath
Than Mawkyne cryit on hie:° high
"Now ma thow sing, for I am schent!° destroyed
Quhat alis° lufe at me?" ails

Mawkyne went hame withowttin faill;
Full wery eftir° cowth° weip:° after / did / weep
Than Robene in a ful fair daill° dale
Assemblit all his scheip.
Be that,° sum pairte of Mawkynis aill° by that time / distress
Outthrow° his hairt cowd creip;° throughout / creep
He fallowit° fast thair till° assaill,° followed / to / confront
And till hir tuke gude keip.° heed

"Abyd, abyd, thow fair Makyne!
A word for ony thing!
For all my luve it sal° be thyne, shall
Withowttin depairting.° dividing
All haill thy harte for till haif myne[8]
Is all my cuvating;° desire
My scheip tomorne quhill° houris nyne till
Will neid° of no keiping." need

"Robene, thow hes° hard° soung° and say° have / heard / sung / said
In gestis° and storeis auld,° tales / old
The man that will nocht quhen he may
Sall haif nocht° quhen he wald. nought
I pray to Jesu every day
Mot eik thair cairis cauld[9]
That first preiss° with the to play press, strive
Be firth,° forrest or fawld."° wood / fold

"Makyne, the nicht is soft and dry,
The wedder is warme and fair,
And the grene woid° rycht neir us by wood
To walk attour° allquhair;° across / everywhere
Thair ma na janglour° us espy, scandalmonger
That is to lufe contrair;° contrary

8. For your heart to have mine all whole (entirely). 9. May their cold cares increase.

Thairin, Makyne, bath ye and I
Unsene we ma repair."

"Robene, that warld° is all away	world
And quyt° brocht° till ane end,	quite / brought
And nevir agane thairto, perfay,°	in faith
Sall it be as thow wend:°	thought
For of my pane thow maid it play,[1]	
And all in vane I spend:°	exerted myself
As thow hes done, sa° sall I say:	so
Murne on! I think to mend."°	improve

"Mawkyne, the howp° of all my heill,°	hope / health
My hairt on the is sett,	
And evirmair to the be leill,°	loyal
Quhill I may leif° but° lett;°	live / without / hindrance
Nevir to faill—as utheris feill—	
Quhat grace that evir I gett."	
"Robene, with the I will nocht deill;°	have intercourse
Adew! For thus we mett."	

Malkyne went hame blyth° annewche°	happy / enough
Attour the holttis hair:[2]	
Robene murnit, and Malkyne lewche,°	laughed
Scho° sang, he sichit° sair—	she / sighed
And so left him bayth° wo° and wrewche,°	both / woeful / wretched
In dolour and in cair,°	care, sorrow
Kepand° his hird under a huche,°	keeping / hut, hovel
Amang the holtis hair.	

[Robert Henryson, ca. 1425–ca. 1500]

76

I shall say what inordinat love is:	
The furiosite and wodness° of minde,	madness
A instinguible brenning, fawting bliss,[3]	
A grete hungre insaciat to finde,°	satisfy
A dowcet° ille,° a evel swetness blinde,	sweet / evil
A right wonderfulle sugred swete erroure,	
Withoute labor rest—contrary to kinde°—	nature
Or withoute quiete to have huge laboure.	

1. For you made jest of my pain.
2. Across the hoar (gray) woods.
3. An inextinguible burning, lacking bliss.

III

I have a gentil cok

77

I have a gentil° cok,   *noble*
  Croweth° me day;   *(who) crows*
He doth° me risen erly,   *makes*
  My matins for to say.

I have a gentil cok,
  Comen he is of gret;[1]
His comb is of red corel,
  His tayel is of jet.

I have a gentil cok,
  Comen he is of kinde;[2]
His comb is of red corel,
  His tail is of inde.°   *indigo*

His legges ben of asor,°   *azure*
  So gentil and so smale;
His spores° arn of silver white,   *spurs*
  Into the worte-wale.°   *root of cock's spur*

His eynen° arn of cristal,   *eyes*
  Loken° all in aumber;   *set*
And every night he percheth him
  In min ladyes chaumber.

78

I have a newe gardin,
  And newe is begunne;[3]

1. He comes of a great family.   3. And it has recently been planted.
2. He is of good lineage.

Swich° another gardin   *such*
    Know I not under sunne.

In the middis of my gardin
    Is a peryr° set,   *pear-tree*
And it wele non per bern
    But a per Jenet.⁴

The fairest maide of this town
    Preyed me
For to griffen° her a grif°   *graft / shoot*
    Of min pery tree.

Whan I hadde hem° griffed   *them*
    Alle at her wille,
The win and the ale
    She dede in fille.⁵

And I griffed her
    Right up in her home;°   *membrane?*
And be° that day twenty wowkes,°   *by / weeks*
    It was quik° in her womb.   *alive*

That day twelfus month,
    That maide I mette:
She seid it was a per Robert,
    But non per Jonet!⁶

79

I pray you, cum kiss me,
My little pretty Mopse.°   *sweetheart ?*
*I pray you, cum kiss me.*¹

"Alas, good man, most° you be kist?   *must*
Ye shall not now, ye may me trust.
Wherefore go where as ye best lust,²
    For, iwis,° ye shall not kiss me."   *certainly*

4. And it will bear no pear/ But an
early pear.
5. She filled me up/ With wine and ale.
6. [Pun on "Jenet" in line 8; the child
was named Robert, not John.]
1. [Refrain repeated after each stanza.]
2. "As ye best lust": it best pleases you.

Iwis, swet hart, if that ye
Had asked a greter thing of me,
So onkind to you I wold not have be;°   *been*
   Wherefore now ye shall not kiss me.

I thinke very well that ye are kind
Whereas° ye love and set yore mind,   *wherever*
But all yore wordes be but as wind;
   Wherefore now ye shall not kiss me."

"I do but talke, ye mow° me trust,   *may*
But ye take everything at the worst."
"Wherefore I say, as I said furst,
   Iwis, ye shall not kiss me."

"I pray you, let me kiss you.
If that I shall not kiss you,
Let me kiss yore carchos° nocke;°   *carcass' / cleft in buttocks*
   I pray you, let me kiss you."

"All so I say as I furst have said,
And ye will not therewith be dismayd.
Yet with that onsar° ye shall be paid;°   *answer / satisfied*
   Iwis, ye shall not kiss me."

"Now I see well that kisses are dere,
And, if I shold labor all the whole yere,
I thinke I shold be never the nerc;°   *nearer*
   Wherefore, I pray you, cum kiss me."

"Never the nere, ye may be shure,°   *sure*
For ye shall not so sone bring me in ure° *use, performance*
To consent unto yore nise° plesure,   *foolish*
   Nor, iwis, ye shall not kiss me."

"I pray you, com and kiss me,
My little pretty Mopse,
And if that ye will not kiss me,
   I pray you, let me kiss you."

"Well, for a kiss I wille not sticke,
So that ye will do nothing but likke;
But, and° ye begin on me for to pricke,   *if*
   Iwis, ye shall not kiss me."

"Now I see well that ye are kind,
Wherefore ye shall ever know my mind,
And ever yore own ye shall me find,
   At all times redy to kiss you."

80

Hogyn cam to bowers° dore—   *boudoir's*
Hogyn cam to bowers dore,
He trild° upon the pin° for love,   *rattled / door-latch*
   Hum, ha, trill go bell—
He trild upon the pin for love,
   Hum, ha, trill go bell.

Up she rose and let him in—
Up she rose and let him in,
She had awent° she had worshipped° all her kin,°
                    thought / honored / family

   Hum, ha, trill go bell—
She had awent she had worshipped all her kin,
   Hum, ha, trill go bell.

When they were to bed brought—
When they were to bed brought,
The old chorle he could do nought,
   Hum, ha, trill go bell—
The old chorle he could do nought,
   Hum, ha, trill go bell.

"Go ye furth to yonder window—
Go ye furth to yonder window,
And I will cum to you within a throw,°   *short time*
   Hum, ha, trill go bell—
And I will cum to you within a throw,
   Hum, ha, trill go bell."

Whan she him at the window wist°—   *knew*
Whan she him at the window wist,
She torned out her ars and that he kist,
   Hum, ha, trill go bell—
She torned out her ars and that he kist,
   Hum, ha, trill go bell.

"Iwis,° leman,° ye do me wrong—   *indeed / lover*
Iwis, leman, ye do me wrong,
Or elles your breth is wonder strong,
   Hum, ha, trill go bell—
Or elles your breth is wonder strong,
   Hum, ha, trill go bell."

81

We ben° chapmen° light of fote,   *are / peddlers*
The foule weyes° for to flee.[1]   *ways*

We bern° abouten° non cattes skinnes,   *carry / about*
Purses, perles, silver pinnes,°   *brooches*
Smale° wimpeles° for ladies chinnes;   *fine / head-dresses*
   Damsele, bey° sum ware° of me.   *buy / merchandise*

I have a poket for the nones,°   *nonce*
Therine ben tweyne° precious stones;   *two*
Damsele, hadde ye asayed° hem onys,°   *tried / once*
   Ye shuld the rathere° gon° with me.   *sooner / go*

I have a jelif of Godes sonde[2]—
Withouten fyt° it can stonde;   *feet*
It can smiten° and hath non honde;°   *smite / hand*
   Ryd° yourself what it may be.   *guess*

I have a powder for to selle,
What it is can I not telle;
It maket° maidenes wombes to swelle: *makes*
   Thereof I have a quantitee.

82

A, a, a, a,
Yet I love wherso I go.[3]

In all this warld nis° a merier life   *is not*
Than is a yong man withouten a wife,
For he may liven withouten strife
   In every place wherso he go.

In every place he is loved over all
Among maidens gret and small,
In daunsing, in pipinge, and renning at the ball,
   In every place wherso he go.

1. [Refrain repeated after each stanza.]   3. [Refrain repeated after each stanza.]
2. I have a jelly sent from God.

They lat light be[4] husbondmen
Whan they at the ball rene;°   *run*
They cast hir° love to yong men   *their*
   In every place wherso they go.

Than sey maides, "Farwell, Jacke,
Thy love is pressed all in thy pake;
Thou berest thy love behind thy back,
   In every place wherso thou go!"

83

A, dere God, what I am fayn,
For I am madyn now gane![1]

This enther day[2] I mete a clerke,
And he was wily in his werke;
He prayd me with him to herke,°   *listen*
   And his counsel all for to layne.°   *conceal*

I trow° he coud° of gramery;°   *believe / knew / magic*
I shall now telle a good skill° why: *reason*
For what I hade siccurly,[3]
   To warne° his will had I no mayn.°   *refuse / strength*

Whan he and me brout° un° us the schete,°   *brought / on / sheet*
Of all his will I him lete;°   *permitted*
Now will not my girdil met°—   *meet*
   A, dere God, what shall I sayn?

I shall sey to man and page°   *youth*
That I have bene of pilgrimage.
Now will I not lete° for no rage°   *allow / sexual passion*
   With me a clerk for to pleyn.°   *play*

84

I have forsworne it whil I live
To wake° the well-ey.[4]   *pass the night by*

4. Lat light be": think little of.
1. Ah, dear God, how worthless I am,/
For I am no longer a virgin. [Refrain
repeated after each stanza.]

2. A day or two ago.
3. Because from my own experience.
4. [Refrain repeated after each stanza.]

The last time I the well woke,
Sir John caght me with a croke;°   *crooked staff*
He made me to swere be° bell and boke   *by*
  I shuld not tell-ey.

Yet he did me a well wors turne;
He leide my hed again the burne;°   *well*
He gave my maidenhed a spurne°   *stroke*
  And rove° my kell°-ey.   *rent / maidenhead*

Sir John came to oure hous to play
Fro evensong time til light of the day;
We made as mery as flowres in May—
  I was begiled-ey.

Sir John he came to our hous;
He made it wonder copious;[5]
He seid that I was gracious
  To beire a childe-ey.

I go with childe, well I wot;°   *know*
I schrew° the fader that it gate,°   *curse / engendered*
Withouten° he finde it milke and pap   *unless*
  A long while-ey.

Brian is my name iet.°   *called*

85

Hey noyney! I will love our Sir John and° I love eny.[1]   *if*

O Lord, so swet° Sir John dothe kis,   *sweetly*
  At every time when he wolde pley!
Of himselfe so plesant he is—
  I have no powre to say him nay.

Sir John loves me and I love him;
  The more I love him, the more I maye.
He says, "Swet hart, cum kis me trim"°—   *nicely*
  I have no powre to say him nay.

---

5. He made it exceedingly well furnished   1. [Refrain repeated after each stanza.]
with gifts.

Sir John to me is profering
  For his plesure right well to pay,
And in my box he puttes his offring—
  I have no powre to say him nay.

Sir John is taken in my mouse trappe;
  Faine wold I have hem bothe night and day.
He gropeth nislye° abought my lappe—   *nicely*
  I have no powre to say him nay.

Sir John geveth me reluys° ringes,   *glittering*
  With praty° plesure for to assay,°   *pleasing / examine*
Furres of the finest with other thinges—
  I have no powre to say him nay.

86

"Kyrie," so "Kyrie,"
Jankin singeth merie,°   *merrily*
  With "aleison."[1]

As I went on Yol° Day in our procession,   *Yule*
Knew I joly Jankin be° his mery ton.°   *by / tone, voice*
  Kyrieleison.

Jankin began the offis° on the Yol Day,   *church service*
And yet me thinketh[2] it dos me good, so merie gan° he say   *did*
  Kyrieleison.

Jankin red the pistil° full fair and full well,   *Epistle*
And yet me thinketh it dos me good, as evere have I sell.°
                                                      good fortune
  Kyrieleison.

Jankin at the *Sanctus* craked° a merie note,   *uttered*
And yet me thinketh it dos me good—I payed for his cote.
  Kyrieleison.

Jankin craked notes an hundred on a knot,[3]

1. *"Kyrie aleison"*: God have mercy   2. "Me thinketh": it seems to me.
upon us. [Refrain repeated after each   3. "On a knot": at a time.
stanza.]

And yet he hakked° hem smaller than wortes° to the pot.   chopped / vegetables
    Kyrieleison.

Jankin at the *Angnus*⁴ bered° the *pax-brede;*⁵   carried
He twinkeled, but said nout,° and on min fot he trede.   nought
    Kyrieleison.

Benedicamus Domino,° Crist fro schame me schilde.   Let us bless the Lord
Deo gracias, therto°—alas, I go with childe!   Thanks be to God, also.
    Kyrieleison.

87

Alas, alas, the while°—   time
Thout° I on no gile,°   thought / guile
So have I good chaunce.
Alas, alas, the while—
That ever I coude daunce.¹

Lad° I the daunce a° missomer° day;   led / on / midsummer
I made smale trippes,° soth° fore to say.   steps / truth
Jak, oure haly water clerk, com° be° the way,   came / by
And he lokede me upon; he thout that I was gay—
    Thout ic° on no gile.   I

Jak, oure haly water clerk, the yonge strippeling,
For the chesone of me° he com to the ring,°
                                                 because of me / circle of dance
And he trippede on my toe, and made a twinkeling.°   winking
Ever he cam ner,° he spared for no thinge—   nearer
    Thout I on no gile.

Jak, ic wot,° priyede° in my faire face;   know / pried
He thout me full worly,° so have I good grace.   attractive
As we turnden oure daunce in a narwe° place,   narrow
Jak bed° me the mouth; a kussinge ther was—   offered
    Thout I on no gile.

Jak tho° began to roune° in min ere: then / whisper
"Loke that thou be privey and grante that thou thee bere

4. *Agnus Dei:* Lamb of God.   Mass.
5. *"Pax-brede":* tablet kissed during the   1. [Refrain repeated after each stanza.]

A peire whit gloves ic ha to thin were!"[2]
"Gremercy,° Jacke," that was min answere— *many thanks*
  Thoute ic on no gile.

Sone after evensong, Jak me mette:
"Com hom after thy gloves that ic thee bihette."° *promised*
Whan ic to his chamber com, down he me sette.
From him mitte° I nat go whan we were mette— *might*
  Thout I on no gile.

Schetes° and chalones,° ic wot, were ispredde. *sheets / blankets*
Forsothe, tho Jak and ic wenten to bedde.
He prikede and he pransede, nolde° he never linne:°
  would (not) / cease
It was the muryest nit° that ever I cam inne— *night*
  Thout I on no gile.

Whan Jak had don, tho he rong the belle;
All night ther he made me to dwelle.
Oft, I trewe,° we hadden iserved the reaggeth° devel of helle!
  suppose / shaggy
Of other smale burdes° kep° I nout° to telle— *frivolities / care / not*
  Thout I on no gile.

The other° day at Prime° I com hom, as ic wene.°
  next / early morning / think
Meth° I my dame copped° and kene:° *met / bad-tempered / sharp*
"Sey, thou stronge strumpet, ware hastu bene?
Thy tripping and thy dauncing well it wol be sene!"
  Thout I on no gile.

Ever by on and by on, my damme reched me clot.[3]
Ever I ber it privey wile that I mout,[4]
Till my gurdel aros, my wombe wax° out. *grew*
"Evel ispunne yern, ever it wole out"[5]—
  Thout I on no gile.

Ribbe ne rele ne spinne ic ne may,[1]
For joye that it is holiday.[2]

2. See that you be discreet and allow
yourself to carry/ A pair of white gloves
(which) I have for your wearing.
3. Again and again, my mistress gave
me a blow.

4. I kept it secret as long as I might.
5. Ill-spun yarn ever will ravel.
1. I may not scrape, wind, or spin
(flax).
2. [Refrain repeated after each stanza.]

All this day ic han° sought,   *have*
Spindel ne werve ne fond I nought.[3]
To miche° blisse ic am brought   *much*
  Agen° this highe holiday.   *in preparation for*

All unswope° is oure fleth,°   *unswept / floor*
And oure fire is unbeth;°   *not built up*
Oure ruschen ben unrepe yeth,[4]
  Agen this highe holiday.

Ic moste feschen° worten° in,   *fetch / herbs*
Thredele° my kerchef under my chin.   *tie, fasten*
Leve° Jakke, lend me a pin   *dear*
  To thredele me this holiday.

Now it draweth to the none,°   *noon*
And all my cherres° ben undone.   *chores*
I moste a lite solas mye schone[5]
  To make hem douge° this holiday.   *useful (soft?)*

I moste milken in this pail.
Outh me bred all this schail.[6]
Yet is the dow° under my nail   *dough*
  As ic knad° this holiday.   *knead*

Jakke wol bringe me onward in my wey,
With me desire for to pleye.
Of my dame stant me non eyghe[7]
  And never a good holiday.

Jacke wol pay for my scoth°   *contribution*
A Sonday atte the ale-schoth.[8]
Jackc wol souse° well my throth°   *drench / throat*
  Every good holiday.

Sone he wolle take me be° the hand,   *by*
And he wolle leye me on the land,
That all my buttockes ben of sand,
  Upon this hye holiday.

In he pult° and out he drow,°   *thrust / drew*
And ever ic lay on him ilow.°   *on the ground*
"By Godes deth, thou dest° me wow°   *cause / woe*
  Upon this heye holiday!"

3. Neither spindle nor reel did I find.
4. Our rushes are still uncut.
5. I must polish my shoes a little.
6. I ought to spread out all this bowl (of dough).
7. I am not afraid of my mistress.
8. On Sunday at the scotale (festival with levies for ale).

Sone my wombe began to swelle
As greth° as a belle.   great
Durst I nat my dame telle
   What me betidde° this holiday.   befell

Cantelena

At the northe ende of Selver° White,   Silver
   My lef° me bat°—   loved one / ordered
At the northe ende of Selver White,
My lef me bat I scholde abide.
I leyde my ware,° a bogeler° brode,   target / buckler
   And ever he smote—
I leyde my ware, a bogeler brode,
And ever he smote by side.[1]
Shalle ther never man just° therat,   joust
   But if° he can—   unless
Shalle ther never man just therat,
   But if he can it smite.

At the suthe ende of Selver White,
   My lef me bat—
At the suthe ende of Selver White,
My lef me bat I scholde abide.
Leyde I my ware, a peckel° wide,   peck
   And ever he smote—
Leyde I my ware, a peckel wide,
And ever he smote by side.
Shalle ther never man just therat,
   But if he can—
Shalle ther never man just therat,
   But if he can it smite.

At the weste ende of Selver White,
   My lef me bade—
At the weste ende of Selver White,
My lef me bade I scholde abide.
Layde I my ware, a bosshelle° brode,   bushel
   And ever he smote—

1. "By side": near the mark.

Layde I my ware, a bosshelle brode,
And ever he smote by side.
Shalle ther never man just therat,
  But if he can—
Shalle ther never man just therat,
  But if he can it smite.

90

Cantelena

May no man slepe in youre halle,
For dogges, madame—for dogges, madame—
But if° he have a tent° of xv inche   *unless / surgical probe*
  With twey° clogges,°   *two / wooden blocks (testicles)*
To drive awey the dogges, madame.
  Iblessed be such clogges,
  That giveth such bogges,°   *movements*
  Bitwene my lady legges,
To drive awey the dogges, madame.

May no man slepe in youre halle,
For rattes, madame—for rattes, madame—
But if he have a tent of xv inche
  With letheren° knappes,°   *leather / knobs*
To drive awey the rattes, madame.
  Iblessed be suche knappes,
  That giveth such swappes,°   *strokes*
  Under my lady lappes,°   *pudenda muliebra*
To drive awey the rattes, madame.

May no man slepe in youre halle,
For flies, madame—for flies, madame—
But if he have a tent of xv inche
  With ... byes,°1   *rings*
To drive awey the flies, madame.
  Iblessed be such byes,
  That maketh such swyes,°   *movements*
  Bitwinne my lady thyes,°   *thighs*
To drive awey the flies, madame.

1. [The line is incomplete.]

91

In secreit place this hyndir° nycht   last
I hard ane beyrne say till ane bricht,[1]
"My huny, my hart, my hoip,° my heill,°   hope / health
I have bene lang your luifar° leill°   lover / loyal
And can of yow get confort nane:
How lang will ye with danger° deill?°   disdain / deal
Ye brek my hart, my bony° ane."°   bonny / one

His bony beird was kemmit° and croppit,°   combed / trimmed
Bot all with cale° it was bedroppit,°   cabbage / spattered
And he wes townysche,° peirt° and gukit.°   uncourtly / bold / foolish
He clappit° fast, he kist and chukkit°   caressed / chucked under the chin
As° with the glaikis° he wer ouirgane;°   as if / sexual desire / overcome
Yit be° his feirris° he wald have fukkit: by / ways
"Ye brek my hart, my bony ane."

Quod he, "My hairt, sweit° as the hunye,   sweet
Sen° that I borne wes of my mynnye°   since / mother
I never wowit° weycht° bot yow;   wooed / creature
My wambe° is of your luif° sa fow°   belly / love / full
That as ane gaist° I glour° and grane,°   ghost / stare / groan
I trymble° sa, ye will not trow:°   tremble / believe
Ye brek my hart, my bony ane."

"Tehe,"° quod scho, and gaif° ane gawfe;°   tee-hee / gave / guffaw
"Be still my tuchan° and my calfe,   calf's skin stuffed with straw
My new spanit° howffing° fra the sowk,°   weaned / oaf / suck
And all the blythnes of my bowk;°   body
My sweit swanking,° saif° yow allane   fine fellow / except
Na leid° I luiffit° all this owk:°   person / loved / week
Full leif° is me° your graceles gane."°   dear / to me / face

Quod he, "My claver° and my curldodie,°   clover / ribwort plantain
My huny soppis,° my sweit possodie,°   sops / sheep's head broth
Be not oure° bosteous° to your billie,°   too / rough / sweetheart
Be warme hairtit and not evill willie;[2]
Your heylis° quhyt° as quhalis° bane,°   heels / white / whale's / bone
Garris° ryis° on loft my quhillelillie:°   makes / rise / penis
Ye brek my hart, my bony ane."

Quod scho, "My clype,° my unspaynit° gyane°
                                                   big softie / unweaned / giant

---

1. I heard a boy say to a fair lady.   2. "Evill willie": malevolent.

With moderis mylk yit in your mychane,°   *mouth*
My belly huddrun,³ my swete hurle bawsy,⁴
My huny gukkis,⁵ my slawsy gawsy,⁶
Your musing waild perse° ane hart of stane: *pierce*
Tak gud confort, my grit° heidit° slawsy,   *great / headed*
Full leif is me your graceles gane."

Quod he, "My kid, my capirculyoun,°   *woodgrouse*
My bony baib° with the ruch° brylyoun,°   *babe / rough / ?*
My tendir gyrle, my wallie° gowdye,°   *fine / goldfinch*
My tyrlie myrlie,⁷ my crowdie mowdie,⁸
Quhone° that oure mouthis dois° meit° at ane   *when / do / meet*
My stang° dois storkyn° with your towdie:°
    sting, penis / stiffen / pudendum
Ye brek my hairt, my bony ane."

Quod scho, "Now tak me be the hand,
Welcum, my golk° of Marie° land,   *cuckoo / fairy*
My chirrie° and my maikles° munyoun,°   *cherry / matchless / darling*
My sowklar° sweit as ony unyoun,°   *suckling / onion*
My strumill° stirk° yit new to spane,°   *stumbling / bullock / wean*
I am applyit° to your opunyoun: *inclined*
I luif rycht weill your graceles gane."

He gaiff to hir ane apill° rubye;°   *apple / red*
Quod scho, "Gramercye,° my sweit cowhubye."°   *thanks / booby*
And thai tway to ane play began
Quhilk° men dois call the dery dan,⁹   *which*
Quhill° that thair myrthis° met baythe° in ane: *while / mirths / both*
"Wo is me," quod scho, "Quhair° will ye, man?   *where*
Best now I luif that graceles gane."

[*William Dunbar, ca.* 1460–*ca.* 1520]

3. "Belly huddrun": big belly, glutton.
4. "Hurle bawsy": dear one.
5. "Huny gukkis": foolish honey.
6. "Slawsy gawsy": handsome fellow.
7. "Tyrlie myrlie": a term of endear-
ment, like "hurle bawsy" above.
8. "Crowdie mowdie": gruel of milk and meal.
9. "Dery, dan": a dance (i.e., copula-tion).

IV

Swete Jhesu

92

Swete Jhesu, king of blisse,
Min herte° love, min herte lisse,°   *heart's / joy*
Thou art swete, mid iwisse:[1]
Wo is him that thee shall misse.

Swete Jhesu, min herte light,
Thou art day withouten night.
Thou geve me strengthe and eke° might   *also*
For to lovien° thee all right.   *love*

Swete Jhesu, my soule bote,°   *remedy*
In min herte thou sette a rote°   *root*
Of thy love that is so swote,°   *sweet*
And wite° it that it springe° mote.°   *guide / grow / may*

93

Louerd, thu clepedest° me   *called*
And ich° nagt° ne answarede thee   *I / nothing*
Bute wordes scloe° and sclepie:°   *slow / sleepy*
"Thole° yet! Thole a litel!"   *be patient (imperative)*
Bute "yet" and "yet" was endelis,
And "thole a litel" a long wey is.

1. "Mid iwisse": certainly, indeed.

92

94

Wele,° herying,° and worshipe be to Crist that dere° us boughte,
joy / praise / at high price
To wham° gradden° "Hosanna!" children clene° of thoughte.
whom / proclaimed / pure

Thou art king of Israel and of Davides kunne,°   *kin*
Blessed king, that comest till° us withoute wem° of sunne.°
to / stain / sin

All that is in hevene thee herieth° under on,[1]   *praises*
And all thin° owen hondewerk and euch° dedlich° mon.
thine / each / mortal

The folk of Jewes with bowes comen° ageinst thee,   *came*
And we with bedes° and with song meketh° us° to thee.
prayers / humble / ourselves

Heo° kepten° thee with worshiping ageinst° thou shuldest deye,
they / cared for / until
And we singeth to thy worshipe in trone° that sittest heye.   *throne*

Here will and here mekinge thou nome tho to thonk;[2]
Queme° thee, thenne, milsful° king, oure offringe of this song.
let please / merciful

Wele, herying, and worshipe be to Crist that dere us boughte,
To wham gradden "Hosanna!" children clene of thoughte.

[*Friar William Herebert, d.* 1333]

95

Com, Shuppere,° Holy Gost, ofsech° oure thoughtes;
Creator / descend into
Ful° with grace of hevene heortes° that thu wroughtest,   *fill / hearts*

1. "Under on": together.
2. Their will and their obedience you then received graciously.

Thou that art cleped° forspekere° and gift from God isent,
called / advocate
Welle of lif, fur,° charite and gostlich° oynement.°
fire / spiritual / ointment
Thou givst the sevene giftes, thou finger of Godes honde,
Thou makest tonge of fleshe speke leodene° of uche° londe.
language / each
Tend° light in oure wittes,° in oure heortes love;   *kindle / senses*
Ther° oure body is leothe-wok,° gif strengthe from above.
where / weak
Shild us from the feonde° and gif us grith° anon,   *Devil / protection*
That we witen us from sunne thorou the lodes-mon.[1]
Of the Fader and the Sone thou gif us knowlechinge,°   *understanding*
To leve° that full of bothe thou ever be lovinge.   *believe*
Wele° to the Fader and to the Sone that from deth aros,   *glory*
And also to the Holy Gost ay° be worshipe and los.°   *ever / praise*

[*Friar William Herebert, d.* 1333]

96

Holy Wroughte° of sterres bright,   *Creator*
Of right bileve° ay° lasting light,   *belief / ever*
Crist, that boughtest mon with fight,
Her° the bone° of meke wight!°   *hear / prayer / creature*

Thou hedest° ruthe° of world forlore°   *had / pity / lost, ruined*
Thorou deth of sunfol° rote;°   *sinful / root*
Thou savedest monkun,° therfore,   *mankind*
To gulty geve° bote.°   *gave / remedy*

Toward the worldes ende
Thy wille was t'alende°   *to take up abode*
  In on° maidenes bour:°   *a / chamber*
Ase° spouse of chaumbre alone   *as*
Out of that clene° wone°   *pure / abode*
  Thou come t'oure honour.

To whas° stronge mightes   *whose*
Knowen of alle wightes
  Bendeth hem imone[2]

1. That we may guard ourselves from   2. They bend together.
sin, through the guide.

Of hevene and eek° of eorthe,   *also*
And knowlecheth° him wourthe° *acknowledge / worthy*
  For bowen° to him one.°   *to bow / alone*

Holy God, we biddeth thee,
That shalt this worlde deme,°   *judge*
From oure fikel° fohes° spere   *deceitful / foe's*
Thou thilke° time us yeme.°   *at that / guard*

Herying,° worshipe, mighte, and wele° *praise / glory*
To Fader and the Sone!
And also to the Holy Gost
And ever mid hem wone!³

[*Friar William Herebert, d.* 1333]

97

Crist, buyere° of alle icoren,°   *redeemer / chosen*
The Fadres olpy° sone,   *only*
On toforen ey ginning boren,⁴
Over alle speche and wone,°   *custom*

Thou light, thou Faderes brightnesse,
Thou trust and hope of alle,
Lust° what thy folk thorou-out the world *listen to*
To thee biddeth and calle.

Wroughte° of oure hele,°   *creator / salvation*
Now have in thine munde⁵
That of o° maide wemless°   *a / spotless*
Thou toke oure kunde.°   *nature*

This day berth° witnesse,   *bears*
That neweth° uche° yer, *renews itself, returns / each*
That-ou alightest from the Fader⁶—
Of sunne° make us sker.°   *sin / clear*

Him hevene and erthe and wilde see
And all that is ther-on

---

3. And ever with them dwell!
4. Born before any beginning.

5. Now remember (have in your mind).
6. That you descended from the Father.

Wroughte, of thy cominge
Hereth with blisfol ron.[7]

And we nomliche° that beoth bought   *especially*
With thine holy blod
For this day singeth a newe song
And maketh blisfol mod:°   *mood, cheer*

Weole,° Louerd, be with thee,   *glory*
Iboren of o may,[8]
With Fader and the Holy Gost
Withouten ende-day.°   *end*

[*Friar William Herebert, d.* 1333]

Thou king of wele° and blisse,   *joy*
Louerd Jesu Crist,
Thou Faderes Sone of hevene,
That never ende bist,[1]

Thou, for to save monkunne,°   *mankind*
That thou haddest wrought,
A meke maides wombe
Thou ne shonedest° nought;   *shunned*

Thou that overcome
The bitter dethes sting,
Thou openedest hevene-riche°   *kingdom of heaven*
To right bileves° thring;°   *belief's / insistence*

Thou sist° in Godes right hond,   *sit*
In thy Faderes blisse;
Thou shalt comen to demen° us,   *judge*
We leveth all to wisse.[2]

Thee, thenne, we biddeth help us
Wham° thou havest iwrought,   *whom*
Whom with thy derewourthe° blod   *precious*
On rode° havest ibought;   *Cross*

7. Heaven and earth and the wild sea/   8. Born of a maiden.
And all that is therein/ Created, for   1. That shall never end.
your (Christ's) coming/ Praise Him   2. We believe assuredly.
(God) with blissful song.

Thee, thenne, we bisecheth,
Help us, thin owne hine,°   *servants*
Whom with thy derewourthe blod
Hast bought from helle pine.°   *suffering*

[*Friar William Herebert, d. 1333*]

99

Jesu our raunsoun,°   *ransom*
Love and longinge,°   *object of desire*
Louerd God almighty,
Wroughte° of alle thinge,   *Creator*
Flesh thou nome°   *took*
And mon bicome
In times endinge.[1]

What milsfolnesse° awalde° thee   *mercifulness / overcame*
That oure sunnes° bere,°   *sins / bore*
So bitter deth to tholien,°   *endure*
From sunne us for t'arere?°   *to raise up*

Helle-clos° thou thorledest°   *prison / pierced*
And boughtest thine of bonde;[2]
With gret nobleye°   *splendor*
Thou opsteye°   *ascended*
To thy Fader° right honde.   *Father's*

Thilke milse nede thee[3]
T'awelde° oure wickenesse   *to overcome*
With thy mercy,
And full° us ay°   *fill / ever*
With thy nebshaftes° blisse.   *countenance's*

Thou be now oure joye
That shalt ben oure mede,°   *reward*
And oure wele° ay be in thee   *happiness*
That shalt us with thee nede.[4]

[*Friar William Herebert, d. 1333*]

1. At the end of time (i.e., in the last days of the world).
2. And redeemed your own from bondage.
3. May that same mercy constrain you.
4. Who will require us to be with you.

100

God, that all this mightes may,[1]
In hevene and erthe thy wille is o;°   *always*
Ich habbe be losed mony a day,[2]
Er° and late, ibe° thy fo;   *early / by*
Ich wes to wite and wiste my lay;[3]
Longe habbe° holde° me therfro.°   *have (I) / kept / from it*
Ful of mercy thou art ay;°   *always*
All ungreithe° ich am to thee to go.   *unprepared*

To go to him that hath us boght,°   *redeemed*
My gode deden° bueth° fol smalle;   *deeds / are*
Of the werkes that ich ha° wrogkt   *have*
The beste is bittrore° then the galle.   *more bitter*
My good ich wiste,° I nolde° it noght,   *knew / wanted*
In folie me° wes luef° to falle;   *to me / pleasant*
When I myself have thourghsoght,°   *thoroughly examined*
I knowe me for the worst of alle.

God, that deyedest° on the rod,°   *died / Cross*
All this world to forthren° and fille,° *benefit / make perfect*
For us thou sheddest thy swete blod;
That° I ha don me liketh ille;   *what*
Bote er° ageyn° thee stith° I stod, *always / against / firmly*
Er and late, loude and stille:[4]
Of mine deden finde I non god;
Lord, of me thou do thy wille.

In herte ne mighte I never bowe,
Ne° to my kunde° Louerd drawe;   *nor / good*
My meste° fo is my loves trowe[5]—   *greatest*
Crist ne stod me never hawe.[6]
Ich holde me vilore° then a Giw,°   *more vile / Jew*
And I myself wolde bue° knowe.°   *be / revealed*
Lord, mercy, rewe° me now;   *pity*
Reise up that° is falle° lowe!   *that which / fallen*

God, that all this world shall hede,°   *heed, care for*
Thy gode might thou hast in wolde;°   *control, power*
On erthe thou come° for oure nede,   *came*
For us sunful° were boght and solde.   *sinful (ones)*

1. God, who can perform all these mighty deeds.
2. I have been brought low many a day.
3. I was to blame and knew my duty.
4. "Loude and stille": loud and quiet (i.e., in all circumstances).
5. "Loves trowe": trust in praise.
6. I never stood in awe of Christ.

When we bueth° dempned° after° ur dede   *are / judged / according to*
A° domesday, when rightes° bueth tolde,   *on / justice*
When he shule suen° thy wounde° blede,   *see / wounds*
To speke thenne we bueth° unbolde.°   *shall be / timid*

Unbold ich am to bidde° thee bote;°   *beg (of) / remedy*
Swithe° unreken° is my rees;°   *very / unpleasant / rashness*
Thy wille ne welk° I ner° afote;°   *walked / never / on foot*
To wickede werkes I me chees.°   *turned*
Fals I wes in crop and rote[7]
When I seide thy lore° wes lees.°   *teaching / false*
Jesu Crist, thou be my bote,
So boun° ich am to make my pees.   *ready*

All unreken° is my ro,°   *uneasy / rest*
Louerd Crist; whet shall I say?
Of mine deden finde I non fro,°   *comfort*
Ne nothing that I thenke may.[8]
Unworth ich am to come thee to;[9]
I serve thee nouther° night ne day.   *neither*
In thy mercy I me do,°   *put*
God, that all this mightes may.

[Harley 2253]

IOI

Swete Jesu, king of blisse,
Min herte° love, min herte lisse,°   *heart's / joy*
Thou art swete mid iwisse.[1]
Wo is him that thee shall misse!

Swete Jesu, min herte light,
Thou art day withoute night,
Thou geve° me streinthe and eke might   *give (imperative)*
For to lovien° thee aright.   *love*

Swete Jesu, min herte bote,°   *remedy*
In min herte thou sete° a rote°   *set (imperative) / root*

7. "Crop and rote": leaf and root.
8. Nor from anything that I can think of.
9. "Thee to": to you.
1. "Mid iwisse": certainly.

Of thy love, that is so swote,°   *sweet*
And leve° that it springe mote.°   *grant / may*

Swete Jesu, min herte gleem,°   *light*
Brightore then the sonnebeem,
Ibore° thou were in Bedleheem;   *born*
Thou make° me here° thy swete dreem.°   *cause (imperative) / to hear / melody*

Swete Jesu, thy love is swete;
Wo is him that thee shall lete!°   *abandon*
Gif me grace for to grete°   *greet*
For° my sinnes teres wete.°   *on account of / wet*

Swete Jesu, king of londe,
Thou make me fer° understonde   *to*
That min herte mote° fonde°   *may, must / experience*
How swete beth° thy love-bonde.   *is*

Swete Jesu, Louerd° min,   *Lord*
My lif, min herte, all is thin;°   *yours*
Undo° min herte and light° therin,   *open / alight, come down*
And wite° me from fendes° engin.°   *guard / Devil's / trick*

Swete Jesu, my soule° fode,   *soul's*
Thin werkes beth bo° swete and gode;   *both*
Thou boghtest° me upon the rode;°   *redeemed / Cross*
For me thou sheddest thy blode.

Swete Jesu, me reoweth[2] sore
Gultes° that I ha° wroght yore;°   *guilts / have / for long*
Tharefore I bidde° thin milse° and ore;°   *beg / mercy / grace*
Mercy, Lord, I nul° namore.   *will (not)*

Swete Jesu, Louerd God,
Thou me boghtest with thy blod;
Out of thin herte orn° the flod;   *ran*
Thy moder it segh° that thee by stod.   *saw*

Swete Jesu, bright and shene,°   *beautiful*
I preye thee thou here my bene°   *prayer*
Thourgh ernding° of the hevene quene,   *intercession*
That thy love on me be sene.°   *seen*

Swete Jesu, berne° best,   *of men*
With thee ich hope habbe rest;
Whether I be south other° west,   *or*
The help of thee be me nest.°   *nearest*

2. "Me reoweth": I regret.

44

4444

Swete Jesu, well may him be
That thee may in blisse see.
With love-cordes drawe thou me
That I may comen and wone° with thee.   dwell

Swete Jesu, hevene king,
Feir and best of alle thing,
Thou bring me of° this longing   out of
To come to thee at min ending.

Swete Jesu, all folkes reed,°   help, counsel
Graunte us er we buen° ded   are
Thee underfonge° in fourme of bred,   to receive
And sethe° to heovene thou us led.°   later / lead (imperative)

[Harley 2253]

102

Jesu Crist, heovene° king,   heaven's
Gef° us alle good ending   give
  That bone° biddeth° thee;   prayer / offer
At the biginning of my song,
Jesu, I thee preye among°   all the while
  In stude° all wher° I be.   place / wherever
For thou art king of alle;
To thee I clepie° and calle,   cry
  Thou have mercy of me!

This ender day° in o morewening,°   a day or two ago / morning
With drery herte and gret mourning
  On my folie I thoghte;
One that is so swete a thing,°   creature, person
That ber° Jesu, the hevene° king,   bore / heaven's
  Mercy I besoghte.

Jesu, for thy muchele° might,   great
Thou graunte us alle hevene light,
  That us so dere¹ boghtest.°   bought
For thy mercy, Jesu swete,
Thin hondywerk nult° thou lete,°   will not / abandon
  That thou well yerne° soghtest.°   eagerly / sought

1. "So dere": at so high a price.

Well ichot° and soth it is   *I know*
That in this world nis no bliss,
  Bote care, serewe, and pine;°   *torment*
Tharefore ich° rede° we wurchen° so   *I / advise / work, behave*
That we mowe° come to   *may*
  The joye withoute fine.°   *end*

[*Harley* 2253]

103

Heye Louerd, thou here my bone,[1]
That madest middelert° and mone,°   *earth / moon*
  And mon of murthes munne;[2]
Trusty king and trewe in trone,°   *heaven*
That thou be with me saghte° sone,°   *reconciled / forthwith*
  Asoile° me of sunne.°   *absolve / sin*

Fol° ich° wes in folies fain,°   *full (fool?) / I / glad*
In luthere° lastes° I am lain,   *base / vices*
  That maketh min thriftes° thunne,° *fortunes / unhappy*
That semly sawes wes woned to seyn.[3]
Now is marred° all my meyn,°   *injured / strength*
  Away is all my wunne.°   *joy*

Unwunne° haveth min wonges° wet,   *grief / cheeks*
  That maketh me routhes° rede.°   *repentance / express*
Ne seme I nout ther I am set,[4]
Ther° me° calleth me fulle-flet° *where / one / useless encumbrance*
And waynoun° wayteglede.°   *good-for-nothing / fire-watcher*

Whil° ich wes in wille° wolde,°   *formerly / pleasure's / power*
In uch° a bour° among the bolde°   *each / house / powerful ones*
  Iholde° with the heste;°   *respected / greatest*
Now I may no finger folde,°   *clasp*
Lutel° loved and lasse itolde,°   *little / esteemed*
  Ileved° with the leste.°   *considered / least*

1. High Lord, hear my prayer.
2. And remind man of pleasures.
3. (I) who was accustomed to say fair speeches.

4. Nor do I befit (the place) where I am set (i.e., nor am I suitable for that station which I now occupy).

A goute me hath igreithed° so   *afflicted*
And other eveles monye° mo;°   *many / more*
 I not° whet bote° is beste.   *know not / remedy*
Thar er wes wilde ase the ro,[5]
Now I swike,° I mey nout so;   *leave off*
 It° siweth° me so faste.° *i.e., gout, or old age / follows / closely*

Faste I wes on horse hegh°   *high*
And werede worly wede;[6]
Now is faren° all my feh,°   *gone / wealth*
With serewe that ich it ever seh.°   *saw*
 A staff is now my stede.

When I see steden° stithe° in stalle   *steeds / strong*
And I go haltinde° in the halle,   *limping*
 Min herte° ginneth° to helde;° *heart / begins / sink*
That° er wes wildest inwith° walle° *what / within / walls*
Now is under fote° ifalle°   *foot / fallen*
 And mey no finger felde.°   *clasp*

Ther° ich wes lef° ich am full loht,° *where / beloved / hateful*
And alle min godes° me atgoht,° *goods / go away*
 Min gomenes° waxeth gelde.° *pleasures / barren*
That feire founden me mete and cloht,[7]
He° wrieth° awey as he were wroght;° *they / go / angry*
 Such is evel° and elde.° *hardship / old age*

Evel and elde and other wo
 Foleweth me so faste
Me thunketh° min herte breketh atwo. *it seems to me*
Swete God, why shall it swo?°   *so*
 How may it lengore° laste?   *longer*

Whil° my lif wes luther° and lees:° *formerly / base / false*
Glotonie my glemon° wes;   *minstrel*
 With me he wonede° a while;   *dwelt*
Prude° wes my plowe-fere,°   *Pride / play-fellow*
Lecherie my lauendere;°   *laundress (harlot?)*
 With hem° is Gabbe° and Gile.° *them / Falsehood / Deceit*

Coveitise° min keyes bere,° *Covetousness / carried*
Nithe° and Onde° were my fere,° *Envy / Anger / companions*
 That bueth° folkes file;°   *are / vile*
Liare° wes my latimer;° *Falsehood / interpreter*
Sleuthe° and Slep° my bediver,° *Sloth / Sleep / bed-fellows*
 That weneth° me umbe while.[8]   *attract*

Umbe while I am to wene,°   *attracted*
 When I shall murthes meten.°   *find*

5. Where, formerly, I was wild as the roe.
6. And wore splendid garments.
7. Those who generously provided food and clothes for me.
8. "Umbe while": at times.

Monne° mest° I am to mene:°   *of men / greatest / lament*
Lord, that hast me lif to lene,°   *grant*
  Such lotes° lef° me leten.°   *evil deeds / grant / to abandon*

Such lif ich have lad fol° yore;°   *full / long time*
Mercy, Louerd, I nul° namore;   *will (not)*
  Bowen ichulle° to bete.°   *I will / atone*
Siker° it siweth° me full sore,   *certainly / follows*
Gabbes° les° and luthere lore;°   *lies / false / teaching*
  Sunnes bueth unsete.°   *evil*

Godes heste° ne huld° I noght,   *command / kept*
Bote ever ageyn° his wille I wroght;   *against*
  Mon lereth° me too lete.°   *teaches / late*
Such serewe hath min sides thurghsoght°   *pierced*
That all I weolewe° away to noght   *wither*
  When I shall murthes mete.°   *find*

To mete murthes ich wes well fous,°   *eager*
  And comely mon ta calle[9]
(I say by other° as° by us)   *others / just as*
Alse° is hirmon° halt° in hous,   *as / retainer / haughty*
  As heved-hount° in halle.   *chief huntsman*

Dredful deth, why wolt thou dare?°   *lie motionless*
Bring° this body that is so bare°   *take / poor*
  And in bale° ibounde.   *torment*
Careful° mon icast° in care,   *sorrowful / cast into*
I falewe° as flour ilet° forthfare,°   *wither / abandoned / to die*
  Ich habbe min dethes wounde.

Murthes helpeth me no more;
Help me, Lord, er then ich hore,°   *become gray*
  And stunt° my lif a stonde.°   *end / time*
That yokkin hath iyirned yore;[1]
Now it sereweth° him full sore,   *grieves*
  And bringeth him to grounde.

To grounde it haveth him ibroght;
  Whet° is the beste bote°   *what / remedy*
Bote° herien° him that hath us boght,   *except / to praise*
Ure Lord that all this world hath wroght,
  And fallen him to fote?[2]

Now ich am to° deth idight;°   *for / prepared*
  Idon° is all my dede.   *finished*

9. And worthy to be called an important man.
1. That desire has long been yearned for.
2. And to humble ourselves before him.

God us lene of his light
That we of sontes° habben sight   *saints*
And hevene to° mede!°   *for / reward*

[*Harley* 2253]

104

As I wandrede her° by weste   *here*
Faste under a forest side,
I seigh° a wight went him to reste;   *saw*
Under a bough he gon° abide.   *did*
Thus to Crist full yeorne° he criyede,   *earnestly*
And bothe his hondes he held on heigh:
"Of povert, plesaunce,° and eke° of pride,   *pleasure / also*
Ay° mercy, God, and graunt-mercy!"[1]   *ever*

God, that I have igrevet° thee   *grieved*
In wille and werk, in word and dede,
Almighty Lord, have mercy of me
That for my sunnes° thy blod gon schede!   *sins*
Of wit and worschupe, weole and wede,[2]
I thonke thee, Lord, full inwardly;
All in this world, howevere I spede,°   *succeed*
Ay mercy, God, and graunt-mercy!

Graunt-mercy, God, of all thy gifte,
Of wit and worschupe, weole and wo;
Into thee, Lord, min herte I lifte;
Let never my dedes twinne° us atwo.   *part*
Mercy that I have misdo,°   *done wrong*
And sle° me nought sodeynly!   *slay*
Though Fortune wolde be frend or fo,
Ay mercy, God, and graunt-mercy!

I am unkinde,[3] and that I knowe,
And thou hast kud° me gret kindenes;   *shown*
Therfore with humbel herte and lowe,
Mercy and forgivenes
Of pride and of unboxumnes!°   *disobedience*
Whatevere thy sonde° be, thus sey I,   *message, gift*

1. "Graunt-mercy": hearty thanks, perhaps punning on "grant mercy."
2. For intelligence and honor, happiness and clothing.
3. "Unkinde": unnatural, perhaps also suggesting "unkind."

In hap° and hele,° and in seknes,   *good fortune / health*
Ay mercy, God, and graunt-mercy!

Graunt-mercy, God, of all thy grace,
That fourmed° me with wittes five,   *created*
With feet and hond, and eke of face,
And liflode,° whil I am alive: *sustenance*
Sithen° thou hast give me grace to thrive,   *since*
And I have ruled me rechelesly,°   *negligently*
I weore to blame and I wolde strive—
But mercy, God, and graunt-mercy!

Mercy that I have misspent
My wittes five! Therfore I wepe.
To dedly sinnes ofte have I asent,°   *consented*
Thy Commaundements couthe° I never kepe;   *could*
To sle my soule in sunne I slepe,
And lede my lif in lechery;
From covetise° couthe I nevere crepe—   *avarice*
Ay mercy, God, and graunt-mercy!

Of othes° grete and glotony,   *oaths*
Of wanhope° and of wikked wille,   *despair*
Bakbite my neighebors for envy,
And for his good I wolde him culle,°   *strike*
Trewe men to robbe and spille,°   *injure*
Of simony and with surquidri°—   *presumption*
Of all that evere I have don ille,
Ay mercy, God, and graunt-mercy!

By lawe I scholde no lengor live
Then° I hedde don a dedly sinne;   *when*
Graunt-mercy that ye wolde forgive,
And geve me space° to mende me inne!   *opportunity*
From wikked dedes and° I wolde twinne,   *if*
To receive me ye be redy
Into thy blisse that never schal blinne:°   *cease*
Now mercy, God, and graunt-mercy!

Graunt mercy, for thou madest me,
Mercy, for I have don amis!
Min hope, min help is hol° in thee,   *entirely*
And thou hast yore° biheight° me this: *long since / promised*
Whos-evere is baptized schal have bliss,
And he rule him rightwisly.[4]
To worche thy wille, Lord, thou me wis°—   *guide*
Now mercy, God, and graunt-mercy!

Sothfast° God, what schal I say?   *true*
How schulde I amendes make,

4. If he order his life righteously.

That plesed thee nevere into this day,
Ne schop me nought my sunnes forsake?[5]
But schrift° of mouthe my sunnes schal slake,   *confession*
And I schal sece° and beo sory;   *cease*
And to thy mercy I me take—
Now mercy, God, and graunt-mercy!

Fader and Sone and Holigost,
Graunt-mercy, God, with herte light,
For thou woldest not that I weore lost.
The Fader hath given me a might;°   *power*
The Sone a science° and a sight,   *knowledge*
And wit to welde me worschupely;[6]
The Holigost ur grace hath dight.°   *appointed*
Now mercy, God, and graunt mercy!

This is the Trone° that twinned nevere,   *throne*
And preved° is persones three,   *proved*
That is and was and schal ben evere
Only God in Trinite:
Help us, Prince of alle pite,
At the day that we schal dy,
Thy swete face that we may see.
Now mercy, God, and graunt-mercy!

105

When I see blosmes springe
    And here° foules° song,   *hear / birds'*
A swete love-longinge
    Min herte thourghout° stong,°   *completely / pierces*
All for a love newe,
That is so swete and trewe,
    That gladieth° all my song;   *makes glad*
Ich wot all mid iwisse[1]
My joye and eke my blisse
    On him is all ilong.[2]

When I miselve° stonde   *myself*
    And with min eyen seo°   *see (him)*

5. Nor aimed to forsake my sins.
6. And wit (intelligence) to rule myself reverently.

1. I know quite certainly.
2. Is wholly caused by him.

Thurled° fot and honde   *pierced*
  With grete nailes threo°—   *three*
Blody wes his heved;°   *head*
On him nes nout bileved,
  That wes of peines freo³—
Well° well oghte min herte   *very*
For his love to smerte
  And sike° and sory beo.°   *sigh / be*

Jesu, milde and softe,°   *gentle*
  Gef me streinthe and might
Longen° sore and ofte,   *to long*
  To lovie° thee aright,   *love*
Pine° to tholie° and dreye°   *torment / endure / suffer*
For thee, swete Marye;
  Thou art so free and bright,
Maiden and moder milde:
For love of thine childe,
  Ernde° us° hevene light.   *obtain by intercession / for us*

Alas, that I ne con
  Turne to him my thoght
And cheosen° him to° lemmon;°   *choose / for / lover*
  So duere° he us hath iboght,   *at such a high price*
With woundes deope° and stronge.°   *deep / severe*
With peines sore and longe;
  Of love ne conne° we noght.   *know*
His blod that feol° to grounde   *fell*
Of° his swete wounde   *from*
  Of peine us hath iboght.°   *redeemed*

Jesu, milde and swete,
  I singe thee my song;
Ofte I thee grete
  And preye thee among;°   *all the while*
Let me sunnes° lete,°   *sins / abandon*
And in this live° bete°   *life / atone for*
  That° ich have do° wrong;   *what / done*
At oure lives ende,
When we shule wende,
  Jesu, us undefong!°   *receive (imperative)*

[*Harley* 2253]

---

3. Nothing was believed about him,/ Who was noble where suffering was concerned.

V

Thirty dayes hath November

106

Thirty dayes hath November,
April, June, and September;
Of xxviii is but oon,
And all the remenaunt xxx and i.

107

I wot a tree xii bowes betake;
lii nestes bethe that up imad;
In every nest beth briddes vii.[1]
Ithanked be the God of hevene
And every brid with selcouth° name.   *strange, wonderful*

108

Januar   By this fire I warme my handes;
Februar   And with my spade I delve° my landes.   *dig*
Marche   Here I sette my thinge° to springe;°   *seeds / grow*

1. I know a tree (the year) that has   of fifty-two nests (weeks);/ In every
twelve boughs (months);/ It is made up   nest are seven birds (days).

Aprile	And here I here the fowles singe.	
Maii	I am as light as birde in bowe;°	*bough*
Junii	And I wede° my corne well enow.°	*weed / enough*
Julii	With my sythe° my mede° I mawe;°	
		scythe / meadow / mow
Auguste	And here I shere my corne full lowe.	
September	With my flail I erne my brede;	
October	And here I sawe° my whete so rede.°	*sow / golden*
November	At Martinesmasse I kille my swine;	
December	And at Cristemasse I drinke redde wine.	

109

In Merche, after the first C,
Loke the prime° wherever he be;   *new moon*
The third Sonday, full iwisse,°   *certainly*
Ester° day trewly it is.   *Easter*
And if the prime on the Sonday be,
Rekene° that Sonday for one° of the three.   *count / the first*

110

If Sanct Paules day¹ be fair and cleir,
Than shall betid ane happie yeir.
If it chances to snaw or rane,
Than shall be deir all kinde of graine.
And if the wind be hie on loft,
Than weir° shall vex the kingdome oft.   *war*
And if the cloudes make darke the skye,
Boith° nowte° and fowl that yeir shall die.   *both / cattle*

---

1. [The Conversion of St. Paul is commemorated on January 25.]

III

xxxii teeth that bethe° full kene,°
cc bones and nintene,
ccc vaines sixty and five,
Every man hathe that is alive.

are / sharp

112

Fleumaticus:°   *phlegmatic*
   Sluggy and slowe, in spetinge° muiche,°   *spitting / much*
   Cold and moist, my natur is suche;
   Dull of wit, and fat, of contenaunce° strange,   *appearance*
   Fleumatike, this complecion may not change.

Sanguineus:°   *sanguine*
   Deliberal° I am, lovinge and gladde,   *liberal*
   Laghinge and playinge, full seld° I am sad;   *seldom*
   Singinge, full fair of colour, bold to fight,
   Hote and moist, beninge,° sanguine I hight.°   *benign / am called*

Colericus:°   *choleric*
   I am sad and soleynge° with heviness in thoght;   *sullen*
   I covet right muiche, leve will I noght;
   Fraudulent and suttill,° full cold and dry,   *subtle*
   Yollowe of colour, colorike am I.

Malencolicus:°   *melancholy*
   Envius, dissevabill,° my skin is roghe;   *deceitful*
   Outrage° in exspence, hardy inoghe;   *extravagant*
   Suttill and sklender,° hote and dry,   *slender*
   Of colour pale, my nam is malencoly.

113

Phebus fonde° first the craft of medecine
By touche of pous° and urine inspections.

practiced
pulse

Esculapius taght the doctrine
To know the qualities of the four compliccions,
Of electuaries, drages,° and pociouns.   *drugs*
Among all other ther is nothing mor mete°   *fitting, proper*
To the help of man then temperat diete.

114

Juce of lekes° with gotes° galle   *leeks / goat's*
For evil heringe° help it shalle.   *hearing*
Too° partes of the juce, the third of galle,   *two*
Melled° small,° and warme withalle.   *mixed / finely*
In noise° or eir° where it be do,°   *nose / ear / put*
For grete hedewark° well° it slo;°   *headache / will / cure*
Broken bones will it knit,
And angrey sores wille it flit.°   *drive away*
Lekes and salt same done,
Helpes a woman to clooe° son.°   *staunch menstrual flow / soon*
It is gud for dronken men
A raw lek to ete, and comforteth the brain.

115

Medicina pro morbo caduco et le fevre.
In nomine Patris et Filii et Spiritus Sancti, Amen.[1]

What° manere of evil thou be,   *whatever*
In Goddes name I coungere° thee.   *conjure*
I coungere thee with the holy crosse
That Jesus was done° on with fors.°   *placed / violence*
I conure thee with nailes three
That Jesus was nailed upon the tree.
I coungere thee with the crowne of thorne
That on Jesus hede was done with scorne.
I coungere thee with the precious blode

1. Medicine for epilepsy and the fever./   Son and of the Holy Ghost, Amen.
In the name of the Father and of the

That Jesus shewed upon the rode.°   Cross
I coungere thee with woundes five
That Jesus suffred be° his live.°   in / life
I coungere thee with that holy spere
That Longeus to Jesus hert can° bere.°   did / bear
I coungere thee nevertheless
With all the vertues of the Masse,
And all the holy prayers of Seint Dorathy.
   In nomine Patris et Filii et Spiritus Sancti, Amen.

116

For the nightemare:
Take a flint stone that hath an hole thorou° of his   through
owen° growing, and hange it over the stabil doore,   own
or ell° over horse, and ell write this charme: else
In nomine Patris, etc.
Seint Jorge, Our Lady° knight,   Lady's
He walked day, he walked night,
Till that he founde that foule wight;°   creature
And whan that he here° founde,   her
He here bete and he here bounde,
Till trewly there here trouthe° sche plight   troth
That sche sholde not come be° nighte,   by
Withinne seven rode° of londe space   rods
Ther° as Seint Jeorge inamed was.   where

St. Jeorge. St. Jeorge. St. Jeorge.
In nomine Patris, etc. And write this in a bille°   letter
and hange it in the hors° mane.   horse's

117

A good medicin for sor eyen:

For a man that is almost blind:
Lat him go barhed° all day agein° the wind   bareheaded / against
  Till the sone° be sette;   sun

At even wrap him in a cloke,
And put him in a hous full of smoke,
   And loke that every hol be well shet.°   *shut*

And whan his eyen begine to rope,°   *water*
Fill hem° full of brinston° and sope,°   *them / brimstone / soap*
   And hyll° him well and warme;   *cover*
And if he see not by the next mone°   *moon*
As well at midnight as at none,
   I schal lese° my right arme.   *lose*

118

Spende, and God schal sende;
Spare,° and ermor° care;   *hoard / evermore*
Non penny, non ware;°   *care (merchandise?)*
Non catel,° non care.   *goods*
   Go, penny, go.

119

Go bet,° penny, go bet, go!   *more quickly*
For thou mat° maken bothe frend and fo.[1]   *may*

Penny is an hardy° knight,   *courageous*
Penny is mekil° of might,   *great*
Penny of wrong he maketh right
   In every cuntry wher he go.

Though I have a man islawe°   *slain*
And forfeted the kinges lawe,
I shall finden a man of lawe
   Will taken min penny and let me go.

1. [Refrain repeated after each stanza.]

And if I have to don fer° or ner,°   *far / near*
And penny be min massanger,
Than am I non thing in dwer°—   *doubt*
    My cause shall be well ido.°   *performed*

And if I have pens° bothe good and fine,   *pence*
Men will bidden me to the wine;
"That I have shall be thine,"
    Sekerly° they will seyn so.   *surely*

And whan I have non in min purs,
Penny bet° ne penny wers,   *better*
Of me they holden but litel fors:°   *care*
    "He was a man, let him go!"

120

Man upon mold,° whatsoever thou be,   *earth*
I warn utterly thou gettest no degree,°   *social position*
Ne° no worship abid with thee,   *nor*
But° thou have the penny redy to tak° to.   *unless / have recourse*

If thou be a yeman, a gentilman wold be,
Into sum lordes cort than put thou thee;
Lok thou have spending large and plenty,
And alwey the penny redy to tak to.

If thou be a gentilman, and wold be a squier,
Ridest out of cuntry as wild as eny fier:°   *fire*
I thee warn as my frend thou failest of thy desir
But thou have the penny redy to tak to.

If thou be a squier, and wold be a knight,
And darest no° in armur put thee in fight,   *not*
Than to the kinges cort hy thee full tight,°   *quickly*
And look thou have the penny redy to tak to.

If thou be a lettred man, to bere° estat in scole,   *have*
A pilion° or taberd° to wer in hete or cole,°   *cap / short coat / cold*
Thee to besy therabout I hold thee but a fole°   *fool*
But thou have the penny redy to tak to.

If thou be a bachelar and woldest ever thrive,
Prekest out of contry and bringest home a wife;

In much sorrow and care ledest thou thy life—
But thou have the penny redy to tak to.

If thou be a marchant to buy or to sell,
And over all the country woldest bere the bell,[1]
I thee consell as a frend at home to dwell
But thou have the penny redy to tak to.

If thou be a yong man in lust thy life to lace,°   *involve*
About chirch and market the bishop will thee chace;
And if thou mayst be get,° thou getes nouther° grace   *caught / neither*
But thou have the penny redy to tak to.

If thou have out° to do with the law to plete,°   *ought / plead*
At London at the parvis° many one will thee rehete:°

                    St. Paul's Church-porch /
                                attack

I warne thee com not ther but° thy purse may swete,°   *unless / sweat*
And that thou have the penny redy to tak to.

121

Money, money, now hay° goode day!   *have*
   Money, where haste thou be?°   *been*
Money, money, thou goste away
   And wilt not bide° with me.[2]   *stay*

Above all thing thou arte a king
   And rulest the world over all;
Who lakethe thee, all joy, parde,°   *by God*
   Will sone then frome him fall.

In every place thou makeste solas,°   *pleasure*
   Gret joye, sporte, and welfare;
When money is gone, comforte is none,
   But thought, sorowe, and care.

In kinges corte, wher money dothe route,°   *go round*
   It maketh the galandes° to jet,°   *gallants / strut*
And for to were° gorgeouse ther gere,°   *wear / apparel*
   Ther cappes awry to set.

In the heyweyes° ther joly palfreys   *highways*
   It maketh to lepe and praunce;

1. "Bere the bell": be the best.   2. [Refrain repeated after each stanza.]

It maketh justinges, pleys, disguisinges,°   *allegorical entertainments*
  Ladys to singe and daunce.

For he that alway wanteth° money   *lacks*
  Stondeth a mated chere,[3]
Can never well sing, long daunce nor springe,
  Nor make no lusty chere.

At cardes and dice it bereth the price
  As king and emperoure;
At tables,° tennes, and all othere games   *backgammon*
  Money hathe ever the floure.°   *flower*

Withe squier and knight and every wighte
  Money maketh men faine°   *glad*
And causeth many in sume compeney
  Their felowes to disdaine.

In marchandise who can devise
  So good a ware, I say?
At all times the best ware is
  Ever redy money.

Money to incresse, marchandes° never to cease   *merchants*
  With many a sotell° wile,   *subtle*
Men say they wolde for silver and golde
  Ther owne faders begile.

Women, I trowe,° love money also,   *fancy*
  To by° them joly gere,   *buy*
For that helpethe and oft causethe
  Women to loke full faire.

In Westminster Hall the criers call;
  The sergeauntes° plede apace;   *sergeants-at-law*
Attorneys appere, now here, now ther,
  Renning° in every place.   *running*

Whatesoever he be, and if that he
  Wante money to plede the lawe,
Do what he can, in his matter° than   *law suit*
  Shalle° prove not worthe a strawe.   *he will*

I know it not, but well I wotte°   *know*
  I have harde oftentimes tell,
Prestes° use this guise, ther benefice   *priests*
  For moieny° to bey and sell.   *money*

Craftesmen, that be in every citee,
  They worke and never blinne;°   *cease*

3. Stands with the air of one checkmated or baffled.

Sume cutte, sume shave, sume knoke, sum grave,
   Only money to winne.

The plowman himselfe dothe digge and delve
   In storme, snowe, frost, and raine,
Money to get with laboure and swete;
   Yet small geines° and muche paine.   *gains*

And sume for money lie by the wey
   Another mannes purse to get,
But they that long use it amonge
   Ben hanged by the neke.

The beggers eke in every strete
   Lie walowing by the wey;
They begge, they crie, oft they cume by,
   And all is but for money.

In every coste° men love it moste,   *coast*
   In Inglonde, Spaine, and France,
For every man lacking it than
   Is clene oute of countenaunce.

Of whate degree soever he be,
   Or vertuouse conning he have,
And wante money, yet men will sey
   That he is but a knave.

Where indede, so God me spede,
   Sey all men whate they can,
It is allwayes sene nowadayes
   That money makethe the man.

122

He that spendes muche and getes nothing,
And owthe° muche and hathe nothing,   *owes*
And lokes in his porse and findes nothing,
He may be sorye and saye nothing.

                           Quothe K.L.

123

I had my ⎫   ⎧and my ⎫
I lent my ⎪ good ⎪to my ⎬ frend.
I asked my ⎬   ⎨of my ⎪
I lost my ⎭   ⎩and my ⎭

I made of my frend my fo:
I will be war I do no more so.

124

Pees° maketh plente.°   *peace / plenty*
Plente maketh pride.
Pride maketh plee.°   *plea (law suit)*
Plee maketh povert.°   *poverty*
Povert maketh pees.

125

Who hath that conning by wisdam or prudence
To know whether his frende be feint or stable?
Ther is no creature, I trow,° that hath that science°
                                 believe / knowledge

To know his frende—the world is so mutable,
And frenship is double and vary° diseivable;°   *very / deceitful*
The mouthe seithe ane,° the hert thinketh another;   *one thing*
Alas to say, it is full lementable,
Unneth° a man now may truste his owne brother.   *scarcely*

126

I conjour hem° in the name of the Fader, and Sone,   *them*
  and Holy Gost;
In hem is vertu° althermost!°✠   *power / most of all*
In the beginning and in the ending,
And in the vertu of all thing
Is, and was, and ever schal be—
In the vertu of the Holy Trinitee—
By the vertu of every Masse,
That ever was seyde, more and lasse—
In the vertu of herbe, grass, ston, and tree—
And in the vertu that ever may be.

If here come eny fon°   *foes*
Me to robbe, other° me to sclon;°   *or / slay*
They stond as stille as eny ston,
They have no powere away to gon,
By the vertu of the Holy Trinitee,
Tille they have life of me.
Lord Jesu, graunte me this,
As ye ben in heven bliss.

127

To the Holy Goste my goodes I bequeth
  That in this place be set,
To the Father and the Sone
  All theves for to let.°   *hinder*
And if any theves hither come
  My goodes away to fet,°   *fetch*
The Holy Goste be them before
  And make them for to let;°   *give up*
And make them to abide
  Till I againe come;
Thorough the vertu° of the Holy Gost,   *power*
  The Father, and the Sonne.

Now I go my way—tide what may betide!
If any theves hither come, here I shall abide.

I bind you theves
And do you conjure,
So° St. Bartelmew bound the Devil   *as*
With his bearde so hoare . . . .[1]

128

Here I ame and fourthe I mouste,[2]
And in Jesus Criste is all my trust.
No wicked thing do me no dare,°   *injury*
Nother° here nor elleswhare.   *neither*
The Father with me; the Sonne with me;
The Holy Goste, and the Trinitee,
Be betwixte my gostely Enimie and me.
  In the name of the Father, and the Sonne,
  And the Holy Goste, Amen.

129

He that in youthe no vertu will yowes,°   *use*
In age all honor shall him refuse.

130

In 8° is alle my love,   ⎫   H *(eighth letter)*
And° 9° be isette before;   ⎬ IHC[4]   *if* / I *(ninth letter)*
So 8 be iclosed[3] above,   ⎬
Thane° 3° is good therefore.   ⎭   *then* / C *(third letter)*

1. [The line is incomplete.]   to indicate contraction.
2. Here I am and forth I must go.   4. [Contraction of the name "Jesus" in
3. "Iclosed": marked with the tilde (~)   Greek.]

131

Kepe well x,[1] and flee fro vii;[2]
Rule well v,[3] and come to heven.

132

Who redes this boke of imagerie,[4]
It will hom° counfort and make redie,   *them*
And understonde hor° witte to clere,   *their*
By thes beestes° purtreyed here;   *beasts*
And full knowing of mikel° treuth   *much*
That now is hidde—it is grete reuth;°   *pity*
What they bemeenen° in hor kinde,   *mean*
Waytnas° tho gloose° and ye shall finde   *witness / gloss*
It is as keye that will unloken
Tho dore that is full faste stoken;°   *stuck shut*
This keye were gode men to finde,
To make hom see that now ben blinde;
God gif us grace that sight to have
To reule us right we may be save.[5]

133

I have twelve oxen that be faire and brown,
And they go a-grasinge° down by the town.   *grazing*
     With hay, with howe, with hay!
Saweste thou not min oxen, thou litel pretty boy?

1. The Ten Commandments.
2. The Seven Deadly Sins.
3. The Five Wits (Senses).
4. I.e., the Apocalypse.
5. To govern ourselves rightly, so that we may be saved.

I have twelve oxen, and they be faire and whight,°   *white*
And they go a-grasing down by the dike.
   With hay, with howe, with hay!
Saweste not thou min oxen, thou litel pretty boy?

I have twelve oxen, and they be faire and blak,
And they go a-grasing down by the lak.°   *lake*
   With hay, with howe, with hay!
Saweste not thou min oxen, thou litel pretty boy?

I have twelve oxen, and they be faire and rede,
And they go a-grasing down by the mede.°   *meadow*
   With hay, with howe, with hay!
Saweste not thou my oxen, thou litel pretty boy?

134

By a forest as I gan° fare,°   *did / go*
Walking all myselven alone,
I hard° a morning° of an hare,   *heard / mourning*
Roufully schew mad here mone.[1]

"Dereworth° God, how schal I leve°   *beloved / live*
And leid° my life in lond?   *lead*
Frow° dale to doune I am idreve;°   *from / driven*
I not° where I may site or stond!   *know not*

I may nother° rest nor slepe   *neither*
By no vallay that is so derne,°   *out of the way*
Nor no covert may me kepe,
But ever I rene° fro herne° to herne.   *run / hiding place*

Honteres will not heire° ther° Masse,   *hear / their*
In hope of hunting for to wend;°   *go*
They coupelleth° ther houndes more and lasse,   *couple (in pairs)*
And bringeth them to the feldes ende.

Roches° rennen on every side   *dogs*
In forrows that hope me to find;
Honteres taketh ther horse and ride
And cast the contray to the wind.

Anon as they cometh me behinde,
I loke and sit full stille and lowe;

1. Piteously she made her moan.

The furst man that me doth finde
Anon he crit,° 'So howe!'° so howe!'   cries / ho

'Lo,' he saith, 'where sitteth an hare—
Arise up, Watte,° and go forth blive!'°   i.e., hare / quickly
With sorroe and with mich care
I schape° away with my life.   escape

At winter in the depe snowe
Men will me seche° for to trace,   seek
And by my steppes I am iknowe;°   known
And followeth me fro place to place.

And if I to the toune come or torne,
Be it in wortes° or in leike,°   herbs / leek
Then will the wives also° yeorne°   as / eagerly
Flece me with here° dogges eke.°   their / also

And if I sit and crope° the koule,°   eat / kale
And the wife be in the waye,
Anon schowe° will swere, 'By cokkes soule!   she
There is an hare in my haye!'

Anon sche wille clepe,° 'Forth, cure,° knave!'   call / cur
And loke right weel where I sitte;
Behind sche will with a stave
Full well porpos me to hitte.

'Go forthe, Watte, with Cristes curse,
And if I leve,° thou schalt be take;°   live / taken
I have an hare-pipe° in my purse,   trap
It schal be set all for thy sauke!'°   sake

Then hath this wyf two dogges grete,°   huge
On me sche biddeth heme° goe;   them
And as a scrowe° sche will me thret,°   shrew / threaten
And ever sche crieth, 'Go, doggee, goe!'

But all way this most° I go,   must
By no banke I may abide;
Lord God, that me is wo!²
Many a happe° hath me betide.°   mishap / befallen

There is no beest in the world, I wene,°   think
Hert, hind, buke, ne dove,
That sufferes halfe so miche tene°   misery
As doth the silly wat—go where he go.

2. "That me is wo": what woe is mine!

If a gentilmane will have any game,
And find me in forme° where I sitte,   *lair*
For dred of losinge of his name
I wot° welle he wille not me hitte.   *know*

For an acures° bred° he will me leve,   *acre's / breadth*
Or° he will let his hondes° rene;   *before / hounds*
Of all the men that beth alive
I am most behold to gentilmen!

As sone as I can ren to the laye,°   *lea, open land*
Anon the greyhondes will me have;
My bowels beth ithrowe awaye,
And I am bore home on a stave.°   *staff*

Als° soon as I am come home,   *as*
I am ihonge hie° upon a pine;   *high*
With leeke-wortes° I am eete anone,   *herbs*
And whelpes play with my skine!"

135

"Pax vobis,"° *quod the fox,*   *Peace be unto you*
"*For I am comen to towne.*"[1]

It fell ageins° the next night   *upon*
The fox yede to[2] with all his mighte,
Withouten cole° or candelight,   *coal*
    Whan that he cam unto the towne.

Whan he cam all in the yarde,
Sore° the gees were ill aferde;°   *sorely / afraid*
"I shall make some of youre berde,[3]
    Or that° I go from the towne!"   *before*

Whan he cam all in the crofte,
There he stalked wunderfull softe;
"For here have I be frayed° full ofte   *frightened*
    Whan that I have come to towne."

He hente° a goose all be the eye,[4]   *seized*
Faste the goos began to creye!°   *cry out*

1. [Refrain repeated after each stanza.]   3. I shall outwit some of you.
2. "Yede to": went about his work.   4. "Be the eye": in a twinkling.

Oute yede° men as they might heye,°   *went / hasten*
  And seide, "Fals fox, ley it downe!"

"Nay," he saide, "so mot° I thee°—   *may / thrive*
Sche shall go unto the wode with me,
Sche and I unther° a tree,   *under*
  Emange° the beryes browne.   *among*

I have a wyf, and sche lieth seke;°   *sick*
Many smale whelpes sche have to eke[5]—
Many bones they muste pike°   *pick*
  Will° they ley adowne."   *until*

136

The fals fox came unto our croft,
And so our geese full fast he sought.
With how fox, how; with hey fox, hey!
Come no more unto our house to bere our geese aweye!

The fals fox came unto our stye,
And toke our geese ther by and by.

The fals fox cam into our yerde,
And ther he made the geese aferde.°   *afraid*

The fals fox came unto our gate,
And toke our geese ther wher they sate.

The fals fox came unto our halle-dore,
And shrove° our geese ther in the flore.   *heard confession of*

The fals fox came into our halle,
And assoiled° our geese both grete and small.   *absolved*

The fals fox came unto our coupe,
And ther he made our geese to stoupe.°   *bow down*

He toke a goose fast by the nek,
And the goose tho° began to quek.°   *then / quake*

The good-wife came out in her smok,
And at the fox she threw her rok.

5. "To eke": also.

The good-man came out with his flaile,
And smote the fox upon the taile.

He threw a goose upon his back,
And furth he went tho with his pak.

The good-man swore if that he might,
He wolde him slee° or° it wer night.   *slay / before*

The fals fox went into his denne,
And ther he was full mery thenne.

He came agene yet the next weke,
And toke awey both henne and cheke.°   *chick*

The good-man saide unto his wife,
"This fals fox liveth a mery life."

The fals fox came upon a day,
And with our geese he made affray.°   *disturbance*

He toke a goose fast by the nek,
And made her to sey, "Wheccumquek!"

"I pray thee, fox," seid the goose tho,
"Take of my feders° but not of my to."°   *feathers / toes*

137

I have a yong suster
Fer° beyonden the see;°   *far / sea*
Many be the drowries°   *love-tokens*
That she sente me.

She sente me the cherye
Withouten ony ston,
And so she ded the dove[1]
Withouten ony bon.

Sche sente me the brer°   *briar*
Withouten ony rinde;°   *branch*
Sche bad me love my lemman°   *lover*
Withoute longing.

1. And also she did (send) the dove.

How shuld ony cherye
Be withoute ston?
And how shuld ony dove
Ben withoute bon?

How shuld ony brer
Ben withoute rinde?
How shuld I love min lemman
Without longing?

Whan the cherye was a flour,
Than hadde it non ston;
Whan the dove was an ey,°   *egg*
Than hadde it non bon.

Whan the brer was onbred,°   *unborn*
Than hadde it non rind;
Whan the maiden hath that° she loveth,   *what*
She is without longing.

138

Maiden in the mor° lay,   *moor*
  In the mor lay,
Sevenight° fulle, sevenight fulle.   *a week*
Maiden in the mor lay,
  In the mor lay,
Sevenightes fulle and a day.

Welle° was hire mete.°   *good / food*
What was hire mete?
  The primerole° and the—   *primrose*
  The primerole and the—
Welle was hire mete.
What was hire mete?
  The primerole and the violet.

Welle was hire dring.°   *drink*
What was hire dring?
  The chelde° water of the—   *cold*
  The chelde water of the—
Welle was hire dring.

What was hire dring?
  The chelde water of the welle-spring.

Welle was hire bour.°   *abode*
What was hire bour?
  The rede rose and the—
  The rede rose and the—
Welle was hire bour.
What was hire bour?
  The rede rose and the lilie flour.

139

Summe men sayen° that I am blac°—   *say / dark-complexioned*
It is a colour for my prow;°   *profit*
Ther° I love, ther is no lac,   *where*
I may not be so white as thou.

Blac is a colour that is good,
So say I and many mo;°   *more*
Blac is my hat, blac is my hood,
Blac is all that longeth° therto.   *belongs*

Blac wol do as good a nede°   *service*
As the white at bord and bedde;
And therto also° trew in dede,   *as*
And therto I ley my lif to wedde.[1]

Wind and water may steyne the white,
Iwis;° the blac it may not so.   *certainly*
Ther° is the blac is all my delite;   *where*
I am iholde be skile therto.[2]

Pepper withoute° it is well blac,   *outside*
Iwis; withinne it is not so.
Lat go the colour and tak the smac,°   *taste*
This I sey by me and mo.

God save all hem° that beth° browne,   *them / are*
For they beth trew as any stel;°   *steel*
God kepe hem bothe in feld and towne,
And thanne schal I be kept full well.

1. "To wedde": for a pledge.   2. I am held by reason to that.

140

Swarte smeked smethes, smattered with smoke,[1]
Drive me to deth with den° of here° dintes!°   *din / their / strokes*
Swech° nois on nightes ne herd men never: *such*
What knavene cry,[2] and clattering of knockes!
The cammede° kongons° crien after "Col, col!"

        snub-nosed / changelings
And blowen here bellewes that all here brain brestes.°   *bursts*
"Huff, puff!" seith that one; "Haff, paff!" that other.
They spitten and sprawlen and spellen° many spelles,°   *tell / tales*
They gnawen and gnacchen,° they grones togedere,   *gnash*
And holden hem° hote with here hard hammers.   *themselves*
Of a bole° hide ben here barm-felles,°   *bull's / leather aprons*
Here schankes° ben schakeled for the fere-flunderes;° *legs / fiery sparks*
Hevy hammeres they han that hard ben handled,
Stark° strokes they striken on a steled° stokke.°   *strong / steel / anvil*
"Luss, buss! lass, dass!" routen be rowe[3]—
Sweche° dolful a dreme° the devil it todrive°!   *so / noise / dispel*
The maister longeth a litel and lascheth a lesse,
Twineth hem twein, and toucheth a treble.[4]
"Tik, tak! hic, hac! tiket, taket! tik, tak!
Luss, buss! luss, dass!" swich lif they leden!
Alle clothemeres,° Crist hem give sorwe,   *horse armorers*
May no man for brenwateres[5] on night han his rest!

141

Wenest° thu, uscher,° with thy cointise,°   *think / teacher / cunning*
Iche° day beten° us on this wise,°   *each / to beat / manner*
    As° thu wer lord of toun?   *as if*
We had lever° scole forsake,   *rather*
And ilche of us another crafte take,
    Then long to be in thy bandoun.°   *power*

1. Black smoked smiths, begrimed with smoke.
2. What noise of assistants.
3. "Routen be rowe": crash in turn.
4. The master lengthens a little (piece of iron) and hammers a smaller (piece),/ Twines the two of them, and touches (strikes with his hammer) a treble (note).
5. "Brenwateres": water-burners; smiths who plunge their hot irons into water.

But wolde God that we might ones°	*once*
Cache thee at the mulne° stones,	*mill*
Or at the crabbe tree—	
We schuld leve in thee such a probeyt°	*proof, evidence*
For° that° thu hast us don and seid,	*because of* / *what*
That alle thy kin shuld rue° thee.	*pity*

And tho Sire Robert,° with his cloke,	*i.e., the Devil*
Wold thee helpe and be thy Poke,°	*Puck*
The werre° thu schust° fare;	*worse* / *should*
And for his prayer the rather we wold	
Given him stripes all uncolde,°	*stinging*
Not for him thee spare.	

For ofte sore we abye°	*pay for*
The twinkelinges of his eye,	
The maister us to bete;	
For he and thu are at assent,	
All day given° agagement°	*give, make* / *agreement*
To given us strokes grete.	

142

Mon in the mone° stond° and strit;°	*moon* / *stands* / *strides*
On his bot-forke° his burthen° he bereth;	*forked stick* / *bundle*
It is muche wonder that he n'adoun° slit°—	*not down* / *falls*
For doute° leste he falle, he shoddreth° and shereth.°	*fear* / *trembles* / *veers*

When the forst freseth, muche chele he bid;[1]	
The thornes beth kene, his hattren to-tereth.[2]	
Nis° no wight° in the world that wot° when he sit,	*there is (not)* / *person* / *knows*
Ne, bote it be the hegge, whet wedes he wereth.[3]	

Whider trowe this mon ha the wey take?[4]	
He hath set his o° fot his other toforen.°	*one* / *in front of*
For non highte that he hath ne sight me him ner shake:[5]	
He is the sloweste mon that ever wes iboren.°	*born*
Wher he were o the feld pitchinde stake,[6]	
For hope of his thornes to dutten his doren,[7]	
He mot mid his twibil other trous make[8]	

1. When the frost freezes, much cold he endures.
2. The thorns are sharp (and) tear his clothes to pieces.
3. Nor, unless it be the hedge, what clothes he wears.
4. Where do you think this man has made his way?
5. Despite any effort one may make, one never sees him move.
6. Whether he be in the field fastening stakes.
7. In the hope of closing his doors with his thorns.
8. He must either make a bundle with his two-edged axe.

Other° all his dayes werk ther were iloren.°   *or / lost*

This ilke° mon upon hegh° whener° he were,   *very / high / whenever*
Wher° he were i'° the mone boren and ifed,°   *whether / in / reared*
He leneth on his forke° as a grey frere;°   *forked stick / friar (Franciscan)*
This crokede° caynard° sore he is adred.°   *bowed / idler / afraid*
It is mony day go⁹ that he was here;
Ichot of his ernde he nath nout isped.¹
He hath hewe° sumwher a burthen of brere;°   *hewn / briars*
Tharefore sum hayward° hath taken his wed.°   *hedge-keeper / pledge*

If thy wed is itake,° bring hom the trous,°   *taken / brush, hedge-cuttings*
Set forth thin other fot, strid° over sty.°   *stride / path*
We shule preye° the haywart hom to our hous   *ask*
And maken him at eyse° for the maistry,²   *ease*
Drinke to him deorly° of fol good bous,°   *affectionately / strong drink*
And oure dame douse° shall sitten him by.   *sweet*
When that he is dronke as a dreynt° mous,   *drowned*
Thenne we schule borewe° the wed ate° baily.°   *obtain / from / bailiff*

This mon hereth me nout thagh° ich to him crye;   *though*
Ichot the cherl is def; the Del him todrawe!³
Thagh ich yeye upon hegh, nulle nout hye:⁴
The lostlase ladde con nout o lawe.⁵
Hupe forth, Hubert, hosede pye!⁶
Ichot th'art amarscled° into the mawe.°   *stuffed full / stomach*
Thagh me teone with him that min teth mye,⁷
The cherl nul nout adoun er the day dawe.°   *dawns*

                              [Harley 2253]

143

Ich° am of Irlaunde,   *I*
And of the holy londe
Of Irlande.

Gode sire, pray ich thee,
For of sainte charitee,⁸
Come and daunce wit me
In Irlaunde.

9. It is many days ago.
1. I know he has not succeeded in his errand.
2. "For the maistry": extremely.
3. I know the fellow is deaf; may the Devil tear him to pieces!
4. Though I cry out on high, he will not at all hurry.
5. The lazy lad knows nothing of law.
6. Go forth, Hubert, (you) magpie in stockings!
7. Though one be so angry with him that one's teeth grate.
8. Good sir, I pray you,/ For the sake of holy charity.

VI

Make we mery

144

Make we mery bothe more and lasse,
For now is the time of Cristimas.[1]

Let no man cum into this hall,
Grome, page, nor yet marshall,
But that sum sport he bring withall,
For now is the time of Cristmas.

If that he say he can not sing,
Sum oder° sport then let him bring,   other
That it may please at this festing,
For now is the time of Cristmas.

If he say he can nought do,
Then for my love aske him no mo;°   more
But to the stokkes then let him go,
For now is the time of Cristmas.

145

Verbum caro factum est
Et habitavit in nobis.[2]
Fetis bel chere,[3]
Drink to thy fere,°   companion

1. [Refrain repeated after each stanza.]   among us.
2. The word was made flesh/ And dwelt   3. Excellent good cheer.

Verse le bavere,[4]
And singe Nouwel!

146

Farewele, Advent; Cristemas is cum;
Farewele fro us both alle and sume.[1]

With paciens thou hast us fedde
And made us go hungrie to bedde;
For lak of mete° we were nighe dedde;   food
Farewele fro us both alle and sume.

While thou haste° be° within oure house,   have / been
We ete° no puddinges ne no souce,°   ate / sauce
But stinking fisshe not worthe a louce;
Farewele fro us both alle and sume.

There was no fresshe fisshe ferre ne nere;[2]
Salt fisshe and samon was too dere,
And thus we have had hevy chere;
Farewele fro us both alle and sume.

Thou hast us fedde with plaices° thinne,   i.e., a kind of fish
Nothing on them but bone and skinne;
Therfore oure love thou shalt not winne;
Farewele fro us both alle and sume.

With muskilles° gaping afture the mone°   mussels / moon
Thou hast us fedde at night and none,°   noon
But ones° a wyke,° and that too sone;   once / week
Farewele fro us both alle and sume.

Oure brede was browne, oure ale was thinne,
Oure brede was musty in the binne,
Oure ale soure or° we did beginne;   before
Farewele fro us both alle and sume.

Thou art of grete ingratitude
Good mete fro us for to exclude;
Thou art not kinde but verey rude;
Farewele fro us both alle and sume.

4. Pour the drink.   2. "Ferre ne nere": far or near.
1. [Refrain repeated after each stanza.]

Thou dwellest with us agenst oure wille,
And yet thou gevest us not oure fille;
For lak of mete thou woldest us spille;°   *punish*
Farewele fro us both alle and sume.

Above alle thinge thou art a meane°   *cause, agent*
To make oure chekes bothe bare and leane;
I wolde thou were at Boughton Bleane!
Farewele fro us both alle and sume.

Come thou no more here nor in Kent,
For, if thou do, thou shalt be shent;°   *punished*
It is enough to faste in Lent;
Farewele fro us bothe alle and sume.

Thou maist not dwelle with none eastate;
Therfore with us thou playest chekmate.
Go hens,° or we will breke thy pate!   *hence*
Farewele fro us both alle and sume.

Thou maist not dwell with knight nor squier;
For them thou maiste lie in the mire;
They love not thee nor Lent, thy sire;
Farewele fro us both alle and sume.

Thou maist not dwell with labouring man,
For on thy fare no skille he can,[3]
For he must ete bothe now and than;
Farewele fro us both alle and sume.

Though thou shalt dwell with monke and frere,°   *friar*
Chanon° and nonne ones every yere,   *canon*
Yet thou shuldest make us better chere;
Farewele fro us both alle and sume.

This time of Cristes feest natall
We will be mery, grete and small,
And thou shalt go oute of this halle;
Farewele fro us both alle and sume.

Advent is gone; Cristemas is cume;
Be we mery now, alle and sume;
He is not wise that wille be dume°   *silent*
In ortu Regis omnium.[4]

[*James Ryman, ca.* 1490]

3. For he cannot get by on your fare.   4. At the birth of the King of all.

147

Hay, ay, hay, ay,
Make we merie as we may.[1]

Now is Yole° comen° with gentil chere,°   *Yule / come / countenance*
Of merthe and gomen° he has no pere;°   *amusement / peer*
In every londe where he comes nere
Is merthe and gomen, I dar wele say.

Now is comen a messingere
Of yore lorde, Ser Nu Yere°—   *Sir New Year*
Biddes us all be merie here
And make as merie as we may.

Therefore every mon that is here
Singe a carol on his manere;[2]
If he con° non we schall him lere,°   *knows / teach*
So that we be merie allway.

Whosoever makes hevy chere,
Were he never to me dere,[3]
In a diche I wolde he were,
To dry his clothes till it were day.

Mende the fire, and make gud chere!
Fill the cuppe, Ser Botelere!°   *butler*
Let every mon drinke to his fere!°   *companion*
Thys° endes my carol, with care awaye.   *thus*

148

Holver° and heivy° mad a gret party:°   *holly / ivy / debate*
Who shuld have the maistrie°   *mastery*
    In londes wher they go?

1. [Refrain repeated after each stanza.]   3. Were he never so dear to me.
2. "On his manere": in his own fashion.

Than spake holver: "I am freshe and jolly;
I wol have the maistrie
  In londes wher they go."

Than spake heivy: "I am loud and proud,
And I will have the maistrie
  In londes wher they go."

Than spak holver, and set him downe on his knee:
"I prey thee, jentil heivy, sey me no veleny°   *villainy*
  In londes wher we go."

149

Alleluia, alleluia,
Alleluia, now sing we.

Here comes holly that is so gent,°   *noble*
To please all men is his intent.
  Alleluia.

But lord and lady of this hall,
Whosoever ageinst holly call—
  Alleluia.

Whosoever ageinst holly do crye
In a lepe[1] shall he hang full hye.
  Alleluia.

Whosoever ageinst holly do sing,
He maye wepe and handes wring.
  Alleluia.

150

Ivy, chefe° of trees it is;   *chief*
  Veni, coronaberis.[2]

---

1. "In a lepe": straightway.   2. Come, you shall be crowned.

The most worthye she is in towne—
  He that seith other do amisse—
And worthy to ber the crowne.
  Veni, coronaberis.

Ivy is soft and meek of spech;
  Ageinst all bale she is blisse;
Well is he that may her rech.°   *attain*
  Veni, coronaberis.

Ivy is green, with colour bright,
  Of all trees best she is;
And that I preve° well now be° right.   *prove / by*
  Veni, coronaberis.

Ivy bereth berys black;
  God graunt us all his blisse,
For there shall we nothing lack.
  Veni, coronaberis.

151

Tidinges I bring you, for to tell
What me in wild forest befell,
Whan me must with a wild best mell[1]—
  With a bor° so brime.°   *boar / fierce*
A bore so brime that me pursued,
Me for to kill sor sharply ameved,°   *aroused*
That brimly° best so cruel and unrid,° *fierce / violent*
  Ther tamed I him,
And reft fro him both lith° and lime.°   *joint / limb*

Truly to shew you that is trew,
His hed with my swerd I hew,°   *sever*
To mak this day to you mirth new.
  Now etes° therof anon.   *eat*
Etes on, much good do it you!
Take you bred and musterd therto;
Joy with me that I have thus done;
I pray you to be glad everichon,°   *everyone*
  And joy all in one.

1. When I had to engage in combat with a wild beast.

152

Po, po, po, po,
Love brane° and so do mo.°¹ — *brawn / more, others*

At the beginning of the mete,° — *feast*
Of a bores hed ye schal ete,
And in the mustard ye shall wete;° — *dip*
   And ye shall singen or° ye gon. — *before*

Wolcum° be ye that ben° here, — *welcome / are*
And ye shall have right gud chere,
And also a right gud fare;
   And ye shall singen or ye gon.

Welcum be ye everichon,° — *everyone*
For ye shall singen right anon.
Hey you fast that ye had don,²
   And ye shall singen or ye gon.

153

Caput apri refero,
Resonens laudes Domino.³

The bores hed in hondes I bringe,
With garlondes gay and birdes singinge!
I pray you all helpe me to singe,
   Qui estis in convivio.⁴

The bores hede, I understond,
Is chef° service in all this londe, — *chief*
Whersoever it may be fonde,° — *found*
   Servitur cum sinapio.⁵

1. [Refrain repeated after each stanza.]
2. Hasten that you be done.
3. The boar's head I bring,/ Singing praises to the Lord. [Refrain repeated after each stanza.]
4. Who are at this banquet.
5. It is served with mustard.

The bores hede, I dare well say,
Anon after the twelfthe day,
He taketh his leve and goth away—
 Exivit tunc de patria.[6]

154

Hey, hey, hey, hey!
The bores hede is armed gay.[1]

The bores hede in hond I bring,
With garlond gay in portoring;°   *carrying*
I pray you all with me to singe,
 With hay!

Lordes, knightes, and squiers,
Persons,° prestes,° and vicars—   *parsons / priests*
The bores hede is the furst mess,°   *course*
 With hay!

The bores hede, as I you say,
He takes his leive° and gothe his way   *leave*
Soon after the tweilfeth° day,   *twelfth*
 With hay!

Then comes in the secund cours with mikel° pride: *much*
The cranes and the heirons,° the bitteres° by ther side,
            herons / bitterns
The pertriches and the plovers, the woodcokes and the snit,° *snipe*
 With hay!

Larkes in hot schow,° ladys for to pik,°   *broth / pick*
Good drink therto, lucius° and fin—   *luscious*
Bluet° of almain,° romnay° and win, *soup / almond / sweet wine*
 With hay!

Gud bred, ale, and win, dare I well say,
The bores hede with musterd armed so gay.

Furmante to pottage, with venisun fin,[2]
And the hombuls° of the dove, and all that ever comes in. *entrails*

Capons ibake,° with the peses° of the row,° *baked / pieces / roe (deer)*
Reisons of corrans, with oder spises mo.[3]

6. He has left the country.
1. [Refrain repeated after each stanza.]
2. Frumenty (wheat boiled in milk) for
pottage, with fine venison.
3. Raisins of currants, with other spices.

155

Bon Joure, bon joure a vous![1]
I am cum unto this hous,
With par la pompe, I say.[2]

Is ther any good man here
That will make me any chere?°   *kind welcome*
And if ther were, I wold cum nere
To wit° what he wold say.   *know*
  A, will ye be wild?
  By Mary mild
  . . . .[3]
I trow° ye will sing gay.   *believe*
  Bon Joure.

Be gladly,° masters everychon!°   *joyful / everyone*
I am cum myself alone
To appose° you on° by on.   *examine / one*
Let see who dare say nay.
  Sir, what say ye?
  Sing on, let us see.
  Now will it be
This or another day?
  Bon Joure.

Lo, this is he that will do the dede!
He tempereth° his mouth, therfore take hede.   *tunes*
Sing softe, I say, leste your nose blede,
For hurt yourself ye may!
  But by God that me bought,°   *redeemed*
  Your brest is so tought,°   *taut*
  Till ye have well cought°   *coughed*
Ye may not therwith away.[4]
  Bon Jour.

Sir, what say ye, with your face so lene?°   *lean*
Ye sing nother° good tenoure,° treble, ne mene.°
                                        neither / tenor / middle voice
Utter not your voice without° your brest be clene,   *unless*
Hartely° I you pray!   *heartily*
  I hold you excused,
  Ye shall be refused,
  For ye have not be° used   *been*

1. Good Day, good day to you!
2. *"Par la pompe"*: ceremonial procession. [Refrain repeated after each
stanza.]
3. [The line is missing.]
4. You may not do away with it.

To no good sport nor play.
  Bon Joure.

Sir, what say ye, with your fat face?
Me thinketh° ye shuld bere a very good bace°   *it seems to me / bass*
To a pot of good ale or Ipocras,°   *sweet wine*
Truly as I you say!
  Hold up your hede,°   *head*
  Ye loke like lede;°   *lead*
  Ye wast° miche° bred   *waste / much*
Evermore from day to day.
  Bon Joure.

Now will ye see wher° he stondeth behinde?   *whether*
Iwis,° brother, ye be unkind.   *certainly*
Stond forth, and wast with me som wind,
For ye have ben called a singer ay.°   *always*
  Nay, be not ashamed;
  Ye shall not be blamed,
  For ye have ben famed
The worst in this contrey!
  Bon Jour.

156

If I singe, ye will me lakke,°   *blame*
And wenen° I wer out of min wit;   *think*
Therfor smale notes will I crake;°   *utter*
So wolde God I wer quit.°   *finished*

Syne me muste[1] take this mery toin°   *tune*
To glade° withal this cumpany,   *gladden*
I rede° or° ony swich° be don,   *advise / before / such*
For Godes love, tey° up your ky!°   *take / key*

Forsothe I may not singe, I say;
My voys and I arn° at discord;   *are*
But we shul fonde° to take° a day   *try / appoint*
To taken min avis° and min acord.°   *advice / agreement, harmony*

1. Since I must.

157

Omnes gentes, plaudite,[1]
I saw miny° briddes seten° on a tree;   *many / sit*
He token her flight and flowen away,[2]
With *ego dixi*,[3] have good day.
Many white federes° hath the pye°—   *feathers / magpie*
I may noon mor singen, my lippes arn° so drye!   *are*
Manye white federes hath the swan—
The mor that I drinke, the lesse good I can!
Ley stikkes on the fer, wil mot it brenne[4]—
Geve° us onys° drinken er we gon henne!°   *give / once / hence*

158

Is° tell you my mind, Anes Tayliur,° dame;°
                                        I shall / Agnes Taylor / madame
I deme° we lak plesur.   *think*
Loke here, dame, unloke your dur!°   *door*
Alacke, we have no likur!°   *drink*

Frende, and° we are fer in dette   *even though*
For your fine gode wine, God watte,°   *knows*
A short gint° has a pint potte;   *measure*
I dranke onys;° I wold drinke yette.   *once*

159

Bring us in good ale, and bring us in good ale;
Fore our Blessed Lady sake, bring us in good ale![5]

1. All people, applaud.
2. They took their flight and flew away.
3. I say.
4. Lay sticks on the fire, well may it burn.
5. [Refrain repeated after each stanza.]

Bring us in no browne bred, fore that is made of brane;°   *bran*
Nor bring us in no whit bred, fore therin is no game;°   *amusement*
  But bring us in good ale.

Bring us in no befe, for ther is many bones;
But bring us in good ale, for that goth downe at onys;°   *once*
  And bring us in good ale.

Bring us in no bacon, for that is passing fat;
But bring us in good ale, and give us inought° of that;   *enough*
  And bring us in good ale.

Bring us in no mutton, for that is ofte lene;
Nor bring us in no tripes, for they be seldom clene;
  But bring us in good ale.

Bring us in no egges, for ther are many schelles;
But bring us in good ale, and give us nothing elles;
  And bring us in good ale.

Bring us in no butter, for therin are many heres;°   *hairs*
Nor bring us in no pigges flesch, for that will make us bores;°   *boars*
  But bring us in good ale.

Bring us in no podinges, for therin is all gotes blood;
Nor bring us in no veneson, for that is not for our good;
  But bring us in good ale.

Bring us in no capons flesch, for that is ofte der;°   *expensive*
Nor bring us in no dokes flesch, for they slobber in the mer;°   *pond*
  But bring us in good ale.

160

How, butler, how! bevis a tout![1]
Fill the boll,° jentil° butler, and let the cup rought!°
                     drinking vessel / noble / go
                                    round

Jentil butler, *bel ami,*[2]
Fill the boll by the eye,[3]

1. *"Bevis a tout"*: drink to all.   3. "By the eye": immediately.
2. *"Bel ami"*: good friend.

That we may drink by and by.
  With how, butler, how! bevis a tout!
  *Fill the boll, butler, and let the cup rought!*4

Here is mete° for us all,   food
Both for gret and for small;
I trow° we must the butler call.   believe

I am so dry I cannot spek,
I am nigh choked with my mete;
I trow the butler be aslepe.

Butler, butler, fill the boll,
Or elles I beshrewe° thy noll!°   curse / head
I trow we must the bell toll.

If the butlers name be Water,°   Walter (pun)
I wold he were a galow-claper,°   gallows-bird
But if° he bring us drink the rather.°   unless / sooner

161

Tappster, fille another ale!
Anonne° have I do;°   anon / done
God send us good sale.°   joy
Avale° the stake,° avale;   wreathe / ale-stake
Here is good ale ifoundc!
Drinke to me,
And I to thee,
And lette the coppe go rounde.

162

Here I was and here I drank;
Farwell dam,° and mikill° thank.   madame / much
Here I was and had gud cheer,
And here I drank well° gud beer.   very

4. [Refrain repeated after each stanza.]

163

D . . . dronken—
Dronken, dronken, idronken—
. . . dronken is Tabart atte° wine.   *with*
Hay . . . suster,° Walter, Peter,   *sister*
Ye dronke° all depe,°   *drank / deeply*
And I shulle eke!°   *also*
Stondet° alle stille—   *stand*
Stille, stille, stille—
Stondet alle stille—
Stille as any ston;
Trippe a lutel° with thy feet,   *little*
And let thy body go.

VII

And all was for an appil

164

Adam lay ibounden,
Bounden in a bond;
Foure thousand winter
Thowt° he not too long.   *thought*
And all was for an appil,
An appil that he took,
As clerkes finden wreten
In here° book.   *their*

Ne hadde the appil take° ben,   *taken*
The appil taken ben,
Ne hadde never our lady
A ben hevene quen.[1]
Blissed be the time
That appil take was!
Therfore we moun° singen   *may*
"Deo gracias!"°   *Thanks be to God!*

165

Off° Februar the fyiftene° nycht   *of / fifteenth*
Full lang befoir the dayis lycht
   I lay in till[2] a trance;
And then I saw baith° hevin and hell: *both*
Me thocht amangis° the feyndis° fell°   *among / fiends / fierce*
   Mahoun° gart° cry° ane dance   *the Devil / began / to call for*

1. Have been queen of heaven.   2. "In till": in.

Off schrewis° that wer nevir schrevin,°   *devils / shriven*
Aganis° the feist of Fasternis evin[3]   *in preparation for*
  To mak thair observance:
He bad gallandis° ga graith° a gyis,°   *gallants / make ready / an entertainment*

And kast° up gamountis° in the skyis   *cast / capers, frolics*
  That last came out of France.

"Lat se," quod he, "Now quha° begynnis?"   *who*
With that the fowll° sevin deidly synnis   *foul*
  Begowth° to leip at anis.°   *began / once*
And first of all in dance wes Pryd,°   *Pride*
With hair wyld bak and bonet on syd
  Lyk to mak waistie° wanis;°   *desolate / dwellings*
And round abowt him as a quheill°   *wheel*
Hang all in rumpillis° to the heill°   *folds / heel*
  His kethat° for the nanis.°   *garment / occasion*
Mony° prowd trumpour° with him trippit;   *many a / imposter*
Throw skaldand° fyre ay° as thay skippit   *scalding / ever*
  Thay gyrnd° with hiddous granis.°   *snarled / groans*

Heilie° harlottis on hawtane° wyis°   *haughty / proud / manner*
Come in with mony sindrie° gyis,°   *sundry / guises, attires*
  Bot yit luche° nevir Mahoun,   *laughed*
Quhill° preistis come in with bair schevin° nekkis: *while / shaven*
Than all the feyndis lewche° and maid gekkis,°   *laughed / derisive gestures*
  Blak Belly and Bawsy Brown.[4]

Than Yre° come in with sturt° and stryfe,   *Ire / violence*
His hand wes ay upoun his knyfe,
  He brandeist° lyk a beir;°   *swaggered / boar*
Bostaris,° braggaris,° and barganeris°   *boasters / braggarts / wranglers*
Eftir him passit in to pairis,
  All bodin° in feir° of weir,°   *arrayed / dress / war*
In jakkis° and stryppis° and bonettis of steill;°   *plated coats / armor / steel*
Thair leggis wer chenyeit° to the heill,   *chained*
  Frawart° wes thair affeir;°   *froward / bearing*
Sum upoun udir° with brandis° beft,°   *others / swords / beat*
Sum jaggit° uthiris° to the heft°   *stabbed / others / haft*
  With knyvis that scherp° cowd scheir.°   *sharply / cut*

Nixt° in the dance followit Envy,   *next*
Fild full of feid° and fellony,   *feud, enmity*
  Hid malyce and dispyte;
For pryvie° hatrent° that tratour trymlit;°   *secret / hatred / trembled*
Him followit mony freik° dissymlit°   *fellow / disguised*
  With fenyeit° wirdis° quhyte,°   *feigned / words / specious*

3. "Fasternis evin": Fasterns Even, the   4. Names of two fiends.
last night of Carnival before Lent.

And flattereris in to menis facis
And bakbyttaris in secreit placis
  To ley° that had delyte, — *lie*
And rownaris° of fals lesingis:° — *whisperers / lies*
Allace,° that courtis of noble kingis — *alas*
  Of thame can nevir be quyte.° — *rid*

Nixt him in dans come Cuvatyce,° — *Covetousness*
Rute of all evill and grund of vyce,
  That nevir cowd be content;
Catyvis,° wrechis, and ockeraris,° — *villains / usurers*
Hud pykis,° hurdaris,° and gadderaris°— — *misers / hoarders / gatherers*

  All with that warlo° went: — *scoundrel, devil*
Out of thair throttis thay schot on udder° — *each other*
Hett° moltin gold, me thocht a fudder,° — *hot / cartload*
  As fyreflawcht° maist fervent;° — *lightning / raging*
Ay as thay tomit° thame° of schot — *emptied / themselves*
Feyndis fild° thame new up to the thrott° — *filled / throat*
  With gold of allkin° prent.° — *every kind of / impression*

Syne° Sweirnes,° at the secound bidding, — *then / Sloth*
Come lyk a sow out of a midding,° — *midden*
  Full slepy wes his grunyie;° — *snout*
Mony sweir bumbard belly huddroun,
Mony slute daw and slepy duddroun,⁵
  Him servit ay with sounyie:° — *care*
He drew thame furth in till a chenyie,° — *chain*
And Belliall° with a brydill° renyie° — *Belial / bridle / rein*
  Evir lascht thame on the lunyie;° — *loin*
In dance thay war so slaw° of feit° — *slow / feet*
Thay gaif thame in the fyre a heit° — *heat*
  And maid thame quicker of counyie.° — *motion*

Than Lichery that lathly° cors° — *loathly / person*
Come berand° lyk a bagit hors,⁶ — *neighing*
  And Ydilnes did him leid;
Thair wes with him ane ugly sort,° — *company*
And mony stynkand° fowll tramort° — *stinking / corpse*
  That had in syn° bene deid:° — *sin / dead*
Quhen° thay wer entrit in the dance — *when*
Thay wer full strenge° of countenance, — *unnatural*
  Lyk turkas° birnand° reid; — *blacksmith's pincers / burning*
All led thay uthir° by the tersis,° — *each other / penis*
Suppois° thay fycket° with thair ersis° — *although / copulated / arses*
  It mycht be na remeid.° — *helped*

Than the fowll monstir Gluttery,
Off wame° unsasiable° and gredy, — *belly / insatiable*
  To dance he did him° dres;° — *himself / address*

5. Many a lazy, idle big-belly (glutton),/ Many a slovenly slattern and sleepy sloven.
6. "Bagit hors": stallion.

Him followit mony fowll drunckart
With can and collep,° cop° and quart,   *flagon / cup*
  In surffet° and exces;   *surfeit*
Full mony a waistles° wallydrag°   *waistless, fat / weakling*
With wamis° unweildable did furth wag   *bellies*
  In creische° that did incres.   *grease*
"Drynk," ay thay cryit° with mony a gaip;°   *cried / yawn*
The feyndis gaif thame hait° leid° to laip,°   *hot / lead / lap*
  Thair lovery° wes na les.°   *allowance / less*
Na menstrallis playit to thame but dowt,[7]
For gemen° thair wer haldin° owt   *minstrels / kept*
  Be day and eik° by nycht: *also*
Except a menstrall that slew a man,
Swa° till° his heretage° he wan° *so / to / inheritance / won*
  And entirt be breif° of richt.°   *writ / right*

Than cryd Mahoun for a heleand° padyane;° *highland / pageant*
Syne° ran a feynd to feche Makfadyane   *then*
  Far northwart in a nuke:°   *corner*
Be° he the correnoch° had done schout, *by the time that / outcry*
Erschemen° so gadderit him abowt,   *Gaels, Celts*
  In hell grit° rowme° thay tuke.° *much / room / took*
Thae tarmegantis, with tag and tatter,[8]
Full lowd in Ersche° begowth° to clatter *Erse / began*
  And rowp° lyk revin° and ruke.° *shout hoarsely / raven / rook*
The Devill sa devit° wes with thair yell, *deafened*
That in the depest pot° of hell   *pit*
He smorit° thame with smuke.   *smothered*

[*William Dunbar, ca. 1460–ca. 1520*]

166

   There blows a colde wind todaye, todaye,
     The wind blows cold todaye;
   Crist suffered his passion for mannes salvacion,
     To kepe the cold wind awaye.[1]

This winde be° reson is called tentacion;° *by / temptation*
  It raugeth° both night and daye.   *rages*
Remember, man, how thy Savior was slaine
  To kepe the colde winde awaye.

7. "But dowt": assuredly.
8. Those boisterous fellows, in tattered, ragged garments.
1. [Refrain repeated after each stanza.]

Pride and presumcion and fals extorcion,
  That meny man dothe betraye—
Man, cum to contricion and axe° confession   *ask*
  To kepe the colde wind awaye.

O Mary mild, for love of the child
  That died on Good Fridaye,
Be our salvacion from mortal damnacion,
  To kepe the cold wind awaye.

He was nailed, his blode was haled,°   *drawn*
  Oure remission for to by,°   *buy*
And for our sinnes all he dronke both eysel° and gall,   *vinegar*
  To kepe the cold wind awaye.

Slouthe, envy, covetis, and lecherie
  Blewe the cold wind, as I dare saye;
Agene° suche pusin° he suffered his passioun   *against / poison*
  To kepe the cold wind awaye.

O man, remember the Lord so tender
  Whiche died withoute denaye;°   *doubt*
His hondes so smert° laye next to his hart   *painful*
  To kepe the cold wind awaye.

Now pray we all to the King celestiall,
  That borne he was of maide,
That we maye love so with other mo,°   *more*
  To kepe the cold wind awaye.

At the daye of dome° when we schal cum   *judgment*
  Our sins not for to denaye,
Mary, praye to the Sone that sighthy° in his trone°   *sits / throne*
  To kepe the cold wind awaye.

At the last ende, man, thou schalt send
  And kepe bothe night and daye;
The moste goodlest tresior° is Crist the Savior   *treasure*
  To kepe the cold wind awaye.

Here let us ende, and Crist us defend
  All be° the night and be daye,   *by*
And bring us to his place where is mirthe and solas
  To kepe the cold wind awaye.

167

Whenneso will wit overstieth,[1]
Thenne is will and wit forlore;°   *ruined*
Whenneso will his hete° hieth,°   *ardor / hastens*
Ther nis nowiht wit icore.[2]
Ofte will to seorwe° sieth,°   *sorrow / proceeds*
Bute if° wit him wite° tofore;°   *unless / warn / before*
Ac° whenneso will to wene° wrieth,°   *but / hope / turns*
The ofo° of wisdom is totore.°   *head covering / torn apart*

168

Herkeneth, lordinges, grete and smale,
Ich° wole you telle a wonder° tale,   *I / wonderful, strange*
How holy churche was brout° in bale°   *brought /misery*
　Cum magna iniuria.°   *with great wrong*

Knightes werone° sent fro Harry king,[3]   *were*
Wickede men, without lesing;°   *lying*
There they dedone° a wonder thing,   *did*
　Frementes insania.°   *raging with madness*

The chef clerk of all this lond,
Of Caunterbury ich understonde,
He was slay° with wickede hond,   *slain*
　Demonis potencia.°   *by the Devil's power*

They soutone° the bischop all aboute,   *sought*
In his paleys withinne and withoute;
Of Jhesu Crist they haddone° no doute°   *had / fear*
　In sua superbia.°   *in their arrogance*

With her° mouthes they yendone° wide   *their / yawned, gaped*
And seide to him with gret pride:
"Traitur, thu here schal abide,
　Ferens mortis tedia."°   *enduring death's weariness*

1. Whenever will surmounts reason.　　　　3. Henry II (1154–89).
2. There reason is not at all chosen.

He answerede with milde chere:°   *demeanor*
"If ich schal die in this manere,
Lat him go that is here,
   Absque contumelia."°   *without affront*

Turmentures abouten him gon° sterte,°   *did / rush*
With wickede wondes° hey° in herte;   *wounds / deep*
Ther he diede, on his moder churche,
   Optans celi gaudia.°   *hoping for heaven's joys*

Clerk, maide, wedede° and wif,   *husband*
Wercheped° Thomas in all her° lif   *honored / their*
For sixtene tokenes[4] of gret strif,
   Contra regis consilia.°   *against the King's councils*

169

Man meye longe him lives wene,
Ac ofte him liyet the wreinch;[1]
Fair weder° ofte him went° to rene,   *weather / turns*
And ferliche maket his blench.[2]
Tharfore, man, thu thee bithench°—   *bethink*
All shel° falwi° the grene.   *shall / fade*
Welawey! nis° king ne° quene   *(there) is not / nor*
That ne shel drinke of dethes drench.°   *draught*
Man, er° thu falle off thy bench,   *before*
Thu sinne aquench.

Ne° may strong ne starch° ne kene°   *nor / imperious / hardy*
Aglye° dethes witherclench;°   *escape / fierce grip*
Yung and old and bright ansiene,°   *of face*
All he riveth° an° his streng.°   *destroys / in / strength*
Fox° and ferlich° is the wreinch,   *ready / sudden*
Ne may° no man thar toyenes,°   *may stand / against*
Weylawey! ne iweping ne bene,°   *prayer*
Mede, liste, ne leches dreinch.[3]
Man, let° sinne and lustes stench,   *forsake*
Well do, well thench!°   *think*

Do by Salomones rede,°   *counsel*
Man, and so thu shelt well do.

4. [The sixteen provisions of the Consti-
tutions of Clarendon (1164) advanced
royal prerogatives in opposition to the
Church and contributed to that hostility
between Henry and Beckett which re-
sulted in the latter's martyrdom (1170).]

1. Man may expect long life for himself,/ But often the sudden turn of fate
lies in wait for him.
2. And suddenly plays his trick.
3. Bribe, art, nor doctor's draught.

Do also° he thee toghte and sede°   *just as / said*
What thin° ending thee bringth to,   *your*
Ne sheltu° nevere misdo.   *shall you*
Sore thu might thee adrede,[4]
Weylawey! swich° wenth° well lede° *such / expects / to lead*
Long lif and blisse underfo,°   *to receive*
Thar° deth luteth° in his sho°   *where / lurks / shoe*
To him fordo.°   *destroy*

Man, why neltu° thee bithenchen?   *will you not*
Man, why neltu thee bisen?°   *look to*
Of felthe° thu ert isowe,°   *filth / sown*
Weirmes° mete° thu shelt ben.° *worms' / food / be*
Here navest° thu blisse days three,   *have not*
All thy lif thu drist° in wowe;   *suffer*
Welawey! deth thee shall dun° throwen   *down*
Thar thu wenest heye° stee.°   *high / to ascend*
In wo shall thy wele° enden,   *prosperity*
In wop° thy glee.   *weeping*

Werld and wele thee bipecheth,°   *deceive*
Iwis hie buth thine ifo;[5]
If thy werld mid wele thee sliket°   *flatters*
That is far° to do thee wo.   *for*
Tharfore let lust overgon,°   *pass by*
Man, and eft° it shall thee liken.° *afterwards / please*
Welawey! hu° sore him wiket°   *how / it fails*
Thar in one stunde° other° two   *time / or*
Wurch° him pine° evermo. *it causes / suffering*
Ne do, man, swo!°   *so*

170

No more ne will I wicked be;
Forsake ich° wille this worldes fee,°   *I / wealth*
This wildes wedes, this folen glee.[1]
Ich wul be mild of chere;°   *bearing*
Of knottes shall my girdil be:
Becomen ich will frere.°   *friar*

---

4. "Thee adrede": be afraid.
5. Indeed they are your foes.

1. These wild people's garments, this foolish entertainment.

Frer menur° I will me make,
And lecherie I wille asake;°
To Jhesu Crist ich will me take
And serve in holy churche:
All in my houres° for to wake,
Goddes wille to wurche.°

minorite (Franciscan)
renounce

canonical hours
work

Wurche I wille this° workes gode,
For him that bought° us in the rode;°
Fram his side ran the blode,
So dere° he gan° us bie.°
For sothe I tell° him mor than wode°
That hanteth° licherie.

these
redeemed / Cross

dearly / did / redeem
consider / mad
practices habitually

171

Yit° is God a curteis° lord,
And mekeliche° con schewe his might;
Fain he wolde bringe til° acord
Monkinde, to live in treuthe aright.
Allas! why set we that lord so light,
And all too foule with him we fare?
In world is non so wis no° wight°
That they ne have warning to be ware.

yet / courteous
meekly
to

nor / brave

We may not seye, but if° we lye,
That God wol vengaunce on us stele;°
For openly we see with eye
Thees warninges beoth wonder° and fele.°
But now this wrecched worldes wele°
Maketh us live in sunne° and care.
Of many merveiles I may of mele,°
And all is warning to be ware.

unless
inflict without warning

wonderful / many
happiness
sin
tell

Whon° the comuynes° bigan to rise,
Was non so gret lord, as I gesse,
That they in herte bigon to grise,°
And leide heore° jolite° in presse.°
Wher was thenne heore worthinesse,
Whon they made lordes droupe and dare?°

when / commons

feel terror
their / gaiety / aside

be dismayed

Of alle wise men I take witnesse,
This was a warning to be ware.

Bifore, if men hedde had a gras,°   *grace*
Lordes mighte wonder weel°   *well*
Han let the rising that ther was,[1]
But that God thoughte yit sumdel°   *to some extent*
That lordes schulde his lordschup feel,
And of heore lordschipe make hem bare.
Trust therto as trewe as steel,
This was a warning to be ware.

And also, whon this eorthe quok,°   *quaked*
Was non so proud he nas° agast,   *was not*
And all his jolite forsok,
And thought on God, whil that it last;°   *lasted*
And alsone° as it was overpast,   *as soon*
Men wox° as evel as they dude° are.°   *became / did / before*
Uche mon in his herte may cast:°   *reflect*
This was a warning to be ware.

Forsothe, this was a lord to drede,
So° sodeynly mad mon agast;   *(who) so*
Of gold and selver they tok non hede,
But out of her° houses full sone they past.   *their*
Chaumbres, chimeneys all tobarst,°   *burst asunder*
Chirches and castels foule° gon° fare,   *foully / did*
Pinacles, steples to grounde it cast;
And all was warning to be ware.

The meving° of this eorthe, iwis,°   *quaking / indeed*
That schulde by kinde° be ferm and stabele,   *nature*
A pure verrey° tokning° it is,   *true / token, symbol*
That mennes hertes ben chaungable,
And that to falsed° they ben most abul;°   *falseness / able*
For with good feith wol we not fare.
Leef° it well withouten fabel,   *believe*
This was a warning to be ware.

The rising of the comuynes in londe,
The pestilens, and the eorthe-quake—
Theose threo thinges, I understonde,
Betokenes the grete vengaunce and wrake°   *devastation*
That schulde falle for sinnes sake,
As this° clerkes conne declare.   *these*
Now may we chese° to leve or take,   *choose*
For warning have we to ben ware.

Evere I drede, be my trouthe,°   *troth*
Ther may no warning stande in sted;[2]

1. To have allowed (i.e., that God allowed) the rising that there was.
2. "Stande in sted": avail.

We ben so full of sinne and slouthe,
The schame is passed the sched° of hed,   *top*
And we lyen right hevy as led,
Cumbred in the fendes snare.
I leeve° this beo ur beste red,°   *believe / counsel*
To thenke on this warning and be ware.

Sikerliche,° I dar well saye,   *undoubtedly*
In such a plyt this world is in,
Mony° for winning° wolde bitraye   *many / profit*
Fader and moder and all his kin.
Now were heigh time to begin
To amende ur mis° and well to fare;   *wrong-doing*
Ur bagge hongeth on a sliper° pin,   *slippery*
Bote° we of this warning be ware.   *unless*

Be war, for I con sey no more!
Be war for vengauns of trespas.
Be war and thenk upon this lore.°   *advice*
Be war of this sodeyn cas.°   *turn of events*
And yit be war while we have spas,°   *opportunity*
And thonke that child that Marye bare,
Of° his gret godnesse and his gras: *for*
Send us such warning to be ware.

172

The law of God be to thee thy rest,
The flesh thy sacrifice, the world exile,
God thy love and thy tresour best,
Heven thy contre° thorogh every while.   *country*
Repentaunce thou take into thy brest
For thin unkinnesse° and wikkidness vile,   *unnaturalness*
And abide at thyself withinne thy nest°   *lodging*
Lest under pite thou be trapped with gile;[1]
Except at° somwhile° as a hasty gest   *that / sometimes*
Thu stert to do good but thorogh no long mile.
Have do,° glutoun, flee to this fest!°   *done / feast*
For herein of all winning lyth° crosse and pile.[2]   *lies*

---

1. Lest you be trapped by guile in the guise of pity.
2. "Crosse and pile": reverse and ob- verse of a coin (i.e., the beginning and the end).

173

Of a mon Matheu° thoghte,   *St. Matthew*
Tho he the winyord wroghte,[1]
  And wrot° it on° his bok.   *i.e., Matthew / in*
In marewe° men he soghte,   *morning*
At under° mo° he broghte, *third hour (9 a.m.) / others*
  And nom,° and non forsok.   *took*
At midday and at non°   *ninth hour (3 p.m.)*
He sende° hem° thider fol son° *sent / them / quickly*
  To helpen hem with hok;°   *hook*
Here° foreward° wes to fon° *their / promise / receive*
So the furmest hevede idon,[2]
  Ase the erst° undertok.°   *first / received*

At evesong even negh,[3]
Idel men yet° he segh°   *still / saw*
  Lomen° habbe an° honde.   *tools / in*
To hem he saide an hegh[4]
That suithe° he wes undregh° *very much / unwilling*
  So idel for to stonde.[5]
So it wes bistad°   *arranged*
That no mon hem ne bad°   *demanded*
  Here lomes to fonde.°   *use*
Anon he was birad°   *resolved*
To werk that he hem lad;[6]
  For night nolde he nout wonde.[7]

Here hure anight he nome,[8]
He that furst and last come,
  A penny brod and bright.
This other swore, alle and some,[9]
That er° were come with lome, *early*
  That so nes° it nout° right, *was (not) / not at all*
And swore somme° unsaght° *a certain / displeased one*
That hem° wes werk bitaght° *to them / assigned*
  Longe er it were light;
For right were that me raght[1]
The mon that all day wraght° *worked*
  The more mede° anight.   *reward*

1. When he (i.e., the man) worked (planted) the vineyard.
2. As the first (men) had done.
3. At a time quite near evensong.
4. "An hegh": aloud.
5. (To see them) stand so idle.
6. That they should do the work he had assigned them.
7. He was not deterred (from employing the laborers) by the fact that night was approaching.
8. Their hire (pay) at night they took.
9. These others swore, one and all.
1. For it were right that one should give.

Thenne seith he, iwis:°	*indeed*
"Why, nath° nout uch mon his?	*has (not)*
Holdeth° now or° pees.	*hold / your*
Away, thou art unwis!°	*foolish*
Tak all that thine is,	
And fare° ase foreward° wees.°	*act / agreement / was*
If I may betere beode°	*offer*
To my latere° leode,°	*more recent / men*
To leve° nam I nout lees;°	*be considered / untrue*
To alle that ever hider eode°	*went*
To do today my neode,°	*need, necessary business*
Ichulle° be wrathelees."°	*I will / without anger*
This world me wurcheth° wo;	*causes*
Rooles° ase the ro,°	*restless / roe*
I sike for unsete,[2]	
And mourne ase men doth mo°	*more*
For doute° of foule fo,	*fear*
How I my sunne° may bete.°	*sin / atone for*
This mon that Matheu gef°	*gave*
A penny that wes so bref,°	*little*
This frely folk unfete,[3]	
Yet he yirnden° more,	*desired*
And saide he come° well yore,°	*came / long before*
And gonne° his love forlete.°	*did / lose*

[*Harley* 2253]

174

Middelerd° for mon wes° mad;°	*earth / was / made*
Unmighty° aren his meste° mede.°	*weak / greatest / rewards*
This hedy hath on honde ihad[1]	
That hevene hem° is hest° to hede.	*to them / most important*
Ich herde a blisse budel us bad[2]	
The drery° domesday to drede,	*terrible*
Of sunful saughting sone be sad	
That derne doth this derne dede.[3]	

2. I sigh because of evil.
3. This (ironically) excellent person, not well-disposed.
1. This Blessed One has brought it about.

2. I heard that a herald of joy commanded us.
3. (Commanded us) soon to be sated with sin/ (Us) who secretly do these secret deeds.

Thagh° he° ben derne done,   *though / they*
These wrakeful° werkes under wede°   *wicked / clothes*
In soule soteleth° sone.°   *are revealed / quickly*

Sone is sotel, as ich ou° say,   *to you*
This sake,° althagh it seme swete.   *sin, guilt*
That I telle° a poure play°   *esteem / pleasure*
That furst is feir and sethe° unsete.°   *later / evil*
This wilde wille° went° away   *lust / passes*
With mone and mourning muchel° unmete.°   *very / excessive*
That° liveth on liking out of lay[4]   *he who*
His hap° he deth° full harde on hete°   *destiny / does / lament*
Ageyns he howeth henne;[5]
Alle his thrivene° thewes° threte° *virtuous / good qualities / rebuke (him)*
That thenketh nout on thenne.°   *that time*

Ageynes thenne us threteth three[6]
If he beth thriven and thowen in theode,[7]
Ur soule bone° so° brotherly be   *slayers / as*
As berne° best that bale° forbeode.°   *men / harm / prevent*
That° wole withstonden streinthe of theo,°   *he who / them*
His rest is reved with the reode.[8]
Fight of other ne darf he flee[9]
That fleishes° fauning° furst foreode,°   *flesh's / caressing / withstood*
That falsest is of five.°   *i.e., the five senses*
If we leveth° eny leode,°   *believe / man*
Werring is worst of wive.[1]

Wives wille were ded wo,[2]
If he° is wicked° for to welde;°   *she / hard / control*
That burst° shall bete° for hem° bo:°   *injury / atone / them / both*
He shall him burewen thah he hire belde.[3]
By body and soule I sugge° also   *say*
That some beoth° founden under felde°   *are / ground*
That hath to° fere° his meste° fo.   *for / mate / greatest*
Of gomenes° he may gon all gelde°   *pleasures / destitute*
And sore ben fered° on folde,°   *frightened / earth*
Lest he to harmes helde°   *sink*
And happes hente unholde.[4]

Hom° unholdest° her° is on°   *home / most disastrous / here / one*
Withouten° helle, as ich it holde,   *outside*
So fele° bueth° founden monnes fon°   *many / are / enemies*
The furst of hem biforen I tolde;

4. "Liking out of lay": unlawful pleasure.
5. By the time he thinks of going hence.
6. With regard to that time, three enemies (the World, the Flesh, and the Devil) threaten us.
7. If they be outstanding and flourishing among men.
8. He is as restless as a swaying reed.
9. He need not flee combat with other enemies.
1. Strife is the worst of wives.
2. Lust of woman is complete woe.
3. He shall save himself, though she defend herself.
4. And receive disastrous fortune.

Ther afterward this worldes won°   *riches*
With muchel unwinne° us woren° wolde.   *grief / disturb*
Sone beth this° gomenes gon   *these*
That maketh us so brag° and bolde   *lively*
And biddeth us ben blithe;
An° ende he casteth° us fol° colde   *in / removes / very*
In sunne° and serewe° sithe.°   *sin / sorrow / time*

In sunne and sorewe I am seint,°   *sunk*
That siweth° me so sully° sore;   *follows / exceedingly*
My murthe is all with mourning meind,°   *mingled*
Ne may ich mithen° it namore.   *conceal*
When we beth with this world forwleint,°   *made proud*
That we ne lustneth° lives° lore,°   *listen to / life's / advice*
The fend° in fight us fint° so feint°   *Devil / finds / feeble*
We falleth so° flour° when it is frore,°   *as / flower / withered*
For° folkes Fader° all fleme;°   *from / Father (i.e., God) / fugitives*
Wo him° was iwarpe° yore°   *to him / destined / for long*
That Crist nul° nowiht° queme.°   *will not / (not) at all / please*

To queme Crist we weren icore°   *chosen*
And kend° his craftes for to knowe.   *taught*
Leve° we nout, we buen forlore,°   *believe / ruined*
In lustes° thagh we leyen° lowe;   *pleasures / lie*
We shule arise ur Fader before
Thagh fon us fallen° umbe throwe;[5]   *overthrow*
To borewen° us alle he wes ibore.°   *save / born*
This bonning when him bemes blowe,[6]
He bit° us buen° of hise°   *commands / to be / his*
And on his right hond hente° rowe,°   *take / position*
With rightwise° men to arise.   *righteous*

[*Harley* 2253]

175

Mercy abid° and loke° all day,   *abides / looks*
Whan man fro senne° will wende awey.   *sin*
If senne ne were, mercy ne were non;
If mercy be cald,° he comet° anon.   *called / comes*

5. "Umbe throwe": at times.
6. When trumpets blow this summons for him.

Mercy is redy there° senne is mest,°   *where / most, greatest*
And mercy is lattest° there senne is lest.°   *latest / least*
Lord, gef° me grace my senne to see,   *give*
That night and day I mow° hem° flee   *may / them*
And comen to that iche blisse to,[1]
That evere shall lesten° withouten wo.   *last*

[*From the Commonplace Book of John Grimestone*, 1372]

176

By west, under a wilde wode-side,[2]
In a launde ther° I was lente,°   *where / arrived*
Wlanke° deor° on grounde gunne° glide;   *fine, proud / animals / did*
And lyouns raumping° upon bente,°   *rearing up / field*
Beores, wolves with mouthes wide,
The smale beestes they all torente.°   *tore to pieces*
Ther haukes unto heore° pray they hide,°   *their / hastened*
Of whuche to one I tok good tente°—   *heed*
A merlion° a brid had hente°   *merlin (falcon) / seized*
And in hire° foot heo° gan it bringe;   *her / she*
It couthe° not speke, but this it mente: *could*
How Mercy passeth alle thinge.

Mercy was in that briddes muynde,°   *mind*
But therof knew the havek° non,   *hawk*
For in hir foot heo gan it binde,
And heold it stille as eny ston;
Heo dude° after the cours of kinde,°   *did / nature*
And fley° into a treo° anon.   *flew / tree*
Thoru° kinde the brid gan Mercy finde,   *through*
For on the morwe heo let it gon.
Full stille I stod, myself alon,
To herken how that brid gan singe:
Awey wol wende bothe murthe° and moon,°   *joy / lamentation*
And Mercy passeth alle thinge.

How Mercy passeth strengthe and right,
Mony a wise seo we may;[3]

1. And come to that very bliss.   3. We may see in many a way.
2. In the west, beside a wild wood.

God ordeined Mercy most of might,
To beo above his werkes ay.
Whon° deore° Jhesu schal be dight°   *when / dear / prepared*
To demen° us at doomes-day,   *judge*
Ur sunne° wol beo so muche in sight   *sin*
We schul not wite° what we schul say.   *know*
Full fersliche° Right wol us affray,°   *fiercely / attack*
And blame us for ur misliving;
Then dar non prese° for us to pray,   *undertake*
But Mercy that passeth alle thing.

Right wolde fleme° us for ur sinne,   *banish*
Might wolde don execucion;
And rightwise° God then wol beginne   *righteous*
For to reherce us this resoun:°   *utterance*
"I made thee, Mon, if that thou minne,°   *remember*
Of feture lich° min owne fasoun,°   *like / nature*
And after crepte into thy kinne,°   *race, kind*
And for thee suffred passioun;
Of thornes kene then was the croun,
Full scharpe upon min hed standing;
Min herte-blood ran from me doun,
And I forgaf thee alle thing.

Min herte-blood for thee gan blede
To buye° thee from the fendes blake,   *redeem*
And I forgaf thee thy misdede—
What hast thou suffred for my sake?
Me hungred,[4] thou woldest not me fede;
Ne never my thurst ne woldestou° slake;   *would you*
Whon I of herborwe° hedde gret nede,   *shelter*
Thou woldest not to thin hous me take.
Thou seye° me among todes° blake,   *saw / toads*
Full longe in harde prison lyng.°   *lying*
Let seo what onswere° constou° make: *answer / can you*
Wher weore thou kinde in eny thing?

And how I quenched all thy care,
Lift up thin eye and thou maist see
My woundes wide, blody, all bare,
As I was raught° on roode-tree.   *stretched*
Thou seye me for defaute forfare,°   *perish*
In seknes° and in poverte;   *sickness*
Yit° of thy good woldestou not spare,   *yet*
Ne ones° come to visite me;   *once*
All eorthly thing I gaf to thee,
Bothe beest and fisch and foul fleoyng,°   *flying*
And tolde thee how that Charite
And Mercy passeth alle thing.

4. I was hungry.

How mightou° eny mercy have   *might you*
That never desiredest non to do?
Thou seye me naked and clothes crave,
Barehed and barefot gan I go;
On me thou vochedest no thing save,[5]
But bede° me wende thy wones° fro.   *bade / dwellings*
Thou seye me ded and boune° to° grave,   *ready / for*
On bere seven dayes and mo;
For litel dette I oughte° thee tho,°   *owed / then*
Thou forbed my burying.
Thy Pater Noster seide not so,
For Mercy passeth alle thing."

Theos° are the werkes of Mercy sevene,   *these*
Of whuche Crist wol us areyne,°   *arraign, call to account*
That alle schul stoney° with that stevene°   *be stupefied / voice*
That ever to resoun mighte ateyne;
For heer but if we make us evene,[6]
Ther may no might ne giftes geyne.°   *avail*
Thenne to the king of hevene,
The Bok seith that we schul seyne:
"Wher hastou,° Lord, in prisoun leyne?   *have you*
Whonne weore thou in eorthe dwelling?
Whon seye we thee in such peyne?
Whon askedest thou us eny thing?"

"Whon ye seye outher° blind or lame   *either*
That for my love asked you ought;°   *aught*
All that ye duden° in min name,   *did*
It was to me bothe deede and thought;
But ye that hated Cristendame°   *Christianity*
And of my wrathe never ne rought,°   *cared*
Your servise schal ben endeless schame,
Hellefuir° that slakes nought.   *hell-fire*
And ye that with my blood I bought,
That loved me in youre livinge,
Ye schul have that ye have sought:
Mercy that passeth alle thinge."

This time schal tide°—it is no nay—   *befall*
And well is him that hath that grace
For to plese his God to pay,[7]
And Mercy seche° while he hath space.°   *seek / time*
For beo ur mouth crommed with clay,[8]
Wormes blake wol us enbrase—
Then is too late, Mon, in good fay,°   *faith*
To seche to amende of thy trespace.

5. On me you bestowed nothing.
6. For unless we make ourselves righteous here.
7. "To pay": to his satisfaction.
8. For if our mouth be crammed with
clay.

With mekeness thou may hevene purchase,
Other meede° thar thee⁹ non bring;   *payment*
But knowe thy God in uche° a case,   *each*
And love him best of any thing.

To God an mon weore holden° meste°   *obligated / most*
To love and his wrathe eschuwe.
Now is non so unkinde° a beeste   *unnatural*
That lasse° doth that weore him duwe;°   *less / due*
For beestes and foules, more° and leeste,° *greater / smallest*
The cours of kinde alle they suwe;°   *follow*
And whonne we breken Godes heste,°   *commandment*
Ageynes° kinde we ben untrewe.   *against*
For kinde wolde that we him knewe,
And dradde° him most in ure doing;   *feared*
It is no right that he us rewe,°   *should pity*
But Mercy passeth alle thing.

Now harlotrie° for murthe is holde,   *profligacy*
And vertues tornen into vice,
And Simonye hath chirches solde,
And Lawe is ledde by Covetise;
Ur feith is frele to flecche° and folde,°   *waver / collapse*
For treuthe is put to litel prise;°   *value*
Ure God is glotenie and golde,
Dronkeness, lecherie, and dise.°   *dice*
Lo! Heer° ur lif and ure delice,°   *here / pleasure*
Ur love, ur lust, and ure liking;
Yet if we wole repente and rise,
Mercy passeth alle thinge.

Unlustily° ur lif we lede,   *slothfully*
Monhod° and we twinne° in two;   *manliness / part*
To heven ne° helle take we non hede,   *nor*
But one day come, another go.
Who is a maister now but Meede,°   *possessions*
And Pride that wakened all ur wo?
We stunte° neither for schame ne drede   *stop*
To teren° ur God from top to to,°   *rend / toe*
Forswere° his soule, his herte also,   *swear profanely by*
And alle the menbres° that we cun° minge°– *members / can / mention*
Full harde vengeaunce wol falle on tho,°   *those*
But Mercy passeth alle thinge.

And corteis° Knighthod and Clergie,   *courteous*
That wont were vices to forsake,
Are now so rooted in ribaudie°   *ribaldry, obscenity*
That other merthes lust hem not make.¹

9. "Thar thee": you need.
1. That they do not care for other pleasures.

Awey is gentil Cortesie,
And Lustiness° his leve hath take;   *vigor*
We love so slouthe and harlotrie
We slepe as swolle° swin° in lake;   *swollen / swine*
Ther wol no worschupe° with us wake   *honor*
Til that Charite beo mad a king—
And then schal all ur sinne slake,°   *slacken*
And Mercy passeth alle thing.

I munge° no more of this to you,   *relate*
Althaugh I couthe° if that I wolde,   *could*
For ye han° herd well why and how   *have*
Bigon this tale that I have tolde.
And this men knowen well inough,
For° merlions feet ben colde,   *because*
It is heor° kinde° on bank and bough   *their / nature*
A quik° brid to haven and holde,   *living*
From foot to foot to flutte° and folde°   *flit / clasp*
To kepe hire from clomesing°—   *numbness*
As I an hawthorn gan biholde,
I saugh myself the same thing.

Whon heo hedde holden° so all night,   *held*
On morwe heo let it gon away.
Whether Gentrie° taught hire so or Righte,   *courtesy*
I con not tell you, in good fay.
But God, as thou art full of might,
Though we plese thee not to pay,
Graunt us repentaunce and respight,
And schrift and hosel or we day;[2]
As thou art God and mon° verray,°   *man / true*
Thou beo ur help at ure ending,
Bifore thy face that we may say:
"Now Mercy passeth alle thinge."

177

The firste stok,° fader of gentilesse—   *i.e., God or Christ*
What man that claymeth gentil for to be
Must folowe his trace,° and alle his wittes dresse°   *footstep / address*
Vertu to sewe,° and vyces for to flee.   *follow*
For unto vertu longeth° dignitee,   *belongs*
And noght the revers, saufly dar I deme,°   *judge*
Al° were° he mytre, croune, or diademe.   *although / wear*

2. And absolution and the Eucharist before we die.

This firste stok was ful of rightwisnesse,°   *righteousness*
Trew of his word, sobre, pitous,° and free,°   *merciful / generous*
Clene° of his gost,° and loved besinesse,   *pure / spirit*
Ayeinst the vyce of slouthe, in honestee;
And, but° his heir love vertu, as dide he,   *unless*
He is noght gentil, thogh he riche seme,
Al were he mytre, croune, or diademe.

Vyce may wel be heir to old richesse;
But ther may no man, as men may wel see,
Bequethe his heir his vertuous noblesse
(That is appropred° unto no degree   *appropriated*
But to the firste fader in magestee,
That maketh hem° his heyres that him queme),°   *them / please*
Al were he mytre, croune, or diademe.

[*Geoffrey Chaucer, ca. 1340–1400*]

178

Somtyme° the world was so stedfast and stable   *once*
That mannes word was obligacioun;
And now it is so fals and deceivable
That word and deed, as in conclusioun,[1]
Ben nothing lyk,° for turned up-so-doun°   *alike / upside-down*
Is al this world for mede° and wilfulnesse,   *reward, bribery*
That al is lost for lak of stedfastnesse.

What maketh this world to be so variable
But lust° that folk have in dissensioun?   *pleasure*
For among us now a man is holde unable,°   *lacking ability*
But if° he can, by som collusioun,   *unless*
Don his neighbour wrong or oppressioun.
What causeth this but wilful wrecchednesse,°   *baseness*
That al is lost for lak of stedfastnesse?

Trouthe is put doun, resoun is holden fable;
Vertu hath now no dominacioun;
Pitee exyled, no man is merciable;
Through covetyse is blent° discrecioun.   *blinded*
The world hath mad a permutacioun
Fro right to wrong, fro trouthe to fikelnesse,
That al is lost for lak of stedfastnesse.

1. "As in conclusioun": as things turn out.

Lenvoy to King Richard

O prince, desyre to be honourable,
Cherish thy folk and hate extorcioun!
Suffre° nothing that may be reprevable°   *permit / blameworthy*
To thyn estat don° in thy regioun.   *to be done*
Shew forth thy swerd of castigacioun,
Dred God, do law, love trouthe and worthinesse,
And wed thy folk agein to stedfastnesse.

[*Geoffrey Chaucer, ca.* 1340–1400]

179

Flee fro the prees,° and dwelle with sothfastnesse,°   *crowd / truth*
Suffyce unto° thy good, though it be smal;   *be satisfied with*
For hord hath hate, and climbing tikelnesse,°   *instability*
Prees hath envye, and wele° blent° overal;   *well-being / blinds*
Savour no more than thee bihove shal;
Reule wel thyself, that other folk canst rede;°   *counsel*
And trouthe thee shal delivere, it is no drede.°   *doubt*

Tempest° thee noght al croked to redresse,   *distress*
In trust of hir° that turneth as a bal: *i.e., Fortune*
Gret reste stant° in litel besinesse;   *stands*
Be war also to sporne° ayeyns an al;°   *kick / awl*
Stryve not, as doth the crokke° with the wal.   *crock*
Daunte° thyself, that dauntest otheres dede;   *control*
And trouthe thee shal delivere, it is no drede.

That° thee is sent, receyve in buxumnesse;°   *that which / submissiveness*
The wrastling for this world axeth a fal.
Her is non hoom, her nis° but wildernesse: *is (not)*
Forth, pilgrim, forth! Forth, beste,° out of thy stal!   *beast*
Know thy contree, look up, thank God of al;
Hold the heye wey, and lat thy gost° thee lede;   *spirit*
And trouthe thee shal delivere, it is no drede.

Envoy

Therfore, thou Vache,° leve thyn old wrecchednesse;   *Sir Philip de la Vache*

Unto the world leve° now to be thral;   *cease*

Crye him mercy, that of his hy goodnesse
Made thee of noght, and in especial
Draw unto him, and pray in general
For thee, and eek for other, hevenlich° mede;°   *heavenly / reward*
And trouthe thee shal delivere, it is no drede.

[*Geoffrey Chaucer, ca.* 1340–1400]

180

Heven, it es° a riche ture.°   *is / tower*
Wele bies him[1] that it may win!
Of mirthes° ma° than hert may think   *pleasures / more*
And tha° joys shall never blin.°   *those / cease*

Sinful man, bot° thu thee mend   *unless*
And forsak thin wikked sin,
Thu mon° singe ay "wailaway!"   *shall*
For comes° thu never mare° tharinne.   *will come / more*

1. Joy be to him.

VIII

I sing of a maiden

181

I sing of a maiden
That is makeles,[1]
King of alle kinges
To° here sone she ches.°   *for / chose*

He cam also° stille   *as*
Ther° his moder was   *where*
As dew in Aprille
That falleth on the gras.

He cam also stille
To his moderes bowr
As dew in Aprille
That falleth on the flour.

He cam also stille
Ther his moder lay
As dew in Aprille
That falleth on the spray.°   *branch, twigs*

Moder and maiden
Was never non but she:
Well may swich° a lady   *such*
Godes moder be.

1. "Makeles": matchless, possibly punning on "mateless." (See pp. 325–349, below.)

182

Salve Regina

Salve	Hail! Oure patron and lady of erthe,	
Regina	Quene of heven and empress of helle,	
Mater	Moder of all bliss thu art, the ferth,°	*fourth*
Misericordiae	Of mercy and grace the secunde welle.	
Vita	Life come of thee, as the sounde of a bell.	
Dulcedo	Swetness, thu art both moder and maide,	
Et spes nostra	Oure hope with thee that we may dwelle.	
Salve	Hail! Full of grace, as Gabriel said.	

Ad te	To thee, oure socour, our helpe, oure trust,	
Clamamus	We crye, we pray, we make oure complaint,	
Exules	Exilde to prison fro gostly° lust.°	*spiritual / pleasure*
Filii	The childer of Adam, that so was ataynte°	*tainted*
Evae	Of Eve, our moder, here are we dreynte.°	*drowned*
Ad te	To thee, that bindes the fendes° whelpe,°	*Devil's / offspring*
Suspiramus	We sighe, we grone; we wax all fainte	
Gementes	Weping for sorow; gode lady, now helpe!	

Et flentes	Weping for sin and for oure paine,	
In hac	In this derkness oure time we spende;	
Lacrimarum	Of teres the comfort is a swete raine;	
Valle	In the vaile of grace it will discende.	
Eia	Have done, gode lady, grace is thy frende;	
Ergo	Therfore send us sum of thy grace.	
Advocata	Oure advocate, make us afore° our ende	*before*
Nostra	Oure sinnes to wesche° whils we have space.°	*wash / time*

Illos tuos	Thy merciful eene° and lufly° loke	*eyes / loving*
misericordes		
oculos		
nos converte	Cast opon us for oure disporte.°	*pleasure*
Et Ihesum	And Jhesu, thy babe, that thy flesche toke,	
Benedictum	So blissed a Lord, make us supporte,	
Fructum	That fruit of life may us comfort,	
Ventris tui	Of thy wome° the fruit may suffise	*womb*
Nobis	To us, whorby° we may resorte,	*whereby*
Post hoc	After this exile, to paradise.	

Exilium	Exile is grevos° in this derk werre;°	*painful / fear*
Ostende	Schewe us thy lust,° the stronger to fight.	*desire*
Benigna	Benigne lady, and our see-sterre,°	*sea-star*
O clemens	O buxum° lanterne, gif us thy light.	*kindly*

O pia   O meke, o chaste, o blisfull sight,
O dulcis   O swete, o kinde, o gentill and free,°   noble
Maria   Mary, with Jhesu that joyful knight,
Salve   Haile and fare wele! And thinke on me!
         Amen.

183

Levedye,° ic° thonke thee—   *Lady / I*
Wid herte swithe° milde—   *very*
That gohid° that thu havest idon° me   *good / caused*
Wid thine swete childe.

Thu art good and swete and bright,
Of alle otheir icorinne;[1]
Of thee was that swete wight
That was Jesus iboren.[2]

Maide milde, bid I thee
Wid thine swete childe
That thu herdie° me   *shelter*
To habben Godes milce.°   *mercy*

Moder, loke one° me   *on*
Wid thine swete eyen;
Reste and blisse gef° thu me,   *give*
My lehedy,° then° ic deyen.   *Lady / when*

184

Thou wommon boute° fere°   *without / peer*
Thin° owne fader bere.°   *your / bore*
Gret wonder this was
That on° wommon was moder   *one*
To fader and hire brother,
So° never other nas.°   *as / was (not)*

1. Chosen above all others.
2. That sweet man, that was Jesus, was born of you.

Thou my suster and moder
And thy sone my brother—
Who shulde thenne drede?
Whoso haveth the king to° broder   *for*
And eek° the quene to moder   *also*
Well aughte° for to spede.°   *ought / prosper*

Dame, suster and moder,
Say° thy sone, my brother,   *say to*
That is domes-mon,°   *judge*
That for thee that him bere,
To me be debonere°—   *gentle*
My robe he haveth opon.[1]

Sethe° he my robe tok,   *because*
Also° ich° finde in Bok,°   *as / I / i.e., Bible*
He is to me ibounde;
And helpe he wole,° ich wot,°   *will / know*
For love the chartre wrot,
The enke° orn° of° his wounde.   *ink / flowed / from*

Ich take to witnessinge°   *witness*
The spere and the crowninge,
The nailes and the rode,°   *Cross*
That he that is so cunde°   *benevolent*
This ever haveth in munde,°   *mind*
That boughte us with his blode.

When thou geve° him my wede,°   *gave / garment*
Dame, help at the nede[2]—
Ich wot thou might fol° well,   *full*
That for no wreched gult°   *guilt*
Ich be to helle ipult°—   *thrust*
To thee ich make apel.°   *appeal*

Now, Dame, ich thee biseche,
At thilke° day of wreche°   *that / vengeance*
Be by thy sones trone,
When sunne° shall ben° sought   *sin / be*
In werk, in word, in thought,
And spek for me, thou one.°   *alone*

When ich mot° nede° apere   *must / needs*
For mine gultes here
Tofore° the domes-mon,   *before*
Suster, be ther my fere°   *companion*
And make him debonere
That my robe haveth opon.

1. My robe he has on (i.e., he wears my clothes).   2. Lady, help in time of need.

For habbe° ich thee and him   *have*
That markes berth° with him,   *bears*
That charite him tok—
The woundes all blody,
The toknes of mercy,
Ase° techeth Holy Bok—   *as*
Tharf me nothing drede;[3]
Sathan shall nout° spede   *not*
With wrenches° ne with crok.°   *tricks / guile*

[Friar William Herebert, d. 1333]

185

Heyl, Levedy,° see-sterre bright,   *Lady*
Godes moder, edy° wight,°   *blessed / person*
Maiden ever furst and late,
Of heveneriche sely gate,[1]
Thilk° *Ave* that thou fonge° in spel° *that / received / speech*
Of° the aungeles mouth cald Gabriel: *from*

In grith° us sette and shild from shome,° *security / shame*
That turnst abakward Eves nome;[2]
Gulty monnes bond unbind;
Bring light til° hem° that beoth blind.   *to / them*
Put from us oure sunne°   *sin*
And ern° us alle wunne.°   *procure for / bliss*

Show that thou are moder one,°   *alone*
And he for thee take oure bone[3]
That for us thy child bicom,°   *became*
And of thee oure kunde° nom.°   *nature / took*
Maide one° thou were mid childe   *only*
Among alle so milde.

Of sinne us quite° on haste   *deliver*
And make us meke and chaste.
Lif thou gif° us clene;°   *give (imperative) / pure*
Wey siker us yarke and lene[4]

3. I need fear nothing.
1. Blessed gate of the kingdom of
heaven.
2. You who reverse Eve's name (i.e.,
"Eva" becomes "Ave").

3. And may he (Christ), for your sake,
receive our prayer.
4. Prepare for us and lend us a sure
way.

That we Jesus isee°   *may see*
And ever blithe° be.   *happy*

To Fader, Crist and Holy Gost be thonk and heryinge;°   *praise*
To three persones and o° God, o menske° and worshipinge.
                                            one / honor

[*Friar William Herebert, d.* 1333]

186

Holy moder, that bere° Crist,   *bore*
Buyere° of monkunde,   *redeemer*
Thou art gat° of hevene blisse   *way*
That prest wey givst and bunde.[1]
Thou sterre of see, rer° op the folk   *raise*
That rising haveth in munde.[2]
In thee thou bere thin holy fader,
That maiden were, after and rather,°   *before*
Wharof° so wondreth kunde.°   *at which / nature*
Of° Gabrieles mouthe   *from*
Thou fonge° thilke° Ave;   *received / that*
Lesne° us of sunne° nouthe,°   *release / sin / now*
So° we bisecheth thee.   *as*

[*Friar William Herebert, d.* 1333]

187

Be glad, of all maidens floure,
That hast in hevene swich° honoure   *such*
  To passe° in hye blisse   *surpass*
Aungeles and other seints also;
The joye is nought like ther-to
  Of eny that ther isse.°   *is*

1. Who gives (us) the way promptly and   2. That have rising in mind (i.e., that
handily.   are bent on rising).

Be gladde, Goddes spouse bright,
That gevest ther gretter light
   To the hevenly place
Than ever dede° sunne on erthe here   *did*
When it was brightest and most clere
   In the midday space.°   *time*

Be glad, of vertues vessel clene,[1]
To whom obeith as right quene
   The court of heven on highe,
And worschipeth withoute stinting°   *ceasing*
Thorwe° thankinges and be° blessing   *through / by*
   And endeles melodie.

Be glad, moder of Jhesu dere,
That spedest alle way[2] thy prayere
   Bifore the Trinite.
As God will, swich is thy wille;
There may no wight° sinful spille°   *person / perish*
   On whom thou hast pite.°   *pity*

Be glad, moder of hevene° king,   *heaven's*
Swich he wol, after plesing,[3]
   To thy servaunt trewe
Graunt bothe mede° and reward   *wages*
Here and also afterward
   In joye that ever is newe.

Be glad, maiden and moder swete,
Next the sone thou hast a sete,
   Iglorified blisfully.
And this we saddely° beleve,   *firmly*
But how, openly descrive
   Ne may no thing erthely.[4]

Be glad, of oure gladnesse welle,
That art seker° ay° to dwelle   *sure / always*
   In mirthe that hath non ende,
Which schal never were° ne wast;°   *wear away / waste*
Ther-to bringe us, moder chast,
   When we hen° wende.   *hence*

Thus, thou blessed quene of hevene,
I worschipe thee with joyes sevene
   In alle that I may.
When I schal leve this soreful° lif,   *sorrowful*

---

1. Clean vessel of virtues.
2. "Alle way": always.
3. Such that he will, according to his
pleasure.
4. But how, no earthly thing may openly
describe.

Be to me redy in that strif,
  Lady, I thee pray.

Lady, for these joyes sevene
And for thy gladnesse five,
Bringe me to the blisse of hevene,
Thorwe grace of clene° life.   *pure*

188

Upon a lady my love is lente,°   *settled*
Withoutene change of any chere°—   *mien*
That is lovely and continent
And most at my desire.

This lady is in my herte pight;°   *fixed*
Her to love I have gret haste.
With all my power and my might
To her I make mine herte stedfast.

Therfor will I non other spouse
Ner° none other loves, for to take;   *nor*
But only to her I make my vowes,
And all other to forsake.

This lady is gentill and meke,
Moder she is and well° of all;   *happiness*
She is never for° to seke,   *far*
Nother° too grete ner too small.   *neither*

Redy she is night and day,
To man and wommon and childe infere,°   *together*
If that they will aught to her say,
Our prayeres mekely for to here.°   *hear*

To serve this lady we all be bounde
Both night and day in every place,
Where ever we be, in felde or towne,
Or elles in any other place.

Pray we to this lady bright,
In the worship of the Trinite,
To bringe us alle to heven light.
Amen, say we, for charite.

189

Blessed be thou, levedy,°   *Lady*
Full of heovene° blisse,   *heaven's*
Swete flur° of parays,°   *flower / paradise*
Moder of mildenesse;
Preye Jesu thy sone
That he me rede° and wisse°   *guide / teach*
So my wey for to gon
That he me never misse.°   *lose sight of*

Of thee, swete levedy,
My song I wile biginne:
Thy deore, swete sones love
Thou lere° me to winne;   *teach (imperative)*
Ofte I sike° and serewe among°—   *sigh / all the while*
May I never blinne!°   *cease*
Levedy, for thy milde mod,[1]
Thou shilde me from sinne.

Mine thoghtes, levedy,
Maketh me full wan.
To thee I crye and calle:
Thou here° me for thy man.   *hear (imperative)*
Help me, hevene quene,
For thin ever ich° am.   *I*
Wisse° me to thy deore sone;   *guide*
The weyes I ne can.°   *know*

Levedy, Seinte Marye,
For thy milde mod
Soffre never that I be
So wilde ne so wod°   *mad*
That ich here forleose°   *lose*
Thee that art so god,
That Jesu me to boghte[2]
With his swete blod.

Brighte and shene° sterre cler,   *beautiful*
Light thou me and lere°   *teach*
In this false fikel world
Myselve so to bere
That I ner° at min ending   *never*
Have the feond° to fere.°   *Devil / fear*
Jesu, mid° thy swete blod   *with*
Thou boghtest me so dere.

1. Lady, on account of your gentle spirit.   2. For whose sake Jesus redeemed me.

Levedy, Seinte Marye,
So fair and so bright,
All min help is on° thee   *fixed on*
By day and by night;
Levedy free,° thou shilde me   *noble*
So° well as thou might,   *as*
That I never forleose
Heveriche° light.   *the Kingdom of Heaven's*

Levedy, Seinte Marye,
So fair and so hende,°   *gracious*
Preye Jesu Crist, thy sone,
That he me grace sende
So to queme° him and thee   *please*
Er ich henne° wende,   *hence*
That he me bringe to the bliss
That is withouten ende.

Ofte I crye "Mercy";
Of milse° thou art welle;   *mercy*
Alle buen false that bueth mad³
Bothe of fleish and felle;°   *skin*
Levedy swete, thou us shild
From the pine° of helle: *torment*
Bring us to the joye
That no tonge it may of telle.

Jesu Crist, Godes sone,
Fader and Holy Gost,
Help us at oure nede
As thou it all well wost;°   *know*
Bring us to thin riche,°   *kingdom*
Ther° is joye most;°   *where / greatest*
Let us never it misse
For non worldes bost!°   *boast, vainglory*

[*Harley* 2253]

190

Now goth sonne under wod:° *wood (forest, or wood of the Cross)*
Me reweth,¹ Marye, thy faire rode.°   *face*
Now goth sonne under tree:
Me reweth, Marye, thy sone and thee.

3. All that are made (created) are false.   1. "Me reweth": I feel pity for.

191

Maiden moder° milde,°   *mother / gentle*
  Oiez cel oreysoun;[1]
From shome° thou me shilde   *shame*
  E de ly mal feloun;[2]
For love of thine childe
  Me menez de tresoun.[3]
Ich° wes wod° and wilde,   *I / mad*
  Ore su en prisoun.[4]

Thou art feir and free°   *noble*
  E plein de doucour;[5]
Of thee sprong the ble,°   *noble person*
  Ly soverein creatour;[6]
Maide, biseche I thee
  Vostre seint socour;[7]
Meke and milde be with me
  Pur la sue amour.[8]

Tho° Judas Jesum founde,   *when*
  Donque ly beysa,[9]
He wes bete and bounde
  Que nus tous fourma.[1]
Wide were his wounde
  Que le Giw ly dona;[2]
He tholede harde stounde,
  Me poi le greva.[3]

On stou° as thou stode,   *place*
  Pucele, tot pensaunt,[4]
Thou restest thee under rode,°   *Cross*
  Ton fits veites pendant;[5]
Thou seye° his sides of blode,   *saw*
  L'alme de ly partaunt;[6]
He ferede uch an fode
  En mound que fust vivaunt.[7]

His siden were sore,
  Le sang de ly cora;[8]

1. Hear this prayer.
2. And from the evil villain.
3. Lead me from wrong-doing.
4. Now I am in prison.
5. And full of gentleness.
6. The sovereign Creator.
7. Your holy aid.
8. For his love.
9. Then kissed him.
1. Who made us all.

2. Which the Jews gave him.
3. He endured times of suffering./ But little did it grieve him.
4. Virgin, quite sorrowful.
5. Saw your son hanging.
6. The soul departing from him.
7. He caused fear in every living crea-ture/ Who was living in the world.
8. The blood ran from him.

That lond wes forlore,°   *ruined*
Mes il le rechata.⁹
Uch° bern° that wes ibore°   *each / man / born*
En enfern descenda.¹
He tholede deth, therfore,
En ciel puis mounta.²

Tho Pilat herde the tidinge,
Molt fu joyous baroun;³
He lette° bifore him bringe°   *commanded / to bring*
Jesu Nazaroun.
He was icrouned kinge
Pur nostre redempcioun.⁴
Whose° wol me° singe   *whoever / i.e., this lyric*
Avera grant pardoun.⁵

[*Harley 2253*]

192

At a springe-well° under a thorn,°   *water spring / thorn-shrub*
Ther was bote of bale, a litel here aforn,⁶
Ther biside stant° a maide,   *stands*
Fulle of love ibounde.°   *bound*
Who-so° wol seche° trewe love,   *whoever / seek*
In hir it schal be founde.

193

Now skrinketh° rose and lilie-flour,   *withers*
That whilen° ber° that swete savour° *once / bore / scent*
In somer, that swete tide;°   *time*
Ne is no quene so stark° ne stour,° *powerful / strong*
Ne no levedy° so bright in bour,°   *lady / chamber*

9. But he redeemed it.
1. To hell descended.
2. To heaven then ascended.
3. He was a very happy nobleman.
4. For our redemption.
5. Will have great pardon.
6. There was relief of misery, a little while ago.

That ded° ne shall by glide.[1]   death
Whose° wol fleish lust forgon°   whoever / forego
And hevene° bliss abide,   heaven's
On Jesu be his thoght anon,°   at once
That thirled was his side.[2]

From Petresbourgh in o° morewening,   a
As I me wende° o° my pleying,°   went out / on / pleasure
On my folie° I thoghte.   folly (illicit love?)
Menen I gon my mourning[3]
To hire° that ber the hevene king,   her
Of mercy hire bisoghte.
Ledy, preye thy sone for us,
That us dere boghte,
And shild us from the lothe° hous   hateful
That to° the fend° is wroghte.°   for / Devil / made

Min herte of° dedes wes fordred,°   on account of / afraid
Of sinne that I have my fleish fed
And folewed all my time,
That° I not° whider I shall be led   so that / know not
When I lye on dethes bed,
In joye or into pine.°   torment
On o° ledy min hope is,   a certain
Moder and virgine;
We shulen° into hevene bliss   shall (proceed)
Thurgh hire medicine.

Betere is hire medicin
Then eny mede° or eny win;   mead
Hire erbes smulleth swete.
From Catenas° into Divelin°   Caithness / Dublin
Nis ther no leche° so fin   physician
Oure serewes to bete.°   cure
Mon that feleth eny sor°   grief
And° his folie wol lete,°   if / leave
Withoute gold other° eny tresor   or
He may be sound° and sete.°   healed / content

Of penaunce is his plastre all,°   wholly
And ever serven hire I shall
Now and all my live;°   life
Now is free that er° wes thrall,°   formerly / slave
All thourgh that levedy gent° and small:°   noble / slender
Heried° be hir joyes five!   praised
Wherso eny sek° is,   sick
Thider hie blive;[4]
Thurgh hire beoth° ibroght to bliss   are
Bo° maiden and wive.   both

1. "By glide": overtake.   3. I did express my grief.
2. Whose side was pierced.   4. Thither let him hasten quickly.

For he that dude his body on tree,[5]
Of oure sunnes° have piete,°   *sins / pity*
That weldes heovene boures.[6]
Wimmon, with thy jolifte,°   *gaiety*
Thou thench° on Godes shoures;°   *think / pains*
Thagh thou be whit and bright on blee,°   *face*
Falewen° shule thy floures.   *wither*
Jesu, have mercy of me,
That all this world honoures.

[*Harley* 2253]

194

As I me rod this ender day[1]
By grene wode to seche° play,°   *seek / pleasure*
Mid° herte I thoghte all on a may,°   *with / maiden*
    Swetest of alle thinge.°   *persons*
Lithe,° and ich° you telle may   *listen / I*
    All of that swete thinge.

This maiden is swete and free° of blod,   *noble*
Bright and feir, of milde° mod;°   *gentle / mind*
Alle heo° may don° us god°   *she / do / good*
    Thurgh hire° bisechinge;°   *her / intercession*
Of hire he tok fleish and blod,
    Jesus, hevene° kinge.   *heaven's*

With all my lif I love that may;
He° is my solas night and day,   *she*
My joye and eke° my beste play,   *also*
    And eke my love-longinge;
All the betere me° is that day   *to me*
    That ich of hire singe.

Of alle thinge I love hire mest,°   *most*
My dayes bliss, my nightes rest;
Heo counseileth and helpeth best
    Bothe elde and yinge;°   *young*

5. For the sake of him who put his body   heaven.
on the Cross.   1. As I rode out a day or two ago.
6. You who rule the chambers of

Now I may—if I wole°—   *will*
   The fif° joyes minge.°   *five / mention*

The furst joye of that wimman,
When Gabriel from hevene cam
And seide God shulde bicome man
   And of hire be bore,°   *born*
And bringe up of helle° pin°   *hell's / torment*
   Monkin° that wes forlore.°   *mankind / condemned*

That other° joye of that may   *second*
Wes on Cristesmasse day,
When God wes bore on thoro lay,²
   And broghte us lightnesse;°   *brightness*
The ster wes seye° bifore day,   *seen, visible*
   This° hirdes° bereth witnesse.   *these / shepherds*

The thridde joye of that levedy,°   *lady*
That men clepeth° the Epiphany,   *call*
When the kinges come wery°   *weary*
   To presente hire sone
With myrre, gold, and encens,
   That wes mon° bicome.   *man*

The furthe joye we telle mawen°   *may*
On Estermorewe° when it gon° dawen:°   *Easter morning / did / dawn*
Hire sone, that wes slawen,°   *slain*
   Aros in fleish and bon;
More joye ne may me° haven,°   *one / have*
   Wif ne maiden non.

The fifte joye of that wimman,
When hire body to hevene cam,
The soule to the body nam,°   *went*
   As it wes woned° to bene.°   *accustomed / be*
Crist, leve° us alle with that wimman   *allow*
   That joye all for to sene.°   *see*

Preye we alle to oure levedy,
And to the sontes° that woneth° hire by,   *saints / dwell*
That heo of us haven mercy
   And that we ne misse
In this world to ben holy
   And winne hevene blisse.

[*Harley* 2253]

2. When God was born in perfect light.

195

Marye, maide milde and fre,°   *noble*
Chambre of the Trinite,
One while lest to me[1]
    Ase° ich° thee grete with songe: *as / I*
Though my fet° onclene be,   *vessel*
    My mes° thou onderfonge.°   *dish of food / receive*

Thou art quene of paradis,
Of hevene, of erthe, of all that is;
Thou bere° thane° kinge of blis   *bore / that*
    Withoute senne° and sore;°   *sin / pain*
Thou hast iright° that° was amis,   *righted, amended / what*
    Iwonne° that was ilore.°   *won / lost*

Thou ert the colvere° of Noe   *dove*
That broute° the braunche of olive tree   *brought*
In tokne that pays° scholde be   *peace*
    Bitwexte God and manne.
Swete levedy,° help thou me,   *lady*
    Whanne ich schal wende hanne.°   *hence*

Thou art the bosche° of Sinai,   *bush*
Thou art the righte Sarrai,[2]
Thou hast ibrought° us out of cry°   *brought / calling distance*
    Of calenge° of the fende.°   *claim / Devil*
Thou art Cristes owene drury,°   *sweetheart*
    And of Davies° kende.°   *David's / kin*

Thou ert the slinge, thy sone the ston,
That Davy slange Golie° opon;   *Goliath*
Thou ert the yerd° all of Aaron   *rod*
    Me dreye isegh springinde.[3]
Witnesse at ham° everechon°   *them / everyone*
    That wiste° of thine childinge.°   *knew / childbearing*

Thou ert the temple Salomon,
In thee wondrede° Gedeon;   *wondered*
Thou hest igladed° Simeon   *gladdened*
    With thine swete offringe
In the temple at the auter-ston,°   *altar-stone*
    With Jhesus, hevene° kinge.   *heaven's*

1. Listen to me for a while.
2. You are the true Sarah (i.e., perhaps, the legitimate wife of Abraham, as opposed to the bondwoman Hagar).
3. Which, though dry, was seen bringing forth a shoot.

Thou ert Judith, that faire wif,
Thou hast abated all that strif;
Holofernes with his knif[4]
    His hevede° thou him binome.°   *head / took away*
Thou hest isaved here° lif   *their*
    That to thee wille come.

Thou ert Ester, that swete thinge,
And Asseuer,° the riche kinge,   *Ahasuerus*
Thee heth ichose to his weddinge
    And quene he heth afonge;°   *taken*
For Mardocheus,° thy derlinge,   *Mordecai*
    Sire Haman was ihonge.°   *hanged*

The prophete Ezechiel
In his boke it witnesseth well
Thou ert the gate so° stronge so° stel,°   *as / as / steel*
    Ac° evere ischet° fram manne;   *but / shut*
Thou erte the righte faire Rachel,
    Fairest of alle wimman.

By righte tokninge° thou ert the hel°   *symbolizing / hill*
Of whan° spellede° Daniel;   *which / spoke*
Thou ert Emaus, the riche castel,
    Thar° resteth alle werie;°   *where / weary*
In thee restede Emanuel
    Of whan° ispeketh Isaie.   *whom*

In thee is God bicome a child,
In thee is wreche° bicome mild;   *vengeance*
That unicorn that was so wild
    Aleyd is of a cheaste;[5]
Thou hast itamed and istild°   *quieted*
    With melke of thy breste.

In the Apocalyps, Sent John
Isegh an wimman with sonne bigon,[6]
Thane mone° all onder hire° ton,°   *the moon / her / toes*
    Icrouned° with twel° sterre:°   *crowned / twelve / stars*
Swil° a levedy nas° nevere non   *such / was (not)*
    With thane fend to werre.°   *make war*

As the sonne taketh hire pas°   *way*
Withoute breche° thorghout that glas,° *fracture / glass*
Thy maidenhod onwemmed° it was   *unblemished*
    For bere° of thine childe.   *bearing*
Now, swete levedy of solas,
    To us senfolle° be thou milde!   *sinful*

---

4. With Holofernes' own knife.   6. Saw a woman clothed with the sun.
5. Is subdued by a chaste woman.

Have, levedy, this litel songe
That out of senfol herte spronge;
Agens the feend thou make me stronge,
　And gif me thy wissinge;°   *guidance*
And though ich habbe ido° thee wrange,   *done*
　Thou graunte me amendinge!

[*William of Shoreham, ca.* 1325]

196

In a tabernacle° of a toure,°   *wall-niche / tower*
As I stode musing on the mone,°   *moon*
A comly quene, most° of honoure,   *greatest*
Apered in gostly° sight full sone.   *spiritual*
She made compleynt thus by hir one,°   *by herself*
For mannes soule was wrapped in wo:
"I may nat leve mankinde allone,
　Quia amore langueo.[1]

I longe for love of man my brother,
I am his vokete° to voide his vice;   *advocate*
I am his moder—I can none other[2]—
Why shuld I my dere childe dispise?
If he me wrathe° in diverse wise,   *provoke to anger*
Through flesshes freelte fall me fro,[3]
Yet must me° rewe° him till he rise,   *one / pity*
　Quia amore langueo.

I bid,° I bide° in grete longing,   *pray / wait*
I love, I loke° when man woll crave;° *look for the time / beg*
I pleyne° for pite of peyning;°   *lament / suffering*
Wolde he aske mercy, he shuld it have.
Say to me, soule, and I shall save;
Bid me, my childe, and I shall go;
Thou prayde me never but my son forgave:[4]
　Quia amore langueo.

O wreche in the worlde, I loke on thee,
I see thy trespas day by day:

1. Because I languish for love.
2. I cannot do otherwise.
3. (If) through flesh's frailty (he) fall
from me.
4. Never did you ask (pray) me, that
my Son did not forgive you.

With lechery ageyns my chastite,
With pride agene my pore aray.
My love abideth, thine is away;
My love thee calleth, thou stelest° me fro;   *steal away*
Sewe° to me, sinner, I thee pray,   *petition*
   Quia amore langueo.

Moder of mercy I was for thee made;
Who nedeth it but thou al-one?
To gete thee grace I am more glade
Than thou to aske it. Why wilt thou noon?°   *none*
When seid I nay, tell me, till° oon?°   *to / anyone*
Forsoth never yet, to frende ne foo.
When thou askest nought, than make I moone,°   *lamentation*
   Quia amore langueo.

I seke thee in wele and wrechednesse,
I seke thee in riches and poverte.
Thou, man, beholde where thy moder is!
Why lovest thou me nat sith° I love thee?   *since*
Sinful or sory° how evere thou be,   *sorrowful*
So welcome to me there ar° no mo;°   *are / more*
I am thy suster, right trust on me,
   Quia amore langueo.

My childe is outlawed° for thy sinne;   *banished*
My childe is bete for thy trespasse;
Yet prikketh mine hert that so ny° my kinne   *near*
Shuld be disseased.° O *Sone, allasse!*   *distressed*
Thou art his brother; his moder I was;
Thou soked my pappe, thou loved man so;
Thou died for him; mine hert he has,
   Quia amore langueo.

Man, leve thy sinne, than, for my sake.
Why shulde I gif thee that thou nat wolde?[5]
And yet if thou sinne, som prayere take
Or trust in me as I have tolde.
Am nat I thy moder called?
Why shuldest thou flee? I love thee, lo!
I am thy frende; thy helpe beholde,
   Quia amore langueo."

Now, Sone, she saide, *wilt thou sey nay,*
Whan man wolde mende him of his mis?°   *wrong-doing*
Thou lete me never in veine yet pray.
Than, sinfull man, see thou to this,
What day thou comest, welcome thou is,

5. Why should I give you what you do not want?

This hundreth yere if thou were me fro;[6]
I take thee full faine!° I clippe,° I kisse,   *gladly / embrace*
   Quia amore langueo.

Now wol I sit and sey nomore,
Leve° and loke with grete longing;   *leave off, cease*
When man woll calle, I wol restore;
I love to save him; he is mine ofspringe;
No wonder if mine hert on him hinge,°   *hang*
He was my neighbore; what may I do?
For him had I this worshipping,°   *honoring*
   And therefore *Amore langueo.*

Why was I crouned and made a quene?
Why was I called of mercy the welle?
Why shuld an erthly woman bene
So high in heven, above aungelle?°   *angels*
For thee, mankinde, the truthe I telle;
Thou aske my helpe, and I shall do
That° I was ordained; kepe thee fro helle,   *what*
   Quia amore langueo.

Nowe, man, have minde on me forever.
Loke on thy love thus languisshing;
Late° us never fro other dissevere;°   *let / part*
Mine helpe is thine owne; crepe under my winge.
Thy sister is a quene, thy brother a kinge,
This heritage is tayled;° sone° come therto;   *entailed / soon*
Take me for thy wife and lerne to singe,
   Quia amore langueo."

6. Even if you were away from me for a hundred years.

IX

A God and yet a man?

197

A God and yet a man?
A maide and yet a mother?
Wit wonders what wit can
Conceave: this, or the other?

A God—and can he die?
A dead man—can he live?
What wit can well replie?
What reason reason give?

God, Truth itselfe doth teach it.
Mans wit senckes° too far under,   *sinks*
By reasons power, to reach it.
Beleeve and leave to wonder!

198

As I lay upon a night
I lokede upon a stronde;°   *shore (or country)*
I beheld a maiden bright—
A child she hadde in honde.

Hire loking° was so lovely,   *aspect*
Hire semblant° was so swete,   *appearance*
Of all my sorwe, sikerly,°   *undoubtedly*
She mighte my bales° bete.°   *pains / relieve*

I wondrede of that swete wight,°   *person*
And to myself I saide:
"She hadde don mankinde unright[1]
But if° she were a maide."   *unless*

Be° hire sat a sergant,°   *by / man*
That sadly° seide his sawe;°   *seriously / speech, utterance*
He sempte° be his semblant   *seemed*
A man of the elde° lawe.   *old*

His her° was hor° on hevede,°   *hair / gray / head*
His ble° began to glide;°   *color / fade*
He herde well what I seide
And bad me faire° abide.   *pleasantly*

"Thu wondrest," he seide, "skilfuly,°   *reasonably*
On thing thu hast beholde;
And I dede° so, treuly,   *did*
Til tales weren me tolde.

How a womman shulde ben° than   *be*
Moder and maiden thore;°   *there*
And withouten wem° of man   *blemish*
The child shulde ben bore.°   *born*

Althou I unworthy be
She is Marye, my wif;
God wot° she hadde nevere child be° me—   *knows / by*
I love hire as my lif.

But or° evere wiste° I   *before / knew*
Hire wombe began to rise;
I telle the treuthe, treuly,
I ne wot nevere in what wise.

I troste to hire goodnesse,
She wolde nothing misdo;
I wot et° well, iwisse,°   *it / indeed*
For I have founden et so,

That rathere a maiden shulde
Withouten man conceive,
Than Marye misdon° wolde   *do wrong*
And so Joseph deceive.

The child that lith° so porely   *lies*
In cloutes° all bewent°   *rags / wound about*
And bounden so misesly°—   *uncomfortably*
From hevene he is isent.

1. She would have done mankind an injustice.

His fader is king of hevene
(And so seide Gabriel),
To wham° that child is evene,°   *whom / equal*
O Emanuel."

But this child that I saw than,
And as Joseph seide,
I wot the child is God and man,
And his moder, maide.

I thanked him of° his lore   *for*
With all min herte° might,   *heart's*
That this sight I saw thore
As I lay on a night.

This child, thanne, worchipe we
Bothe day and night,
That we moun° his face see   *may*
In joye that is so light.

[*From the Commonplace Book of John Grimestone, 1372*]

199

This yonder° night I sawe a sighte: *other*
A sterre as bright as ony daye;
And ever amonge[1] a maidene songe,
"By by, lully, lullaye."

This maiden hight° Mary, she was full milde,   *called*
She knelede bifore here owne dere childe.
   She lullede, she lappede,°   *wrapped*
   She rullede,° she wrapped,   *turned*
   She wepped° withoutene nay;[2]   *wept*
   She rullede him, she dressede him,
   She lissed° him, she blessed him,   *comforted*
   She sange: "Dere sone, lullay."

1. "Ever amonge": at the same time.   2. "Withoutene nay": assuredly.

She saide: "Dere sone, ly still and slepe.
What cause hast thu so sore to wepe,
  With sighing, with snobbinge;°   *sobbing*
  With crying and with scrycchinge,°   *screeching*
  All this londe-day;°   *livelong day*
  And thus wakinge with sore wepinge,
  With many salt teres droppinge?
  Ly stille, dere sone, I thee pray."

"Moder," he saide, "for man I wepe so sore
And for his love I shall be tore
  With scorging, with thretning,°   *rebuking*
  With bobbing,° with beting—   *mocking*
  For sothe, moder, I saye—
  And on a crosse full hy hanging,
  And to my herte foll sore sticking
  A spere on Good Fridaye."

This maidene aunswerde with hevy chere:°   *countenance*
"Shalt thu thus sofere,° my swete sone dere?   *suffer*
  Now I morne, now I muse,
  I all gladness refuse—
  I, ever for this day.
  My dere sone, I thee pray,
  This paine thu put away,
  And if it possibil be may."[3]

200

Herodes, thou wikked foe, wharof is thy dredinge?°   *dread*
And why art thou so sore agast° of Cristes tocominge?°
     aghast / coming
Ne reveth he nouth erthlich good that maketh us hevene kinges.[1]

The kinges wenden° here° way and foleweden the sterre, *went / their*
And sothfast° light with sterre-light soughten from so ferre, *true*
And shewden° well that he is God in gold and stor° and mirre.
     showed / incense

Crist, icleped° hevene lomb,° so com to Seint Jon *called / lamb*

3. If it may be possible.   does not take away earthly goods.
1. He that makes us kings of heaven

And of him was iwashe that sinne ne hadde non,[2]
To halewen our follouth water, that sinne havet fordon.[3]

A newe mighte° he cudde° ther° he was at a feste:

power / showed / where

He made fulle with shir° water six cannes by the leste;[4]   *clear*
Bote the water turnde into wyn thorou Cristes owne heste.°   *bidding*

Wele,° Louerd, be mid thee, that shewedest° thee° today

happiness / revealed / yourself

With the fader and the holy gost withouten ende-day.°   *end*

[*Friar William Herebert, d.* 1333]

201

Lullay, lullay, litel child, why wepest thu so sore?[1]

Lullay, lullay, litel child,
Thu that were so sterne and wild,
Now art become meke and mild,
To saven° that° was forlore.°   *save / that which / lost*

But for my senne° I wot° it is   *sin / know*
That Godes sone suffret° this;   *suffers*
Mercy, Lord! I have do° mis°—   *done / wrong*
Iwis° I wile no more.   *indeed*

Agenis° my fadres wille I ches°   *against / chose*
An appel with a reuful° res;°   *pitiful / rush*
Wherfore min heritage I les,°   *lost*
And now thu wepest therfore.

An appel I tok of a tree,
God it hadde forboden me;
Wherfore I shulde dampned be,
If thy weping ne wore.[2]

Lullay for wo, thu litel thing,
Thu litel barun, thu litel king;
Mankinde is cause of thy murning,
That thu hast loved so yore.°   *long since*

2. And by him (i.e., Saint John) was
washed (Christ), who had no sin.
3. To hallow baptismal water for us,
whom sin had destroyed.

4. "By the leste": at least.
1. [Refrain repeated after each stanza.]
2. If it were not for your weeping.

For man that thu hast ay loved so
Yet shaltu° suffren peines mo,°   *shall you / more*
In heved,° in feet, in hondes two,   *head*
And yet wepen well more.

That peine us make of senne free,
That peine us bringe, Jhesu, to thee,
That peine us helpe ay to flee
The wikkede fendes° lore.°   *fiend's / teaching*

[*From the Commonplace Book of John Grimestone*, 1372]

202

Lullay, lullay, litel child, child reste thee a throwe;°   *space of time*
Fro heye° hider° art thu sent with us to wone° lowe.
                                                          high / hither / dwell
Pore and litel art thu mad,° unkut° and unknowe,°
                                                       made / strange / unknown
Pine° and wo to suffren her° for thing° that was thin owe.°
                                                  suffering / here / creature / own
   Lullay, lullay, litel child, sorwe mauth° thu make;   *may*
   Thu art sent into this world, as tu were forsake.[1]

Lullay, lullay, litel grom,° king of alle thinge,   *boy*
Whan I thenke of thy methchef,° me listet wol litel singe;[2]
                                                                    adversity

But caren I may[3] for sorwe, if love wer in min herte,
For swiche° peines as thu shalt drien° were nevere non so smerte.
                                                             such / endure

   Lullay, lullay, litel child, well mauth thu crie,
   For than thy body is bleik and blak, sone after shall ben drie.[4]

Child, it is a weping dale that thu art comen inne;
Thy pore clutes it proven well,[5] thy bed mad in the binne;°   *manger*
Cold and hunger thu must tholen° as° thu were geten° in senne,
                                                    endure / as if / begotten

1. As if you were forsaken.
2. I (full) little wish to sing.
3. But I may be anxious.

4. For when your body is wan and pale,
soon after it will be dry (of blood?).
5. Your poor rags prove it well.

And after deyen on the tree for love of all mankenne.
  Lullay, lullay, litel child, no wonder thou° thu care;°
                                        though / are anxious
  Thu art comen amonges hem° that thy deth shulen° yare.°
                                        them / shall / prepare

Lullay, lullay, litel child, for sorwe mauth thu grete;°   *weep*
The anguis that thu suffren shalt shall don the blod to swete;[6]
Naked, bunden° shaltu° ben, and seithen° sore bete,
                              bound / shall you / afterwards
No thing free upon thy body of pine shall be lete.[7]
  Lullay, lullay, litel child, it is all for° thy fo,   *because of*
  The harde bond of love longing that thee hat° bunden so.   *has*

Lullay, lullay, litel child, litel child thin ore!°   *grace*
It is all for oure owen gilt that thu art peined sore;
But wolde we yet kinde be, and liven after thy lore,°   *teaching*
And leten senne for thy love, ne keptest thu no more.[8]
  Lullay, lullay, litel child, softe slep and faste,°   *deeply*
  In sorwe endet° every love but thin at the laste.   *ends*

[*From the Commonplace Book of John Grimestone*, 1372]

203

It wes upon a Shere Thorsday° that ure Louerd aros.   *Holy Thursday*
Full milde were the wordes he spec to Judas:
"Judas, thou most° to Jurselem, oure mete° for to bugge;°
                                        must go / food / buy
Thritty platen° of selver thou bere upon thy rugge.°   *pieces / back*
Thou comest° fer° i' the brode stret,° fer i' the brode strete;
                                        will come / far / road
Summe of thine cunesmen° ther thou meist imete."°   *kinsmen / meet*

Imette° wid his soster, the swikele° wimon:°
                              (he) met / deceitful / woman
"Judas, thou were wurthe me stende thee[1] wid ston.

6. The anguish that you will suffer will make the blood sweat.
7. Nothing will be left free of suffering upon your body.
8. And abandon sin for your love, you would suffer no more.
1. Judas, you deserve to be stoned.

Judas, thou were wurthe me stende thee wid ston,
For° the false prophete that thou bilevest upon."   *on account of*

"Be stille, leve° soster; thine herte thee tobreke!²   *dear*
Wiste° min Louerd Crist, full well he wolde be wreke."°
if knew / avenged

"Judas, go thou on the roc, heye upon the ston;
Ley thine heved° i' my barm;° slep thou thee anon."   *head / lap*

Sone so° Judas of slepe was awake,°   *as soon as / aroused*
Thritty platen of selver from him weren itake.°   *taken*
He drow° him selve by the top° that all it lavede° ablode;
tore / crown of the head / streamed
The Jewes out of Jurselem awenden° he were wode.°   *thought / mad*

Foret him° com the riche Jew that heiste° Pilatus:
forth to him / was called
"Wolte sulle° thy Louerd that heite° Jesus?"   *will you sell / is called*

"I nul sulle my Louerd for nones cunnes eiste,³
Bote° it be for the thritty platen that he me bitaiste."°
unless / entrusted

"Wolte sulle thy Lord Crist for enes° cunnes golde?"   *any*

"Nay, bote it be for the platen that he habben° wolde."°
to have / wanted

In him com ur Lord gon as his postles setten at mete:⁴
"How sitte ye, postles, and why nule ye ete?
How sitte ye, postles, and why nule ye ete?
Ic° am aboust° and isold today for oure mete."   *I / bought*

Up stod him Judas: "Lord, am I that frec?°   *man*
I nas never o' the stude ther me thee evel spec."⁵

Up him stod Peter and spec wid all his miste:°   *might*
"Thau° Pilatus him come wid ten hundred cnistes,°   *though / knights*
Thau Pilatus him come wid ten hundred cnistes,
Yet ic wolde, Louerd, for thy love fiste."°   *fight*

"Stille thou be, Peter! Well I thee iknowe;
Thou wolt fursake me thrien° ar° the cok him crowe."   *thrice / ere*

2. May your heart burst asunder!
3. I will not sell my Lord for any kind of possessions.
4. In came Our Lord as his apostles sat at table.
5. I was never in the place where they spoke evil of you.

204

At the time of matines, Lord, thu were itake,°   *taken*
And of° thine disciples sone° were forsake;° *by / soon / forsaken*
The felle° Jewes thee token° in that iche° stounde,°
          cruel / took / same / hour
And ledden thee to Caiphas, thin handes harde ibounde.
 We honuren thee, Crist, and blissen thee with vois,
 For thu boutest° this werld with thin holy croys. *redeemed*

At prime, Lord, thu were ilad° Pilat beforn,   *led*
And there wol° fals witnesse on thee was iborn;   *very*
He° smiten° thee under the ere and seiden, "Who was that?"
            they / smote
Of° hem° thy faire face foule was bespat.   *by / them*

At underne,[1] Lord, they gunnen° thee to crucifiye, *began*
And clotheden thee in pourpre° in scoren° and in envye;
         purple robe / scorn
With wol kene° thornes icorouned thu were,   *sharp*
And on thy shulder to thy peines° thin holy croys thu bere.
            sufferings

At midday, Lord, thu were nailed to the rode,°   *Cross*
Betwixen tweye° theves ihanged all on blode;   *two*
For thy pine° thu wexe° athirst and seidest, "Sicio."°
      suffering / grew / I am thirsty
Galle and eysil° they geven° thee to drinken tho.°
        vinegar / gave / then

At the heye noon,[2] Lord, thu toke thy leve,
And into thy fader° hond the holigost thu geve. *father's*
Longis° the knight a sharp spere all to thin herte pighte;°
    Longinus (or Longius) / drove home
The erthe quakede and tremlede, the sunne les° hire lighte. *lost*

Of° the rode he was idon° at the time of evesong; *from / taken*
Mildeliche° and stille he suffrede all here° wrong. *mildly / their*
Suich a deth he underfeng° that us helpen may. *experienced*
Allas! The crune° of joye under thornes lay! *crown*

At cumplin° time he was ibiriyed° and in a ston ipith,°
     compline / buried / placed

1. Third hour of the day (9 A.M.).
2. "Heye noon": ninth hour of the day (3 P.M.).

Jhesu Cristes swete body, and—so seith holy writh°—   *writ*
Enoint with an oniment°; and than was cumpliyed°
                                        ointment / accomplished
That° beforn of Jhesu Crist was ipropheciyed.   *that which*

This iche° holy orisoun° of thy passioun   *same / prayer*
I thenke° to thee, Jhesu Crist, with devocioun;   *i.e., pray*
That thu, that suffredest for me harde pininge,°   *suffering*
Be my solas and my confort at my last endinge.

[*From the Commonplace Book of John Grimestone,* 1372]

205

Somer is comen° and winter gon,   *come*
This day° biginneth to longe;°   *these days / grow long*
And this foules everichon[1]
Joye hem° wit songe.   *themselves*
So° stronge care me bint,°   *such / binds*
All wit[2] joye that is funde°   *found*
  In londe,
All for a child
That is so milde
  Of honde.°   *hand*

That child, that is so milde and wlonk°   *splendid*
And eke of grete munde,°   *power*
Bothe in boskes° and in bank   *bushes*
Isout me havet astunde.[3]
Ifunde° he hevede° me,   *found / had*
For° an appel of a tree   *on account of*
  Ibunde;°   *bound*
He brak the bond
That was so strong
  Wit wunde.°   *wounds*

That child that was so wilde and wlonk
To me alute° lowe;   *stooped, bowed*

1. And these birds, every one.   3. Has sought me for a time.
2. "All wit": along with.

Fram me to Jewes he was sold:
Ne cuthen hey him nout knowe.[4]
"Do we,"° saiden he,°   *let us / they*
"Naile we him opon a tree
  A lowe;°   *on a hill*
Ac° arst° we shullen°   *but / first / shall*
Scumi° him   *shame*
  A throwe."°   *awhile*

Jhesu is the childes name,
King of all londe;
Of the king he meden game[5]
And smiten° him wit honde   *smote*
To fonden° him; opon a tree   *test*
He geven° him wundes two and three   *gave*
  Mid honden;
Of bitter drinck
He senden° him   *sent*
  A sonde.°   *serving*

Det he nom o' rode-tree,
The lif of us alle;
Ne mighte it nout other be
Bote we sholden falle
And fallen in helle dep.
Nere nevere so swet
  Wit alle,
Ne mighte us save
Castel, tur,
  Ne halle.[6]

Maide and Moder thar° astod,°   *there / stood*
Marye full of grace,
And of here eyen heo let blod[7]
Fallen in the place.
The trace° ran° of here blod,   *track / flowed*
Changed here fles° and blod   *flesh*
  And face.
He was todrawe,°   *torn to pieces*
So dur° islawe°   *grievously / slain*
  In chace.°   *chase*

Det° he nam,° the swete man,   *death / took*
Well heye opon the rode;
He wes ure sunnes everichon[8]

4. They were not able to know him at all.
5. They made fun of the king.
6. Death he took on the Cross,/ (He who was) the life of us all;/ Nor could it have been otherwise/ Unless we were to fall/ And fall into deep hell./ Were it never so sweet/ Withal,/ (Neither) castle, tower,/ Nor hall/ Could save us.
7. And from her eyes she let blood.
8. He washed our sins, every one.

Mid his swete blode.
Mid flode° he lute° adun°   *flood / bowed / down*
And brac the gates of that prisun
      That stode,
And ches° here   *chose*
Out that° there   *those who*
      Were gode.°   *good*

He ros him ene° the thridde day,   *on*
And sette him on his trone;
He wule° come a° domes-day,   *will / on*
To dem° us everich one.   *judge*
Grone he may and wepen ay,°   *ever*
The man that deiet° withoute lay° *dies / law, faith*
      Alone.
Grante us, Crist,
With thin uprist°   *resurrection*
      To gone.°   *go*

206

Lutel° wot° it any mon   *little / knows*
How love him haveth° ibounde° *has / bound*
That for us on the rode° ron°   *Cross / bled*
And boghte° us with his wounde. *redeemed*
The love of him us haveth imaked sounde,[1]
And icast° the grimly° gost° to grounde.
          cast / terrible / spirit (Devil)
Ever and o,° night and day, he haveth us in his thoghte;
He nul nout leose that he so deore boghte.[2] *always*

He boghte us with his holy blod.
What shulde he don° us more?   *give*
He is so meoke, milde, and good,
He nagulte° nout therfore.   *did not sin*
That we han idon, I rede we reowen sore,[3]
And cryen ever to Jesu: "Crist, thin ore!"° *grace*

1. "Imaked sounde": healed.
2. He will not at all lose that which he bought so dearly. [Refrain repeated after each stanza.]
3. What we have done, I say we should regret sorely.

He segh° his fader so wonder° wroth°   *saw / extremely / angry*
With mon that wes ifalle,°   *fallen*
With herte sor° he seide his oth:°   *sad / oath*
We shulde abeyen° alle.   *pay the penalty*
His swete sone to him gon° clepe° and calle,   *did / cry*
And preyede he moste° deye for us alle.   *might*

He broght us alle from the deth
And dude° us frendes° dede.°   *did / a friend's / deed*
Swete Jesu of Nazareth,
Thou do° us hevene° mede.°   *give / heaven's / reward*
Upon the rode why nulle° we taken hede?   *will not*
His grene wounde so grimly conne blede.[4]

His deope° wounden bledeth fast;   *deep*
Of hem° we oghte° munne.°   *them / ought / to be mindful*
He hath us out of helle icast,°   *removed*
Ibroght us out of sunne.°   *sin*
For love of us his wonges° waxeth thunne;°   *cheeks / thin*
His herte blod he gef° for all monkunne.°   *gave / mankind*

[*Harley* 2253]

207

The kinges baneres beth° forth ilad;°   *are / led*
The rode tokne is now tosprad,[1]
Whar he that wrought° havet° all monkunne,°   *created / had / mankind*
Anhonged° was for oure sunne.°   *hanged / sin*

Ther he was wounded and furst iswonge,°   *scourged*
With sharpe spere to herte istonge;°   *stabbed*
To washen us of sunne clene,
Water and blod ther ronne° at ene.°   *ran / once*

Ifolfuld° is Davides sawe,°   *fulfilled / utterance*
That soth° was prophete of the olde lawe,   *truly*
That saide: "Men, ye mowen° isee   *may*
How Godes trone° is rode tree."   *throne*

Ah, tree! that art so fair ikud,°   *made known*
And with kinges pourpre° ishrud,°   *purple / clothed*

4. His fresh wounds so grievously did bleed.   1. The Cross token is now spread out.

Of wourthy stok ikore° thou were,   *chosen*
That so holy limes opbere.°   *bore up*

Blessed be thou that havest ibore
The worldes raunsoun that was forlore;[2]
Thou art imaked Cristes weye;°   *way, path*
Thorou thee he tok of helle preye.

Ah, croyz! min hope, onliche° my trust,   *alone*
Thee nouthe° ich° grete with all my lust!°   *now / I / desire*
The milde sped° in rithfolnesse;°   *prosper (imperative) / justice*
To sunfole° men shew milsfolnesse.°   *sinful / mercy*

Ah God, the heye° Trinite,   *high*
Alle gostes° herye° thee!   *spirits / praise*
Hem° that thou boughtest on rode tree   *them*
Here° wissere° evermore thou be.   *their / guide*

[*Friar William Herebert, d.* 1333]

208

Helpe, crosse, fairest of timbres three,[3]
In braunches beringe° bothe frute and flowr!   *bearing*
Helpe, bannere beste, my fon° to do° flee,   *foes / make*
Staff and strengthinge° full of socour!°   *strengthening / help*
On londe, on see, where that I be,
Fro fire brenninge° be me beforne;   *burning*
Now Cristes tree, signe of pitee,
Helpe me ever I be nought lorne.[4]

209

Stedefast crosse, inmong° alle other   *among*
Thou art a tree mikel° of prise;°   *much / worth*

2. The ransom (i.e., Christ) of a world   which Christ and the two thieves were
that was lost.   crucified.
3. "Timbres three": the three crosses on   4. Help me ever (that) I be not lost.

In braunche and flore° swilk° another   *flower / such*
I ne wot° non in wode no° rys.°   *know / nor / thicket*
Swete be the nales,°   *nails*
And swete be the tree,
And sweter be the birdin° that hanges upon thee!   *burden*

210

What is he, this lordling that cometh from the fight
With blod-rede wede° so grisliche° idight,°   *garment / terribly / arrayed*
So faire° icointised,° so semlich° in sight,   *fairly / apparelled / goodly*
So stifliche° gongeth,° so doughty a knight?   *resolutely / goes*

"Ich° it am, ich it am, that ne speke bote° right,   *I / except*
Chaunpioun to helen° monkunde° in fight."   *heal / mankind*

Why, thenne, is thy schroud° red with blod all imeind,°
                     clothing / mingled
Ase troddares in wringe with most all bispreind?[1]

"The wringe ich habbe° itrodded all mysulf on,°   *have / alone*
And of all monkunde ne was non other won.°   *hope*
Ich hem° habbe itrodded in wrethe° and in grome,°
                 them / wrath / anger
And all my wede is bispreind with here° blod isome,° *their / together*
And all my robe ifuled° to here° grete shome.° *fouled / their / shame*
The day of thilke° wreche° leveth° in my thought,
                 that / vengeance / lives
The yer° of medes° yelding° ne forget ich nought.
                year / reward's / payment
Ich loked all about° som helpinge mon;   *about for*
Ich soughte all the route,° bote help nas° ther non.
                company / was (not)
It was min owne strengthe that this bote° wroughte,   *cure*
Min owne doughtinesse that help ther me broughte."

On Godes milsfolnesse° ich wole bithenche me,[2]   *mercifulness*
And herien° him in alle thing that he yeldeth° me.   *praise / gives*

1. As treaders in the wine-press all spat-   2. "Bithenche me": reflect.
tered with must.

"Ich habbe itrodded the folk in wrethe and in grome,
Adreynt° all with shennesse,° idrawe° down with shome."
drowned / humiliation / drawn

[*Friar William Herebert, d.* 1333]

211

Abide, gud men, and hald your pays,°	*peace*
And here what God himselven says	
Hingand° on the rode:°	*hanging / Cross*
"Man and woman that by me gase,°	*go*
Luke up to me and stint° thy pase,°	*stop / pace*
For thee I sched my blode.	
Behald my body or° thou gang,°	*before / go*
And think opon my pains strang,	
And still as stane° thou stand;	*stone*
Behald thy self the soth,° and see	*truth*
How I am hinged° here on this tree	*hanged*
And nailed fute and hand.	
Behald my heved,° behald my fete,	*head*
And of thy misdedes luke thou lete;°	*abandon*
Behald my grisely° face,	*terrible*
And of thy sins ask aleggance,°	*relief*
And in my mercy have affiance,°	*trust*
And thou shall get my grace."	

212

Men rent me on rode°	*Cross*
With woundes woliche° wode,°	*woefully / savage*
All blet° my blode.	*bled*
Thenk, man, all it is ye to gode.[1]	

1. Think, man, it is all for your good.

Thenk who ye first wroghte,[2]
For what werk helle you soughte;
Thenk who ye agein boughte:°   *redeemed*
Werk warly,° faile me noughte.°   *prudently / not*

Biheld° my side,   *behold*
My woundes sprede so wide;
Restless I ride:
Lok upon me! Put fro° ye pride.   *from*

My palefrey is of tree,
With nailes nailede thurgh me.
Ne° is more sorwe to see: *nor*
Certes° non more no may be.   *certainly*

Under my gore°   *clothes*
Ben° woundes selcouthe° sore.   *are / exceedingly*
Ler,° man, my lore:°   *learn / teaching*
For my love, sinne no more!

Fall nought for° fonding;°   *because of / temptation*
That schal ye most turne to goode;
Mak stif° withstonding:°   *strong / resistance*
Thenk well who me rent on the rode!

213

Undo° thy dore, my spuse dere!   *open*
Alas, why stond I loken° out here?   *locked*
  For am I thy make!°   *mate*

Loke my lokkes and eek min heved[1]
And all my body with blod beweved°   *enveloped*
  For thy sake.

Alas! Alas! evel° have I sped;°   *evilly / prospered*
For senne° Jesu is fro me fled,   *sin*
  My trewe fere.°   *companion*

Withouten° my gate he stant° alone,   *outside / stands*
Sorfuliche° he maket his mone   *sorrowfully*
  On° his manere.   *in*

---

2. Think who first created you.   1. Look at my locks (of hair) and also my head.

Lord, for senne I sike° sore,   *sigh*
Forgef° and I ne will no more,   *forgive*

With all my might senne I forsake;
And opne min herte thee inne to take.

For thin herte is cloven° oure love to kecchen;°   *cleft / catch, obtain*
Thy love is chosen us alle to fecchen;

Min herte it therlede° if I wer kende°   *would pierce / well-disposed*
Thy swete love to haven in mende.°   *mind*

Perce min herte with thy lovinge,°   *affection*
That in thee I have my dwellinge.

[*From the Commonplace Book of John Grimestone,* 1372]

214

Thenk, man, of min harde stundes;°   *hours, times*
Thenk of mine harde wundes.[1]

Man, thu have° thine thout° one° me;   *(imperative) / thought / on*
Thenk how dere I bouthe° thee;   *redeemed*
I let me nailen to the tree—
Hardere deth ne may non be—
Thenk, man, all it was for thee.

I gaf° my fles,° I gaf my blod,   *gave / flesh*
For thee me let idon on rod,[2]
Out of my side ern° the flod;   *ran, flowed*
I tholed° it all wid milde mod°—   *endured / mind, mood*
Man, it was all for thy god.°   *good*

Mine peines weren harde and stronge—
My moder thouth° es° swithe° longe: *thought / them / very*
Thenk, man, er thu do thy sinne
What I tholede for mankinne;°   *mankind*
Min harde deth thee shall don° blinne.°   *make / cease (to sin)*

1. [Refrain repeated after each stanza.]
2. For you, I let myself be put on the Cross.

215

Senful man, bethink and see
What peine I thole° for love of thee.   *suffer*
Night and day to thee I grede,°   *cry aloud*
Hand and fotes on rode° isprede.°   *Cross / spread*
Nailed I was to the tree,
Ded and biried, man, for thee;
All this I drey° for love of man.   *endured*
But werse me dot, that he ne can[1]
To me turnen onis° his eye   *once*
Than all the peine that I drye.°   *endured*

[*From the Commonplace Book of John Grimestone,* 1372]

216

Ye that passen by the weye,
Abideth a litel stounde!°   *time*
Beholdeth, all my felawes,
If any me lik is founde.
To the tree with nailes three
Wol° fast° I hange bounde;   *very / firmly*
With a spere all thoru my side,
To min herte is mad a wounde.

[*From the Commonplace Book of John Grimestone,* 1372]

217

Water and blod for thee I swete,°   *sweat*
And as a thef° I am itake;°   *thief / seized*

1. But it is worse to me that he cannot.

I am ibounden, I am ibete,°   *beaten*
And all it is, man, for thy sake.

I suffre Jewes on me to spete,°   *spit*
And all night with hem° I wake,   *them*
To loken° whan thu woldest lete°   *see / abandon*
Thy senne° for love of thy make.°   *sin / mate*

My body is as red as ro,°   *rose*
Thornes prikken min hed fol° sore;   *full, very*
My visage waxeth wan° and blo;°   *pale / livid*
I have so bled I may no more.

Min herte is forsmite° ato,°   *smitten / in two*
All, mankinde, for love of thee:
To loken whan thu woldest go
Fro thy senne for love of me.

Thou° thu will nought loven me,   *though*
Sithen° I thee my love schewe,   *since, even though*
Nedes I mot° loven thee,   *must*
Ne be thu nevere so untrewe.[1]

The nailes, the scourges, and the spere,
The galle, and the thornes sharpe—
Alle these moun° witnesse bere   *may*
That I thee have wonnen with min harte.

[*From the Commonplace Book of John Grimestone,* 1372]

218

Wofully araide,°   *afflicted*
My blode, man,
For thee ran.
It may not be naide,°   *denied*
My body blo and wanne,[2]
Wofully araide.[3]

---

1. Though you be never so untrue.   3. [Refrain repeated after each stanza.]
2. "Blo and wanne": black and blue.

Beholde me, I pray thee, with all thine whole reson,
And be not hard-herted for this encheson:°   *reason*
That I for thy saule° sake was slaine, in good seson,   *soul's*
Begiled and betraide by Judas fals treson,
Unkindly intreted°   *treated*
With sharp corde sore freted.°   *gnawed*
The Jues me thretted,°   *rebuked*
They mowed,° they spitted and dispised me,   *grimaced*
Condemned to deth as thu maiste see.

Thus naked am I nailed, O man, for thy sake.
I love thee: thenne love me. Why slepest thu? Awake!
Remember my tender hert-rote° for thee brake,   *heart's core*
With paines my vaines constrained to crake.°   *crack*
Thus was I defased
Thus was my flesh rased°   *torn*
And I to deth chased.
Like a lambe led unto sacrefise
Slaine I was in most cruel wise.

Of sharp thorne I have worne a crowne on my hed:
So rubbed, so bobbed,° so rufulle, so red;   *beaten*
Sore pained, sore strained, and for thy love ded;
Unfained, not demed,° my blod for thee shed;   *condemned?*
My fete and handes sore
With sturde° nailes bore.   *strong*
What might I suffer more
Then I have sufferde, man, for thee?
Com when thu wilt, and welcome to me!

Dere brother, non other thing I desire
But geve me thy hert free, to rewarde mine hire.°   *service*
I am he that made the erth, water and fire.
Sathanas,° that sloven° and right lothely sire,   *Satan / knave*
Him have I overcaste,
In hell presoune° bounde faste   *prison*
Wher ay° his wo shall laste.   *always*
I have purvaide° a place full clere°   *provided / bright*
For mankinde, whom I have bought dere.

219

Love me broughte
And love me wroughte,°   *created*
Man, to be thy fere.°   *companion*

Love me fedde
And love me ledde
And love me lettet° here.   *abandoned*

Love me slou°   *slew*
And love me drou°   *drew*
And love me leyde on bere.°   *bier*
Love is my pes,°   *peace*
For love I ches,°   *chose*
Man to buyen° dere.°   *redeem / dearly*

Ne dred thee nought,[1]
I have thee sought
Bothen° day and night,   *both*
To haven thee;
Well is me,
I have thee wonnen in fight.

[*From the Commonplace Book of John Grimestone*, 1372]

220

I am Jesu, that cum to fight
Withouten sheld and spere;
Elles° were thy deth idight,°   *otherwise / appointed*
If my fighting ne were.[2]

Sithen° I am comen and have thee brought   *since*
A blisful bote° of bale,°   *remedy / pain*
Undo thin herte, tell me thy thought,
Thy sennes° grete and smale.   *sins*

[*From the Commonplace Book of John Grimestone*, 1372]

1. Do not fear.   2. If it were not for my fighting.

221

My folk, what hab*he*° I do° thee	*have / done to*
Other° in what thing tened° thee?	*or / injured*
Gin° nouthe° and onswere thou me.[1]	*begin / now*
For from Egypte ich° ladde° thee,	*I / led*
Thou me ledest to rode° tree.	*Cross*
Thorou wildernesse ich ladde thee,	
And fourty yer bihedde° thee,	*protected*
And aungeles bred ich gaf° to thee,	*gave*
And into reste ich broughte thee.	
What more shulde ich haven idon°	*done*
That thou ne havest nouth° underfon?°	*not / received*
Ich thee fedde and shrudde° thee;	*clothed*
And thou with eysel° drinkest to me,	*vinegar*
And with spere stingest me.	
Ich Egypte bet° for thee,	*beat*
And here° tem° I shlou° for thee.	*their / offspring / slew*
Ich delede° the see for thee,	*divided*
And Pharaon dreynte° for thee;	*drowned*
And thou to princes sullest° me.	*sell*
In bem° of cloude ich ladde thee;	*beam*
And to Pilate thou ledest me.	
With aungeles mete ich fedde thee;	
And thou buffetest and scourgest me.	
Of the ston ich dronk to thee;	
And thou with galle drinkst to me.	
Kinges of Canaan ich for thee bet;	
And thou betest min heved° with red.°	*head / reed*
Ich gaf thee crowne of kinedom;°	*kingdom, rule*
And thou me givst a crowne of thorn.	
Ich muchel worshipe° dede° to thee;	*honor / did*
And thou me hongest on rode tree.	

[*Friar William Herebert, d. 1333*]

1. [Refrain repeated after each stanza.]

222

My folk, now answere me
And sey what is my gilt:
What might I mor ha° don for thee   *have*
That I ne have fulfilt?

Out of Egipte I broughte thee,
Ther° thu wer in thy wo;   *where*
And wikkedliche° thu nome° me,   *wickedly / seized*
As° I hadde ben thy fo.   *as if*

Over all abouten I ledde thee
And oforn° thee I yede;°   *before / went*
And no frenchipe fond I in thee
Whan that I hadde nede.

Fourty wenter I sente thee
Angeles mete° fro hevene;   *food*
And thu heng me on rode° tree   *Cross*
And greddest° with loud stevene.°   *cried / voice*

Heilsum° water I sente thee   *healthful*
Out of the harde ston;
And eysil° and galle thu sentest me—   *vinegar*
Other gef° thu me non.   *gave*

The see° I parted osunder for thee,   *sea*
And ledde thee thoru wol° wide;   *very*
And the herte blod to sen° of me,   *see*
Thu smettest° me thoru the side.   *smote*

Alle thy fon° I slou for thee,   *foes*
And made thee cout° of name;   *famous*
And thu henge me on rode tree,
And dedest° me michil° schame.   *did / much*

A kinges yerde° I thee betok°   *scepter / granted*
Til thu wer all beforn;°   *before*
And thu heng me on rode tree
And corounedest° me with a thorn.   *crowned*

I made thin enemies and thee
For to ben knowen° osunder;° *distinguished / apart*
And on an hey hill thu henge me,
All the werld on me to wonder.

[*From the Commonplace Book of John Grimestone,* 1372]

223

Why have ye no reuthe° on my child?   *pity*
Have reuthe on me, ful of murning!
Taket doun on rode my derworthy child,[1]
Or prek° me on rode with my derling.   *impale*

More pine° ne may me° ben° don   *suffering / to me / be*
Than laten° me liven in sorwe and schame;   *to let*
As love me bindet° to my sone,   *binds*
So lat us deyen bothen isame.°   *together*

[*From the Commonplace Book of John Grimestone,* 1372]

224

A sory beverech it is, and sore it is abought.[2]
Now in this sharpe time this brewing hat° me brought.   *has*
Fader, if it mowe° ben° don as I have besought,   *may / be*
Do awey this beverich, that I ne drink it nought.

And if it mowe no betre ben, for alle mannes gilt,
That it ne muste nede that my blod be spilt,
Swete fader, I am thy sone, thy will be fulfilt!
I am her° thin owen child: I will don° as thu wilt.   *here / do*

[*From the Commonplace Book of John Grimestone,* 1372]

1. Take down from the Cross my pre-cious child.
2. A sorrowful beverage it is, and sorrowfully it is paid for.

225

Swete sone,° reu° on me,	*son / have pity*
And brest° out of thy bondes;	*burst*
For now me thinket° that I see—	*it seems to me*
Thoru° bothen thin hondes—	*through*
Nailes dreven into the tree,	
So reufuliche° thu honges.°	*pitifully / hang*
Now is betre that I flee	
And lete° alle these londes.	*leave, abandon*

Swete sone, thy faire face	
Droppet° all on blode,	*drips*
And thy body dounward	
Is bounden to the rode.°	*Cross*
How may thy modres herte	
Tholen° so swete a fode,°	*endure / child*
That blissed was of alle born	
And best of alle gode!°	*good*

Swete sone, reu on me	
And bring me out of this live,°	*life*
For me thinket that I see	
Thy deth, it neyhet° swithe;°	*draws nigh / quickly*
Thy feet ben° nailed to the tree—	*are*
Now may I no more thrive,	
For all this werld withouten thee	
Ne shall me maken blithe.°	*happy*

[*From the Commonplace Book of John Grimestone, 1372*]

226

"Stond well, moder, under rode!°	*Cross*
Bihold thy sone with glade mode;°	*mind*
Blithe,° moder, might° thou be."	*happy / must*

"Sone, how shulde I blithe° stonde?   *happily*
I see thin° fet, I see thin honde   *your*
Nailed to the harde tree."

"Moder, do wey° thy wepinge.   *cease*
I thole° deth for monkinde;   *endure*
For my gult° thole I non."°   *guilt / none*

"Sone, I fele the dedestounde,°   *hour of death*
The swert° is at min herte° grounde°   *sword / heart's / bottom*
That me bihet° Simeon."   *promised*

"Moder, mercy! Let me deye,
For° Adam out of helle beye°   *in order to / redeem*
And his kun° that is forlore."°   *kin / condemned*

"Sone, what shall me to rede?[1]
My peine° pineth° me to dede.°   *suffering / torments / death*
Lat me deye thee bifore."

"Moder, thou rewe° all of thy bern,° *have pity (imperative) / son*
Thou woshe away the blody tern;°   *tears*
It doth me worse then my ded."

"Sone, how may I teres werne?°   *restrain*
I see the blody stremes erne°   *flow*
From thin herte to my fet."

"Moder, now I may thee seye:
Betere is that ich one° deye   *alone*
Then all monkunde to helle go."

"Sone, I see thy body biswongen,°   *scourged*
Fet and honden thourghout stongen;°   *pierced*
No wonder thagh° me be wo!"   *though*

"Moder, now I shall thee telle:
If I ne deye, thou gost to helle;
I thole ded for thine sake."

"Sone, thou art so meke and minde,°   *present in my thoughts*
Ne wit° me naught, it is my kinde°   *blame / nature*
That I for thee this sorewe make."

"Moder, now thou might well leren°   *teach*
Whet sorewe haveth that children beren,[2]
Whet sorewe it is with childe gon."°   *to go*

---

1. Son, what counsel (advice) shall I take? 2. What sorrow they have who bear children.

"Sorewe, iwis,° I con° thee telle;   *indeed / can*
Bote° it be the pine° of helle,   *except / torment*
More serewe wot° I non."   *know*

"Moder, rew of moder kare,[3]
For now thou wost° of moder fare,°   *know / destiny*
Thou° thou be clene° maiden-mon."°   *though / pure / virgin*

"Sone, help at alle nede
Alle tho° that to me grede,°   *those / cry out*
Maiden, wif, and fol° wimmon."   *foolish*

"Moder, may I no lengore dwelle;
The time is come I shall to helle;
The thridde° day I rise upon."   *third*

"Sone, I will with thee founden;°   *go*
I deye, iwis, for thine wounden;
So soreweful ded nes° never non."   *was (not)*

When he ros, tho° fell° hire sorewe;   *then / abated*
Hire blisse sprong the thridde morewe.
Blithe, moder, were thou tho!

Levedy,° for that ilke° blisse,   *Lady / same, very*
Bisech thy sone of sunnes° lisse;°   *sin's / remission*
Thou be oure sheld ageyn oure fo!

Blessed be thou, full of blisse!
Let us never hevene misse,
Thourgh thy swete sones might.

Louerd, for that ilke blod
That thou sheddest on the rod,
Thou bring us into hevene light.

[*Harley* 2253]

227

Jesu, for° thy muchele° might,   *because of / great*
Thou gef° us of thy grace,   *give (imperative)*
That we mowe° day and night   *may*

3. Mother, have pity on mothers' sorrow.

Thenken o° thy face.   *about*
In min herte it doth me god°   *good*
When I thenk on Jesu° blod,   *Jesus'*
That ran doun by his side,
From his herte doun to his fot;°   *foot*
For us he spradde his herte blod—
His wondes° were so wide.   *wounds*

When I thenke on Jesu ded,°   *death*
Min herte overwerpes;°   *is cast down*
My soule is won° so° is the led°   *pale / as / lead*
For° my fole° werkes.°   *on account of / foolish / deeds*
Full wo is that ilke° mon   *same, very*
That Jesu ded ne thenkes on,
What he soffrede so sore.
For my sinnes I will wete,°   *weep*
And alle° I wile hem° forlete,°   *completely / them / abandon*
Now and evermore.

Mon that is in joye and bliss
And lith° in shame and sinne,   *lies down*
He is more then unwis°   *foolish*
That therof nul° nout blinne.°   *will (not) / cease*
All this world it geth° away;   *goes*
Me thinketh° it neyith° domesday;   *it seems to me / approaches*
Now man gos to grounde.
Jesu Crist, that tholede° ded,   *endured*
He may oure soules to hevene led°   *lead*
Withinne a lutel° stounde.°   *little / time*

Thagh° thou have all thy wille,   *though*
Thenk on Godes wondes;
For° that we ne shulde spille,°   *in order / perish*
He tholede harde stoundes.¹
All for mon he tholede ded;
If he wile leve on his red²
And leve° his folie,   *abandon*
We shule have joye and bliss,
More then we conne seien,° iwis,°   *say / indeed*
In Jesu compagnie.

Jesu, that wes milde and free,°   *noble*
Wes with spere istongen;°   *pierced*
He was nailed to the tree,
With scourges iswongen.°   *flogged*
All for mon he tholede shame,
Withouten gult, withouten blame,
Bothe day and other.°   *i.e., continually*

1. He endured times of suffering.   2. If he will believe in his teaching.

Mon, full muchel he lovede thee,
When he wolde make thee free°   *free*
And bicome thy brother.

[*Harley* 2253]

228

I sike° when I singe   *sigh*
For sorewe that I see,
When I with wepinge
Biholde upon the tree
And see Jesu the swete
His herte° blod forlete°   *heart's / lose*
For the love of me;
His woundes waxen wete;°   *wet*
They wepen stille° and mete.°   *continually / fittingly*
Marye, reweth° thee.   *it grieves*

Heye upon a doune,°   *hill*
Ther° all folk it see may,   *where*
A mile from uch toune,¹
Aboute the midday
The rode° is up arered;°   *Cross / raised*
His frendes aren afered°   *afraid*
And clingeth° so° the clay.   *become dispirited / as*
The rode stond° in stone;°   *stands / rock*
Marye stont° hire one²   *stands*
And seith, "Weylaway!"

When I thee biholde
With eyen° brighte bo°   *eyes / both*
And thy body colde—
Thy ble° waxeth blo,°   *complexion / leaden*
Thou hengest° all of blode   *drip*
So heye upon the rode,
Bitwene theves two—
Who may sike more?
Marye wepeth sore
And siht° all this wo.   *sees*

The nailles beth too stronge,
The smithes are too sleye;°   *skillful*
Thou bledest all too longe,
The tree is all too heye;

1. "Uch toune": habitation.   2. "Hire one": alone.

The stones beoth all wete.
Alas! Jesu, the swete,
For now frend hast thou non
Bote° Seint Johan mourninde°   *except / mourning*
And Marye wepinde°   *weeping*
For pine that thee is on.³

Ofte when I sike
And makie° my mon,°   *make / moan*
Welle ille thagh me like,⁴
Wonder is it non,
When I see honge° heye   *hang*
And bittre pines dreye°   *suffer*
Jesu, my lemmon:°   *beloved*
His wondes sore smerte,
The spere all to his herte
And thourgh his sides gon.

Ofte when I sike
With care I am thourghsoght;°   *pierced through*
When I wake, I wike;°   *grow weak*
Of serewe is all my thoght.
Alas! Men beth wode°   *mad*
That swereth° by the rode   *swear*
And selleth him for noght
That boghte us out of sinne.
He bring us to winne°   *joy*
That hath us dere° boght.   *at a high price*

[*Harley* 2253]

229

Mery it is in May morning
Mery ways for to gone.°¹   *walk*

And by a chapel as I came
Met I with Jhesu to chircheward gone,
Peter and Paule, Thomas and John,
And his desiples everichone.°   *each one*
    Mery it is.

3. For the suffering that is upon you.   1. [Refrain repeated after each stanza.]
4. Though I am much distressed by it.

Sente Thomas the belles gane° ring,   *did*
And Sent Collas° the Mass gane sing,   *Nicholas*
Sent John toke that swete offering,
And by a chapel as I came.
    Mery it is.

Oure Lorde offered what he wolde:
A challes° alle of riche red golde.   *chalice*
Oure Lady, the crowne of hir mowlde,°   *head*
The sone° oute of hir bosome shone.   *sun (or Son)*
    Mery it is.

Sent Jorge that is oure Lady° knighte,   *Lady's*
He tende° the taperes faire and brighte,   *kindled*
To min eye a semley sighte,
And by a chapel as I came.
    Mery it is.

230

Lully, lulley; lully, lulley;
The faucon° hath born my mak° away.[1]   *falcon / mate*

He bare° him up, he bare him down;   *bore*
He bare him into an orchard brown.

In that orchard ther was an hall,
That was hanged with purpil and pall.°   *rich fabric*

And in that hall ther was a bede;
It was hanged with gold so rede.

And in that bed ther lithe° a knight,   *lies*
His woundes bleding day and night.

By that bedes side ther kneleth a may,°   *maiden*
And she wepeth both night and day.

And by that beddes side ther stondeth a ston,
Corpus Christi° wreten° theron.   *Body of Christ / written*

1. [Refrain repeated after each stanza.]

231

I have laborede sore and suffered deth,
And now I rest and draw my breth.
But I schall come and call right sone°   *soon*
Hevene and erth and hell to dome;°   *judgment*
And thane schall know both devil and man
What I was and what I am.

X

When the turuf is thy tour

232

When the turuf° is thy tour,°	turf / tower
And thy put° is thy bour,°	pit / bower
Thy wel° and thy white throte	skin
Shulen wormes to note.[1]	
What helpet° thee thenne	will help
All the worilde° wenne?°	world's / bliss

233

If man him bithoghte	
Inderlike° and ofte	inwardly
Hu° harde is the fore°	how / going
Fro bedde to florc,	
Hu reuful° is the flitte°	sorrowful / flight
Fro flore to pitte,	
Fro pitte to pine°	torment
That nevre shall fine,°	end
I wene° non° sinne	suppose / no
Shulde his herte winnen.	

1. Worms shall have for their use.

234

Whanne mine eyhnen° misten,°	*eyes / become dim*
And mine eren° sissen,°	*ears / stop*
And my nose koldeth,°	*becomes cold*
And my tunge foldeth,°	*folds*
And my rude° slaketh,°	*complexion / shows impairment*
And mine lippes blaken,°	*become black*
And my mouth grenneth,°	*grimaces*
And my spotel° renneth,°	*spittle / runs*
And min her° riseth,°	*hair / falls out*
And min herte griseth,°	*trembles*
And mine honden bivien,°	*tremble*
And mine fet° stivien°—	*feet / become rigid*
All too late, all too late,	
Whanne the bere° is ate° gate.	*bier / at the*

Thanne I schel flutte°	*flit*
From bedde to flore,	
From flore to here,°	*hair-cloth, shroud*
From here to bere,	
From bere to putte,°	*pit*
And the putt fordut:°	*shut up*
Thanne lyd° min hous uppe° min nose.	*lies / upon*
Of all this world ne give ic° a pese.°	*I / pea*

235

Nu thu, unsely body, upon bere list:[1]	
Where bet° thine roben° of fau and of gris?[2]	*are / robes*
Suic day havet icomen, thu changedest hem thris,[3]	
That maket° the Hevin erthe that thu on list;	*made*
That rotihin shall so dot the lef that honget on the ris.[4]	
Thu ete° thine mete° imaket in couses;°	*ate / food / cauldrons*
Thu lettes the poore stonden thrute in forist and in is;[5]	

1. Now you, wretched body, lie upon (your) bier.
2. "Of fau and of gris": of ermine.
3. Such a day has been (that) you changed them thrice.
4. That shall rot as does the leaf that hangs on the branch.
5. You let the poor stand outside in frost and in ice.

Thu noldest not thee bithenchen for to ben wis:[6]
Forthy, havestu forloren the joye of parais.[7]

236

Biseth° you in this ilke° lif — *provide / same*
Of liflode° in that other lif. — *sustenance*

Sethe° mon shall henne° wende — *because / hence*
And nede° deyen at then° ende, — *necessarily / the*
  And wonien° he not° whare,° — *dwell / knows not / where*
Good is that he trusse° his pak — *tie up*
And timliche° pute his stor° in sak, — *speedily / possessions*
  That not° when henne fare.° — *knows not / to journey*

Euch° mon thenche° for to spede° — *each / let think / prosper*
That° he ne lese° the grete mede° — *so that / lose (not) / reward*
  That God us dighte yare.[1]

This lif nis° bote° sorewe alway, — *is not / but*
Unnethe° is mon gladfol° o° day — *scarcely / happy / one*
  For sorewe and tene° and care; — *affliction*
Mon with sorewe is furst ibore,° — *born*
And eft with sorewe rend° and tore° — *rent / torn*
  If he right° thenkth of his ware.° — *directly / goods*

What is lordshipe and heynesse,° — *high rank*
What helpth catel° and richesse? — *possessions*
  Gold and selver awey shall fare;
Thy gost° shall wonye° thou ne wost° nout where; — *spirit / dwell / know*
Thy body worth wounde in grete other here[2]—
  Of other thing thou worst° all bare. — *will be*

Bithench, mon, yerne on euche wise[3]
Er thou be brought to thilke° asise,° — *that / court*
  On what thou shalt truste thare.
What good thou havest, mon, here idon
Prest° ther thou shalt underfon,° — *promptly / receive*
  Elles° ever thou worst in care. — *or else*

6. You would not reflect upon yourself in order to be wise.
7. Therefore, you have lost the joy of paradise.
1. That God prepared for us long ago.

[Refrain repeated after each stanza.]
2. Your body will be wrapped in soil or in a hair-shirt.
3. Man, consider seriously in every way.

Be mon yong other° be he old,   or
Non so strong ne° well itold°   nor / regarded
  That hennes° ne mot° fare.   hence / must
Deth is hud,° mon, in thy glove,   hidden
With derne° dunt° that shall he prove   secret / blow
  And smite thou nost° whare.   know not

Tofore the deth is betere o dede
Then after tene, and more of mede,[4]
  And more quencheth care:
Be monnes wittes him bireved,[5]
His eyen° blind, his eren° deved,°   eyes / ears / deafened
  The cofres beth° all bare.   will be

Be the gost from body reved,°   taken
The bernes° sone shulle ben sheved,°   barns / emptied
  Ne shall me° nothing spare;   one
Be the body with greth° biweved,°   earth / enveloped
  The soule sone shall be leved,°   left
  Alas! of frendes bare.

                               [*Friar William Herebert, d. 1333*]

237

Kindely° is now my coming   according to nature
Into this werld with teres and cry;
Litel and povere° is min having,°   poor / property
Britel° and sone° ifalle° from hi;   frail / soon / fallen
Scharp and strong is my deying,
I ne woth whider schal I:[1]
Foul and stinkande° is my roting.°   stinking / rotting
On me, Jhesu, you have mercy!

238

Now bernes,° buirdes,° bolde and blithe,°   men / ladies / happy
To blessen you her° now am I bounde;   here

4. Before death, one deed is better/   5. When man's wits are taken from him.
Than ten after, and of more value.   1. I know not whither I shall go.

I thonke you alle a thousend sithe,°   *times*
And prey God save you hol° and sounde;   *hale*
Wherever ye go, on gras or grounde,
He you governe withouten greve.°   *grief*
For frendschipe that I here have founde,
Ageyn° my wille I take my leve.   *against*

For frendschipe and for giftes goode,
For mete and drinke so gret plente,
That Lord that raught° was on the roode—   *stretched*
He kepe thy comely cumpayne.°   *company*
On see or lond, wher that ye be,
He governe you withouten greve.
So good disport ye han° mad me,   *have*
Ageyn my wille I take my leve.

Ageyn my wille althaugh I wende,
I may not alwey dwellen here;
For every thing schal have an ende,
And frendes are not ay° ifere.°   *always / together*
Be we never so lef° and dere,°   *dear / precious*
Out of this world all schul we meve;°   *move*
And whon we buske° unto ur bere,   *go*
Ageyn ur wille we take ur leve.

And wende we schulle, I wot° never whenne,   *know*
Ne whoderward° that we schul fare;   *whitherward*
But endeles blisse or ay to brenne°   *burn*
To every mon is yarked° yare.°   *prepared / ready*
Forthy° I rede° uch mon beware,   *therefore / advise*
And lete ur werk ur wordes preve,°   *justify*
So that no sunne° ur soule forfare°   *sin / destroy*
Whon that ur lif hath taken his leve.

Whon that ur lif his leve hath laught,°   *taken*
Ur body lith° bounden by the wowe,°   *lies / wall*
Ur richesses alle from us ben raft,
In clottes° colde ur cors is throwe.°   *clods / thrown*
Wher are thy frendes who wol thee knowe?
Let see who wol thy soule releve.
I rede thee, Mon, ar° thou ly° lowe,   *ere / lie*
Be redy ay to take thy leve.

Be redy ay, whatever bifalle,
All sodeynly lest thou be kight;°   *summoned*
Thou wost° never whonne thy Lord wol calle;   *know*
Loke that thy laumpe be brenninge bright;
For leve° me well, but° thou have light,   *believe / unless*
Right foule thy Lord wol thee repreve,°   *reprove*
And fleme° thee fer out of his sight,   *banish*
For all too late thou toke thy leve.

Now God that was in Bethleem bore,
He give us grace to serve him so
That we may come his face tofore,°   *before*
Out of this world whon we schul go;
And for to amende that° we misdo,   *that which*
In cley or° that we clinge and cleve,°   *ere / are lodged*
And mak us evene° with frend and fo,   *just*
And in good time to take ur leve.

Now haveth good day, gode men alle,
Haveth good day, yonge and olde,
Haveth good day, bothe grete and smalle,
And graunt-mercy° a thousend folde!   *hearty thanks*
If evere I mighte, full fain I wolde,
Don° ought that were unto you leve;°   *do / dear*
Crist kepe you out of cares colde,
For now is time to take my leve.

239

Wrecche° mon, why artou° proud,   *wretched / are you*
That art of erth imaked?
Hider ne broutestou no schroud,[1]
Bot pore thou come° and naked.   *came*

When thy soule is faren° out,   *has journeyed*
Thy body with erthe iraked,°   *covered over*
That body that was so ronk° and loud   *haughty*
Of alle men is ihated.

240

Fare well, this world! I take my leve for evere;
I am arrested to appere at° Godes face.   *before*
O mightiful God, thu knowest that I had levere°   *rather*
Than all this world to have one houre space°   *time*

1. You brought no garment hither.

To make asithe° for all my grete trespace.   *reparation*
My hert, alas! is brokene for that sorowe;
Som be this day that shall not be tomorow.

This life, I see, is but a cheyre° feyre.°   *cherry / fair*
All thinges passene, and so most I, algate.°   *in any case*
Today I sat full ryall° in a cheyere,°   *royal / throne*
Till sotell° deth knoked at my gate,   *subtle*
And on-avised° he seid to me: "Chek-mate!"   *without warning*
Lo! How sotell he maketh a devors,°   *divorce, separation*
And, wormes to fede, he hath here leyd my cors.

Speke softe, ye folk, for I am leyd aslepe.
I have my dreme; in trust is moche treson.°   *treachery*
From dethes hold feyne° wold I make a lepe,   *gladly*
But my wisdom is turned into feble resoun.
I see this worldes joye lasteth but a season.
Wold to God, I had rememberd me beforne!
I sey no more but "Be ware of ane horne!"°
                              i.e., the call of Judgment Day

This feeble world, so fals and so unstable,
Promoteth his° lovers for a litel while,   *its*
But at the last he yeveth° hem° a bable°   *gives / them / toy*
Whene his peinted° trouth is torned into gile.   *feigned*
Experience causeth me the trouth to compile,°   *tell*
Thinking this: too late, alas! that I began,
For folly and hope disseiveth many a man.

Farewell, my frendes! the tide° abideth no man.   *time*
I moste departe hens, and so shall ye.
But in this passage the beste song that I can°   *know*
Is *Requiem Eternam*:° I pray God grant it me.   *Eternal Rest*
Whan I have ended all min adversite,
Graunte me in Paradisc to have a mansion,
That shede his blode for my redempcion.
  Beati mortui qui in domino moriuntur.
  Humiliatus sum vermis.[1]

241

I wende to dede, knight stithe in stoure![2]
Thurghe° fight in felde I wane° the flour.   *through / won*

1. Blessed are the dead who die in the   2. I depart to death, a knight stout in
Lord./ I am brought low with the   battle.
worms.

Na° fightes me taght the dede to quell: no
Wend to dede, soth° I you tell.   truth

I wende to dede, a kinge, iwisse!°   indeed
What helpes honor or werldes blisse?
Dede is to man the kinde° way: natural
I wende to be clade in clay.

I wende to dede, clerk full of skill,
That couth° with worde men mare° and dill.°   could / mar / benumb
Sone has me made the dede ane ende:[3]
Bese° ware with me! To dede I wende!   be

242

Erthe tok° of erthe erthe with woh;°   took / wrong
Erthe other erthe to the erthe droh;°   added
Erthe leide erthe in erthene throh.°   grave
Tho° hevede° erthe of erthe erthe inoh.°   then / had / enough

[*Harley* 2253]

243

This is no lif, alas, that I do lede;
It is but deth as in lifes likenesse,
Endeless sorrow assured oute of drede,°   doubt
Past all despeire and oute of all gladenesse.
Thus well I wote° I am remedylesse,   know
For me nothing may comforte nor amende
Till deth come forthe and make of me an ende.

3. Death has soon made an end of me.

244

All ye that passe be° this holy place,   *by*
Both spiritual and temporal of every degree,
Remember yourselfe well during time and space:
I was as ye are nowe; and as I, ye shall be.
Wherfor I beseche you of your benignitee,
For the love of Jhesu and his Mother Marye,
For my soule to say a *Pater Noster* and an *Ave*.

245

Alanus calvus
Iacet hic sub marmore duro;
Utrum sit salvus,
Non curavit, necque curo.[1]

Anglice:°   *in English*
Here lieth under this marbill ston,
Riche Alane, the ballid° man;   *bald*
Whether he be safe° or noght,   *saved*
I recke° never—for he ne roght!°   *care / cared*

1. [The Latin is accurately translated by the Middle English.]

Abbreviations

AH	*Analecta Hymnica*
A.V.	Authorized (King James) Version of the Bible
Add.	Additional (Manuscript)
B.M.	British Museum
Bk.	Book
Bodl.	Bodleian Library, Oxford
Brook	G. L. Brook, ed., *The Harley Lyrics*, fourth ed. (Manchester, 1968)
Brown XIII	Carleton Brown, ed., *English Lyrics of the Thirteenth Century* (Oxford, 1932)
Brown XIV	Carleton Brown and G. V. Smithers, eds., *Religious Lyrics of the Fourteenth Century*, second ed. (Oxford, 1957)
Brown XV	Carleton Brown, ed., *Religious Lyrics of the Fifteenth Century* (Oxford, 1939)
c., ca.	*circa* (about)
Camb.	Cambridge
cap., ch.	chapter
C.E.	*College English*
cent.	century
col.	column
Coll.	College
Corp. Christi	Corpus Christi (College)
d.	died
dist.	distich
E.E.T.S.	Early English Text Society (Publications)
Encyl. Brit.	*Encyclopaedia Britannica*
Eng.	English
Ex^r	Exchequer
F(f)	folio(s)
Greene	R. L. Greene, ed., *The Early English Carols* (Oxford, 1935)
Index	Carleton Brown and R. H. Robbins, eds., *The Index of Middle English Verse* (New York, 1943)
L(l)	Line(s)
Lat.	Latin
Lib.	*Liber* (Book)
Lib.	Library
Mackenzie	W. M. Mackenzie, ed., *The Poems of William Dunbar* (London, 1932; reprinted 1960)
Magd.	Magdalen (College)
M.E.	Middle English
Misc.	Miscellany

M.L.R.	*Modern Language Review*
Mod. Phil.	*Modern Philology*
MS.	Manuscript
n.	note
N. & Q.	*Notes and Queries*
Nat.	National
no(s)	number(s)
NS	New Series
O.E.D.	*Oxford English Dictionary*
Oxf.	Oxford
P.G.	*Patrologiae Graecae Cursus Completus* (Migne)
P.L.	*Patrologiae Latinae Cursus Completus* (Migne)
P.M.L.A.	*Publications of the Modern Language Association*
poet.	poetry
pt.	part
q.v.	*quid vide* (which see)
r.	recto
Rawl.	Rawlinson
Robbins	R. H. Robbins, ed., *Secular Lyrics of the Fourteenth and Fifteenth Centuries,* second ed. (Oxford, 1955)
Robinson	F. N. Robinson, ed., *The Works of Geoffrey Chaucer,* second ed. (Boston, 1957)
st.	stanza
Sum. theol.	*Summa Theologica*
Univ.	University
v.	verso, or verse
vv., vs.	verses
vol.	volume
Wood	H. H. Wood, ed., *The Poems of Robert Henryson* (Edinburgh and London, 1933; second ed., 1958)
†	died

Table of Textual Sources and Dates

Poem numbers refer to the present collection; index numbers, to Brown and Robbins' *Index of Middle English Verse*; an asterisk after poem number indicates that music has survived, but not always in the manuscript printed here.

POEM	INDEX	MANUSCRIPT	DATE OF POEM	SOURCE
1*	4223	Bodl. 14751	Second half of 13th cent.	Brown XIII
2*	4221	Corp. Christi Camb. 8	13th cent.	Brown XIII
3*	3223	B.M. Harley 978	First half of 13th cent.	Brown XIII
4	1861	B.M. Harley 2253	Early 14th cent.[1]	Brook
5*	2163	Bodl. 14755	c. 1225	Brown XIII
6*	864	Bodl. 21713	c. 1270	Brown XIII
7	196	Eton Coll. 36, Part II	Mid 14th cent.	Brown XIV
8	3408	Camb. Univ. Oo. 7.32	Early 14th cent.	Brown XIV
9	12	Camb. Univ. Ff. 1.6	Late 15th cent.	Brown XV
10	3873	Jesus Oxf. 29, Part II	13th cent.	Brown XIII
11	3787	Bodl. 3896	1399	Robinson
12	3310	Bodl. 1687	13th cent.	Brown XIII
13	4177	B.M. Harley 2253	Early 14th cent.	Brook
14	4083	Univ. Coll. Oxf. 33	15th cent.	Brown XV
15	1002	Nat. Lib. Scotland, Advocates 18.7.21	Second half of 14th cent.[2]	Brown XIV
16	360	Lincoln's Inn, Hale 135	c. 1300	Brown XIII
17	194	Bodl. 13679	14th cent.	Robbins
18	2260	Nat. Lib. Scotland, Advocates 18.7.21	Second half of 14th cent.	Brown XIV
19	2009	Bodl. 1687	13th cent.	Brown XIII
20	2622	Bodl. 13679	14th cent.	Robbins
21*	4199	Bodl. 21956	c. 1390	Robbins
22*	521	King's Camb. Muniment Roll, 2.W.32	Early 14th cent.	Robbins
23	1121	Caius Camb. 54	Late 14th cent.	Robbins
24	3465	B.M. Harley 682	Mid 15th cent.	Robbins
25	2243	B.M. Harley 682	Mid 15th cent.	Robbins
26	1394	B.M. Harley 2253	Early 14th cent.	Brook

1. Brook, p. 3, suggests that all the lyrics in Harley 2253 should be dated c. 1314–25.
2. Brown XIV, p. viii, dates this manuscript 1372.

POEM	INDEX	MANUSCRIPT	DATE OF POEM	SOURCE
27	515	B.M. Harley 2253	Early 14th cent.	Brook
28	4194	B.M. Harley 2253	Early 14th cent.	Brook
29	2207	B.M. Harley 2253	Early 14th cent.	Brook
30	1449	B.M. Harley 2253	Early 14th cent.	Brook
31	105	B.M. Harley 2253	Early 14th cent.	Brook
32	1504	B.M. Harley 2253	Early 14th cent.	Brook
33	1395	B.M. Harley 2253	Early 14th cent.	Brook
34	2236	B.M. Harley 2253	Early 14th cent.	Brook
35	4037	B.M. Harley 2253	Early 14th cent.	Brook
36	1921	B.M. Harley 2253	Early 14th cent.	Brook
37	3898	Bodl. 13679	14th cent.	Robbins
38*	2185	Caius Camb. 383	Mid 15th cent.	Robbins
39	1333	Huntington Lib., California, EL 1160	c. 1500	Robbins
40	3782	B.M. Harley 4294	Early 16th cent.	Robbins
41	1280	Caius Camb. 383	Mid 15th cent.	Robbins
42	1768	Bodl. 12653	Early 16th cent.	Robbins
43	2421	Bodl. 12653	Early 16th cent.	Robbins
44	2756	Bodl. 3896	Late 14th cent.	Robinson
45	2518	B.M. Harley 2252	Early 16th cent.	Robbins
46	1010	Kilkenny Castle, Ormond	Second half of 15th cent.	Robbins
47*	2231	Bodl. 21956	c. 1390	Robbins
48*	3722	Bodl. 6668	c. 1445	Robbins
49*	925	Bodl. 6668	c. 1445	Robbins
50*	146	Bodl. 6668	c. 1445	Robbins
51	1334	Bodl. 14530	Late 15th cent.	Robbins
52*	266	London Public Record Office: Ex^r Misc. 23/1/1	c. 1530	Robbins
53*	2381	Bodl. 6668	c. 1445	Robbins
54	1240	B.M. Harley 682	Mid 15th cent.	Robbins
55	926	Bodl. Lat. Misc. c.66	c. 1500	Robbins
56	3418	Camb. Univ. Add. 5943	15th cent.	Robbins
57*	1330	Caius Camb. 383	Mid 15th cent.	Robbins
58	2654	B.M. Sloane 1584	Early 16th cent.	Robbins
59	3222	Bodl. 1687	13th cent.	Brown XIII
60	3874	B.M. Harley 2253	Early 14th cent.	Brook
61	3078	Trinity Camb. 323	Second half of 13th cent.	Brown XIII
62	1485	Balliol Oxf. 354	Late 15th cent.	Robbins
63	3999	Balliol Oxf. 354	Late 15th cent.	Robbins
64	3919	Bodl. 29734	c. 1480	Robbins
65	1829	Bodl. 1797	Late 14th cent.	Robbins
66	1938	B.M. Sloane 2593	15th cent.	Robbins
67	*63	Bodl. 21831	15th cent.	Robbins
68	4279	B.M. Sloane 2593	15th cent.	Robbins
69	210	Bodl. 29734	c. 1480	Robbins
70*	3879	Bodl. 3340	Mid 15th cent.	Robbins
71	1278	Bodl. 10234	Mid 15th cent.	Robbins

POEM	INDEX	MANUSCRIPT	DATE OF POEM	SOURCE
72	3832	Bodl. 14530	Late 15th cent.	Robbins
73	2437	Bodl. 14530	Late 15th cent.	Robbins
74	3171	Bodl. 29734	c. 1480	Greene
75	2831	Nat. Lib. Scotland, Advocates 1.1.6	15th cent.	Wood
76	1359	Copenhagen 29264	15th cent.	Brown XV
77	1299	B.M. Sloane 2593	15th cent.	Robbins
78	1302	B.M. Sloane 2593	15th cent.	Robbins
79	150	Canterbury Cathedral, Christ Church Letters, Vol. II, No. 173	c. 1500	Robbins
80	1222	Balliol Oxf. 354	Late 15th cent.	Robbins
81	3864	B.M. Sloane 2593	15th cent.	Robbins
82	1468	Bodl. 29734	c. 1480	Robbins
83	3594	St. John's Camb. 259	Mid 15th cent.	Robbins
84	3409	Camb. Univ. Ff. 5.48	15th cent.	Robbins
85	2494	Huntington Lib., California, EL 1160	15th cent.	Robbins
86	377	B.M. Sloane 2593	15th cent.	Robbins
87	1849	Caius Camb. 383	Mid 15th cent.	Robbins
88	225	Caius Camb. 383	Mid 15th cent.	Robbins
89	438	Camb. Univ. Add. 5943	15th cent.	Robbins
90	2135	Camb. Univ. Add. 5943	15th cent.	Robbins
91	1527	Magd. Camb. Maitland Folio	c. 1500	Mackenzie
92	3236	Bodl. 1687	13th cent.	Brown XIII
93	1978	New Coll. Oxf. 88	Early 14th cent.	Brown XIV
94	3872	B.M. Add. 46919	Early 14th cent.	Brown XIV
95	643	B.M. Add. 46919	Early 14th cent.	Brown XIV
96	1235	B.M. Add. 46919	Early 14th cent.	Brown XIV
97	600	B.M. Add. 46919	Early 14th cent.	Brown XIV
98	3676	B.M. Add. 46919	Early 14th cent.	Brown XIV
99	1742	B.M. Add. 46919	Early 14th cent.	Brown XIV
100	968	B.M. Harley 2253	Early 14th cent.	Brook
101	3236	B.M. Harley 2253	Early 14th cent.	Brook
102	1678	B.M. Harley 2253	Early 14th cent.	Brook
103	1216	B.M. Harley 2253	Early 14th cent.	Brook
104	374	Bodl. 3938	Late 14th cent.	Brown XIV
105	3963	B.M. Harley 2253	Early 14th cent.	Brook
106	3571	B.M. Harley 2341	15th cent.	Robbins
107	1396	B.M. Harley 3362	15th cent.	Robbins
108	579	Bodl. 1689	Mid 15th cent.	Robbins
109	1502	Camb. Univ. Ff. 6.8	Early 16th cent.	Robbins
110	1423	Dunrobin, Scotland	15th cent.	Robbins
111	3572	Bodl. 14526	c. 1470	Robbins
112	3157	Lambeth Palace 523	15th cent.	Robbins
113	2751	Huntington Lib., California, HU 1051	15th cent.	Robbins
114	1810	Huntington Lib., California, HU 1051	15th cent.	Robbins

POEM	INDEX	MANUSCRIPT	DATE OF POEM	SOURCE
115	3911	B.M. Sloane 747	Early 16th cent.	Robbins
116	2903	Bodl. 15353	Early 15th cent.	Robbins
117	813	Bodl. 29734	c. 1480	Robbins
118	3209	Caius Camb. 261	14th cent.	Robbins
119	2747	B.M. Sloane 2593	15th cent.	Robbins
120	2082	Bodl. 29734	c. 1480	Robbins
121	113	B.M. Royal, 17.B	15th cent.	Greene
122	1163	Corp. Christi Oxf. 237	16th cent.	Robbins
123	1297	B.M. Harley 116	15th cent.	Robbins
124	2742	Camb. Univ. Ff. 1.6	Late 15th cent.	Robbins
125	4092	Bodl. 12900	15th cent.	Robbins
126	939	Camb. Univ. Add. 5943	15th cent.	Robbins
127	3771	Bodl. 7798	Late 15th cent.	Robbins
128	1199	Bodl. 7798	Late 15th cent.	Robbins
129	1151	Camb. Univ. Gg. 2.8	15th cent.	Robbins
130	717	Magd. Camb. Pepys 1236	15th cent.	Robbins
131	1817	Camb. Univ. Ee. 4.37	15th cent.	Robbins
132	4096	Magd. Camb. 5	15th cent.	Robbins
133	1314	Balliol Oxf. 354	Late 15th cent.	Robbins
134	559	Nat. Lib. Wales, Porkington 10	15th cent.	Robbins
135	1622	B.M. Royal 19.B.iv	15th cent.	Robbins
136	3328	Camb. Univ. Ee. 1.12	15th cent.	Robbins
137	1303	B.M. Sloane 2593	15th cent.	Robbins
138	3891	Bodl. 13679	14th cent.	Robbins
139	3174	Caius Camb. 383	Mid 15th cent.	Robbins
140	3227	B.M. Arundel 292	Mid 13th cent.	Robbins
141	3895	Lincoln Cathedral 132	14th cent.	Robbins
142	2066	B.M. Harley 2253	Early 14th cent.	Brook
143	1008	Bodl. 13679	14th cent.	Robbins
144	1866	Balliol Oxf. 354	Late 15th cent.	Robbins
145*	795	Bodl. 3340	Mid 15th cent.	Robbins
146	4197	Camb. Univ. Ee. 1.12	Late 15th cent.	Greene
147	2343	B.M. Add. 14997	4 October 1500	Robbins
148	1225	Bodl. 29734	c. 1480	Robbins
149	1195	Bodl. 29734	c. 1480	Robbins
150	3438	Bodl. 29734	c. 1480	Robbins
151	3735	Bodl. 29734	c. 1480	Robbins
152	436	Bodl. 29734	c. 1480	Robbins
153	3313	Balliol Oxf. 354	Late 15th cent.	Robbins
154	3314	Nat. Lib. Wales, Porkington 10	15th cent.	Robbins
155	1609	Balliol Oxf. 354	Late 15th cent.	Robbins
156	1417	B.M. Sloane 2593	15th cent.	Robbins
157	2675	B.M. Sloane 2593	15th cent.	Robbins
158	1608	B.M. Add. 14997	Early 16th cent.	Robbins
159	549	Bodl. 29734	c. 1480	Robbins
160	903	Balliol Oxf. 354	Late 15th cent.	Robbins

POEM	INDEX	MANUSCRIPT	DATE OF POEM	SOURCE
161*	3259	Bodl. 3340	Mid 15th cent.	Robbins
162	1201	Trinity Dublin 214	15th cent.	Robbins
163	*24	Bodl. 13679	14th cent.	Robbins
164	117	B.M. Sloane 2593	15th cent.	Brown XV
165	2623.3	Nat. Lib. Scotland, Advocates: Bannatyne	c. 1500	Mackenzie
166	3525	Bodl. 7683	c. 1500	Greene
167	4016	B.M. Cotton Caligula, A.ix	13th cent.	Brown XIII
168	1892	Caius Camb. 383	Mid 15th cent.	Brown XV
169*	2070	Maidstone A.13	Early 13th cent.	Brown XIII
170	2293	Bodl. 1603	13th cent.	Brown XIII
171	4268	Bodl. 3938	Late 14th cent.	Brown XIV
172	3410	B.M. Add. 37788	15th cent.	Brown XV
173	2604	B.M. Harley 2253	Early 14th cent.	Brook
174	2166	B.M. Harley 2253	Early 14th cent.	Brook
175	2155	Nat. Lib. Scotland, Advocates 18.7.21	Second half of 14th cent.	Brown XIV
176	583	Bodl. 3938	Late 14th cent.	Brown XIV
177	3348	B.M. Cotton Cleopatra D.vii	Second half of 14th cent.	Robinson
178	3190	B.M. Cotton Cleopatra D.vii	Second half of 14th cent.	Robinson
179	809	B.M. Add. 10340	Second half of 14th cent.	Robinson
180	1179	Nat. Lib. Scotland, Advocates 18.8.1	Mid 14th cent.	Brown XIV
181	1367	B.M. Sloane 2593	15th cent.	Brown XV
182	1073	B.M. Add. 37049	15th cent.	Brown XV
183	1836	Trinity Camb. 323	Second half of 13th cent.	Brown XIII
184	3700	B.M. Add. 46919	Early 14th cent.	Brown XIV
185	1054	B.M. Add. 46919	Early 14th cent.	Brown XIV
186	1232	B.M. Add. 46919	Early 14th cent.	Brown XIV
187	465	Huntington Lib., California, HM 127	15th cent.	Brown XV
188	3836	B.M. Cotton Caligula A.ii	15th cent.	Brown XV
189	1407	B.M. Harley 2253	Early 14th cent.	Brook
190	2320	Bodl. 3462	Second half of 13th cent.	Brown XIII
191	2039	B.M. Harley 2253	Early 14th cent.	Brook
192	420	Magd. Oxf. 60	Late 14th cent.	Brown XIV
193	2359	B.M. Harley 2253	Early 14th cent.	Brook
194	359	B.M. Harley 2253	Early 14th cent.	Brook
195	2107	B.M. Add. 17376	Early 14th cent.	Brown XIV
196	1460	Bodl. 21896	c. 1400	Brown XIV
197	37	Bodl. 11670	c. 1500	Brown XV
198*	353	Nat. Lib. Scotland, Advocates 18.7.21	Second half of 14th cent.	Brown XIV

POEM	INDEX	MANUSCRIPT	DATE OF POEM	SOURCE
199	3628	Bodl. 6777	Early 16th cent.	Brown XV
200	1213	B.M. Add. 46919	Early 14th cent.	Brown XIV
201	2024	Nat. Lib. Scotland, Advocates 18.7.21	Second half of 14th cent.	Brown XIV
202	2023	Nat. Lib. Scotland, Advocates 18.7.21	Second half of 14th cent.	Brown XIV
203	1649	Trinity Camb. 323	Second half of 13th cent.	Brown XIII
204	441	Nat. Lib. Scotland, Advocates 18.7.21	Second half of 14th cent.	Brown XIV
205	3221	B.M. Egerton 613	Late 13th cent.	Brown XIII
206	1922	B.M. Harley 2253	Early 14th cent.	Brook
207	3405	B.M. Add. 46919	Early 14th cent.	Brown XIV
208	1182	Stockholm Royal Lib., Medical Misc. XIV	15th cent.	Robbins
209	3212	Merton Oxf. 248	14th cent.	Brown XIV
210	3906	B.M. Add. 46919	Early 14th cent.	Brown XIV
211	110	Bodl. 14667	Mid 14th cent.	Brown XIV
212	2150	B.M. Harley 2316	Mid 14th cent.	Brown XIV
213	3825	Nat. Lib. Scotland, Advocates 18.7.21	Second half of 14th cent.	Brown XIV
214	3565	B.M. Royal 12. E. i	Early 14th cent.	Brown XIV
215	3109	Nat. Lib. Scotland, Advocates 18.7.21	Second half of 14th cent.	Brown XIV
216	4263	Nat. Lib. Scotland, Advocates 18.7.21	Second half of 14th cent.	Brown XIV
217	3862	Nat. Lib. Scotland, Advocates 18.7.21	Second half of 14th cent.	Brown XIV
218	497	B.M. Harley 4012	15th cent.	Brown XV
219	2012	Nat. Lib. Scotland, Advocates 18.7.21	Second half of 14th cent.	Brown XIV
220	1274	Nat. Lib. Scotland, Advocates 18.7.21	Second half of 14th cent.	Brown XIV
221	2241	B.M. Add. 46919	Early 14th cent.	Brown XIV
222	2240	Nat. Lib. Scotland, Advocates 18.7.21	Second half of 14th cent.	Brown XIV
223	4159	Nat. Lib. Scotland, Advocates 18.7.21	Second half of 14th cent.	Brown XIV
224	94	Nat. Lib. Scotland, Advocates 18.7.21	Second half of 14th cent.	Brown XIV
225	3245	Nat. Lib. Scotland, Advocates 18.7.21	Second half of 14th cent.	Brown XIV
226*	3211	B.M. Harley 2253	Early 14th cent.	Brook
227	1705	B.M. Harley 2253	Early 14th cent.	Brook
228	1365	B.M. Harley 2253	Early 14th cent.	Brook
229	298	Nat. Lib. Wales, Porkington 10	15th cent.	Brown XV
230	1132	Balliol Oxf. 354	Late 15th cent.	Greene
231	1308	Nat. Lib. Scotland, Advocates 19.1.11	15th cent.	Brown XV

POEM	INDEX	MANUSCRIPT	DATE OF POEM	SOURCE
232	4044	Trinity Camb. 323	Second half of 13th cent.	Brown XIII
233	1422	B.M. Arundel 292	Mid 13th cent.	Brown XIII
234	3998	Trinity Camb. 43	13th cent.	Brown XIII
235	2369	Trinity Camb. 323	Second half of 13th cent.	Brown XIII
236	3135	B.M. Add. 46919	Early 14th cent.	Brown XIV
237	1818	B.M. Harley 2316	Second half of 14th cent.	Brown XIV
238	2302	Bodl. 3938	Late 14th cent.	Brown XIV
239	4239	Bodl. 1550	Late 14th cent.	Brown XIV
240	769	Trinity Camb. 1157	15th cent.	Brown XV
241	1387	B.M. Cotton Faustina B.vii, Part II	15th cent.	Brown XV
242	3939	B.M. Harley 2253	Early 14th cent.	Brook
243	3613	Camb. Univ. Ff. 1.6	Late 15th cent.	Robbins
244	237	Trinity Camb. 366	15th cent.	Robbins
245	1207	B.M. Harley 665	15th cent.	Robbins

Critical and Historical
Backgrounds

PETER DRONKE

Performers and Performance: Middle English Lyrics in the European Context†

The men and women who sang and played in medieval Europe were the heirs of both a Roman and a Germanic musical tradition. In Rome the vogue for music of every kind seems to have increased enormously from the first century of the Christian era. Writers such as Quintilian and Seneca see in the newfangled music signs of moral as well as of artistic degeneration, and look back nostalgically to a time when music was more serious or more sacred, a time when, after a patrician banquet, the lute would circulate among the guests, who performed songs in praise of heroes and of gods; when dances were not lascivious in character, but ceremonial or religious. Under the Empire, it appears, a more sensual quality came to pervade both vocal and instrumental music, the songs and dances of private feast and public spectacle alike. The musicians were mostly Greeks, whether from Europe, Alexandria, or Asia Minor; the most celebrated dancers, girls from Cadiz (the provocative *puellae Gaditanae* described by Martial and Juvenal), or again from Syria—women such as the *copa* so vividly evoked in a poem that was long attributed to Vergil:

> The Syrian cabaret-hostess, whose hair is bound back by a
> Grecian headband,
> whose quivering thighs sway to the rhythm of castanets,
> dances, intoxicated, voluptuous, in the smoky tavern . . .

Music played a part in every aspect of Roman life. The highest art was considered to be that of the citharode, who sang accompanying himself or herself on the lute. Quintilian gives a precise account of the mode of performance:

> Must not the lute-playing singers (*citharoedi*) attend simultaneously to their memory, to the sound of their voice and to the many inflections, and while striking the chords [with a plectrum] with their right hand, with their left they draw their fingers along them, silence them, and prepare the chords to come; and even their foot does not remain idle but observes the formal regulation of the tempo.

The song was often preceded by an instrumental prelude; more rarely, the soloist sang unaccompanied. The other instrument that was important for lyrical performance was the flute (*tibia*, generally

† From Peter Dronke, *The Medieval Lyric* (New York: Harper & Row, 1969), pp. 13–27, 63–70, 144–147. Reprinted by permission of the Hutchinson University Library and the author.

the double flute), which accompanied the actor on the stage. Cicero is reported to have said: 'Those who cannot become luta-nists become flautists.' Both the lute and the double flute were used polyphonically. Dances and mimes were performed to the accompa-niment of the flute and the *scabellum* (an instrument like a casta-net, but played with the foot), or of a small orchestra with percus-sion instruments. Trumpets, and other brass instruments, were employed for martial music, and played a large part in military life. There was special music for funerals, and funeral-songs (*naeniae*). The first-century records often suggest an excess of music, both in private and public life. In Petronius' fantasy of the banquet of the parvenu Trimalchio, almost everything is done to music—a waiter cannot bring a goblet without bursting into song. Nero made fre-quent and embarrassing public appearances as a singer. Seneca men-tions a concert performed by a huge ensemble of orchestra and choir, a choir in which men and women sang in harmony, singing in three registers (as men and boys were to do later in medieval organum). Many references in Suetonius show the passion of the Roman public, high and low, for musical mime, lyric plays and musical spectacle of every kind. From an anecdote he tells of the Emperor Galba we can see how strikingly a song could become 'popular':

> Galba's arrival [in Rome, A.D. 68] was not altogether well received, as became apparent at the very next show, for, when the players of an Atellane [a farce that often contained elements of topical satire] began the well-known song 'Here comes Onesimus, down from his farm', all the spectators finished it in chorus and mimed it, repeating that particular verse again and again. [No doubt they meant it as an allusion to the churlishness of the Emperor.]

At the same time we must reckon with a rich tradition of popular songs associated with many aspects of the everyday life of the people. There is a remarkable passage about this in a sermon of St. John Chrysostom, the 'golden-mouthed' preacher who became patri-arch of Constantinople in 397:

> By nature we take such delight in song that even infants cling-ing at the breast, if they are crying and perturbed, can be put to sleep by singing. This is how the nurses who carry them in their arms, walking them up and down many times and singing them childish ditties, make their eyelids close. So too journeymen, driv-ing their yoked oxen in the noonday, often sing as they go, making the way less weary by their songs. Not only journeymen but wine-growers, treading the winepress, or gathering grapes, or dressing the vines, or doing any other piece of work, often do it to a song. And the sailors likewise, as they pull the oars. Again,

women who are weaving, or disentangling the threads on their spindle, often sing: sometimes each of them sings for herself, at other times they all harmonise a melody together.

This was the living reality of popular lyric in the fourth century, and a number of later allusions indicate that such traditions lived on in the early Middle Ages. Many scholars today are so sceptical about this that if a modern literary historian had suggested what St. John suggests—that for instance the *chanson de toile* (usually thought to be a learned or aristocratic invention of the late twelfth century) had been current among the common people ever since late antiquity—he would be dismissed as a naive, incurable romantic. But the testimony of St. John—himself an implacable enemy of profane music—cannot be refuted or ignored.

The musical repertoire of the Christians arose in the Roman world, and in many ways reflected and continued the Roman traditions: the range of instruments remains, and the technique of solo singing to the accompaniment of a *cithara*; the ceremonial and sacred uses of song, as well as popular songs with their choruses, are converted to Christian ends. At the same time the erotic songs and dances of the girls of Spain continued into the Middle Ages, and the entertainers, mimes and actors went on performing in hall and fairground, market-square and village green, even when there were no more theatres in Rome. The Christian moralists, like the Roman ones, could deplore the players but not eradicate them. In popular entertainment their techniques and repertoire survive, as is recollected (not in tranquillity, nor perhaps entirely from hearsay) by the Church Father Lactantius, for example, in the early fourth century:

> As for the utterly shameless movements of the actors, what do they teach and arouse but lust—they whose effeminate bodies, supple enough to ape a girlish walk and posture, impersonate loose women by unseemly gesturing? What shall I say of the mime-players, who cultivate the very science of seduction, who teach adulteries by playing them, and mould reality through what they act . . . as each young man and woman sees a model for their sex in those portrayals.

There are literally hundreds of such ecclesiastical condemnations—not only of acting but of singing and dancing, and in particular of the erotic element in all of these—from the time of Tertullian (born *c.* 160) to the high Middle Ages and beyond. It seems that Thomas Aquinas was the first theologian to argue expressly that the entertainer's profession was not in itself sinful!

From ancient times the Germanic peoples, like those of the Mediterranean, had had their own rich traditions of oral poetry and song. From Tacitus alone (our earliest witness) we know of their songs of cosmogony, their heroic lays, panegyric songs, genealogical poems, magical incantations, songs of victory and dirges. Other allusions, in both Greek and Roman writers of the following centuries, testify to further lyrical genres in the Germanic repertoire: Alemannic songs of joy (Emperor Julian, mid-fourth century); Rhenish lampoons (Ausonius, *c.* 370); Merovingian epithalamia and love-songs (Sidonius, fifth century); a Vandal king's elegy (Procopius, sixth century); Merovingian dance-songs and songs of young girls (Council of Autun, late sixth century). Behind a legend of the birth of Clovis (457), told in Latin prose by Gregory of Tours in the late sixth century, we may surmise a romantic vernacular ballad. Childeric is banished from France: he has seduced too many of the daughters of the Franks. As he leaves, he breaks a gold coin with a friend, who says, 'When I send you this half of the coin, and it fits with yours, then it is safe for you to come home.' Childeric goes into exile in Thuringia, at the court of King Bysinus and his wife Basina. It is eight years before the coin comes and he can return to France. So far this need be no more than a prose anecdote; but the climax of Gregory's story, and especially the direct speech, seem to me to reflect a traditional *poetic* shaping of the narrative. The queen from the court of his exile suddenly realises Childeric's worth:

> Queen Basina left her husband
> and came to Childeric.
> Anxiously he asked her
> why she had come to him
> from so far away,
> and she answered, it is said:
> 'I can depend on you;
> I know you are very strong;
> so I have come to live with you.
> But know this: if in lands beyond the sea
> I could have found a bolder man than you,
> I would have sought him out and lived with him.'
> Joyfully he seized her as his wife,
> and she conceived and bore a son,
> and she named him Clovis.
> He was a great man,
> and an outstanding fighter.

In an Anglo-Saxon poem, *Widsith* ('the far-wanderer'), which contains some of the earliest Germanic poetry still extant, we have not only a poetic compendium of rulers and of peoples, but a portrait of the Germanic poet, the *scop* himself. The portrait is larger than life: here the *scop* has an aura that brings him close to Cocteau's myth of the *poète*. He has about him something of the primordial poet, who is all-seeing and divine, whether his name is

Óthinn or Orphée. His role is the most poignant on earth and the most glamorous; he is the loneliest of men and the most sought after; he is both the servant and the uncrowned legislator of mankind:

> So I have traversed many strange lands
> across the wide world, lands where I met with
> good and with ill—cut off from my kindred,
> my own noble race; I served far and wide.
> Thus I can sing, and tell a tale
> to the crowd gathered in the mead-hall,
> tell how lavish great men were in their kindness to me.
> I was with the Huns, and the glorious Goths,
> with the Swedes, the Geats, and the southern Danes . . .
> I was with the Saracens, and the central Asians,
> I was with the Greeks, with the Finns, and with Caesar,
> who had wine-flowing cities in his power . . .
> And I was with Ermanaric for all that time
> that the king of the Goths showed me bounty:
> he, lord of cities, gave me a bracelet
> in which it was reckoned were a full six hundred
> shilling pieces of pure gold.
> I presented it to my lord Eadgils,
> my protector, when I came home,
> to reward the loved prince for the land,
> my father's land, that he left to me.
> Then Ealhhild, daughter of Eadwine,
> royal lady of the court, gave me another.
> Her praise has spread across many lands,
> whenever I was to proclaim in song
> where beneath heaven I knew the best
> of gold-clad queens bestowing gifts.
> When Scilling and I, with ringing voice,
> performed a song before our conquering lord,
> the singing in clear harmony with the harp,
> many a proud-spirited man,
> of great discernment in the art, admitted
> he had never heard a better song . . .
> As the minstrels among mankind
> are fated to walk through many lands,
> they say what is needed, they express thanks,
> and always, south or north, they meet some man
> expert in songs, not slow in giving,
> who wants to exalt renown before his courtiers,
> to do what is noble till all is gone,
> light and life alike; such a one wins praise:
> beneath the heavens, fixed high, his glory.

This passage of triumphant hyperbole can serve as a focal point for a number of sober facts relating to the performance of lyric in the Middle Ages.

The Performer's Travels

While no one man could have visited as many nations as Widsith claims, or have lived so long that he could have sung in the presence of both Ermanaric († 375) and the Frankish Theodoric († 534), the medieval poet-musician was essentially a traveller. This is true not only of the less reputable strolling-players and variety-artists, and of the singers and musicians who performed the songs of others, but also of the early Germanic *scop* and of the many later troubadours, trouvères and Minnesinger who composed as well as performed their songs. Some received a steady patronage and so became 'minstrels' in the strict sense of *ministeriales*, permanent members of a noble, royal, or episcopal household. Their services were then required at certain times of the year, as for the greater feasts. At other times, however, these minstrels too would travel to other courts, often with a letter of recommendation from their patron, which would give them a certain social advantage over the travelling musicians of no fixed abode. In the mid-fifth century the Hunnish Emperor Attila has two Gothic minstrels and a Scythian buffoon performing at his court on the Danube; in 507 Emperor Theodoric at Ravenna sends a singing lutanist to Clovis; at the Parisian court of Clovis' son Childebert we find a Celtic bard Hyvarnion, prized for his composition of songs and lays. In 764 Cuthbert, abbot of Jarrow and Wearmouth, writes to Lullus, archbishop of Mainz, asking him to send over two men: one is an expert glass-blower, the other (Cuthbert is afraid it may sound frivolous) is a *citharista*:

> It would delight me too to have a lutanist, who could play on the kind of lute that we call a *rotta*; for I have one here, and no one to play it. If it is no trouble, please send me over such a man as well. I hope you will not despise this request or laugh at it.

Clearly it was a small matter for a musician to travel from the Rhine to the north of England. From Byzantium, where there was a permanent orchestra attached to the imperial court, an orchestra employed to play sacred as well as profane music, musicians travel to the court at Kiev from the late ninth century onwards. From the tenth century Icelandic scalds travel to Norway, Sweden and Denmark, and are received in honour there as court poets, and later in the twelfth century they too at times travel as far as Kiev. From the eleventh century onwards we know of Byzantine minstrels at the Polish court. In the twelfth century some of the greatest poets are also the most widely travelled ones: the troubadour Raimbaut de Vaqueiras goes from Provence to Italy, to Barcelona, and later follows his friend and patron the Marquis of Montferrat overseas to Byzantium and Thessalonica; the Latin Archpoet follows his patron, who is Barbarossa's chancellor, from Cologne to Vienne to Pavia and Milan. At the close of the twelfth century Peire Vidal, born in Toulouse, makes voyages to Hungary, Spain, Italy, Cyprus and Palestine. In 1192 King Béla III of Hungary sends a *clerc* Elvinus to Paris to learn music—and the chronicler's phrase, *ad discendam melodiam*, suggests practice rather than theory. King Manfred of Sicily (1258–66) has seventeen German musicians at his court in Palermo, while in Castile, at the court of Sancho IV (1284–95), the palace accounts mention salaries paid to fourteen Arabic musicians (among them two women), one Jewish and twelve Christian ones. Such was the internationality of song at every period.

The Performer's and Composer's Social Status

Widsith is both composer and performer; he is of noble birth, and received with honour at every court. Even a king could on occasion assume the role of *scop*, as we see in *Beowulf* when Hrothgar takes his turn at playing the harp—recounting ancient legends, singing elegies on historic events, elaborating tales of fantasy (*syllic spell*), and finally lamenting the passing of his own youthful strength (*Beowulf* 2105 ff.). So too in the Finnsburg lay recalled within the poem, it is Hildeburg, herself of royal race, who sings the dirge over her dead son and brother. A harp was found in the royal ship-burial at Sutton Hoo.

It is likely that from the earliest times the Germanic peoples knew not only Widsiths but musical entertainers of a humbler kind, not only a *scop* but a *gleomon* or *spilman*. The distinction between different classes of singer is difficult to establish philologically, however, as the various terms are often used loosely and interchangeably, as are words such as *jongleur* and *ménestrel* in the later Middle Ages. There is no *appellation contrôlée!*

In the twelfth and thirteenth centuries a number of the great princely patrons of poetry and music composed lyrics themselves: Guillaume IX of Aquitaine, Thibaut de Champagne, who became King of Navarre, the Hohenstaufen Emperors Henry VI in Germany and Frederick II in Sicily, King Alfonso the Wise of Castile and King Denis of Portugal are outstanding examples. The vast majority of poets and singers, on the other hand, had to earn their living by their profession. While a distinction was sometimes drawn between performers and composers, and was sometimes insisted on by the composer, the *trobador*, at the *joglar's* expense, the social boundaries between the two professions remained fluid. In Provence talented *joglars* of humble origins—Marcabru, Bernart de Ventadour, Guiraut de Borneil—become great *trobadors*, welcomed in the highest circles. Arnaut Daniel and Raimbaut de Vaqueiras, though nobly born, become professional *joglars* through poverty; the other Arnaut, of Marueil, becomes a *joglar* after having been a *clerc*. In Portugal the first outstanding poet whose name we know, Martin Codax, rose from the ranks of playing to composing. An exceptional performer could be as proud of his art and as much prized as any composer—in the Russian chronicle of Hypatios we read that (in 1241) a famous singer Mitusa thought so highly of himself that he refused to serve Prince Daníil, and comparable anecdotes are told of singers at earlier courts in Moslem Spain, though I know of none from northern Europe. There even the fact that *joglars* tend to have a different type of name from *trobadors* is suggestive of social differences: the *joglar* tends to adopt a 'stage-name', a name that is striking, piquant, witty, or self-mocking: Alegret, Esperdut, Falconet, Brisepot, Mal Quarrel, Quatre-oeufs. It is tempting to think of the name of Widsith's companion Scilling (i.e. shilling) in this connection and to envisage him as an accompanist and singer of lower status, employed by the distinguished *scop*.

The Minnesinger comprise the widest social range, but whatever their birth they nearly always travel, from court to court or from town to town. The more exalted might employ *joglars*—Ulrich von Lichtenstein required 'many a fiddler to accompany him'—but mostly the German poets acted as their own *joglars*. Some of the principal French trouvères (Gace Brulé, the Chastelain de Couci, Conon de Béthune) were great lords who went to the crusades; but the most gifted and many-sided of all, Adam de la Halle and Rutebeuf, burghers in their background and *clercs* in their education, became impoverished *déclassés*. Being married, they could not hope for great advancement in the clerical world, and they were too bohemian to be accepted by the worthier bourgeoisie.

The wide range of Latin lyrics with profane, topical, satirical or amatory themes, on the other hand, were principally composed, as far as we have evidence, not by a ragged band of bohemians ('the wandering scholars', 'the goliards') but by hard-working, intellectually distinguished professional men. We know five outstanding 'goliard' poets by name: three of these (Hugh Primas, Serlo of Wilton, and Walter of Châtillon) spent the greater part of their lives as professors at some of Europe's leading centres of learning; the other two, Peter of Blois, and Philip, Chancellor of the University of Paris, were among the most prominent administrators of their day. Only the already mentioned 'Archpoet', whose name we do not know, would seem to embody the goliardic myth. His 'confession', with its eloquent plea that the poet's inspiration is bound up with his freedom to live freely, to live dangerously, is perhaps the best-known poem in Medieval Latin. But who was this poet? A knight by birth, he was in fact a court poet, perhaps also a civil servant or minor diplomat, in the service of the Imperial Chancellor, and so almost certainly a member of the circle around Frederick Barbarossa himself. I am convinced that his leitmotif of the wayward, wretched vagabond-poet who is compelled to beg from his patron and his audience contains far less autobiography than literary craft. Each of his poems reveals at a closer look stanza after stanza of deft and brilliant play on both classical and Biblical language, and an intimate knowledge of Roman poetry such as even a Renaissance humanist would have envied. Yet the Archpoet's art is to conceal his art—he makes his verse seem almost effortless, the tone is personal and spontaneous. The Archpoet's picture of the vagabond-poet (whatever element of literal truth it may have contained) has been drawn for the sophisticated entertainment of that international set of diplomats and legislators, high-born scholars and prelates who surrounded the Emperor, whose *lingua franca* was Latin, and among whom the Archpoet probably, by his birth and position, moved as an equal. So too the Sicilian love-poets who surrounded Barbarossa's grandson Frederick II were predominantly courtier-administrators. Those of the Tuscan school, on the other hand, were poets of town rather than court: they tended to come from the educated élite in a wealthy urban milieu. They were seldom travelling poets—unless, like Dante, they had suffered banishment from their own city.

The bracelet that Widsith received from Ermanaric sounds as fabulous as his other claims. But jewellery was indeed one of the more frequent gifts that a patron would give to his poet or singer. The twelfth-century Flemish poet Heinrich von Veldeke describes minstrels being presented with 'precious garments of fur, gold and treasures of every kind, silver and gold vessels, mules and stallions, skins and samite whole and uncut, many a red ring of hammered gold, sable and ermine'. At the other extreme we have Rutebeuf's terrible evocations of poverty, or the jongleur of the *Dit de la maaille*, who does not refuse even a ha'penny (*maaille*), for the ha'pennies mount up soon enough; besides, living in Paris is not dear:

> In Paris with a ha'penny we could buy a large half-pound loaf of bread, or you could have a hefty wench just as you please, or plenty of good coal and wood to cook your meal, or else—there's no denying it—butter or lard, oil or fat enough to make your peas taste good, or a huge ha'penny's worth of wine, a big measure, filled to the top, which would cost twopence anywhere else.

The travelling minstrel had, since Roman times, laboured under certain legal disadvantages, and he might at any time incur the wrath of a fanatic churchman. But it is the bourgeoisie of the rising towns in the twelfth and thirteenth centuries who practise systematic discrimination, by denying *varund volkch* the right of legal appeal, or by limiting them to a quota: thus Strasbourg, around 1200, allows four *ioculatores* and no more.

For the poets and musicians dependent on patronage, therefore, the acquiring of property was their highest material hope. It meant both security and new prestige. Widsith gives his most precious treasure from Ermanaric to his own lord in exchange for land: it is a vassal's act of homage, but also an excellent bargain. In the Domesday Book we find the name of Berdic, the royal *jongleur* (*ioculator regis*), who holds land from the Conqueror, also a *ioculatrix* called Adelinda, who holds land from Earl Roger. In 1246 in Cologne 'Henry the Fiddler and his wife Matilda, lutanist' buy a house in St. Severin's Lane. And even today one cannot read without being moved Walther von der Vogelweide's shout of joy (followed swiftly by an irony born of despair) when around 1220 Emperor Frederick II gave him tenure of some land near Würzburg. This came to Walther, the most original and many-sided poet of his age, the artist too proud to let himself be classed as *spilman* or to receive gifts of 'cast-off clothes', after more than a quarter of a century of insecurity at the mercy of diverse patrons:

> I have my land—all the world hear me!—I have my land!
> Now I am not afraid of frostbite on my toes,
> now I'll no longer beg from worthless lords!
> The noble king, the gracious king, has shown his care for me—
> now summer's air is fresh, winter is warm for me.
> Among my neighbours too I am far more highly prized:
> they no longer look at me as at a poltergeist!
> I was poor too long, through no fault of my own;
> I was so full of railing words, my breath became unclean.
> The king has made it pure, and has made my song serene.

The Mode of Performance

A medieval soloist could sing unaccompanied, or he could accompany himself (especially on harp or lute), or again he could be accompanied by one or more *joglars*. The *joglar* might be expected to play not only harp or lute, guitar or psaltery, but also bowed instruments such as the viol or rebec, or a small portative organ. The *trobador* Guiraut de Calanson demands of a *joglar* that he be able to play no fewer than nine instruments. By and large, the literary allusions leave the impression that, as in the Roman world, unaccompanied singing was much less common than accompanied, and that more often than not the solo singer accompanied himself.

Widsith and his partner Scilling both sing and play the harp. What is striking is that they seem to perform a duet, whether by singing together or (as I think far likelier) by singing in alternation. So too it was a *pair* of Gothic minstrels who performed at Attila's court. The likelihood that alternate singing was an ancient and widespread Germanic practice is of particular interest in that the outstanding lyrical form of the medieval clerical world, the sequence, is one in which either soloists or two half-choirs repeat each new melodic phrase by singing it alternately. We know, moreover, that many early religious sequences adapt the melodies of prior secular songs. In a far-reaching sense, medieval secular and sacred song can be seen as two strands of a single tradition.

* * *

The Performer's Repertoire

Medieval song has three main functions: formal commemoration, entertainment, and cult.

Seigneurial authority presupposes retainers. A ruler maintains around him a body of courtiers and officials; they try to win praise and glory in his eyes, and he in theirs. For praise and glory to be truly won, however, they must be celebrated in some lasting mode. Hence the very nature of a court implies the need for the arts, and in particular for the art of celebration by poetry and song, which has the greatest potentiality of diffusion. The songs of Widsith are essentially celebrations: of the kings and queens he visits; of the deeds present and past that deserve to be remembered; of the ideals by which ruler and ruled aspire to live; and last not least, of the vocation of the *scop* himself, who makes such celebration possible. Widsith can stand as a symbol for the 'official' poetry and song that played so large a part in the life of the courts of medieval Europe —the panegyrics and dirges, the songs that recorded battles, splendid weddings, coronations, great historical moments or moments that have become legend.

In every social group, song appears in its greatest variety when its purpose is entertainment. Tristan, proving himself on arrival at the court of King Mark, sings lays to the harp in Breton, Welsh, Latin and French, and, when pressed, admits to playing six instruments (Gottfried, *Tristan*, lines 3624 ff.). Isolde, at the court in Dublin, entertains her father, King Gurmun, by fiddling an *estampie* (an elaborate kind of dance-song) and a *Leich*[1] (*Tristan*, lines 8062

1. **Leich/lai lyrique**: a composition built of varied stanzas, ABCDEF ..., with a flexible repetition of strophic patterns within the whole. **Descort**: a lyric in lines and sections of unequal length.

ff.); she performs French songs about saints; she plays lyre and harp exquisitely; she sings *pastourelle, rotrouenge* (a monorhymed song with refrain—Richard Coeur-de-Lion's prison song is a famous example), *rondeau* and *canzone, refloit* (another song with refrain) and *folate* (a genre about which no information survives). In the fascinating Provençal romance *Flamenca* (lines 583–731), Lord Archambaut, when the King of France brings him Flamenca, his bride, holds a feast to end all feasts, in which the full spectrum of medieval entertainment is displayed. 'After eating, the guests washed their hands once more, but remained in their places and had wine, as was the custom. Then the tablecloths were removed, cushions and fans were brought, and the *joglars* arose, each longing to be heard. Then you could hear chords of many a different tone echoing. Whoever could perform a new tune on the viol, a new *canzone* or *descort* or *lai*,[1] came forward with the greatest eagerness. One played the lay of Chèvrefeuil on the viol, another the lay of Tintagel [two songs from the Tristan cycle], one sang the lay of the perfect lovers, another the lay composed by Yvain.'

Next come instrumentalists, playing on a wide range of string and wind instruments. They are followed by (or perhaps provide background music for) a marionettist, a knife-juggler, tumblers and acrobats. Those who wished could then hear stories of kings, marquises and counts of old. An earlier line suggests that for these 'one *joglar* recites the words and another accompanies'. There are stories from antiquity: the matter of Troy and Thebes, and of Alexander, and ancient love-stories such as those of Hero and Leander, Orpheus and Eurydice; poems recounting the more romantic Biblical episodes: David and Goliath, Samson and Dalilah, Judas Maccabeus, as well as a curious story of 'how Julius Caesar walked the waves all on his own: he did not pray for help to Our Lord—don't imagine that he was afraid!' Next there are all the themes of Arthurian romance; and finally stories and songs seem to come pell-mell—the star of Merlin, the Assassins, Charlemagne's conquest of Germany, 'the whole story of Clovis and Pepin', Lord Lucifer's fall from glory, two *chansons de geste*, a song by the troubadour Marcabru, and lastly the tale of Daedalus and Icarus. Many of these were going on at the same time in different parts of the hall. Then the host, Archambaut, calls for dancing, and two hundred *joglars* form a string orchestra to play the dance-tunes. Such, at least in ideal, was the range of entertainment expected of medieval performers in the best circles. By this I do not mean these were exclusive types of entertainment—there is no single item here that could not equally have been performed at a fair or on a public holiday. But in less refined circles, or on a less grand occasion, the performers' repertoire would have been still wider—the songs, for instance, would include a range of fabliaux, satires, ribald jests, ballads, dialogues of witty repartee and mock-abuse, drinking songs—all that is customarily, though rather one-sidedly, understood to be 'jongleuresque'.

The third great function of medieval song, in religious cult and contemplation, is discussed in some detail in the next chapter. Here I should like only to glance at some of the relations between the secular repertoire and the clerical world. It is only through the *clercs* (not necessarily priests, but whoever had received a clerical education) that any pagan Germanic poetry has been preserved in writing; it is chiefly from secular songs composed in Latin, especially from the ninth to the early twelfth century, that we can infer with some accuracy the characteristics of secular songs in the Romance languages in the centuries before such songs were written down. The frequent attempts to discourage or prevent the clergy from occupying themselves with profane song are eloquent testimonies to how much they continued to do so; it is only through two famous Carolingian prohibitions, for instance, that we know that monks were singing heroic lays (of the Heathobard king Ingeld) and nuns composing love-songs (*winileodas*) in the late eighth century. Wherever a monastery or bishop's court, and later a cathedral school or university, had any pretensions to musical culture, it admitted to a greater or lesser extent songs intended for entertainment and not for cult, songs performed in hall rather than in church or oratory, which were thus far less restricted in their choice of themes.

* * *

Early English Lyrics

The combination of simple and spectacular expression that we find in Jacopone is also characteristic of the finest religious lyrics in Middle English. Before the thirteenth century, little survives. A few verses by the hermit St. Godric († 1170) are our earliest testimony—a childlike invocation to the Virgin, and one to Saint Nicholas:

Sainte Nicholaes, godes druth,   4: champion[2]
tymbre us faire scone hous!   4: lovely
At thi burth, at thi bare,   6: bearing
Sainte Nicholaes, bring us wel thare!

The image is freshly conceived, and at one with the disarming modesty of the language: Godric's image of heaven is not the bejewelled golden Jerusalem designed by the divine architect, but a

2. The number preceding the gloss indicates the place in the line of the Middle   English word glossed.

plain man's house, beautiful but small enough to be built by one carpenter, a saint with whom he has a special bond. When Godric has a vision of his sister reaching heaven, the Latin life of the hermit gives it utterly conventional hagiographic trappings: two angels, preceded by the Virgin Mary, bring the woman's soul to the altar of Godric's oratory, where she sings a hymn of thanksgiving. Godric's own rendering of his sister's words is less pretentious and far more beautiful:

> Crist and sainte Marie
>   swa on scamel me iledde   1–3: so on a crutch[3]
>   that ic on this erthe ne silde   7: should
>   wid mine bare fote itrede.

Godric can dispense with angels: it is Christ himself who, with Mary, guides his sister (a real woman, bare-footed, not a mere soul) on the heavenward journey; the crutch, sign of the cripple's infirmity on earth, now becomes an instrument of freedom—she can take the road to heaven by leaps and bounds, her foot never touching ground. Any day one might have seen on the village street a woman on crutches, supported in the first moments by a friend on either side, then finding her freedom of movement—but it takes a poet's eye to see the latent possibilities of meaning.

The thirteenth-century lyrics are for the most part anonymous. To the earlier decades of the century belongs the quatrain at once elegiac and radiant:

> Nou goth sonne under wod—
> me reweth, Marie, thi faire rode.   6: face
> Nou goth sonne under tre—
> me reweth, Marie, thi sone and the.

The sun grew dark at the moment of Christ's death; the death of the divine Sun was re-enacted in nature, the physical sun showed compassion for the other by dying at the same moment as he. This conceit had become traditional in Christian hymnody. So for instance Walter of Châtillon writes

> Sol eclypsim patitur
> dum sol verus moritur;

(the sun suffers an eclipse as the true sun dies). What is new and creative in the English quatrain is to begin *now*: a particular moment at nightfall, as the sun sinks behind a wood, can bring to mind the sunset of Good Friday, and the setting of the greater Sun that it reflects. Any sunset—even the one at this moment—can become the historic and the omnitemporal moment; any tree—or this tree—can become the tree of the cross. But the poet particular-

---

3. The normal meaning of *scamellum* in Medieval Latin.

ises further: the forest sunset evokes not the crucifixion itself but
the image of Mary watching; it evokes a surge of pity for a lovely
woman's face that has lost its beauty by weeping too much. The
author of the *Stabat mater* exclaims 'Oh how sad and afflicted she
was!', but he cannot *imagine* it. The English poet does not have to
say to Mary 'Let me mourn with you'—his compassionate insight
shows itself, without need of protestations. In four moments of
vision—the sun among the trees, the beautiful face ravaged, the sun
beneath one particular tree, the mother with her dead son—he has
seen everything, and said all that needs saying.

The sufferings of Christ and of Mary at the crucifixion loom large
in thirteenth century religious lyric, especially in England, where a
devotional movement inspired by meditation on Christ's passion
and on the joys and sorrows of the Virgin can be traced back at
least as far as the *Meditationes* of John of Fécamp († 1078). This
movement, given new force by the Cistercians in the twelfth century and the Franciscans in the thirteenth, became widespread in all
Europe, but its deepest roots seem to have been in England. It is
probably no mere accident of preservation that in medieval European vernacular lyric England alone shows a striking preponderance
of sacred lyrics over profane.

At times we can observe the vernacular lyric growing out of the
Latin meditation: where John of Fécamp wrote 'Candet nudatum
pectus, rubet cruentum latus, tensa arent viscera, decora languent
lumina, regia pallent ora, procera rigent brachia, crura dependent
marmorea, et rigat terebratos pedes beati sanguinis unda,'[4] the vernacular poet sings

Whyt was hys nakede brest
and red of blod hys syde,
bleyc was his fair andlet,   1: pale, 5: countenance
his wunden depe and wide;
starke weren his armes
i-streht upon the rode;   1: stretched, 4: cross
on fif stedes on his body   3: places
the stremes ran on blode.

Compared with this, the Latin makes a lifeless, almost mechanical impression. It is too symmetrical, it is determined to leave nothing out. The English poet selects, and varies his syntactic pattern,
though indeed through his dominant opening syllables—whyt,
bleyc, starke—and through the force of his alliteration, he imposes
a rhythm of his own. But most important is that he is more specific
at the close: where John speaks of 'a wave of blessed blood', the poet

4. The naked breast shows white, the
bleeding flank grows red, the tense reins
wither, the lovely eyes languish, the
royal face grows pale, the long arms
grow stiff, the marble legs hang down,
and a wave of blessed blood drenches
the perforated feet.

ignores the non-visual 'blessed', but *sees* five places on the body
from which streams of blood run out. It may be objected that these
are nothing but the traditional five wounds. And so they are. But
the poet does not use the formulistic concept 'five wounds' (which
would have prevented him from seeing)—he looks, and sees afresh.

So too in another contemporary song of the passion, every detail
is newly visualised and brought to life:

Hey a-pon a dune	
as al folke hit se may,	
a mile wythute the tune	
abute the mid-day,	
the rode was op a-reride;	5: raised
his frendis werin al of-ferde,	5: afraid
thei clungin so the cley.	2–5: shrivelled like (parched) clay
The rod stonit in ston,	3: stands
Mari hir-selfe al-hon;	3: alone
hir songe was way-le-way.	

It is not only specific, it brings to the divine moment the living
immediacy of everyday, the sense of shameful publicity, the collo-
quialism with which any man might taunt his friends for cowardice,
the wordless wail that would spring to the lips of any woman who
had been left alone.

In the finest early English lyrics, even very complex thoughts
and images can be unfolded with the same vivid and personal lucid-
ity. A Latin poet had worked out an elaborate conceit about the
Virgin at the cross: her sorrows then were only the labour-pains she
had not felt at the nativity, but had to feel before the rebirth, the
resurrection, could take place:

> Now harsh Natura, seizing the time, demands her rights, now
> sharpens her pains: now she extorts with usury the moans Mary
> had denied her before giving birth. ... The new birth of Christ
> from the closed sepulchre preserves the form of the virgin birth;
> there he proceeded, here arose, in both he comes forth through a
> seal preserved intact.[5]

Intellectually it is admirable, but a little difficult, a little pedantic
or dry. The English poet, adapting these stanzas, performs an aston-
ishing feat: suddenly all is direct and passionately alive:

In that blisful bearnes buirde	3–5: child's blissful birth
wrong wes wroht to wommone wirde,	5–6: women's lot
ah Kinde craved nou the right.	1: but

5. Tempus nacta trux Natura
nunc exposcit sua iura,
  nunc dolores acuit;
nunc extorquet cum usura
gemitus quos paritura
  Naturae detinuit ...

Christi novus hic natalis
formam partus virginalis
  clauso servat tumulo;
hinc processit, hinc surrexit,
hinc et inde Christus exit
intacto signaculo.

Then thu loch ah nou thu wep,	3: laughed
thi wa was waken that thenne slep—	2–4: woe awakened
childing-pine haves the nou picht . . .	1: labour-pains,
	5: stabbed

Thi luve sone uprisinge	2–3: dear son's/sun's
was selli liik to his birdinge—	2–3: wondrously like,
	6: birth
bitwene two is litel schead—	5: distinction
for, so gleam glides thurt the glas,	5: through
of thi bodi born he was,	
and thurt the hoale thurch he gload.	2–7: through the intact coffin he glided

The goddess Natura (Kinde) is here given a motive: she becomes
a jealous rival who thinks 'It's not fair, not natural, that a woman
should give birth without pain'. The vividness increases when
(unlike the Latin) the Virgin is addressed directly, quite possibly
by the gloating 'midwife' Natura herself; the colourless Latin word
gemitus (moans) becomes the stabbing *childing-pine*. In the later
stanza, where the Latin laboriously *explains* the resemblance
between Christ's birth and resurrection, the English lets us see it.
The poet introduces a new (though traditional) image: the gleam
that glides through glass. It is prepared by the word-play in the first
line: Christ the sun *is* that gleam. The image of the window unites
those of the hymen and the tomb; the divine ray of light glides
through window, hymen and tomb, leaving each unscathed. The
analogies are not expounded conceptually but perceived in an
image.

The English poet's freedom of invention in the thirteenth-century religious lyric could also by-pass learned sources altogether—for
instance in a ballad-like song of Judas, for most details of which no
parallel has been found. Christ sends Judas to buy food in Jerusalem, giving him thirty pieces of silver, and saying very blandly (*ful
milde*) 'You may meet some of your relatives on the way'. The song
continues in swift, taut scenes, throwing dialogue in such sharp
relief that even 'he said', 'she said' become superfluous:

Imette wid his soster, the swikele wimon:	1: Met, 6: deceitful
'Iudas, thou were wurthe me stende the wid ston!	5–6: one should stone

Iudas, thou were wurthe me stende the wid ston—
For the false prophete that thou bilevest upon.'

The 'sister' is of course Judas' mistress, in a euphemism sanc-
tioned not only by the Song of Songs and all its poetic imitations

but also, as a passage in *Piers Plowman* (B V 651) tells us, by a deception current in everyday life. Her harsh teasing provokes in Judas nothing but panicky fear of his master: will that mind-reader not guess her thoughts and take revenge on them both? Reassuring him lovingly, she leads him to the top of a cliff, where he lies, her arms around him; then as he sleeps she takes his money and runs away. By this she thinks she has drawn her lover away from Christ: he will not dare to go back to his employer now. Judas awakes and flies into a mad rage: he is in an impasse, afraid to lose honour and employment with Christ, and afraid to lose his mistress. At that moment Pilate comes in—he is presented as a 'rich Jew', a carica-ture of a money-lender. When Judas names his fee for betraying Christ, he is so astonished at its smallness (thirty silver coins for a piece of espionage!) that he probes further—'You mean you want gold?' But Judas wants the exact amount he has lost, nothing else: only thus, he imagines, will he not be found out when Christ asks for a reckoning. In a flash the scene changes to the Last Supper: Christ's opening words ring terrifyingly, but Judas controls himself and tries to brazen it out:

'Wou sitte ye, postles, ant wi nule ye ete?—   1: How, 7: will not
Ic am iboust ant isold today for oure mete.'   3: bought
Up stod him Iudas: 'Lord, am i that?
I nas never o the stude ther me the evel spec.'

Christ does not answer. He does not need to, for Judas in his excitement has given himself away. His non-sequitur 'I was never in a place where anyone spoke evil of you' is the very thing that Christ knows to be false. In a moment Judas will remember: he had had his answer at the outset of his errand, in the apparently nonchalant but deeply ironic "You *may* meet some of your relatives'. Peter gets up and brags how he would fight to protect Christ, even against a thousand knights. As the Gospel narrative shows, Peter is no physi-cal coward: he can draw his sword on Pilate's soldiers, though (like the Judas of this ballad) he cannot stand up to the taunts of a girl. With Christ's crushing answer:

'Stille thou be, Peter! Wel i the icnowe:
Thou wolt fursake me thrien ar the coc him crowe'   5–6 three
                                                       times before

the poem comes to a subdued close. The two deserters are left standing, with no more to say.

Seldom in medieval poetry has such dramatic compression been achieved in lyrical form. A notable Middle English scholar, George Kane, has recently written that this poem 'apart from the attraction of the antique, has little to recommend it'. I would say it has everything to recommend it—*except* 'the attraction of the antique'. It is one of the most 'modern' of medieval poems: with its swiftly changing tableaux, its terse, explosive use of dialogue, its sharp moments of tension and climax, one could well call it the first masterpiece of expressionism.

There are still other ranges of achievement in the early Middle English religious lyric, which it is difficult to convey in brief compass. Perhaps three short songs can at least signal three streams of tradition that were to flow copiously in England until the end of the Middle Ages. One is the contemplation of mortality and death:

Wen the turuf is thi tour	3: turf
and thi put is thi bour,	3: pit
thi wel and thi wite throte	2: skin
ssulen wormes to note.	1–4: shall profit worms
Wat helpit the thenne	2: helps
al the worlde wunne?	4: bliss

Cognate with such reflections are the lyrical dialogues between body and soul, in which the body is constantly reminded of its corruptibility, the wistful elegies on the theme of *Ubi sunt*—'Where are Paris and Elayne? . . .'—and later, the dances of death. Often in all these, as in the lines just cited, there are the light, aphoristic touches, and the flickers of sardonic humour, that tend to distinguish the English mortality lyrics both from the shrill agonies of the Italian penitential movement and from that horrified fascination with death associated—not always unjustly—with the Gothic in northern Europe.

Then there is a stream of joyful personal devotion to the Virgin Mary, not as a sufferer at the crucifixion but as a romantic heroine in her own right. Perhaps its most perfect expression is in a stanza in a fourteenth-century manuscript:

At a sprynge-wel under a thorn	
ther was bote of bale, a lytel here a-forn;	3–5: remedy for ills
ther by-syde stant a mayde	
full of love y-bounde.	
Ho-so wol seche true love,	1, 3: Whosoever, seek
yn hyr yt schal be founde.	

It was at a fountain, beside a thornbush, that, according to some of the early Christian apocryphal writings, the angel's annunciation to Mary took place. This is the moment of the incarnation, the 'bote of bale' for all mankind. It is to a fountain, too, that girls in the *romances* and dance-songs of medieval Europe often come to meet, or dream about, their beloved. The poet is aware of both associations: impalpably he makes the bridge that joins the omni-temporal moment to the particular one. The annunciation took

place 'a little while ago'; but still a maiden is standing at that fountain, rapt in the fullness of love. It is at once the Virgin, whose true
love can absorb all human love, and any girl made beautiful by
loving. The image is left unbroken, hence enigmatic: this girl opens
the gate of poetic imagination behind which 'heavenly things are
joined to earthly ones, divine to human'.

Finally, there is a stream of lyrical poetry filled with mystical
aspiration towards union with Christ:

Gold and al this werdis wyn	5–6: world's joy
is nouth but Cristis rode.	2: nought
I wolde ben clad in Cristes skyn	
that ran so longe on blode,	6: blood
and gon t'is herte and taken myn in—–	2–4: go to his, 9: lodging
there is a fulsum fode!	4: abundant
Than gef I litel of kith or kyn,	2–3: I would give (care)
for ther is alle gode.	

It is in songs of this stream that we encounter some of the most
striking images in the English religious lyric, whether as here they
are new creations—the cross compounded of the world's gold and
felicity, the shape-changing into the torn skin of Christ—or traditional images re-lived—such as Christ the knight who meets his
death jousting for mankind, the bridegroom enticing his bride to
the wedding-night, the vintner bespattered by the grapes he has
trodden, the lover rejected by the far-off princess, mankind. Here as
in all early English lyric the most distinctive and brilliant achievements lie in the briefest songs, songs that in their sharp but supple
language—not yet over-worn or over-familiar—create moments of
magnetic vitality and concentration.

* * *

English and Galician Love-Songs

Apart from the Latin tradition, there are two vernaculars in which
love-lyric tends to have the same underlying innocence: Middle
English and Galician. The specific qualities of poetic expression,
however, are very different in these languages. When we first
encounter love-lyric in Middle English (shortly after 1200), the
form and diction are without elegance. They are plain and pithy
and concise:

> Though I have wit in plenty,
> in the world's joy I am poor,
> because of a peerless lady,
> crown of all who tread in bower.
> Since she first belonged to him,

> locked in a castle wall of stone,
> I have not been whole or glad,
> or a prosperous man.
> No man lives who heartens me
> to stay and to live merrily—
> it is down to my death I long;
> on me, I can say truthfully,
> woes are harshly hung.

What is remarkable here is not the evocation of the lover's state of feeling (though this has a rueful, down-to-earth tone that carries its own conviction), but the suggestion of a vivid background of events, swiftly adumbrated in two lines—

> sethen furst the heo was his,
> iloken in castel wal of ston—

which lend concreteness and dramatic power to the complaint. Behind the forthrightness of the language we perceive the adroitness and tact of a narrator who knows how to work evocatively.

The song is rounded with a phrase, *herde thet wo hongeth*, that has an almost proverbial ring. So too in the first three lines of a brief song written down half a century later, the proverbial effect allied with the effect of alliteration enables a poet to achieve an intense, gnomic compression:

> Foweles in the frith,
> the fisses in the flod—
> and I mon waxe wod.
> Mulch sorw I walke with
> for beste of bon and blod.

Birds [are] in the woodland, the fishes in the sea—and I must grow mad. I walk with great sorrow for the best of bone and blood.

It begins with the contrast characteristic of the stylised, often highly rhetorical, nature-prelude common in love-lyrics: the implication is that the birds and fishes, being in their element, are happy and fulfilled. The lover's languishing state is conveyed (far more effectively than in many more elaborate complaints) by the two stark words *waxe wod*. The close has a haunting quality: the lover does not describe his state further, nor does he describe the woman who causes it; he reiterates his sorrow with utter simplicity, and mentions his beloved only in a phrase which was probably even then an alliterative cliché. Why then does it have this strangely powerful effect? Is it not because the opening words still reverberate in one's mind, and compel one to associate the last line with them? —She too is bone and blood, a physical being—what right has she to be different from the rest of the living world? If she is the best in

nature, can the blood in her veins be colder than that of the birds
and fishes? These may be only subjective explications of the effect;
what I feel certain of is that the poet intended the opening and
close of his stanza to react on each other and to release associations
of unhappy love, and that his intention was not merely to juxtapose
familiar phrases so as to fit a sweet tune but to achieve a conjunc-
tion that would enrich poetic meaning.

From near the end of the century a song of more joyful love-long-
ing begins:

Bryd one brere, brid, brid one brere,	1–3: Bird on briar
Kynd is come of Love love to crave.	1: Nature
Blithful biryd, on me thu rewe	2: lady/bird, 6: take pity
Or greyth, lef, greith thu me my grave.	2–3: quickly/prepare, dear one

Still the language has that seemingly unpremeditated quality, the
effect at first is almost of a birdlike chatter, bubbling over with
excitement. But the word-play here reveals a keen sense of meaning
and of ambiguity. The second line once more brings to mind the
nature-prelude, but it is more 'metaphysical' than hitherto: it is a per-
sonified Nature who comes in spring to beseech the love-god to
release love in the world—alternatively, Kynd, daughter of the
supreme God, who is Love, descends from on high to crave love (in
the world); both meanings may be implied. The allusion to the
goddess 'of philosophers and scholars', light as it is, is unmistakable.
The third line puns on the first, when *b[i]ryd* is repeated, now
with the overt meaning of 'lady' rather than 'bird'; the fourth line
continues the verbal conjuring (*greyth* can mean both 'quickly' and
'prepare'). All this points to an essentially literary playfulness; but
we cannot exclude from these lines yet another meaning, latent as a
possibility, of the bird as the confidant of lovers, who can take pity
on the lover by bringing him a joyful message from his mistress—
this time a convention deeply rooted in popular song.

In the two remaining stanzas the lover confides his longing to the
bird. Here too it may be possible to detect in the language a conscious echo of popular balladry. With

> She is huit of lime, loueli, trewe,   5: limb
> she is fayr, and flur of alle

we are not far from *As ye came from the holy land*—

> She is neither white nor brown,
> but as the heavens fair ...

just as, in the opening stanza, we come close to Sir Walter Scott—

> 'Who makes the bridal bed,
> Birdie, say truly?'

> 'The grey-headed sexton
> That delves the grave duly.'

For all its many-sided artifice, the language of *Bryd one brere* is still composed wholly of native elements. So too in many stanzas among the love-lyrics in the Harley collection, some of which may go back to before 1300:

> Levedy of alle londe,
> les me out of bonde;
> broht icham in wo.
> Have resting on honde,
> ant sent thou me thi sonde
> sone, er thou me slo;
> my reste is with the ro.
> Thah men to me han onde,
> to love nuly noht wonde,
> ne lete for non of tho.

Lady of all lands, free me from my bonds, I have been brought to woe. Bring about peace for me, and send a message to me now, before you kill me; I rest as little as the roe. Though men are hostile towards me, I shall not swerve from loving, nor cease for any of their sakes.

At a time when such pleas and protestations, and motifs such as the message and the spiteful enemies of love, had become stale elsewhere in Europe through excessive and unimaginative use, they could still be treated in plain English freshly and directly. Again a quatrain of c. 1300, only recently discovered, uses witty hyperbole with an adroitness and vivacity worthy of Kürenberc. The lover, out in the cold night, makes his rueful serenade:

> So longe ic have, lavedi,   5: lady
> yhoved at thi gate,   1: lingered
> that mi fot is ifrore, faire lavedi,   3–5: foot is frozen
> for thi luve faste to the stake!

Here, too, as in *Bryd one brere*, we must reckon with the possibility of word-play—the stake as gatepost, and as the place of execution for love's victim. The fourteenth century in England, however, sees the lyrical language transformed under French influence, all too often an effete and epigonic influence:

> Mercy me graunt off that I me compleyne,
> to yow my lyfis soveraigne plesauns;
> And ese your servaunt of the importabyl peyne
> that I suffre in your obeysauns . . .

Language of this kind, alas, comes to dominate the late medieval English love-lyric. At times, however, as in the finest of the Rawlin-

son lyrics, this newfangled language could still be set aside; or again
an exceptionally subtle and alive personality such as Chaucer could
shape it to his pleasure and thereby win nuances of meaning and
emotion as individual as those of Guillaume or Kürenberc.

* * *

STEPHEN MANNING

Game and Earnest in the Middle English and Provençal Love Lyrics†

Recent criticism of the mediaeval love lyric offers little comfort
to the modern reader in search of personal feeling and emotion. "Le
caractère commun de la poésie 'romane' [c. 1000–1200], dans
toutes ses manifestations, est son objectivité"[1] writes Paul Zumthor, who devotes the major part of his study to the lyric.[2]
"L'oeuvre médiévale est *style*."[3] he insists—as does Roger Dragonetti in his study of the trouvères[4]. A third critic, John Stevens,
observes in his study of the early Tudor lyric and its mediaeval
backgrounds, "the uncertainty remains that it was rarely, if ever, the
first duty of music to express emotion for its own sake. It should
rather be regarded as part of worship, part of ceremony, part of an
allegorical entertainment or a moral play." He then refers to the
similar "applied" nature of the other mediaeval arts.[5] Similarly,
Zumthor emphasizes that the poem, by its being perfectly fashioned, excites admiration and joy, "mais il n'émeut pas. Du moins,
s'il émeut, c'est là un effet secondaire et de surabondance"[6] (p.
180).

All this recalls D. W. Robertson's warning that the mediaeval
poet was not so much interested in his own moods or emotions as

---

† From Stephen Manning, "Game and
Earnest in the Middle English and Provençal Love Lyrics," *Comparative Literature*, 18 (1966), 225–241. Reprinted by
permission of *Comparative Literature*
and the author.
1. The common characteristic of "romanesque" poetry [c. 1000–1200], in all
its manifestations, is its objectivity
[*Editors*].
2. *Langue et techniques poétiques à l'é-
poque romane* (Paris, 1963), p. 12.
3. The mediaeval work is *style*
[*Editors*].
4. *Ibid.*, p. 126; R. Dragonetti, *La Technique poétique des trouvères dans la*
chanson courtoise (Bruges, 1960), *passim.*
5. *Music and Poetry in the Early Tudor
Court* (Lincoln, 1961), p. 235. In speaking of love poetry specifically he emphasizes that "it was chiefly the social *use*
of poetry that mattered. . . . Love-songs
were a part of his [the courtier's] contribution to the social life of the court"
(p. 206). See also p. 156 for reasons
why the art of living approximates the
art of loving.
6. But it does not move one. At least, if
it does move one, this is a secondary
and superfluous effect [*Editors*].

in a reality outside of himself.[7] If we interpret this generalization with Stevens' comments, then the reality outside himself which the courtly lyrist reflects is the ritual of courtly living, which Stevens characterizes as gamesmanship. It is the courtier's business to please, and since all the world loves a lover, the courtier should set about falling in love. Or, as the next best thing, if he is not in love, he must act the lover.

> The "game of love" [says Stevens] was a way of behaving in a way befitting your own and others' dignity, and it inculcated not so much an attitude to others as a *manner* towards them ... Despite his vaunted humility towards his lady, the courtly lover is full of self-respect; he is a model of good breeding, and knows it.

Under such circumstances what happens to personal feeling and emotion? Must we reduce the poets' "clear focus on real women," that various critics have admired, to astigmatism or myopia?

To dismiss the problem by saying that the mediaeval love lyric simply does not reveal subjective feeling does not face the complexities of the situation. Some of the trouvères tell us that their public wanted to know in effect if they were sincere in their singing;[8] moreover the Provençal biographies of the troubadours generally take the lyrics at face value. The touching biography of Jaufré Rudel is a case in point; lacking details, the author takes Jaufré at his word about his far-away love, has him fall in love with the Countess of Tripoli (whom he has never seen), become a Crusader in order to see her, fall sick on board the ship, arrive in Tripoli almost dead, and die in his lady's arms. The biographer has mistaken, in Stevens' valuable distinction, the poet acting as lover for an actual lover posing as poet.[9] Jaufré's emphasis upon his far-away love evidently proved sincere enough to his later mediaeval audience, if not to a modern audience accustomed to looking for the man *behind* the mask. The question of subjectivity, then, is not a modern phenomenon; Bernart de Ventadorn, in a familiar passage, has his say on the subject:

> Chantars no pot gaire valer,
> si d'ins dal cor no mou lo chans;
> ni chans no pot dal cor mover,
> so no i es fin' amors coraus.[1]

> There's not much use singing
> if the song doesn't come from the heart;

7. *A Preface to Chaucer* (Princeton, 1962), p. 15. Stevens' comments are on pp. 151, 156, 194.
8. Dragonetti prints examples on pp. 22–23.
9. His three distinctions are Lover speaking as Lover, Lover posing as Poet, Poet dramatizing himself as Lover (pp. 206–207).
1. *The Songs of Bernart de Ventadorn*, ed. Stephen G. Nichols et al., (Chapel Hill, 1965), No. 15.

and the song can't come from the heart
if no true love is there.

The trouvères, moreover, are anxious to distinguish themselves as
true lovers from false, inconstant lovers who are merely *bel parlers*.[2]
Thus, to emphasize the subjective element is to misunderstand the
nature of the mediaeval love lyric, but to minimize it out of existence is equally short-sighted.

What separates the modern reader from the mediaeval love lyric
is above all his sense of reality. The ritual of courtly existence
means little or nothing to him; he seeks a different kind of reality.
Although familiar enough with unrequited love and the cult of the
Beautiful Woman, the modern reader finds it difficult to respond to
a situation in which the lover goes on loving despite a lifetime of
scorn, or contenting himself with a glance, a token, or in rare
instances a kiss. In order to accept such lyrics the modern reader
demands some authenticating touch which will relieve the incredul-
ity and suggest the genuineness of the experience. But apart from
the issue of historical taste, the modern reader is inclined to forget
that most of the mediaeval love lyrics seem to have been actual
songs set to music. If we draw analogies to our own popular songs,
how realistic do we find the experiences in country music, rock-n-
roll, or even in the so-called "torch" song? The conviction comes
rather from the performance, and indeed performers are often
judged on the degree of conviction with which they perform. Also,
a sophisticated audience detects stylistic differences among performers, which can lead both to a sense of individuality and to a "sincerity" more or less by comparison.

We have no reason to assume matters differed greatly in the
Middle Ages; some means were familiar, others not. The individuality gained from performance might have been achieved by the use
of a different melody for a particular text;[3] by a simple instrumental
counterpointing of the melody rather than a mere doubling of it; by
a difference in interpretation: "it has frequently been pointed out
that singers, in all countries and at all periods of history, have
reserved the right to interpret music in their own way, slowing
down a little here to swell out the tone on a high note, or quicken-
ing up to heighten the effect of a decorative figure or run. There is
indeed no proof that *rubato*, the playing with time-values so often
attributed exclusively to romantic composers and executants, was

2. Dragonetti, pp. 26–28.
3. "The music . . . was used time and
time again for different texts, and some
melodies can be traced across Europe
through three or even four centuries.
Similarly, one and the same text is often
given different melodies, so it becomes
difficult at times to discover who is the
real author and composer"; Denis Stevens, "Ars Antiqua," in *The Pelican*

History of Music, ed. Denis Stevens and
Alec Robertson, I (Baltimore, 1960),
253. Moreover, Gustave Reese points out
that the slightest variation in a melody
was enough to make a troubadour's song
his own; *Music in the Middle Ages*
(New York, 1940), p. 214. On instrumental accompaniment, see Denis Stevens, p. 251. The quotation on singers'
interpretation is from *ibid.*, pp. 255–256.

not known and practiced in the Middle-Ages." But these are stylistic points, external to the experience presented by the actual text.

When we look at the emotion purportedly being experienced by the speaker in today's popular song, we can better appreciate the role of the cliché in the mediaeval love lyric. The popular song writer constructs his text on clichés, and what separates one lyric from another is the choice, combination, arrangement, and expression of these clichés. The recognition of the familiar creates a peculiar aesthetic pleasure, whether the familiar is an idea, a stereotyped expression, or a June/moon rime. Indeed there is an expectation of the familiar, and when the expectation is gratified, it creates a particularly pleasing response. Similarly, in the Middle Ages the cliché played a structural and dynamic role in the lyric, as Dragonetti insists (p. 541); it is, he says, "source d'émotions et des pensées" which "résume et stylise des siècles de vie spirituelle; il est abstraction en ce sens qu'il retient virtuellement la part durable d'une culture, et c'est par quoi il est appel, relai et source des valeurs d'une tradition"[4] (pp. 543–544). The uniqueness of the beloved is one such cliché with structural and dynamic possibilities. Since the lady is unique, her lover undergoes unique sensations of joy, despair, or whatever, which in turn reinforces the often incidental illusion of an actual experience. Paradoxically, moreover—and we are inclined to overlook this—the presentation of the beloved in terms of the ideal might well have been a means of individuation. Leo Spitzer has spoken of the lady's uniqueness "consisting in the potentiated generic,"[5] i.e., the ideal has been embodied in one woman, and this fact marks her as unique. Basically, this technique is also Chaucer's in his portrayal of his pilgrims: the best shipman, the best physician, "the beste beggere in his hous" all rise above the type to emerge as unique embodiments of all that is best—or worst—in the type. The lyrists do not always state the nonpareil, but at least they imply it. The technique seems quite similar to personification allegory.[6]

The suitability of such idealization of the lady is obvious; the feudal basis of the courtly code demands a distance between the lover and his beloved, and such rhetorical exaggeration measures this distance. The feudal basis also makes the emotive connotations more precise or at least more numerous, as does whatever suggestion the poet may make of a comparison to the Virgin Mary. These means of elevating the subject bear emotive and cultural values

4. Source of emotions and thoughts [which] sums up and conventionalizes centuries of spiritual life; it is abstraction in the sense that it virtually preserves the durable part of a culture, and thus it is the summons, transmission, and source of the values of a tradition [*Editors*].

5. "*Explication de texte* Applied to Three Great Middle English Poems," *Archivum Linguisticum*, III (1951), 1–22, reprinted in *Essays on English and American Literature*, ed. Anna Hatcher (Princeton, 1962), p. 198.
6. E.g., the concept of *Lady* Fortune [*Editors*].

beyond what E. R. Curtius calls the topos of outdoing.[7] These extensions of the ideal verify the speaker's feelings and objectify them; the lover consequently introduces not his own impressions but opinions shared by all who behold his lady. He deals, in short, with facts, not impressions. The ideal, then, functions as a kind of objective correlative, even when feeling seems singularly absent. Whatever emotion is lacking in a given poem seems at times to be automatically built into the ideal. The poet evokes the ideal and the emotion is created. On the other hand, we should not underestimate the emotive potential of the ideal in the Middle Ages.

But if the courtly love lyric deals in clichés, like its modern counterpart, then it, too, is to be distinguished from others of its type by the choice, combination, arrangement, and expression of these clichés. The individuality which arises on this level of form seems thus intended to suggest the individuality of the experience itself; that is, insofar as the question of the experience arises at all on this level. Here rather the element of gamesmanship or artifice enters strongly; as Dragonetti says, "tout l'art consiste à en varier la disposition par le renouvellement des combinaisons formelles" (p. 253)[8]. This suggests attention to minutiae, things the modern reader will tend to let slip by. For example, the lady's uniqueness is expressed in various ways. One way is to praise her by comparing her to other people or to natural objects. Long or short catalogues enter here, intended to give only the roughest indication of all the excellences which constitute the beloved. One English lyrist praises his lady by a selective head-to-foot description for three stanzas; then spends part of the next stanza cataloguing her virtues; then, by way of transition, remarks that there is neither viele nor fiddle that creates such mirth. He then compares his lady to gems and to flowers—a third variation on the theme of praise.[9] Another English lyrist uses comparisons as his principal structural device: he describes his beloved in succeeding stanzas as the choicest of gems, of flowers, of birds, of plants, and of human beings. Of the three gems which the first lyrist uses, only the coral overlaps with the ten gems of the second; the three plants of the former are all found in the eleven in the latter. Although both work in the tradition of heavy alliteration, their syntax and diction vary:

> heo is lilie of largesse,
> heo is paruenke of prouesse,
> heo is solsecle of suetnesse . . .

7. *European Literature and the Latin Middle Ages* (New York, 1953), pp. 162–165. Dragonetti discusses feudal and religious vocabulary, pp. 61–121. James J. Wilhelm places great emphasis on the religious vocabulary and suggests replacing the term "courtly love poetry" with "Christian secular poetry," a phrase he finds "both more descriptive and less literal"; *The Cruellest Month* (New Haven, 1965), p. 224.

8. All art consists in varying the arrangement through the renewal of formal combinations [*Editors*].

9. G. L. Brook, ed., *The Harley Lyrics* (Manchester, 1956), No. 14. The next poem referred to is No. 3.

Hire rode is ase rose þat red is on rys;
wiþ lilye-white leres lossum he is;
þe primerole he passeþ, þe peruenke of pris . . .

And, of course, their prosody differs. Conceivably, a third poet could have achieved a sense of individuality by composing two stanzas, the first comparing his lady to flowers and birds, the second to gems and plants, and by alternating the syntactic patterns of the two lyrics just quoted. If the use of this cliché demonstrates the lady's uniqueness, that uniqueness lies in its stylistic demonstration, so that once again the emphasis falls more on the poem as poem rather than as experience.

To analyze these lyrics in terms of their clichés is to see them as songs; the modern reader, however, wants to evaluate the lyrics as poems apart from their being words set to music—a legitimate approach, to be sure—and he is therefore inclined to evaluate the clichés as realistic or not, depending largely upon modern criteria, and in general to evaluate the poem as it creates the illusion of actual experience. Thus, those lyrics in which the lady is less a paragon than a creature of flesh and blood, and those in which the lover is concerned less with service than with physical desire are more "realistic" and therefore "better" poems, unless the poet is able to surmont his handicap and suggest a personal experience. The difference lies, in effect, in the emphasis upon poetic externals. One type of lyric is extremely form-conscious, the other suggests the immediacy of the emotion, and may therefore be called dramatic.

Two different handlings of the cliché of the seasonal opening will clarify the distinction. One is Arnaut Daniel's "L'aura amara," but the time of year is winter, not spring; as Maurice Valency points out, "The song itself seems to shiver in the bitter wind which its sharp sounds evoke, and the sense stutters forth spasmodically, as if forced out between the chattering teeth of the poet."[1] The stanza form is so complex, however, that constant repetition draws attention to it, and the mood cannot be sustained over seven such stanzas. Instead of creating the illusion of an actual experience, the poem instead centers its originality in the stanza form. Instead of individualizing the speaker by his experience, the poem individualizes the poet by his formal tour de force. On the other hand, an anonymous English poem, "Lenten ys come wiþ loue to toune," treats the usual *reverdie* with a deft touch of humor.

* * *

Formally, the whole poem consists of variations upon the theme announced in the first three lines. Usually, the poet names specific flowers and plants (daisy, woodruff, rose, lily, fennel, wild thyme);

1. *In Praise of Love* (New York, 1965), p. 123. He comments further (p. 125) on the distortion of speech patterns; this is not unusual in such lyrics where the meaning created by the sound supersedes logical or grammatical meaning. . . .

once he refers to the leaves in the wood. Some specific animals are mentioned (nightingale, threstlecock, drake, worm), but the poet usually uses a more generic term ("fowl," "briddes," "miles," "deores"). Two references are made to the moon, one to the sun, and one to the dew, all associated with the time of year. This hodge-podge of items suggests both the randomness of the speaker's gaze (or recollection) and a certain lack of emotional control. Only after twenty-two lines does the speaker mention the human reaction to spring, and his own personal application is almost incidental, liable to get lost in the catalogue, which he resumes in the final stanza. The transition to his own feelings is thus gradual. In lines 31–32 he observes that worms woo underground and women grow exceedingly proud, a significant juxtaposition which recalls the cliché of the decay of the human body and suggests a *carpe diem* theme. Then the whole point of the lyric emerges openly in the last three lines: if he can't get what he wants from one particular woman, the speaker will flee to the woods. A strong wave of pent-up feeling thus finally breaks, revealing what we might well call a typical adolescent petulance. Consequently a sharply-etched personality emerges as a result of the presentation of the emotion, and the modern reader appreciates this "dramatic" quality. The poem's formal elements are handled well enough, but here is no technician like Arnaut Daniel.

But the personality which emerges from the mediaeval lyric does not always create a sense of individuality in the sense a modern reader anticipates. One of the most important techniques in the Provençal lyrics, marking them off from their Middle English counterparts, is the identity of the speaker. The speaker is, in many instances, clearly a poet-lover. Moreover, the poet is at times explicitly the poet who composed the poem: "Cercamons ditz . . ." "Ieu sui Arnautz qu'amas l'aura," "Bernartz de Ventadorn l'enten." The relationship between the two identities of the speaker often grows complex; as lover he loves so intensely that his emotion guarantees the quality of the poem. The poem thus becomes the measure of his love, the quality of the poem reflects the degree of his love, and his insistence on his role as poet marks his individuality as lover. Bernart de Ventadorn says that there is not much use singing if the song does not come from the heart; his song does and is therefore superior. Indeed, Bernart gives an additional reason for the perfection of his verse:

> Lo vers es fis a naturaus
> e bos celui qui be l'enten;
> e melher es, qui-l joi aten.
>
> The verse is perfect and well-formed,
> and good to the one who understands it well;

and it is better to the one who hopes for joy
from it.

The lady thus is not only the source of the poem but its ultimate
critic as well; on its perfection depends her reaction and the lover's
reward. Consequently, there is more emphasis upon the poem than
upon the experience. The Provençal troubadour did not try to present a novel experience but to present his experience to his courtly
audience in recognizable and acceptable terms. Thus he reflected
the code of social behavior bequeathed by courtly love and his own
superlative worth therein. The emphasis falls on the poet rather
than on the lover, since the poem bears in itself the subjectivity, the
individuality of the lyric experience. A complex interrelationship, to
be sure, but complicated further by the fact that the poem also may
be the messenger by which the lover makes known his love to his
lady.[2]

All this, of course, was part of the game which the troubadour
played, and it was not so important whether he won or lost, but
how he played it. This mixture of specific poet and lover sometimes
anticipates Dante the Poet-Lover in *La Vita nuova* and the Poet-
Pilgrim in the *Commedia,* and Chaucer the Poet-Pilgrim in the
Canterbury Tales. Dante, in fact, in the earlier work heightens his
fiction, and gives the whole work an air of authenticity, a dramatic
quality, which the lyrics themselves, taken out of context, do not
possess. What he does is in one sense merely to substitute a more
elaborate written context for the live context of the troubadour per-
formances. But in another sense he explores the possibilities inherent in the form of elaborating upon the identity of the poet, of creating a greater dramatic intensity, of suggesting more of a personal
experience. The romanesque emphasis upon form does not yield to
a gothic humanism in a nineteenth-century sense, but the romanesque form does yield to a gothic exploitation of the humanizing
possibilities within that form. Here is the area where mediaeval and
modern tastes can coincide. But the older emphasis upon form is
still there; here is an example of the older tradition from Raimbaut
d'Aurenga:

Escotatz, mas no sai que·s es,
Senhor, so que vuelh comensar;
Vers, estribotz ni serventes
Non es, ni nom no·l sai trobar,
Ni gres no sai co·l me fezes,
S'aital no·l podi acabar,
    que hom mais no vis fach aital per home ni per femna en est
    segle, ni en l'autre qu'es passatz.

---

2. The later ME envoys beginning "Go, little bill" have ample precedent in troubadour verse.

Si tot m'o tenetz a foles,
Per tan no·m poiria laissar
Que ieu mon talan non disses;
No m'en poiria hom castiar;
Tot quant er no pretz un poges
Mas so qu'ades vei et esguar.

    E dir-vos-ai per que: quar s'ieu vos o avia mogut e no-us a trazia a cap, tenriatz m'en per folh: quar mais amaria seis deniers en mon punh que mil soltz al cel.

Ja no·m tema ren far que·m pes
Mos amicx, aquo·l vuelh preguar,
S'als ops no·m vol valer manes,
Pus m'o profer ab lonc tarzar.
Pus leu que selh que m'a conques
No·m pot nulh autre gualiar.

    Tot aisso dic per una dona que·m fai languir ab belhas paraulas et ab loncx respiegz, no sai per que. Pot mi bon esser, senhor?

Que ben a passat quatre mes,
Oc, e mais de mil ans, so·m par,
Que m'a autreiat e promes
Que·m dara so que m'es pus car.
Domna, pus mon cor tenetz pres,
Adoussatz mi ab dous l'amar.

    Dieus, aiuda, *in nomine Patris et Filii et Spiritus sancti!* Dieus, aisso que sera?

Qu'ieu sui per vos guais, d'ira ples,
Iratz, jauzens mi faitz trobar;
E sui m'en partitz de tals tres
Qu'el mon non a, mas vos, lur par;
E sui folhs chantaire cortes
Tan qu'om m'en apela joglar.

    Domna, far ne podetz a vostra guiza, quo fetz n' Aima de l'espatla, que l'estuget lai on li plac.

Er fenisc mon non-sai-que·s-es,
Qu'aissi l'ai volgut bateiar;
Pus mais d'aital non auzi ges,
Be·l dey enaissi apellar;
E diga·l, quan l'aura apres,
Qui que s'en vuelha azautar;

    e si hom li demanda qui l'a fach, pot dire que cel que sap ben far tota fazenda, quan se vol.

    Listen, lords, but I don't know what it is that I've begun; it's not a *vers*, an *estribot*, or a *sirventes*; I don't know how to find a name for it, nor do I know what to do with it, and I can't finish it, for no one has ever seen such a thing made by man or woman in this century or in the preceding one.

Even though you consider me mad, I can't stop without telling you about my desire; nor can anyone make me stop; all that isn't worth a coin, except what I immediately see and behold. And I'll tell you why: because if I've begun a song for you and haven't finished it, you'd think me mad. I much prefer six deniers in my fist than a thousand sous in the sky.

Don't be afraid to do anything that distresses me, my friend, this I pray you; and if you're in need and don't want to help me right now, then offer it to me later since no one can deceive me more than she who has conquered me. I say this because of a lady who has made me languish with beautiful words and long delays, I don't know why. Can this be good for me, sirs?

A good four months has passed, yes, and it's seemed to me more than a thousand years since she assured and promised that she would give me what is dearest to me. Lady, since you hold my heart completely, sweeten my bitterness with sweetness. Help, O God, *in nomine Patris et Filii et Spiritus sancti!* God, how will this turn out?

Because of you, I, merry, am full of care; sad, to compose makes me rejoice; and I am separated from three such that the world doesn't have—except you—their equal; and I am made to sing courteously, so much that men call me a *jongleur* for it. Lady, you can do as you like, as Aima did with the shoulder, which she put where it pleased her.

Now my I-don't-know-what-it-is has ended, as I baptize it; since its like has never been heard, I might well give it such a name; and let me say to him who hears it later, whoever finds pleasure in it: if anyone asks him who made it, he can say that it was one who can do all things well, when he wants to.

The gamesmanship is immediately apparent: the sophisticated stanza form reinforces the speaker's role as poet at the same time that it reflects his role as lover. The erratic course of the poem with its stanzas falling apart after a sestet riming *ababab* throughout mirrors the lover's erotic course. The lover does not know where his love is going any more than the poet can predict the course of his poem. The poem's inconclusive but hopeful ending sums up the lover's attitude as well, and the uniqueness of his song argues for the uniqueness of his love and his beloved. But despite the seeming nonchalance of the stanzaic sequence, the poet has carefully if loosely structured his work so that stanza five climaxes three related motifs: the poet-lover relationship, the poetic worthlessness-beloved's worth—therefore poem's worth, and the poet's madness.

The first motif, the poet-lover relationship, has two principal strands: the poem's uniqueness and the poet's reward. The emphasis upon uniqueness prepares for the poet's concern about payment for his song but only incidental concern from his immediate audience. If they hesitate to give him anything, this is only the same treatment to which he has been subjected in the payment he really craves (lines 20–21 vs. 22–23). His willingness to accept six deniers (line 16) is not a not-so-subtle hint for his lady. But although unique, his song is shapeless and therefore worthless, and the second major motif appears. If worthless because it seems to lack direction, the song is even more so by comparison with the worth of his lady, which he sees and beholds (lines 13–14). Paradoxically, his lady does give it value because of her inspiration; in fact, she is so much responsible for the poem that the poet is but a jongleur, not a troubadour at all (line 39, contrasting with *trobar*, lines 4 and 35). The poet's love has been vaguely hinted at in stanza two, then developed more fully but gradually until all of stanza five is devoted to it. This stanza therefore clarifies the hints the poet has given about his hopes for payment. Finally, it ties in the third motif, that of madness. The poet has spoken of his fear of being thought mad (lines 9, 16), but this poetic madness mirrors his foolishness in loving a certain lady. He himself questions his wisdom in line 25, then develops this thought in the following lines. The height of his poetic folly is the measure of his love-madness: he has been forced to the role of jongleur (line 39).

The tone of resigned helplessness which begins the final stanza now is given a kind of resolution. The poetic helplessness is at any rate a sign of careful poetic training in that the poet is able to compose at least six stanzas such as have never been seen before, and this is in itself no small accomplishment. It has been possible, of course, also because of his lady's inspiration, so that its value is doubled. The poet has not yet been paid, and his reference to his ability to perform all sorts of enterprises well (line 49) is a hopeful, if not subtle, hint to the lady about his reward, suggesting the same implications as lines 40–41. A cure for his madness is his hinted payment. The poem thus ends, as the poet had indicated it would in line 11, once he has spoken of his desire, and it concludes as affirmation of the poet's ability and insistence on the poem as objective correlative to the lover's emotions. The poem is unique; the poet emerges as an emphatically delineated character, with a suggestion of individuality in the cryptic lines 36–37; but there isn't much "sincerity." The mediaeval audience probably never even noticed.

This high degree of formalism which characterizes the mediaeval love lyrics as a whole and marks them as more or less objective, also paradoxically enables the poets to achieve effects which yield a sense of actuality. I have already commented on the potentiality for the development of the narrator's character. The rhetorical tradition also provides the poet with emotive possibilities, as Dragonetti has so excellently demonstrated (*passim*); the use of *exclamatio, interrogatio, ratiocinatio, addubitatio* can illumine the lover's emotional state by his sighs, his questioning of Love's treatment of him, his internal debate, his not knowing what to say. The lover's timidity is a commonplace; in his lady's presence he is embarrassed and fearful, and has "la langue endormie" (Dragonetti, p. 26). His mood changes from fearfulness to abjection to hope to despair; he is torn between his physical desire and his lady's displeasure. Bernart de Ventadorn is for modern readers the most satisfactory of the troubadours because he does manipulate these rhetorical devices and clichés so convincingly:

> Amors, e qu·us es vejaire?
> Trobatz mais fol mas can me?
> Cuidatz vos qu'eu si' amaire
> e que ja no trop merce?
> Que que·m comandetz a faire,
> farai o c'aissi·s cove,
> mas vos non estai ges be
> que·m fassatz tostems mal traire.

> Love, what do you think?
> Have you ever found a greater fool than I?
> Do you think I should be a lover
> even though I find no favor?
> Whatever you command me to do,
> I'll do, as is fitting,
> but it's not good of you
> to treat me badly all the time.

The complaining tone, the touch of humorous self-pity suggest a definite characterization. Here is a man torn between the ritualistic externals of the wooing procedure and the impatience which his genuine love dictates.

> Grans enois es e grans nauza
> tot jorn de merce clamar,
> mas l'amor qu'es en me clauza
> no posc cobrir ni celar.

> It's a great nuisance and a great bother
> every day to be crying for mercy,
> but the love which is locked up in me
> I can't cover up nor hide.

The shift in tone and emotions strikes a psychologically valid note for someone in love, but the regularity of the stanza form serves as a check on emotional display. Occasionally, as in "Lancan vei folha," the underlying emotion causes the thoughts to tumble too rapidly together for strict logical connections. We also see a kind of false opening here, an attempt to bring the subject into proper focus. The speaker is too agitated to accept the seasonal objective correlative—"don't think that *I* want to see either flower or leaf, for the one I want behaves most arrogantly toward me."

The mediaeval poet thus had at his disposal the means by which he could sound as though he meant what he said—in more than one sense. For sometimes the sound is what creates the impression of earnestness: the rhythm, rime, syntax, alliteration, etc. It is the sound which gives vitality to the cliché. Take the following English lyric for an example:

> Foweles in þe frith,
> þe fisses in þe flod,
> And I mon waxe wod.
> Mulch sorw I walke with
> for beste of bon and blod.[3]

> Birds in the trees,
> Fishes in the sea,
> And I must grow crazy.
> Much sorrow I walk with
> for best of bone and blood.

One likely interpretation of this rather cryptic little poem is that it exhibits the clichés of courtly love, it is filled with clichés of diction, yet it succeeds admirably in depicting the speaker's sense of isolation, of distance between himself and his beloved (best of bone and blood).[4] The rime scheme (*abbab*) reflects the division in thought, unifying two related emotions. The first part depicts the isolation of man on earth from the birds in the air and the fishes in the sea, yet the *b* rime groups the earth with the sea, suggesting it is just as natural for man to become mad, and thus counterpointing the emotional contrast. The second part, lines 4–5, depicts the isolation of the speaker from his beloved, a heightened varying of the alienation in the first three lines. The rime scheme (*ab*) also varies the pattern of the first three lines (*abb*), and underscores the analogy in the two parts. As man stands aloof in the first part from the rest of nature, so the beloved in the second half is isolated from the lover. The emotional impact is underscored by alliteration. The alienation in line 3 is heightened by the fact that lines 1 and 2 alliterate with one another, but not with line 3. Similarly, lines 3–4

3. Carleton Brown, ed., *English Lyrics of the XIIIth Century* (Oxford, 1932), No. 8.
4. Edmund Reiss admits the possibility of a complaint in the courtly love tradition, but prefers to read it as a religious poem, suggesting that it paraphrases Matt. viii:20, "Foxes have their holes, the birds their roosts," etc., "A Critical Approach to the Middle English Lyric," *CE*, XXVII (1966), 376–377.

with the "w" alliteration unite the speaker's feelings against the indifference of the beloved in line 5. This last line stands apart from the rest of the poem since it does not alliterate with any preceding line, just as the beloved stands aloof. The use of alliteration and of other devices of sound gives us the impression that the speaker is actually experiencing the emotion of which he speaks. The tightness and compactness of the form contributes a suggestion of tightly-controlled, half-coherent phrases, which betray a smoldering emotion behind the understatement.

The whole question of subjective feeling and emotion in the Provençal and Middle English love lyrics is thus a complex one. In a very real sense, as Zumthor has demonstrated, it is irrelevant to the whole concept of the troubadour poem. But even in the Middle Ages, with the concern of biographical information in the late thirteenth century and the consequent *razos* and *vidas*, the question of "sincerity" arises. John Stevens has made a valuable distinction, pointing out that "concern with emotional *effects* is a quite separate thing from concern with emotional *expression*" (p. 65). In those lyrics where the emotional effects are convincing enough, the historical critic can have his gamesmanship and the modern reader his sincerity. The other lyrics present difficulties. But even the insipid, flat, stereotyped pieces may have had more of a subjective element for their mediaeval audience than we can imagine today, because the audience knew the poet and could measure what he said with what they knew of his actual love affairs and/or his poetic techniques; or because they did not know him and could accept a stranger's songs as personal experience; or because they were so thoroughly versed in the conventions that they could recognize the novelty which a particular lyric offered, thereby suggesting a sense of individuality; or because of the "social context"—as John Stevens suggests, "The spice and piquancy of debate, the saucy-solemn atmosphere of 'problems of love' may have given the love-lyric the individuality it so conspicuously lacks when regarded as 'words on the page' " (p. 208); or finally, because the performer could successfully convince the audience of the sincerity of his sentiments by his performance. But in addition to the sincere and the insipid, there is a large third group, the *jeux*, which emphasizes the cleverness, wit, grace, and elegance of the poet. The individuality of the emotional experience relies solely on the individuality of the style.

Both the Provençal and the Middle English love lyrics provide abundant examples of all three categories. If we are to distinguish the two provenances briefly, we can observe that the earlier English lyrics tend to be less courtly, less elegant than the Provençal; the speaker creates more of an impression of being a lover-poet than a poet-lover; and the emphasis consequently is in general on more of

a "no-nonsense" approach.[5] The later English poems, in the fifteenth and sixteenth centuries, tend toward an amateur poetic or at
any rate toward an extreme self-consciousness which does not come
off with anything near the *brio* of the Provençal.[6] The more professional poets, Chaucer and Charles d'Orleans, for instance, possess a
gracefulness and especially a gentleness rather than the bravado of
many of the Provençal writers. Whether dealing with an English or
a Provençal lyric, however, the modern reader must be aware of the
gamesmanship involved, of the courtly ritual and the "good life"
which these lyrics reflect. The historical critic is there to remind
him, as Chaucer does in another context, "And eek men shal nat
maken ernest of game." If he tries to, he does so at his own risk.

RAYMOND OLIVER

The Three Levels of Style†

The style of a poem is analogous to the atmosphere of a place, if
we remember that poems are more intentional than places. If style
is "a characteristic manner of expression," then the prevailing style
of Middle English poetry is impersonal, down-to-earth, general, and
practical. That is, style can be described in nearly the same terms I
have already used to describe words and metaphor. It varies mainly
with the diction, which varies according to the poet's intention. But
the level of style should be discussed in its own right because it
colors whole poems, not just words or phrases, and because it can be
analyzed into three fairly distinct categories—low, middle, and high
—each with distinct uses. These three levels, however different they
may be in their origins and effects, are all more or less popular,
never esoteric; they are *relatively* low, middle, and high.

Because nearly all the short poems are written in a single poetic
language, whose "grammar" I am describing in this study, the dif-

5. Cf. Brian Stone, *Medieval English Verse* (Baltimore, 1964), p. 178: "The poet celebrates her beauty in frankly sensual terms, and woos her directly, with sharp, urgent protestation and no circumlocution: possession of her body is the aim."
6. The vehicle in English is often not the poem as poem, but poem as letter: see, e.g., Rossell Hope Robbins, *Secular Lyrics of the XIVth and XVth Centuries*, 2nd ed. (Oxford, 1955), Nos. 129, 130, 189, 190. Wilhelm observes that "The notion of the lover as letter-writer, and the love song as letter, is a continuing and much ignored factor in Provençal verse" (p. 209). Robbins, No. 177

asks for correction from the lady and contains a variation of the humility formula: the speaker lists (correctly) his inabilities in "conning and experience, / Maner of enditing, reason, and eloquence"—a sentiment arising more from the trouvère tradition of the gaucherie of the lover's language than in sympathy with the characteristic Provençal insistence upon the perfection of the verse.
† From Raymond Oliver, *Poems Without Names: The English Lyric 1200–1500* (Berkeley and Los Angeles: University of California Press, 1970), pp. 74–85. Reprinted by permission of the Regents of the University of California.

ferences among levels of style are essentially semantic. I do not find it useful to speak as if style and meaning were separate entities, combined in particular poems with varying degrees of skill. The poet finds his meaning by finding his style, his words, which, after all, comprise his meaning. I will use only one ultimate term, "total meaning," which includes tone, diction, and the rest, rather than two terms such as "meaning" and "style." In this way I can avoid speaking as if one style were "better suited" to expressing idealistic attitudes, and another style "better suited" to a materialistic view of reality. The style *is* the attitude, just as it *is* the denotative meaning and everything else one can understand from the words. To say otherwise is to say that "fresh roses" is a good phrase for dealing with pleasant experience, whereas "rotting corpses" is better suited to conveying unpleasant experience. It is much simpler to say that the two phrases mean different things.

I shall define the three levels of medieval style, then, as a function of verbal meaning, and try to keep them distinct from the three classical levels of style. But although there is not, to my knowledge, any documented connection between the anonymous Middle English poems and the earlier doctrine of the three styles, medieval poets did have an atrophied classical tradition at their disposal. A few historical remarks are therefore in order.

Among the classical sources for medieval rhetoric, the *Ad Herennium* has an especially compact definition of the three styles:

> There are, then, three kinds of style, called types, to which discourse, if faultless, confines itself: the first we call the Grand; the second, the Middle; the third, the Simple. The Grand type consists of a smooth and ornate arrangement of impressive words. The Middle type consists of words of a lower, yet not of the lowest and most colloquial, class of words. The Simple type is brought down even to the most current idiom of standard speech.[1]

The corresponding passage from Geoffroi de Vinsauf's *Documentum de Arte Versificandi* reads:

> There are, then, three styles: low, middle, grand. And the styles are given these names according to the persons or things we are talking about. For when we talk about persons or things of general importance, then the style is grand; about low subjects, it is low; about middling subjects, it is middle. Virgil makes use of each style: low in the *Bucolics*, middle in the *Georgics*, grand in the *Aeneid*.[2]

The classical definition is wholly verbal; it deals with the choice and

1. Harry Caplan, trans., *Rhetorica Ad Herennium* (Cambridge, Mass., 1954), pp. 252–253.

2. Edmond Faral, *Les Arts Poétiques du XIIe et du XIIIe Siècle* (Paris, 1958), p. 312.

arrangement of words. The medieval definition is social, in a rather simpleminded way: we use fine language on fine subjects. This confirms the judgment of Rossell Hope Robbins that "the poets who wrote at the request of some nobleman introduced a Latinized or 'aureate' vocabulary, in an effort to create a 'noble' style for their 'noble' readers" (apropos of the Aureate Collections, a group of very expensive manuscripts). When the English poets were conscious of style at all, they must have fit it into some such framework of social decorum. The grandest poems were for God and His Mother—or the poet's mistress—and the lowest were for man the sinner, born and dead in corruption.

Low Style

The terms *colloquial* and *familiar* are both misleading, and *plain* is too mild, so I have settled on the pejorative but accurate term *low* to describe the first level of style. To some extent, the level of a poem's style depends on its particular intention; but even so, there are broad similarities of style in *contemptus* poems, Christmas carols, drinking songs, love lyrics, and others. All are direct and physical, sometimes vulgar, obscene, or boorishly good-humored. The atmosphere of these poems has been well described by Charles Muscatine in connection with medieval bourgeois literature:

> The literature of the bourgeois tradition is "realistic" or "naturalistic," but it neither attempts nor achieves the reportorial detail of the modern fiction describable by these labels. ... [it has] a remarkable preoccupation with the animal facts of life. ... the literature at its best gives the impression of dealing with life directly, with something of life's natural shape and vitality.[3]

Among *contemptus* poems, the low style is usually colored by graphic images of death, decay, old age, and other tokens of mortality. These poems, in their themes, functions, and style, resemble Anglo-Saxon gnomes, riddles, and assorted types of practical verse. I do not know of any direct historical link, but the Middle English verses are similarly earthy and epigrammatic; there is certainly a generic if not a historical relationship. For example:

> Wrecche mon, wy artou proud,
> þat art of herth I-maked?
> hydyr ne browtestou no schroud,°   *clothing*
> but pore þou come & naked.
> Wen þi soule is faren° out,   *passed*
> þi body with erthe y-raked,
> þat body þat was so ronk° and loud,   *rank, haughty*
> Of alle-men is i-hated.

3. Charles Muscatine, *Chaucer and the French Tradition* (Berkeley, 1964), p. 59.

There are many other such epigrams which are knit together with tightly reasoned didacticism, especially from the earlier Middle English period; but longer poems set in a low style are also prominent, as are poems which include low elements or passages.

Certain drinking songs and Christmas carols have as much physicality as the *contemptus* poems, but its effect is quite different. In one Advent carol, for instance, the details are often unlovely, and the language is colloquial and comically abusive:

2

While thou [Advent] haste be within oure howse
We ete no puddynges ne no sowce,
But stynking fisshe not worthe a lowce;
    Farewele [fro vs both alle and sume.]

4

Thou has vs fedde with plaices thynne,
Nothing on them but bone and skynne;
Therefore oure loue thou shalt not wynne;
    Farewele [fro vs both alle and sume.]

5

With muskilles gaping afture the mone
Thou hast vs fedde at nyght and none,
But ones a wyke, and that to sone;
    Farewele [fro vs both alle and sume.]

6

Oure brede was browne, oure ale was thynne,
Oure brede was musty in the bynne,
Oure ale soure or° we did begynne;   *ere*
    Fare[wele fro vs both alle and sume.]

11

Thou maist not dwelle with none eastate;
Therfore with vs thou playest chekmate.
Go hens, or we will breke thy pate!
    Farewele [fro vs both alle and sume.]

Even the best kinds of food mentioned are not gourmet items, and the colorful turns of phrase in stanza 2, line 3, and stanza 11, line 3, are well suited to the familiar "thou." Poems of direct address especially lend themselves to this kind of phrasing:

I am so dry I can-not spek,
I am nygh choked with my mete—
I trow° þe butler be a-slepe.   *believe*
  with how, butler, how! bevis a towght!°   *drink to all (?)*
  ffill þe boll, butler, [& let þe cup rowght!°]   *move around*

Butler, butler, ffill þe boll,
or elles I beshrewe thy noll!°   *head*
I trow we must þe bell toll.
with how, butler, how! bevis a towght!
ffill þe boll, [butler, & let þe cup rowght!]

Iff þe butlers name be water,°   *(pun on "Walter")*
I wold he were a galow-claper,°   *gallows-bird*
but if° he bryng vs drynk þe raþer°   *unless; more quickly*
  with how, butler, how! bevis a towght!
  ffill [þe boll, butler, & let þe cup rowght]

In general, the tone of such poems is homely, boisterous, and crudely good-natured; and the themes are the simple joys of eating and drinking, with or without reference to religious occasions.

    There are a good many popular love songs in a similar vein; the famous "De Clerico et Puella" has low phrasing, especially in the "puella's" speeches ("be stille, þou fol, y calle þe riht; cost [canst] þou neuer blynne [stop]?"); and the satires lend themselves to reasonably coarse language:

        how! hey! it is non les,°   *no lie*
    I dar not seyȝ quan che seyȝt "pes!"

    ȝyng men, I warne ȝou euerychon:
    Elde wywys tak ȝe non;
    for I my-self haue on° at hom—   *one*
      I dar not seyn quan che seyȝt "pes!"

    Quan I cum fro þe plow at non,
    In a reuen° dych myn mete is don;   *riven, cracked*
    I dar not askyn our dame a spon—
      I dar not [seyn quan che seyȝt "pes!"]

    If I aske our dame bred,
    che takyt a staf & brekit myn hed,
    & doþ me rennyn vnder þe bed—
      I dar not [seyn quan che seyȝt "pes!"]

    If I aske our dame fleych,
    che brekit myn hed with a dych:
    "boy, þou art not worȝt a reych!"°   *rush*
      I dar [not seyn quan che seyȝt "pes!"]

    If I aske our dame chese,
    "boy," che seyȝt, al at ese,
    "þou art not worȝt half a pese."
      I dar not sey quan che seyȝt "pes!"

Whatever the specific purpose of the poem, the low style creates a sense of forthright intimacy, usually between speaker and audience.

High Style

At the opposite end of the scale is the high style, which is polite and ethereal where its opposite is gross. In the medieval high style, as it appears in romances, the "setting, landscape, and paraphernalia . . . tend to be exotic, superlative in quality and economy, and, in the best poetry, generating a meaning by their presence without regard for their practical utility in the action. . . ."[4] Two very important foreign influences, one French and the other Latin, have colored this level of style: courtly and aureate diction.

Courtly diction can easily be used in small quantities, like a powerful dye; for this reason it sometimes adds its upper-class tone to poems of a distinctly popular sort. In this case the effect is, of course, ironical. For instance, in the *contemptus* poems, courtly diction is usually a means of stressing the irony in the truth that all mortal beauty, all the *gloria mundi*, must perish—not only perish, but suffer the humiliation of rotting:

Wen þe turuf is þi tuur,°	*tower*
& þe put° is þi bour,	*pit*
þi wel° & þi wite° þrote	*skin; white*
ssulen wormes to note.	*shall be of use to worms*
Wat helpit þe þenne	
al þe worilde wnne?	*all the world's pleasure*

The courtly elements, clichés taken from the poetry of graceful compliment, are "þi tuur," "þi bour," and "þi wite þrote." By juxtaposing them with the turf, the pit, and the usual gnawing worms, the poet has created a piece of obvious but effective irony, rather like a simple woodcut. He has only to name a few key words, and the whole world of courtly love, with all its precarious grace, is present to the mind's eye—only to shrivel from contact with burrowing worms and cold earth.

The tone of this epigram is grimly material, even despairing. But the usual effect of courtly diction in the poems of tragedy is to cast a gentle, elegiac mood over the facts of death and decay, not falsifying the situation but making it poignant rather than grossly shocking. This effect is strengthened by the use of such commonplaces as the *ubi sunt*, descriptions of mortal beauty, or by rare dignity of phrasing. These techniques suggest the general character of a high-style poem: it is on the one hand formal and elegiac, gently mourning the glorious past, while on the other hand it describes present reality *sub specie aeternitatis*. In both cases only beautiful, idealized details are admitted. These graceful laments are very similar in mood to Anglo-Saxon poems such as "The Ruin" and "The Wanderer" and to the elegiac passages in *Beowulf*. The Middle English lyrics normally put more emphasis on the penitential theme, but

4. Muscatine, p. 17.

they have the same lofty sadness as the Anglo-Saxon, the same pal-
pable sense of worldly delights long past—goblets of wine or mead,
brave comrades, beautiful women, splendid dwelling places:

Where are the horses gone to? Where are the men gone? Where
are the givers of treasures gone?
Where are the places of feasting gone? Where are the joys of the
hall?
Alas, the bright cup! Alas, the armed warrior!
Alas, the prince's glory! How that time has passed,
Gone under night-helm, as though it had never been!
· ·
All is hardship in the kingdom of the earth;
the workings of fate change this world under heaven.
Here goods are only lent us, here friends are only lent,
here men are only lent, here women are only lent us;
all this earthen foundation becomes empty.

*Hwaer cwom mearg? Hwaer cwom mago? Hwaer cwom maþþum-
gyfa?
Hwaer cwom symbla gesetu? Hwaer sindon seledreamas?
Eala beorht buna! Eala byrnwiga!
Eala þeodnes þrym! Hu seo þrag gewat,
genap under nihthelm, swa heo no waere.*
· ·
*Eall is earfoðlic eorþan rice,
onwendeþ wyrda gesceaft weoruld under heofonum.
Her bið feoh laene, her bið freond laene,
her bið mon laene, her bið maeg laene,
eal þis eorþan gesteal idel weorþeð!*[5]

French diction is, however, most prominent in the courtly love
poems, which are normally written in a high style. One would
expect the English translator of Charles d'Orléans to use French
words,[6] especially in rhymes, where French suffixes are so convenient (gouernans, plesans, obeyssance, repentance, greuance); but
the same French diction may be found in anonymous courtly
poems:

O mestres, whye
Owtecaste am I
all vtterly
  from your pleasaunce?
Sythe ye & I

5. *The Exeter Book*, ed. George Philip
Krapp and Elliott Van Kirk Dobbie
New York, 1936), pp. 136–137.
6. Theo Stemmler has shown conclu-
sively that Charles D'Orléans could not
have written the English poems traditionally ascribed to him. Stemmler suggests
that the English lyrics, which are free
rather than literal translations from the
French of Charles D'Orléans, were written by a single anonymous poet, probably a minstrel, who had a good but incomplete knowledge of French. See "Zur
Verfasserfrage der Charles D'Orleans zu-
geschriebenen englischen Gedichte," *Anglia* 82 (1964): 458–473.

or° thys, truly,   ere
famyliarly
   haue had pastaunce.°   *diversion, pleasure*

And lovyngly
ye wolde aply
þy company
   to my comforte;
But now, truly,
vnlovyngly
ye do deny
   Me to resorte.°   *"resort" (to you)*

And me to see
as strange° ye be,   *aloof, distant*
as thowe þat ye
   shuld nowe deny,
or else possesse
þat nobylnes
To be dochess
   of grete Savoy.

But sythe þat ye
So strange wylbe
As toward me,
   & wyll not medyll,°   *"meddle," have to do (with me)*
I truste, percase,°   *perhaps*
to fynde some grace
to haue free chayse,°   *hunting (of other women)*
   & spede° as welle!   *succeed*

Although these words bring their own graceful, slightly exotic connotations into English verse, they are elegant mainly because they
refer to elegant things, just as French *dinner* is a more distinguished
meal than English *breakfast.*[7] But even at its most Gallic and
refined, the tone of Middle English poems never approaches the rare-
fied elegance of some modern verse:

> And light
> That fosters seraphim and is to them
> Coiffeur of haloes, fecund jeweller—
> Was the sun concoct for angels or for men?[8]

Aureate diction, which has been more thoroughly studied than
other aspects of Middle English diction,[9] also raises the style of

---

7. See Otto Jespersen, *Growth and
Structure of the English Language,* 9th
ed. (New York, 1956), p. 92. The light
rhythms also add to the elegance.
8. From "Evening Without Angels,"
Collected Poems of Wallace Stevens, p.
137.

9. See, for example, John C. Menden-
hall, *Aureate Terms: A Study in the Literary Diction of the Fifteenth Century*
(Lancaster, Pa., 1919), and John Allen
Conley, "Four Studies in Aureate
Terms," unpublished dissertation (Stan-
ford, 1956–1957).

many anonymous poems, especially devotional poems of praise. There are many examples of jewel-encrusted praise for the Virgin Mary, and indeed for earthly ladies, but one is enough:

Tota pulcra° and principall	*wholly beautiful*
of plente that is plenitude,	
Castell of clennes, I hyr call,	
that beldith° in beatitude,	*dwells*
beyng as clene as clere crystall	
Whose meuynge° is mansuetude.°	*prompting, desire; gentleness*
hyr sete° is sett sempeternall	*seat*
In excelsis so celsitude.	*In the highest loftiness (?)*

The heavy Latin nearly crowds the English out of the lines, as it actually does in macaronic poems. The Latin words in this Marian lyric have not been assimilated to English; one feels them to be foreign, strained, and very formal, like many of the classical Latin words imported into English during and since the Renaissance.[1] The result is a stilted high style, the very opposite of down-to-earth, idiomatic writing. This effect is greatly enhanced, once again, by the meanings of the words, which were felt to be inherently lofty and attractive: clennes, beatitude, clere crystall, mansuetude, in excelsis, celsitude.

A high style is naturally one of the requisites for religious poems of celebration. Christmas songs and carols are often filled with emblematic praise for Christ or the Virgin; they tend to have a strong theological emphasis; and at best they give a rare sense of wonder and sublimity. The burden of one famous carol has a sensuous-theological pun on "vertu" as "strength or fragrance" and "virtue" in the modern sense:

[T]her [is n]o rose of swych° vertu	*such*
As is the rose that bare Jhèsu.	

1

Ther is no ro[se of] swych vertu	
As is the rose that bar Jhesu;	
Alleluya.	

2

For in this rose conteynyd was	
Heuen and erthe in lytyl space,	
Res miranda.	*a marvelous thing*

3

Be° that rose we may weel see	*By*
That he is God in personys thre,	
Pari forma.	*in equal form*

The aungelys sungyn the sheperdes to:⁴
'Gloria in excelcis Deo.'   *"Glory to God in the highest"*
  Gaudeamus.   *Let us rejoice*

[L]eue we al this wordly merthe,⁵
And folwe we this joyful berthe;
  Transeamus.   *Let us pass on*

The same carol celebrates the mysteries of the Incarnation (stanza
2) and the Trinity (stanza 3). And the famous "I syng of a
myden" is not only built on a flawlessly apt metaphor—the coming
of the Holy Spirit to Mary is as imperceptible, refreshing, and total
as the spreading of dew upwards from grass to flower to branches—
it is also compounded of natural details that we still find lovely in
themselves:²

I syng of a myden þat is makeles,°   *peerless, mateless*
kyng of alle kynges to here sone che ches.° *chose*

he cam also stylle° þer his moder was   *as silently*
as dew in aprylle, þat fallyt on þe gras.

he cam also stylle to his moderes bowr
as dew in aprille, þat fallyt on þe flour.

he cam also stylle þer his moder lay
as dew in aprille, þat fallyt on þe spray.° *twigs*

moder & mayden was neuer non but che—
wel may swych a lady godes moder be.

These Christmas poems are no less "high" than the poems of praise
or *vanitas* that I have discussed; but their affective coloration is naturally quite different.

Middle Style

I have chosen the obvious term *middle* to cover the broad range
between low and high, the two extremes on the scale. This is simply
to say that not all the poems are clearly low or high. The middle
style, then, must be defined negatively: it excludes the distinctive
marks of the two more noticeable styles. It is not shockingly realistic, idiomatic, coarsely good-humored, aureate, Frenchified, or
gently elegiac. Poems in the middle style are usually made of
straightforward statements, often explanatory and rarely eccentric.

2. For an excellent discussion, see Leo
Spitzer, *"Explication de Texte* Applied
to Three Great Middle English Poems,"
Archivum Linguisticum 3 (1949): 152 ff.

Some typical examples are "Spende, and god schal sende", "By thys fyre I warme my handys", and this mild admonition:

Euen,° it es a richʒ ture°—	*Heaven; tower*
wele bies im þat itte may win—	*well be him that may win it*
of Mirthes ma° þan ert° may think	*more; art*
and þa iois sal neuer blin.°	*cease*
Sinful man, bot þu þe mend	*unless you mend yourself*
and for-sak þin wikkid sin,	
þu mon° singge hay, 'wailaway!'°	*may; (exclamation of despair)*
for comes þu neuer mare þar-I[nne].	

It should be apparent that the three levels of Middle English style are not the same as the three classical levels, in spite of strong resemblances. The medieval low style, like its classical counterpart, is often didactic and logical, and the high style, also like the classical, eschews coarseness; but the whole center of gravity in medieval short poems is lower than in classical Latin. Even the loftier poems are didactic and plain in comparison to the Vergilian grand style. And the classical styles are arranged on a scale of emotional intensity: the grand style was expected to be overpowering, the low style subdued, and the middle style merely pleasing. The Middle English low style, however, is often more emotionally powerful than its opposite, and the middle style is not conspicuously pleasing.

The level of style, as a function of words and syntax, necessarily reflects the public nature of Middle English short poems. One can see this reflection most distinctly in contrast with Latin and modern English poetry: the medieval poem does not achieve or attempt the grandness of classical Latin, as exemplified by much of the *Aeneid*, or the refined elegance and irony of such moderns as Stevens, Ransom, or Wilbur. Unlike these men, the medieval poet was not writing for a select audience with a high degree of literary culture. There were no Roman aristocrats or American literary critics in the Middle Ages. Medieval poets had to write in simple styles because their verses dealt with general themes and situations, and were meant to be understood at one hearing.

* * *

ROSEMARY WOOLF

Lyrics on Death†

The Middle English verses on death are structurally very similar to those on the Passion, though there is a considerable difference in the proportions between the various kinds. Inevitably those set in

† From Rosemary Woolf, *The English Religious Lyric in the Middle Ages* (Oxford: The Clarendon Press, 1968), pp. 67–85. Reprinted by permission of the publisher.

the third person are the commonest, though there are quite a number in which the meditator reflects on death or in which he is directly addressed by the dead. Whilst some of the lyrics are discursive, most of them also resemble the Passion lyric in that the aim is to fix the mind of the meditator on a meditative object, which here cannot be the moment of death itself, since this scarcely exists in time and may be imperceptible, but is rather some moment in the process of dying and burial: the appearance of the dying man, the poverty of the winding-sheet and the grave, or the repulsiveness of the decaying body. Just as meditation on the Passion stirred the response of love, so meditation on these aspects of death provoked the response of fear. However, that fear should be the emotion generated in these poems as a proper response to death requires some comment from both the literary and the doctrinal points of view, for neither the propriety of fear to a semi-lyric form nor the propriety of fear as a Christian response to death is self-evidently right.

It is obvious that one of the aims of the Passion lyric was to prevent the emotional distancing that is the normal effect of transforming experience into poetry. Careful craftsmanship in the choice of material and vocabulary makes an emotion seem more poignant but less immediate than in everyday life. The meditative structure of the Passion lyric and the direct language prevent a sense of poetical remoteness. Love, however, is usually a pleasurable emotion, whether poetically transmuted or not: the method of the Passion lyric therefore does not raise any particular aesthetic problem. But this is clearly not true of fear, for this emotion, unless given poetic transformation, is repellent to all, and people shun situations that will provoke it. The writer of the Passion lyric could therefore expect an imaginative co-operation from the reader, whilst the writer of the death lyric would have to expect an evasive, self-protecting response. The latter was compelled to get under his reader's guard by some kind of art, and so the death lyric from its very beginnings shows far more poise and contrivance than does the Passion lyric. This was perhaps made possible by the fact that it benefited from a living tradition behind it in Anglo-Saxon and to some extent in Anglo-Norman literature, but it was demanded by the subject-matter. The result is a paradox: in that the death lyric stirs an emotion which the audience does not want to feel, it could more properly be called sermon than poetry, but in that it uses the skill and artfulness of poetry to win its reluctant hearers' attention, it has in its technique more of the obvious qualities of poetry than has the early Passion lyric. Nowadays, when we are spectators rather than participants in the meditative scheme, or at most but half involved, there is an undoubted pleasure in seeing how a short verse will suddenly compel the imagination to focus on what it would normally exclude and forget.

The sermon affiliations of death lyrics are very clearly shown in the fact that, unlike most of the Passion lyrics, they are not complete experiences in themselves. In the kind of fear prompted by the death lyrics there is no value unless it issues in action: the foundation of the death lyric is the Biblical text, 'Memorare novissima tua et in eternum non peccabis'.[1] Whereas love, when it has issued in action, remains love, fear, when it has issued effectively in action, rightly ceases to be fear. Fear is thus a transitional emotion.

The homiletic nature of the death lyric is also seen in the limited range of emotion it expresses. The Passion lyric too is dominated by one simple but strong emotion that controls the whole. But this exclusiveness to the point of intense simplicity is agreeable and moving. It will not constrict the average sensibility, which is not likely to bring to the subject thought or emotion more subtle or profound than that contained within the lyric: on the contrary, without the guidance of the lyric, meditation on the Passion may well elude the average Christian altogether. In this there is, perhaps, no difference between the reactions of a medieval audience and those of a twentieth-century reader. The same, however, is not true of the death lyric, for death is a subject to which everybody brings a powerful and instinctive emotion, and nowadays also an imaginative awareness, partly formed by the classical reflections on death that became a part of English literature during the Renaissance.

The thought of transience and of its arch-example, death, can stimulate a variety of responses. Death can, for instance, be imagined, not as a state to be feared, but as a peaceful sleep, a longed-for harbour after the weariness and uncertainties of life. This classical idea, so familiar from Renaissance literature, is found only exceptionally in the English medieval lyric. and then only at the very end of the period. It occurs occasionally as a minor theme in late moralizing lyrics: in the lines 'Thynk þat ded is opynly / Ende off werdes wo,'[2] for instance, and, in the form of a classical metaphor, it is expressed in a single clumsy stanza, written by an early sixteenth-century hand in the margin of a thirteenth-century manuscript of Gregory's *Decretals*:

> Howe cometh al ye That ben y-brought
>   In bondes,—full of bitter besynesse
> of erthly luste, abydynge in your thought?
>   Here ys the reste of all your besynesse,
>   Here ys the porte of peese, and resstfulnese
> to them that stondeth In stormes of dys[e]se,
>   only refuge to wreches In dystrese,
> and all comforte of myschefe and mys[e]se.[3]

1. Ecclesiasticus vii. 40. 'Remember your end and you will never sin.'
2. 'Thynk man, qware-off thou art wrought', Brown xv, 163, p. 258.
3. Brown xv, 164.

Although this verse is included in Carleton Brown's fifteenth-century volume, in literary terms it belongs with medieval poetry for style rather than content: it shows a characteristic fault of medieval style at its worst, that is a fragmentary appearance resulting from the expression of a single, isolated thought in a verse lacking epigrammatic poise and polish. But in date and content this stanza belongs to the Renaissance. Such a view of death, which sees it as a release from care rather than as a gateway to heaven or hell, could obviously not form part of Christian didactic literature[4]—unless, of course, presented as a temptation, as is so skilfully and movingly done in Despair's temptation of the Red Cross Knight.

However, even if death is to be feared, it is still possible to consider it and to treat it in literature in a number of different ways. Of these one of the best known is the *Carpe diem* or *Carpe florem* theme, whether developed independently or subsumed into love poetry. In its first form it occurs in one of the most famous of medieval Latin secular songs, the *Gaudeamus*, with its exhortation to enjoyment combined with the traditional, didactic invitation to visit the tomb:

> Gaudeamus igitur,
> Juvenes dum sumus;
> Post molestam senectutem
> Nos habebit tumulus.
> Ubi sunt, qui ante nos
> In mundo vixere?
> Abeas ad tumulos,
> Si vis hos videre.
> Vita nostra brevis est
> Breve finietur:
> Venit mors velociter
> Neminem veretur.[5]

This attitude to death has its ancestry in debased Epicureanism, and there is a famous and early example of it in Petronius's description of the handing round of a silver skeleton at the gluttonous and grotesquely opulent Feast of Trimalchio in the *Satyricon*; there are

4. In the homiletic tradition this idea, if mentioned at all, was mentioned to be rebutted. In the *Summa praedicantium*, for instance, the story is told of the man who laughed at the approach of death, but out of pleasure at returning to his own country, not from relief at leaving a troublesome world.

5. F. P. Weber, *Aspects of Death and Correlated Aspects of Life* (London, 1922), pp. 54–55. 'Let us therefore make merry whilst we are young for after burdensome old age the grave will enclose us. Where are they who lived before us in the world? If you wish to see them go to the graveyard. Our life is short and will quickly be ended. Death comes speedily and shows respect to no man.' With this Weber compares 'Scribere proposui de contemptu mundano' (E. du Méril, *Poésies populaires latines du moyen âge* (Paris, 1847), 125–27), which contains the lines, 'Ubi sunt qui ante nos in hoc mundo fuere? / Venies ad tumulos, si eos vis videre'. The last two lines of the second stanza quoted above also occur in this poem.

traces of it too in the dancing skeletons engraved on some Roman gems and drinking cups. But a macabre reminder of death could in general hardly serve effectively as an injunction to renewed dissipation for those brought up in a deeply rooted Christian society. No doubt for all Christians, as for St. Paul, the Epicurean attitude of 'Let us eat and drink; for tomorrow we die' had lost its force in face of the Resurrection. The Latin song derives its power from the bravado with which it parodies and reverses the sentiments of Christian didacticism: it fits with the ironic tone of Goliardic poetry, and is far removed from the earnestness of the Middle English lyric.

The *Carpe diem* theme, however, was perhaps ignored in medieval love poetry, not primarily through didacticism, but through the influence of the courtly love code, by which such an unadorned and pungent argument would certainly have seemed indecorous. Though this theme was made use of by Petrarch, and later by Ronsard, it does not seem to occur in English literature until nearly the beginning of the seventeenth century: even Shakespeare, according to Leishman, does not employ it in his sonnets. It is interesting, incidentally, to notice that whilst Boccaccio's Criseida responds to Pandaro's *Carpe diem* advice with the words 'tu di' vero',[6] and then repeats it to herself in her first monologue,[7] Chaucer's Criseyde ignores Pandarus's warning of crow's feet beneath the eyes,[8] reproaching him instantly with lack of faith,[9] and, whilst she reasons prudently in her monologue, she does not consider this cogent but pagan argument. There could be no better evidence for the medieval attitude to the *Carpe diem* theme than Chaucer's very delicate modification of his source at this point. That writers of the Middle English lyric should have eschewed the *Carpe diem* theme is not surprising: it became in itself a convention, but was not one that could blend with theirs. But there are other attitudes to transience and death, which seem not so much arguments appropriate to an occasion as a common part of human feeling, and therefore their exclusion, at least nowadays, seems an unwelcome limitation of human sensibility. For instance, whilst sermons logically reiterate that to the Christian the transience of an object is a sign of its worthlessness, human feeling, and in particular the poetic imagination, finds that, on the contrary, transience confers on things a poignant beauty and vitality. This opposition between the homiletic and the poetic is, as we shall see, particularly clear in the treatment of the *Ubi sunt* form, of which the potential nostalgia in English is

6. Pt. II, stanza 55, *Tutte le opere di Giovanni Boccaccio*, ed. Vittore Branca, ii (1964), 56.
7. Pt. II, stanza 71, ed. cit. 61.
8. Bk. ii, 1. 403. *Works*, ed. Robinson,

473. Chaucer has amplified Pandarus's speech with the help of the *Ars amatoria*, iii. 59–80.
9. Bk. ii, 11. 408 ff. *Works*, p. 474.

nearly always constrained by the moralizing content of the context, provided nearly always by the Body and Soul debate or the visit to the tomb. There is, for instance, nothing in English comparable to Villon's well-known *Ballade des dames du temps jadis*. Indeed the only time that the evocativeness is allowed to break through fully is in the 'Love Ron':

> Hwer is paris and heleyne
> þat weren so bryht and feyre on bleo,
> Amadas and dideyne,
>   tristram, yseude and alle þeo,
> Ector, wiþ his scharpe meyne,
>   and cesar, riche of wordes feo.
> Heo beoþ i-glyden ut of þe reyne
>   so þe schef is of þe cleo.[1]

—and here the insidious nostalgia is exploited by the transference of the saddened longing from the world to Christ.

It is clear even from the briefest consideration of the potentialities of death as a subject for lyric poetry that the medieval treatment is so limited that it cramps the sensibility. Nevertheless, within its homiletic confines the English death lyric is extremely powerful; and, as with the meditative poetry on the Passion, it gains its strength from the force of the doctrinal and spiritual traditions lying behind it, and from the appropriateness to them of the literary potentialities of the period.

The exclusive and didactic emphasis upon the fear of death had its roots as firmly grounded in doctrine as had the loving meditation on the Passion. The value of fear had been recurrently analysed by the Fathers,[2] and their theory of it seems to have arisen from the need to synthesize two texts, Christ's own exhortation in Matthew x. 28, '. . . sed potius timete eum qui potest et animam et corpus perdere in gehennam',[3] and the statement from 1 John iv. 18, 'Perfecta caritas foras mittit timorem.'[4] They therefore distinguished between two kinds of fear, the one *timor servilis*, by which a man would refrain from evil actions through fear of punishment in hell, the other *timor filialis* or *castus*, by which a man, already loving God, might fear through sin to lose Him. The second is compatible with love of God in this world, the first not. This distinction was maintained in the Middle Ages. It is, for instance, amply set out in St. Thomas's analysis of fear,[5] and appears most importantly in the

1. Brown xiii, 43, p. 70. *Bleo*: appearance; *scharpe meyne*: keen strength; *wordes feo*: worldly possessions; *cleo*: hill-side.
2. An historical discussion is provided by A. W. Hunzinger, *Das Furchtmotiv in der katholischen Busslehre* (Naumburg, 1906).
3. 'But rather fear Him which is able to destroy both soul and body in hell.' (A.V.)
4. 'Perfect love casteth out fear.' (A.V.)
5. *De dono timoris, Summa theologica* II. ii. 19.

Sentences of Peter Lombard, at the point where he discusses fear as one of the Seven Gifts of the Holy Ghost:

> Timor autem servilis est, ut ait August. super psal. 127, cum per timorem gehennae continet se homo a peccato, quo praesentiam judicis et poenas metuit, et timore facit quidquid boni facit, non timore amittendi aeternum bonum quod non amat, sed timore patiendi malum quod formidat. Non timet ne perdat amplexus pulcherrimi Sponsi, sed timet ne mittatur in gehennam.[6]

What, however, distinguishes the medieval treatment of servile fear from that of the Fathers is the place that it finds, not in theological treatises, but in the work of mystical and affective writers. In this it is often made the beginning of the soul's return to God: St. Bernard, followed by many others, such as St. Catherine of Siena, describes how the sinful soul's path to divine union leads from servile fear through cupidity to love. It is not surprising that, as with meditation on Christ in His humanity, this first and lowly step in the upward turning of the soul became detached from the pattern of ascent, and was presented to the non-contemplative layman as a self-sufficient meditative exercise.

In the earlier theological tradition the object of servile fear was said to be hell, and from this there arose the horrific and detailed descriptions of the torments of hell, which are commonplaces of sermon literature.[7] A clear example of this in early Middle English literature is *Sawles Warde*, where the allegorical outline of Wit's household being moved, first through fear of hell and then through cupidity for heaven, derives directly from Hugh of St. Victor's treatise *De anima*, but where the detailed content of Fearlac's speech has its ancestry in the Anglo-Saxon sermon.[8] It is interesting to see how a learned work has supplied the theory and how the native tradition has provided most of the meditative, visual description. Examples of such descriptions of hell, designed to stimulate servile fear, could be multiplied from English sermon literature, but they are rare in the lyric,[9] perhaps because of the inherent unsuitability

6. Lib. III, dist. xxxiv, *P.L.* 192, 823–27. 'Fear is servile, as Augustine says on Ps. cxxvii, when a man refrains from sin through fear of hell, when he fears the presence of the judge and the punishments, and he does out of fear any good that he does, not fear of losing the eternal good which he does not love, but fear of suffering the punishment of which he is afraid. He does not fear that he may lose the embrace of the most beautiful bridegroom, but he fears lest he be sent to hell.' Cf. *P.G.* 49, 153 ff. and *P.L.* 38, 882.
7. In the meditative passages in the work of St. Bernard fear is aroused by descriptions of hell, e.g. in the sixteenth of the *Sermons on the Song of Songs, P.L.* 183, 852; cf. *Sermones de diversis*, xlii,

P.L. 183, 664.
8. Ed. R. M. Wilson, *Leeds School of English Language Texts and Monographs*, iii. In the *De anima* the messenger's name is *timor mortis*: the English adaptor perhaps omitted the reference to death in order that his long description of hell might be more appropriate to the speaker.
9. The few there are enumerate the traditional list of the pains of hell, e.g. 'Unsely gost' (E.E.T.S. 49, 147–55), and an unprinted mnemonic list, 'Fyre and colde and tereshating [shedding]' from MS. Merton 248. Some early death lyrics, such as 'þene latemeste dai' (Brown XIII, 29), have the torments of hell as a subordinate theme.

of the subject-matter, perhaps because the fear they invoke is less immediate and intimate than that of death. People have to be taught to fear hell, they naturally fear death. This truth—so obvious from experience—was in the Middle Ages supported by the authority of Aristotle. St. Thomas, in his analysis of fear, quotes from the *Ethics*, iii. 6, 'Inter omnia terribilissimum est mors.'[1] But, though fear of death is a natural emotion, of which the potential effectiveness would be obvious to homilists and spiritual writers, its propriety must be explained in terms of theological doctrine. At first sight it may seem a contradiction in terms that the Christian should fear death: and, indeed, in the consolatory literature of the patristic period the faith of the Christian in the Resurrection is emphasized in contrast to the hopelessness of the pagan: but the reference is, of course, to the death of others, not to one's own. But, whilst the Resurrection was an answer also to man's instinctive horror of ceasing to be, and in religious terms an answer to the second death (the death of the soul), it did not alter the fact that death was unnatural, and that the most intense demonstration of the immediate consequence of the Fall was that the body was no longer subject to the soul. According to a classical tag, 'Lex non poena mors',[2] it is the way of the world which can be faced only by acceptance and resignation. But, according to St. Augustine, death is 'a sharp, unnatural experience', and a direct penalty for the Fall. He makes, however, a distinction between the death of the good and that of the bad, for, as a result of the Redemption, 'the first breach of nature' is 'good to the good, and bad to the bad',[3] '. . . by God's ineffable mercy the punishment of sin is become the instrument of virtue, and the pain due to the sinner's guilt is the just man's merit'.[4] This doctrine was often repeated in the Middle Ages. A convenient statement of it, combined with a meditative injunction, may be found in the *De disciplina claustrali* of Peter of Celle, in Chapter 23, *de meditatione mortis*, where he describes death as a debt to be paid, but one which for the good is eclipsed by the rewards that will follow:

> Non ergo expavescat solvere debitum mortis, qui expectat soluto debito dotes tantae remunerationis. Debitum tamen est, quod omnibus et ab omnibus debetur et solvitur.

There follows from this the injunction, 'Depinge mortem ante oculos tuos, quam horrenda facies . . .'[5] Paradoxically, man has to be made to fear death in order that he may become the kind of

1. *Sum. theol.* I, 2, xlii, 2. 'That which inspires the greatest fear is death.'
2. Weber, op. cit. 10. 'Death is the law of nature not a punishment.'
3. Bk. xiii, ch. 2. *De civitate dei*, trans. John Healey (London, 1945), II, 2.
4. Bk. xiii, ch. 4, ed. cit. 3.
5. *P.L.* 202, 1131–32. 'The man, who, when his debt is paid expects to be rewarded with a great gift, shall not fear to pay the death which he owes. This is a debt that is owed by all and is payed by all and is everybody's share . . . represent death before your eyes and see how horrifying is his face.'

man who need not fear death. The average Christian must fear it, for, not being like the martyr who has conquered its terrors, he is only freed from the fear by the unmeritorious method of not thinking about it. Few people, except in time of danger, fear death regularly in any pressing sense. St. Thomas stated this, again quoting Aristotle, 'Quae valde longe sunt, non timentur: sciunt enim omnes, quod morientur; sed quia non prope est, nihil curant.'[6] The response of everybody is epitomized in the words of Partridge in Tom Jones: 'I know all human flesh must die; but yet a man may live many years for all that.'

The aim of the death lyric was to dispel this comforting remoteness by emphasizing both the uncertainty and the inevitability of death, and most frequently by, as it were, looking through a magnifying-glass at all the minutiae of death, so that time or aversion might not make its image blurred to the imagination. But this examination of the details of death can not only frighten the meditator into virtue, but also persuade him into a lesser estimation of the objects of his cupidity, for self-aggrandizement and reliance upon material splendour or prosperity seem insecurely based when measured against the eventual squalor and decay of the body in the grave. Explicit warnings to the proud make this subsidiary, didactic intention quite plain: in the Fasciculus morum death is discussed under the heading of humility; in a later vernacular treatise, the Disce mori, meditation on death is recommended as a remedy against the sin of covetousness.[7]

Though there are traces of didacticism and irony in the Passion lyric—the latter springing from the disproportion between God's love and man's sinfulness—it is only in the death lyric that they are common and arise naturally from the subject-matter. This awareness of the moral implications of a remembrance of death is not peculiar to Christianity, and it can be developed in a manner which is satiric rather than penitential. A famous and early example of this

6. I. 2, xlii. 2. 'Things that are very far off do not cause fear; all men know that they must die, but, because death is not near, they pay no heed to it.'
7. MS. Laud Misc. 99, 55ᵛ. The passage, containing many of the traditional themes of death that will later be described, is as follows: Ayenst this synne of covetise the best remedie is to a man to thenke besili on his deth, for as seith Seint Jerome, lightli he forsakith all thing that ofte thenkith he shal deye, and Seint Austyn biddeth a man consider what he shal be here aftir: Consider the sepulchres riche and povere, and what thei that lye in hem were somtyme and what now profited to hem their richesses and the vanyte of the world þat thei hunted so besily. Now is nought seen of theim but asshes. Loke than if ther be difference betwix a king and a knave, the faire and the foule, the stronge and the weyke, whiche and thei might speke wold say to you thees wordes: 'O ye unhappi wrecches to what entent renne ye so beseli to gete the richesses and vanite of the world? Whereto fille ye you wit covetise and wit vices? Considere ye our bones, so that at the hardest your covetise and miserie fere you therby. Suche as ye be, suche were we, and suche as we be, suche shal ye be.' Ymagine the richeste and mightiest of the world and now is he passed; alle his frendes, richesses, worshippes, and all other vanite or pompe of the world have left him naked, and nothing bereth wit him but synne or merit of his werkes.

kind of treatment is Lucian's *Dialogues of the Dead*: in it the vices
and worldly pursuits of contemporary society are discussed within
the framework of a conversation amongst the shades in Hades, so
that their folly and pointlessness becomes plain; and, whilst the
speakers are said to be mere shades, they are also little collections of
bones and skulls, and by this means, in a manner common also in
later preaching literature, the levelling power of death can be shown,
and the uselessness of pride in beauty, in fine clothing, in physical
strength, etc.:

> *Menippus* Where are all the beauties, Hermes? Show me round;
>   I am a new-comer.
> *Hermes* I am busy, Menippus. But look over there to your right,
>   and you will see Hyacinth, Narcissus, Nireus, Achilles, Tyro,
>   Helen, Leda,—all the beauties of old.
> *Me.* I can see only bones, and bare skulls; most of them are
>   exactly alike.
> *Her.* Those bones, of which you seem to think so lightly, have
>   been the theme of admiring poets.
> *Me.* Well, but show me Helen; I shall never be able to make her
>   out by myself.
> *Her.* This skull is Helen.[8]

There is, of course, no question of there being any influence from
Lucian's *Dialogues* on medieval literature. Though the reference to
Lucian is often made in modern works on death in medieval literature and art, it is useful only in showing how excellent a standard of
measurement the fact of death provides for the satirist. It was, however, natural that English medieval literature, in which there was a
strong semi-homiletic, semi-satiric vein, should make use of this
inherent possibility. Amongst the lyric poetry the most striking
example, the Dance of Death, is of the the later period, but, though
in the earlier centuries, which we are at the moment considering,
purely satiric poems do not exist, the meditative often merges into
the satiric.

The theory of the salutary value of servile fear is, in comparison
with the doctrine of the value of love, of so ancient an origin that it
is far more difficult to trace the meditative passages formed by it,
which in turn provided the sources for the medieval lyric. The new
stress on the value of fear in the spiritual writers of the twelfth century admittedly led to Latin treatises, which both enjoined the fear
of death and provided appropriate meditative thoughts: of these
the two most famous were the *De contemptu mundi* of Innocent
III and the *Meditationes piissimae de cognitione humanae condi-
tionis* long attributed to St. Bernard, but now known to be by Wil-

---

8. *The Works of Lucian of Samosata*, trans. H. W. Fowler and F. G. Fowler, i
(Oxford, 1905), 137.

liam of Tournai. These works circulated widely in England (they
survive in a large number of manuscripts), and they provided the
sources for some of the lyrics, and perhaps in some sense the
authority for them all. But these Latin works themselves have
sources, and individual themes in them can be traced back, for
instance, to the *De xii abusivis saeculi* of the eighth century, to
some of the earliest sermons in the pseudo-Augustinian collection,
the *Sermones ad fratres in eremo*, and further still, back to the work
of St. Ephraem of Syria. The long and sometimes indistinct ancestry of various death themes is relevant to the lyric, for some of these
themes had already passed into English literature in the late Anglo-
Saxon period—into the sermons in the Vercelli Manuscript and the
pseudo-Wulfstan collection, and into the poem on the Body and
Soul debate—and from these directly into early Middle English literature. With the early lyrics it is therefore often not possible to tell
whether the immediate source lies in the native vernacular tradition
or in the international learned Latin tradition. This question, however, is of historical rather than literary importance, for there was
no direct stylistic influence from Old English literature. The early
lyrics are as remote from the rhetoric of the Old English sermon or
the patterned style and rhythms of the Old English Body and Soul
poem, as they are from any Latin original. For, though some death
themes continued after the Norman Conquest unaltered in content,
the vernacular in which they were expressed no longer retained the
same range of associations: the metre was no longer that borrowed
from courtly poetry, and the language had none of the dignified leisure of poetic diction. Had the subject-matter of the poetry been
classical reflection on death, this change would also have been an
impoverishment. The medieval death themes, however, like the
meditation on the Passion, did not require nobility of language, but,
on the contrary, their reference to ordinary, unheightened experience was best expressed by quick, exact, colloquial language: therefore the unique diminution of the vernacular in England made it a
perfect medium for this kind of poetry. The immediate, uncomplex
effect of the poetry was not in danger of being modified by an unin-
tended learned or courtly air, for the vocabulary, since it was rarely
used for literary or learned work or for courtly conversation, could
have no overtones except those of everyday communication, and the
style naturally remained close to the popular proverbial sayings
which the poems so often quote: 'Al to late, al to late, /
Wanne þe bere ys ate gate'[9] or 'Man may longe lyves wenen, / ac

9. Brown XIII, 71. Cf. *Proverbs of Hendyng* (H. Varnhagen, 'Zu mittelen-
glischen Gedichten', *Anglia*, iv, 1881, p.
191, from MS Camb. Gg. 1. I), 'Al to
late, al to late,/ Wan þe deth is at the
ȝate'; *Pricke of Conscience*, iii. 2000-
2001, 'For when þe dede es at þe yhate,
/ Þan es he warned over late'.

offte hym legeþt se wrench.'[1]

Therefore, although some of the early death lyrics, such for instance as 'þene latemeste dai' may borrow some of their content from native predecessors and also echo them verbally, they are quite different in effect from Anglo-Saxon literature, for no poetic diction, rhetorical inflation, or any sophisticated literary art softens, or adds grandeur to, the horror of death or the reproach accorded to a sinful life. There is a grim lack of pretentiousness, for the style is not one which could potentially be used for a magnificent subject, and there is no elevation of tone which might suggest remoteness from daily life. The language has not the dignity or subtlety that would come from a long ancestry of literary use, but has instead the immediate effect of everyday speech. This makes it particularly suitable for brief, vivid, hortatory poetry, though perhaps less suitable for the longer, more reflective poems, where the absence of shades of meaning and the comparative smallness of vocabulary can lead to monotony in tone and feeling.

There are a number of brief verses, written in quick-moving, metrically free, two-stressed couplets, which illustrate well the excellence of these early meditative and mnemonic poems. The extremely popular verse, 'If man him biðocte', which was copied and orally repeated consistently from the thirteenth to the fifteenth century, is a typical example:

> If man him biðocte
> inderlike and ofte
> Þu arde is te fore
> fro bedde te flore,
> Þu reuful is te flitte
> fro flore te pitte,
> fro pitte te pine
> ðat nevre sal fine,
> i Þene non sinne
> sulde his herte winne.[2]

The simplicity of the diction, combined with the alliteration and the repetition of key-words from one couplet to another, drive home the pattern of descent from bed to floor to grave to hell. Verses of this kind have a 'catchiness' both poetically and morally effective, whereby they haunt the memory and readily recur to it, even when there is no conscious wish to retain them. The structure is the common meditative one, an emotive description followed by the appropriate moral reflection, and the content is traditional, the recollection of the death-bed, the corpse laid on the floor, the grave

1. Brown XIII, 10 B. *Hym legeþt se wrench*: he is deceived. Cf. *Proverbs of Alfred*, ll. 153–56, ed. E. Borgström (Lund, 1908), 7; *Proverbs of Hendyng* (from MS. Digby 86, *Anglia*, iv. 200),

47. The first stanza of XIII, 10 B is quoted in the *Ayenbite of Inwyt*, E.E.T.S. 23, 129–30.
2. Brown XIII, 13. L. 10 *Winne*, MS. *winnen*.

302 · *Rosemary Woolf*

dug in the ground, and hell, thought of as lying at the centre of the earth. But, whilst the content is traditional and grimly realistic, the arrangement into stages of a falling journey to hell has an intellectual and ironic crispness. Whether this ingenuity was the author's own cannot be told and scarcely matters. No exact source has been identified, though there is a strong probability that somewhere there are some lines of Latin prose, which describe clearly but less pungently a similar pattern of descent.

In some manuscripts this verse is followed by a text of the most popular of all Middle English death lyrics, that on the Signs of Death. Its popularity is partly accounted for by the fact that it was included in the section on death in the *Fasciculus morum*, but the very high number of manuscripts containing it, and the large number of variant versions, show clearly the intrinsic value of the text to the Middle Ages. Nowadays the subject is chiefly familiar from the description of the death of Falstaff, whose feet were 'cold as any stone' and whose 'nose was as sharp as a pen'. It is not known where Shakespeare derived these details: it is not inconceivable that some Middle English version circulated orally, but, since the Signs were still part of received medical knowledge, he could have come across them in some less popular source. For instance, a short work containing them, entitled *The Boke of Knowledge, whether a sycke person beynge in perylle shall lyve, or dye*, was printed in 1535.[3] In this work the Signs appear in a purely medical context, and it was in this way that they originated in the *Prognosticon* of Hippocrates. At the beginning of this work Hippocrates describes with precision the symptoms by which a physician, when he first sees his patient, may know whether he will live or die: 'Nose sharp, eyes hollow, temples sunken, the ears cold and contracted with their lobes turned outwards, the skin about the face hard and parched, and the colour of the face as a whole being yellow or black . . .',[4] and, scattered through the *Prognosticon* and also the *Aphorisms*, these details are repeated and increased. The works of Hippocrates, translated and commented upon by Galen, were preserved, studied, and esteemed in Benedictine monasteries abroad from the time of Cassiodorus, and they appear in English manuscripts from the twelfth century onwards. A diagnosis of approaching death, which included the Signs, was often copied in Anglo-Latin medical manuscripts of the Middle Ages, and there are even a number of similar Middle English medical texts.[5] But in the

3. Marjorie Walters, 'The Literary Background of Francis Bacon's Essay "Of Death" ', *M.L.R.* xxxv (1940), 7, quotes two other examples. Cf. also *Henry V*, ed. J. H. Walter (London 1954), note to II, iii. 14–17.
4. Ed. W. H. S. Jones (Loeb Classical Library, 1959), ii. 8–9.
5. The Signs, for instance, occur in the Latin medical manuscript, Sloane 1313, 29ᵛ, and amongst the vernacular medical notes printed by T. Wright and J. O. Halliwell, *Reliquiae antiquae*, i (London, 1841), 54.

twelfth century the Signs of Death were detached from their medical context and incorporated also into death literature. To the Middle Ages this would almost certainly not have seemed a substantial rerooting of the subject: there would be no reason why symptoms, scientifically observed by a physician, should not also serve as a moral warning. That the medical and the didactic were not unrelated can be seen in the fact that medical manuscripts quite often contain texts of one or two of the death lyrics.[6] However, no doubt often the medical origin of the Signs was forgotten or not known. Some manuscripts of the *Fasciculus morum* ascribe a Latin version to St. Jerome,[7] probably by analogy with the attribution to him of the Fifteen Signs of the Last Judgement. In other words, they are thought of as a solemn and prophetic warning from which the Christian should appropriately take fright.

The Signs of Death first appear in a didactic context in the twelfth-century Worcester Fragments, but, though it is not impossible that this adaptation was first made by the vernacular writer, it remains more probable that it first occurred in some Latin treatise now lost or unidentified. In the Worcester Fragments, which are the remains of a Body and Soul poem, The Signs form part of a prelude, describing the painfulness of dying and the loneliness and humiliation of the corpse. The Signs are as follows:

> Him deaveð þa aeren, him dimmeð (þa) eigen
> Him scerpeð þe neose, him scrinckeþ þa lippen,
> Him scorteð (þe) tunge, him trukeð his iwit,
> Him teoreð his miht, him coldeð his (fet).[8]

The Worcester Fragments were known to some of the writers of the early Middle English death lyric. They directly influenced 'þene latemeste dai' (as we shall discuss later), they perhaps contributed to the tradition of describing the preparations for burial which lies behind 'If man him biþocte,' and finally they may have provided the source for the earliest lyric version of the Signs. There is not here any obvious, intermediary Latin source: the Signs do not, for instance, occur in the *De contemptu mundi* or in the *Meditationes*, though versions are often found adjoining these works in manuscripts, and works based upon them, such as *The Prick of Conscience*,[9] often amplify their original by including the theme. A description of the Signs was also a commonplace of medieval preaching on death.

6. MS. Sloane 1313, for instance, contains an *exemplum* verse about a dying sinner on f. 134r-v (*Index*, 2307).
7. Brown XIII, p. 220. Some of the manuscripts that I have examined, such as MS. Rawl. C. 670, 20v, do not contain this ascription.

8. *Die Fragmente der Reden der Seele an den Leichnam*, ed. R. Buchholz (Erlangen, 1889), I. Ll. 3–4, His tongue ceases, his senses fail, his strength droops.
9. Bk. i, ll. 812–27, ed. Morris, 23.

Alongside the Middle English verses there occur Latin and also Anglo-Norman couplet versions, but these may well derive from the English rather than vice versa, since there is no evidence of their having a circulation independent of the native tradition. Certainly the Latin and Anglo-Norman versions are inferior, lacking the quality of the vernacular couplets, which have a colloquial laconicism that makes them particularly forceful as moral verse. The Latin and Anglo-Norman also show far less variety—there are only minor verbal differences between the versions—whilst, despite the restriction imposed by rhyme in the brief two-stress couplet, the English reinvigorates the unchanging form by fresh detail, or by combinations which often constitute almost a new poem. Many groups of verses, however, are related as variants of one original which has been handed on orally—this is true of the largest group, that of the *Fasciculus morum*, MS. Harley 7322, and MS. Trinity 43—but others are independent and by no means stale treatments of the theme. The version of the *Fasciculus morum*, with its stark combination in each line of noun plus verb, is perhaps the most effective:

> When þe hede quakyth
> And þe lyppis blakyth
> And þe nose sharpyth
> And þe senow starkyth
> And þe brest pantyth
> And þe breþe wantyth
> And þe teþe ratelyʒt
> And þe þrote roteleþ[1]

A slightly later and quite unrelated version of the theme occurs in MS. Arundel 507:

> When þe hee biginnis til turne
> And þe fote biginnis to spurne,
> And þe bak makes þe bowe,
> And þe mouthe makes þe mowe:
> þerby may þu see sone
> þat he sall go to þe dome.[2]

Here the leisure of the slightly longer line has enabled the poet to describe the distorted mouth and eye from Hippocrates and the bent back from a different list (that of the Signs of Old Age), in a way that catches the imagination by a cynical sprightliness, and to use a rhyme scheme which completely escapes the pairs of verbs necessarily recurring in the shorter-lined versions. An effective,

1. MS. Rawl. C. 670, 148ᵛ, Brown xiii, p. 222. *Blakyth*: grow pale; *ratelyʒt*: chatter; *roteleþ*: makes a rattling noise. This version occurs in the four Bodleian manuscripts which I have examined. The entry at *Index* 4035 is therefore misleading.
2. C. Horstman, *Yorkshire Writers*, i (London, 1895), 156.

though more learned, version of the Signs is found in some fif-teenth-century manuscripts. In it the moral, instead of being reserved to the end, in accordance with the usual meditative struc-ture, is interspersed between the Signs, the latter being the list from the *Fasciculus morum*:

When thy hede quakyth:	Memento.
Then thy lyppys blakyth:	Confessio.
When thy noose sharpyth:	Contricio.
Then thy lymmys starkyth:	Satisfaccio.
When thy brest pantyth:	Nosce teipsum.
Than thy wynde wantyth:	Miserere.
When thy nyen hollyth:	Libera me domine.
Then deth folowyth:	Veni ad judicium.[3]

There is here a striking counterpoint between the static English description and the developing warning and prayer of the Latin. The use of significant phrases from Latin liturgical prayer is charac-teristic of some fifteenth-century poetry, and here it has given new force to what was by that time a well-worn theme.

Though the Signs of Death are still effective through their grim accumulation of disagreeable detail, their full power is probably lost in a period that no longer appreciates the medieval much-used rhe-torical formula of the catalogue. The catalogue of feminine beauty, for instance, may nowadays seem a list of dismembered parts, which never become imaginatively integrated: nowadays the impressionis-tic is often more evocative than the meticulously precise. But this type of catalogue could not have been so popular in the Middle Ages, if the very form had weakened its effect.

Another effective little Middle English verse, which has the sting and force of an epigram, is 'Wen þe turuf is þi tuur.' This too has its ancestry in the literary no-man's land of the twelfth century, when the metre used was still the alliterative line with its length and leisure, but when the style already showed the ironic edge and colloquial directness that are characteristic of the death lyrics in the Middle Ages. The subject of the poem is the smallness and poverty of the grave contrasted with the splendour enjoyed by the dead man when he was alive:

> Wen þe turuf is þi tuur,
> and þi put is þi bour,
> þi wel and þi wite þrote
> ssulen wormes to note.
> Wat helpit þe þenne
> al þe worilde wnne?[4]

3. M. R. James, *Catalogue of the Manu-scripts in Queens' College, Cambridge* (Cambridge, 1905), 15. Cf. *Cambridge Middle English Lyrics*, ed. H. A. Person (Seattle, 1953), 16–19.
4. Brown XIII, 30. *Put*: grave; *wel*: skin; *note*: benefit.

The theme itself is an ancient one, and can be found in the homi-
lies of the Eastern Church, where most of the death themes begin.
St. John Chrysostom, for instance, in a passage whose point is the
despising of worldly glory, thus commented upon the death of a
rich man: 'He has departed to the grave which has seized all, and is
buried within the space of three cubits.'⁵ This emphasis on the
physical smallness of the grave, which was to be a commonplace of
medieval death literature, occurs in an early and striking form in
England in the account of the death of William the Conqueror in
the Anglo-Saxon Chronicle, where the style is obviously influenced
by sermon rhetoric:

> Eala hu leas and hu unwrest is þysses middaneardes wela. Se
> þe wæs ærur rice cyng and maniges landes hlaford, he næfde þa
> ealles landes buton seofon fot mæl; and se þe wæs hwilon ges-
> crid mid golde and mid gimmum he læg þa oferwrogen mid
> moldan.⁶

A grimmer, less nostalgic, and more ingenious expression of the
same idea had already occurred in Vercelli Homily ix, where the
grave is briefly described as one of the five images of hell,⁷ and its
shallowness is emphasized by the harshly quaint description of the
roof of the dead man's house lying above his chest: an ironic idea,
which was to be repeated over and over again, and probably stimu-
lated further elaborations of the theme in twelfth-century poetry.

The idea of the smallness of the grave, ironically expressed, recurs
almost as a refrain in the Worcester Fragments,⁸ but the outstanding example of it is the twelfth-century poem now known as 'The
Grave.' This poem has a cleverness, which is neither typically
Anglo-Saxon nor typically medieval: it plays with the conceit of the
grave as a house, exploiting with ironic wit the discords that arise
from this basic metaphor. The oddity of the grave, thought of as a
house, is stressed: the walls are disproportionately low, there are no
doors, and the roof lies immediately above its inhabitant's chest;
and the older idea of the loneliness of the corpse is here expanded
into the idea that no friends will call upon the dead to ask him how
he likes his new home.

* * *

No thirteenth-century lyric treats the theme with such elaborate
and grimly inventive ingenuity, but the idea of the roof lying upon

5. P.G. 55, 511–12. See also 'Das Grab
und seine Länge', Kleinere Schriften von
Reinhold Köhler, ed. J. Bolte, ii (Berlin,
1900), 24–27.
6. Ed. J. Earle and C. Plummer (Oxford, 1952), i. 219. 'Alas, how false and
untrustworthy is the prosperity of this
world. He, who had been a powerful
king and ruler over wide lands, of all
this land is now left with but seven feet;

and he who was formerly clothed in gold
and jewels now lies covered only with
earth.'
7. Der Vercelli-Codex cxvii, ed. Max
Förster (Halle, 1913), 92. The four
other images are: pain, old age, death,
torment.
8. 'Die Fragmente der Reden der Seele
an den Leichnam', ed. Buchholz, A 35-
36, C 29–31, etc.

the breast, chin, or nose remained a favourite commonplace, and with it variations such as that of 'þene latemeste dai', where the dead man's house is said to be constructed with a spade.[9] There is at play here the same kind of wit as we have already seen in descriptions of the armour of Christ, but here, at least from the modern point of view, it is well suited to the theme.

'Wen þe turuf is þi tuur' is a very neat and pointed example of this kind of wit, with the incongruity of the image made sharp by the simplicity of the syntax, and with the yoking together of the nouns, by alliteration in the first line and by the assonance of plosive consonants in the second, as though these devices echoed a similarity of meaning. In its manuscript, MS. Trinity 323, this poem is preceded by a Latin couplet version, but it does not follow that the copyist was right in taking the English to be the translation rather than vice versa. Certainly the English is the more ironically effective with its alliteration, and with the phrase *wormes to note* (cf. Old English *wyrmum to hroðre*) for the Latin *cibus vermium*.

A comparably ironic treatment of a similar subject occurs in the very popular 'Erþe toc of erþe,'[1] which is a punning elaboration of the well-known Genesis-based text, 'Memento homo quod cinis es et in cinerem reverteris', frequently quoted in Latin death literature and in the liturgy of Ash Wednesday at the imposition of the ashes.[2] There are also long, non-epigrammatic versions of these lines, and parallels of these longer texts are found in Latin and Anglo-Norman. This is, therefore, a text whose literary development cannot be unravelled to the point of proof. It seems likely, however, firstly that it is the Latin and Anglo-Norman versions that are the translations,[3] and that the vernacular is their original; and secondly that it is the riddling epigram that has been expanded into the clear and inclusive but diffuse texts, rather than that these have been condensed into an epigram.[4] The verse itself is as follows:

> Erþe toc of erþe, erþe wyþ woh,
> Erþe oþer erþe to þe erþe droh,
> Erþe leyde erþe in erþene þroh—
> Þo hevede erþe of erþe erþe ynoh.[5]

In estimating the quality of these lines it is important to remember that the Middle Ages held a view of puns quite different from that

9. 'Nu sal þin halle wid spade ben wrout', Brown xiii, 29, l. 25, p. 47.
1. Brown xiii, 73; E.E.T.S. 141, 1.
2. 'Remember man that you are dust and to dust you shall return', *Sarum Missal*, ed. J. Wickham Legg (Oxford, 1916), p. 51, footnote 5.
3. Nearly all the material (or references to it) is assembled in E.E.T.S. 141.
4. The arguments for the theory that the Latin is a translation from the English

are set out in E.E.T.S. 141, xxix–xxxiii. Against the possibility that the present verse was the opening of a longer poem, the copyist having forgotten the rest (see E.E.T.S. 141, xv), is the undeniable effect of completeness given by the verse. If the related opening of the long text from MS. Harley 913 (op. cit. 1–4) had survived alone, it would not have given this impression of literary self-sufficiency.
5. Brown xiii, 73. *Woh*: sin; *þroh*: pit.

of later centuries. Nowadays puns imply confusion and they are therefore used only when the intention is jesting or at least unserious. But in the Middle Ages puns implied synthesis, for they were thought of as a rhetorical means of revealing underlying correspondences. Ambiguities of meaning were not random, nor similarities of sound comic coincidences, but both were linguistic indications of the intricate unity of the divine plan. Puns were therefore used for the most august subject-matter, particularly when a paradoxical treatment was appropriate, as for the Incarnation: the play on the similarity of sound in *virgo: virga* (rod, i.e. of Jesse) or the idea of the Infant Christ as *Verbum infans*, the Word that could not speak, are commonplaces of Latin religious poetry.[6] The subject-matter of 'Erþe toc of erþe,' the end of man and of his riches in the grave, through the paradoxical clash between two standards of judgement, is admirably suited to punning expression, and the total effect is of a harsh and uneasily obscure riddle. Not everyone would agree on the meaning of the first two lines, but the following is a possible interpretation of the whole: Man, whose body is made of earth, is born in sin; in his lifetime he accumulates riches for himself; in death he is laid in an earth-grave, and then has he his fill of earth. This bare history of man is satirically hidden behind the word *erþe*, which is substituted for every noun except *woh*, and it is particularly effective, in that most Middle English lyrics decline in tension on account of their moralizing conclusions, whereas this begins quietly and enigmatically, and increases in force until the last line, which is bluntly clear in meaning and gives a savagely ironic summing up of the end of the avaricious man.

* * *

6. An excellent discussion of puns in Latin literature is given by W. J. Ong, 'Wit and Mystery: a Revaluation in Me- diaeval Latin Hymnody', *Speculum*, xxii (1947), 310–41.

Perspectives on Six Poems

A. K. MOORE

[On "Sumer is icumen in"]†

* * *

The celebrated *Cuckoo Song* has usually been exhibited in surveys and discussions of medieval lyric as a superb example of early thirteenth-century poetical and musical art, having been composed, it was supposed, before 1240.[1] Though the excellence of the so-called *Reading Rota* remains undiminished, recent investigation indicates for the music, at least, a much later date than the one traditionally accepted. Bukofzer has shown that the *Summer-canon* could not have been composed prior to 1280, as "duple rhythm," a demonstrated characteristic of the music, was previously unknown in England.[2] On this and other grounds,[3] he dates the accompaniment *ca.* 1310.[4] Considered unaccountably advanced as thirteenth-century song, the *rota* is entirely explicable in terms of the musical practice of the following century. Bukofzer declares that the composer's gift is all the better understood and appreciated by the musicologist as it is examined within the limits of a known tradition. The new dating of the notation proves nothing about the age of the text, though the phonological evidence by no means precludes a date later than 1240.

Sumer is icumen in is the only English song among several French and Latin specimens entered in a commonplace book (now MS. Harley 978) which was kept over a period of many years by monks of Reading Abbey. There are no clues as to the identity of poet or composer or indications of the occasion for which the lyric was written. It belongs to the general class of spring songs cultivated extensively on the Continent. The *Cuckoo Song*, however, is apparently not an imitation, as it lacks the gaudy description and love interest of the songs of greeting to the spring in the *Carmina Burana* and the nature introductions of Old French poetry. The deceptive naïveté of the lyric has led some readers to the conclusion that it was popular in character, notwithstanding the altogether learned environment in which it has come down. A recent editor of

† From A. K. Moore, *The Secular Lyric in Middle English* (Lexington, Ky.: University Press of Kentucky, 1951), pp. 50–52. [See p. 4, above.] Reprinted by permission of the publisher.
1. The evidence for this dating has been summarized by Brown, *Lyrics XIIIth Cent.*, pp. 168 f.
2. M. F. Bukofzer, *Sumer is icumen in: A Revision* (Univ. of Calif. Publications in Music, Vol. II, No. 2; Berkeley and Los Angeles, 1944), pp. 92 f.
3. Among others, the development of the rota out of motet, *conductus,* and *rondellus*; the use of the term *pes* for tenor; the frequency of sixth-chords.
4. George Saintsbury, *A History of English Prosody* (2d ed.; London, 1923), I, 120, shrewdly guessed that the lyric was too good for a period earlier than the late thirteenth century.

the text, Carleton Brown, considered it "easier to believe that it was an imitation of Welsh folk-song than it was the invention of a learned composer"[5]—and this on Gerald's statement in the *Descriptio Kambriae* that the Welsh cultivated counterpoint in the twelfth century.[6] The music, it is hardly necessary to remark, shows no exceptional features by Bukofzer's dating, though it remains the first English composition for six voices. The text, moreover, exhibits a good many notable characteristics besides the "freshness and simplicity" which struck R. M. Wilson as the marks of folk song.[7] Whatever its ultimate origin, the *Cuckoo Song* is immediately the product of a finished poetic talent.[8]

One morning on the southern countryside, the poet becomes suddenly aware of the arrival of joyous "sumer" (probably April).[9] Realization comes in a moment so brief that he cannot hope by ordinary means to give concrete representation to the complex of impulses which unite almost as a single sense-impression to inform him of the happy fact. Nor can he by conventional methods animate the symbols which have flashed "sumer" upon his conscious mind. The composer properly takes rapid movement as the common factor of all that he sees or imagines, and this characteristic of the season he manages to introduce into the song. By mechanical means—the short line and the racing musical score—the poet creates an illusion of speed; but by a far subtler method, he co-ordinates the motion of the prominent objects with the meter.

The choice of onomatopœic *cuccu* (both note and bird) was a fortunate one. The bird suggests not only "sumer" but motion as well, and, as a consequence, "sing, cuccu" laces the parts together. Two kinds of movement are represented in the lyric—the slow, deliberate growth of plant life and the fast, erratic capering of animal life. These diverse sorts of activity are reconciled by verbs of motion. Thus "groweth sed and bloweth med" become for the moment discernible and imaginatively no less rapid than,

5. Brown, *Lyrics XIIIth Cent.*, pp. xv f.
6. Giraldus Cambrensis, *Opera*, Rolls Series, XXI, London, 1868, vi, 189–90, Lib. I, cap. xiii.
7. R. M. Wilson, *Early Middle English Literature*, 1939, p. 260.
8. E. K. Chambers and F. Sidgwick, *Early English Lyrics*, London, 1907, p. 273, where Chambers regards it with considerable justice as a "learned composer's adaptation of a *reverdie*."
9. For the lack of an unequivocal term for the springtime, Middle English poets were compelled to use *somer* to comprehend the interval between the vernal and the autumnal equinoxes. This usage corresponds to the medieval Latin *aestas*, which in several songs of the *Carmina Burana* (cf. Nos. 51, 106, 107, 122) obviously signifies spring. Since the Julian calendar had fallen nearly two weeks behind by the fourteenth century, the season was well advanced in April; the Harleian poet who wrote "Lef & gras & blosme springes in aueryl" was unquestionably correct. The cuckoo arrives on the southern coast of England about the second week of April (*Encyl. Brit.*, 14th ed., *cuckoo, q.v.*), or, by Julian computation, some twelve days earlier. According to medieval reckoning, then, the circumstances fit April rather better than May.

awe bleteth after lomb,
lhouth after calue cu;
Bulluc sterteth, bucke uerteth.[1]

And the persistent *cuccu*, the eternal note of spring, sounds a merry accompaniment to the animals frisking in the flowering meadow. Yet all is objectivity, all realism. The language is homely, the situation probable. In the fourteenth century, as now in isolated regions, the dun deer must have consorted with domesticated bovines. There is nothing essentially "poetic" about the elements which make up the song, and the composer has made no effort to elevate his subject. This is nevertheless art of a high order and an exceptional fusion of sense and melody.

* * *

ROSEMARY WOOLF

[On "In a frith as I con fare fremede"]†

This poem, found amongst the Harley Lyrics,[1] is the earliest extant and also the best of the English pastourelles. Unfortunately its merits have been obscured by textual and verbal difficulties in the last twelve lines—the very point at which the punch in a good pastourelle normally comes—and it has therefore not received the praise that it deserves: many readers would probably agree with Arthur Moore's judgment that '*In a fryht* is clumsy beside the really good *pastourelles*, in both conception and execution' and that 'The end is obscure and inconclusive.'[2] But it requires only a small emendation in l. 40 and the elucidation of the reference in ll. 45–6 for the coherent and subtle construction of the poem to become plain. Indeed, though its slightly cumbersome stanza form, made heavy by alliteration, deprives it of the metrical gaiety and grace normally found in French pastourelles, in the spiritedness of its dialogue and witty manipulation of argument, it is the equal of its French counterparts. Furthermore the greater leisureliness of the stanza form allows for a thoughtful and imaginative expansion of argument in a way that the French metre does not.

1. The older anthologists sometimes made ludicrous attempts to gloss "bucke uerteth" in a way tolerable to Victorian sensibilities. Most recent editors have recognized what every farm boy knows —that quadrupeds disport themselves in the spring precisely as the poet has said. To the fourteenth century, the idea was probably inoffensive.
† From Rosemary Woolf, "The Con-

struction of *In A Fryht As Y Con Fare Fremede*," *Medium Aevum*, 38 (1969), 55–59. [See p. 27–28, above.] Reprinted by permission of Basil Blackwell Publisher.
1. *The Harley Lyrics*, ed. G. L. Brook (Manchester 1948), pp. 39–40.
2. *The Secular Lyric in Middle English* (Lexington 1951), p. 60.

Up to l. 32 the development of the poem is clear: the poet-narrator woos, bribes and wheedles, whilst the maiden first dismisses him with the colloquial directness characteristic of the initial stage of a pastourelle ('Heo me bed go my gates lest hire gremede'), and then progresses to an admirably moral resolve:

> Betere is were þunne boute laste
> þen syde robes ant synke into synne.

* * *

Up to this point, 'In a fryht' conforms to the familiar pattern of a pastourelle, but thereafter a new method of argument develops, one apparently peculiar to this poem. This method consists in each character drawing upon typical dramatic situations from allied lyric genres to give alarming prophecies of the future. The maiden sees herself in the role of the betrayed maiden who so often speaks a lyric complaint:

> Þenne mihti hongren on heowe,
>   in vch an hyrd ben hated ant forhaht,
> ant ben ycayred from alle þat y kneowe,
>   ant bede cleuyen þer y hade claht.

As a parallel to these lines Stemmler has quoted a Provençal pastourelle, in which the maiden says that she does not wish to exchange her virginity *per nom de putayna* [for the name of a whore];[3] and similar parallels can be found in allied Latin dialogues. * * * The lines in 'In a fryht,' however, are not quite the same as these straightforwardly expressed fears of the maiden that she will gain the reputation of a harlot, as the fears are far more precisely and dramatically conceived. For, with the reference to future heartbreak in the first line of the quotation and the emphasis upon social ostracization in the next two, they are strikingly reminiscent of the lyric genre of the complaint of the betrayed maiden, and the predicament which the maiden here foresees is most probably that of bearing a fatherless child: it is for this that she will become an outcast from all whom she knows, in every family hated and scornfully rejected. A poem in the *Carmina Burana*, 'Huc usque, me miseram', describes with extraordinary vividness a situation of this kind:[4] the girl has to sit alone at home, though bitterly reproached by her parents; when she goes out, people look at her as though she were a monster, nudging each other, and pointing their fingers at her. Lyrics that allude to this fate in a more melancholy and less realistic

---

3. Theo Stemmler, *Die englischen Liebesgedichte des MS. Harley 2253* (Bonn 1962) p. 151, and, for the whole poem, Carl Appel, *Provenzalische Chrestomathie* (Leipzig 1920) pp. 101–2.
4. *Carmina Burana* ed. Alfons Hilka and Otto Schumann I, 2 (Heidelberg 1941) p. 209.

way span mediaeval English literature from what is probably an
early fragment, 'Bryd on brere, y telle yt to none othur, y ne dar'[5]
to the lyrics set to music in Ritson's Manuscript:

> A wanton chyld
> Spake wordes myld
> To me alone,
> And me begylyd,
> Goten with child
> And now ys gone.
> . . . .
> Now may I wynd
> Withoute a frynd
> With hert onfayn;
> In ferre cuntre
> Men wene I be
> A mayde agayn.[6]

The would-be lover caps this argument with an equally horrifying
picture of the future, one drawn from another lyric genre, that of
the *chansons de mal mariées*, in which a married woman complains
of her life with an aged and jealous husband and longs for her
young lover from whom she is now cut off or whom it is dangerous
to see. In England there is a scrap of such a verse in Anglo-Norman
preserved in MS. Rawl. D. 913: 'Amy tenetz vous ioyous / si moura
lui gelous',[7] and in the *Red Book of Ossory* there is a more appropriate parallel:

> Alas hou shold Y singe? Yloren is my playnge.
> Hou shold Y with that olde man
> To leuen, and let my leman,
>   Swettist of all thinge[8]

The ingenuity of this reply has been obscured by a textual corruption in l. 40, as a result of which scholars and critics have either
supposed these lines to be spoken by the maiden or else have pro-
duced tortured explanations of ll. 39–40 that necessarily diminish
the force of the whole. It would, however, be a small and reasonably conservative emendation if 'þah he me slowe ne myhti him
asluppe' were changed to: 'þah he þe slowe ne myhtu him asluppe'.
Whenever lyrics survive in more than one manuscript, there are
substantial textual variations between them, and one of the most
recurrent mistakes is the misapportioning of speeches in dialogue

5. *The Early English Carols* ed. R. L.
Greene (Oxford 1935) p. 448.
6. John Stevens, *Music and Poetry in
the Early Tudor Court* (London 1961)
pp. 346–47; cf. also 348–49.

7. Peter Dronke, 'The Rawlinson Lyrics',
N & Q NS viii (1961), 245; cf. *Altfran-
zösische Romanzen Pastourellen* ed. Karl
Bartsch (Leipzig 1870) p. 37.
8. Greene op. cit. xci.

poems. This of course is not the kind of mistake that arises from manuscript copying but from copying from memory, but again the texts of lyrics indicate that this was very common indeed in the Middle Ages.

At this point in 'In a fryht as y con fare fremede', the narrator is shown to become emboldened by his own argument so that he gives an open and colloquially expressed invitation:

> þe beste red þat y con to vs boþe
> þat þou me take ant y þe toward huppe.

And at this, as in so many pastourelles, the maiden suddenly yields. Her capitulation, however, is at first allusively expressed, and the point of the allusion has nowadays not been understood. She says:

> Mid shupping ne mey hit me ashunche;
> nes y never wycche ne wyle.

This may be translated: 'I cannot escape by shape-shifting: I am not a witch or sorceress'. This conceit is derived from the so-called *chanson des transformations* which Jeanroy regarded as a popular forerunner of the pastourelle:[9] in some versions this consists of a verbal game, in which the maiden posits various shapes that she will assume in order to elude her suitor, and the suitor outwits her by inventing shapes for himself that will capture hers (for instance, if she becomes a star, he will become a cloud). In other versions, such as the unique surviving example in English, the ballad of 'The Twa Magicians', the metamorphosis actually takes place:

> Then she became a turtle dow,
> To fly up in the air,
> And he became another dow,
> And they flew pair by pair.
>
> She turned hersell into an eel,
> To swim into yon burn,
> And he became a speckled trout,
> To gie the eel a turn.[1]

Child describes this as 'a base-born cousin of a pretty ballad known all over southern Europe'. The versions containing a magical transformation seem to be close to folklore, those, which are verbal games, are sophisticated variants. The author of 'In a fryht' may have known either or both kinds. The allusion to the *chanson des transformations* is also interesting in that it casts light upon the imaginative development of the preceding argument, in which evasion and capture are expressed, not by postulating metamorphoses,

9. Alfred Jeanroy *Les origines de la poésie lyrique en France* (Paris 1965) pp. 14–15; cf. also W. P. Jones *The Pastourelle* (Cambridge Mass. 1931) pp. 114–15. 1. F. J. Child, *English and Scottish Ballads* (London 1904) p. 78.

but by the citing of typical social situations portrayed in other lyric genres.

In 'In a fryht' this capitulation, so ingeniously expressed, leads straight into the strikingly frank admission: 'ych am a maide, þat me of þunche'. The *Virginitas placuit* argument is usually retracted by actions rather than words, but the unexpected verbal explicitness is a dramatically effective departure from convention. The final line, 'luef me were gome bute gyle', which misled Stemmler into thinking that the maiden finally refused the narrator,[2] is also unusual in carrying a hint of wistfulness, since the maiden is so obviously about to make do with something less desirable. It may, however, be that 'gome boute gyle' was an alliterative collocation that did not then bear the weight of meaning that we now find in it.

This interpretation shows that the poem is carefully constructed throughout and does not trail away after l. 37. It is also interesting in that it reveals a poet who was at home in the traditional French genres, which are so sparsely represented in mediaeval English literature. It may also suggest a knowledge of Latin dialogues between *Amicus* and *Amica,* for in its wit it is reminiscent of the French and in its thoughtfulness and solidity it recalls the Latin. It is anyway clear that the poet thoroughly understood the form and was thus able to invent freely and ingeniously within it.

EDMUND REISS

[On "Now goth sonne under wod" and "Foweles in the frith"]†

* * *

Commonly called "Sunset on Calvary," this piece contains imagery that plays on the related double meanings of certain words. Through this imagery it comments on the crucifixion and also acts as a celebration of the Virgin. The words *son(n)e, wod, Rode,* and *tre,* all ambiguous, are all key words. From what would seem to be in the first line an innocent description of a sunset, with the sun setting behind the trees, the tone changes in the second line to one of foreboding, *reweth* being the strongest word in the line and, indeed, in the whole poem. We may wonder here what Mary's countenance, *Rode,* has to do with the sunset, except that the setting sun has perhaps struck the Virgin's face at such an angle and

2. Op. cit. p. 150.
† From Edmund Reiss, "A Critical Approach to the Middle English Lyric," *College English,* 27 (February 1966), 373–379. [See pp. 7 and 179, above.]

with such a color of light that the face contains a strangeness for the narrator. But then, in the last two lines we realize that, like the sun in the sky, Mary's son is also going under, as it were, on *his* tree — a parallel existing whether or not *sonne* and *sone* are homophonic—and at this point we may also realize that *Rode* in line 2 contains the meaning of cross.

Wod, Rode, and *tre* are all suggestive of the cross, without in any instance the poet's stating denotatively the specific subject of his poem. The indirect approach is, of course, effective in allowing the crucifixion to be the background of the poem, with the foreground being the narrator's compassion for Mary at the foot of the cross. But even this is not the theme being brought out here. The poem begins as an apparent description of nature, then changes to a lament for Mary, a reflection of her grief, and finally becomes a realization of suffering and of the coming of death and night to the world. Sunset and the death of Christ are made to parallel and give further implications to each other.

The power and suggestiveness of these few lines may be seen further by attempting to translate them into modern English. In the recent disappointing book, *Medieval English Verse* (Penguin, 1964, p. 36), Brian Stone writes as follows:

> Now sinks the sun beneath the wood
> (Mary, I pity your lovely face):
> Now sinks the sun beneath the Rood
> (Mary, I pity your Son and you).

The translation has reduced and altered the Middle English original, limiting its suggestiveness, changing its tone, and causing the integral connection between the two subjects, the crucifixion and Mary, to be lost. Here lines 2 and 4 are subordinated to the thought in lines 1 and 3, and act as a refrain of sorts. In its original this poem seems to use reverse ballad meter, with what I view as a trimeter line preceding a tetrameter one. Lines 1 and 3, the action of the crucifixion, are, in any case, short and, as it were, final; lines 2 and 4, longer and more drawn out, are reflective.

A large part of the poem's success lies in its interwoven incremental repetition and in its paronomasia. The incremental repetition, another ballad technique, results in the thought of line 1 being made more particular and concrete in line 3—the collective *wod* is replaced by the singular *tre*—and, similarly, in the meaning of line 2 developing in line 4. The final line, it should be noted, also contains and expands the sun-son idea as first suggested in line 1. Moreover, the paronomasia, taking the form of secular words having religious significance, gives additional suggestiveness to the lines.

II

The second poem I cite here is a good example of those lyrics
that give a personal emotional reaction to something general:

> Foweles in the frith,
> the fisses in the flod,
> And I mon waxe wod.
> Mulch sorw I walke with
> For beste of bon and blod.

This lyric is in some ways similar to "Nou goth sonne vnder wod,"
although the something that is the occasion of this poem is not so
explicit as it was in the other and although the sorrow of the narrator seems here less formal and more personal than in the previous
poem. While "Foweles in the frith" may be similar in tone to a
complaint poem in the courtly love tradition, the nature of the narrator's sorrow is ambiguous; and, as I read the poem, it is every bit
as religious as the other. It may even be recognized as a paraphrase
in personal terms of the familiar passage in Matthew viii. 20 and
Luke ix. 58: "Foxes have their holes, the birds their roosts; but the
Son of Man has nowhere to lay his head."

This poem also contains verbal ambiguity as relevant as that in
the earlier lyric. For instance, *wod* in line 3 continues in a sense the
places represented by *frith*, forest, and *flod*, sea, of the two preceding lines—functioning in one respect like *wod* in line 1 of "Nou
goth sonne vnder wod." It thus acts in a series—*frith, flod, wod*—
that parallels the series, *foweles, fisses,* and *I*. But, at the same time,
in its most applicable meaning here of "mad," *wod* serves to distinguish and separate man from the rest of nature. The fowls and
fishes are content in their environment, but man is deranged and
out of harmony with the world around him. While *wod* as wood
and *wod* as mad are not phonologically exact, a play on words may
still be possible, at least in the context of this particular poem.

The last two lines give meaning to and expand the idea of isolation suggested in the first three lines. Although man may seem to
be initially joined with the other living beings, he is really different
from them: they fly above and swim beneath the surface of the
earth, but he is limited to its surface. He walks and, furthermore,
walks alone with "mulch sorw," while the fowls and fishes apparently are with others of their own kind. The *w*-sounds in lines 3 and
4 tend to join *walke* with "waxe wod," and suggest that the two
actions are related. *Waxe* also serves to link the growth of the I to
that of the fowls and fishes and, again, to contrast with their
growth; for the narrator grows *wod*, mad.

Nor is madness to be regarded as merely a temporary state in his life; it is, on the other hand, the result of living after original sin. To be a beast (*beste*) of bone and blood means, as it were, to experience "mulch sorw." Furthermore, at least insofar as its orthography indicates, *beste* may signify "best," a meaning that shows the term to be doubly ironic. To be the "best" of bone and blood, to be man, is to "waxe wod" and to be the most sorrowful of creatures. The separation of man from the rest of nature is like that seen in Alain de Lille's *Complaint of Nature*, where Nature's garb is shown rent by man's actions, an idea going back to the description of Philosophy in Boethius' *Consolation of Philosophy*.

A further implication here may be that the narrator, like a scapegoat, carries on his shoulders the weight of human sin and its resultant sorrow. Along with being fallen man, he also approximates Christ as man of sorrows. Indeed, *beste* as "best" may be a more pointed reference to Christ, to him who was the best of living beings. Because of Christ and his suffering, the narrator sorrows; also, because of Christ, he has additional responsibility in that he now knows his obligations and the need for redemption. Not to stretch the point too much, the predicament of the narrator here is like that Sartre says is the human condition when responsible man feels the anguish, forlornness, and despair of being alive. If the narrator were one of the "foweles in the frith" or the "fisses in the flod," such problems would not be his.

While recognizing that much of the power of this piece, really a two-part song, is due to its understatement—that is, the author does not work out a moral or give us anything explicitly didactic—we should also realize the nature and effectiveness of its verbal ambiguities. "Nou goth sonne vnder wod" centered on the ambiguities of a few words; this poem, on the other hand, uses primarily contrasting elements to make its point. With the exception of *beste*, with its two possible meanings, this lyric tends to use patterns of words that create meaning through their relationships to each other.

The rhythms here are also worth noting. Lines 1 and 2 have two major stresses each, but then in line 3—the key line of the poem—the rhythm changes. As I read it, *I, mon, waxe,* and *wod* should all be stressed, the basic pattern of the first two lines thus being replaced by this essentially spondaic line. Line 4 again contains two stresses, but the line is different from 1 and 2, as the narrator is different from the fowls and fishes. This difference is marked principally by the feminine ending, "walke with"; after stressed *walke* appears an unaccented syllable, giving the line the impression of stumbling and thereby reflecting the narrator's state of mind. The final line contains three major stresses and, although regularly iambic, continues the sorrow through the *h*-alliteration of the stressed words, *beste, bon,* and *blod.*

* * *

D. W. ROBERTSON, JR.

[On "Maiden in the mor lay"] †

* * *

An excellent example of poetic *aenigma* is afforded by the four-teenth-century poem called "The Maid of the Moor." The interpretation offered here was developed in collaboration with Professor Huppé, who also shares responsibility for the approach as a whole. * * *On the surface, although the poem is attractive, it cannot be said to make much sense. Why should a maiden lie on a moor for seven nights and a day? And if she did, why should she eat prim-roses and violets? Or again, how does it happen that she has a bower of lilies and roses on the moor? The poem makes perfectly good sense, however, if we take note of the figures and signs in it. The number seven indicates life on earth, but life in this instance went on at night, or before the Light of the World dawned. The day is this light, or Christ, who said "I am the day." And it appears appropriately after seven nights, or, as it were, on the count of eight, for eight is also a figure of Christ. The moor is the wilderness of the world under the Old Law before Christ came. The primrose is not a Scriptural sign, but a figure of fleshly beauty. We are told three times that the primrose was the food of this maiden, and only after this suspense are we also told that she ate or embodied the violet, which is a Scriptural sign of humility. The maiden drank the cool water of God's grace, and her bower consisted of the roses of martyrdom or charity and the lilies of purity with which late medie-val and early Renaissance artists sometimes adorned pictures of the Blessed Virgin Mary, and, indeed, she is the Maiden in the Moor, the maiden who was at once the most beautiful of all women and the divinity whose humility made her the most accessible of all saints.

* * *

† From D. W. Robertson, Jr., "Histori-cal Criticism," *English Institute Essays: 1950,* ed. A. S. Downer (New York: Columbia University Press, 1951), pp. 3–31. [See pp. 128–129, above.] Reprinted by permission of the author and the publisher.

E. T. DONALDSON

[On "Maiden in the mor lay"]†

* * *

I cannot find that the poem, as a poem, makes any more "sense" after exegesis than it did before, and I think it makes rather more sense as it stands than the critic allows it. Maidens in poetry often receive curiously privileged treatment from nature, and readers seem to find the situation agreeable. From the frequency with which it has been reprinted it seems that the "Maiden in the Moor" must have offered many readers a genuine poetic experience even though they were without benefit of the scriptural exegesis. I do not think that most of them would find it necessary to ask the questions of the poem that Robertson has asked; indeed, it seems no more legitimate to inquire what the maiden was doing in the moor than it would be to ask Wordsworth's Lucy why she did not remove to a more populous environment where she might experience a greater measure of praise and love. In each case the poetic *donnée* is the highly primitive one which exposes an innocent woman to the vast, potentially hostile, presumably impersonal forces of nature; and the Middle English lyric suggests the mystery by which these forces are, at times, transmuted into something more humane, even benevolent, by their guardianship of the innocent maiden. The poetic sense is not such as necessarily to preclude allegory, and I shouldn't be surprised if medieval readers often thought of the Virgin as they read the poem, not because they knew the symbols and signs, but because the Virgin is the paramount innocent maiden of the Christian tradition: such suggestivity is one of poetry's principal functions. Robertson's hard-and-fast, this-sense-or-no-sense allegory, however, seems to me so well-concealed and, when explicated, so unrevealing that it can be considered only disappointing if not entirely irrelevant. The function of allegory that is worth the literary critic's attention (as opposed to cryptography, which is not) cannot be to conceal, but is to reveal, and I simply do not believe that medieval poets veiled their poems in order to hide their pious message from heretics and unbelievers. In allegory the equation is not merely *a* equals *b*, the literal statement reanalyzed equals the suggested meaning, but is something more like *a* plus *b* equals *c*, the literal statement plus the meaning it suggests yield an ultimate meaning that is an inextricable union of both. Patristically the primrose may be a figure of fleshy beauty, but actually (and the actual is what

† From E. T. Donaldson, "Patristic Exegesis in the Criticism of Medieval Literature: The Opposition," *Critical Approaches to Medieval Literature*, ed. D. Bethurum (New York: Columbia University Press, 1960), pp. 1–26. Reprinted by permission of the author and the publisher.

poetry is made of) it is one of the commonest of the lovely flowers which nature in its benevolent aspect lavishes upon mankind and, in this case, all-benevolent lavishes upon the maiden of the moor. Robertson asks the question "Why should she eat primroses?" I hope that if I answer "Because she was hungry," it will not be said of me that a primrose by the river's brim a yellow primrose was to him, and it was nothing more.

* * *

JOHN SPEIRS

[On "Maiden in the mor lay"]†

* * *

Who is this 'maiden' who has spent a seven-nights' vigil on the moor beside a well? It is unlikely that we can ever know exactly, and there is perhaps no need that, as readers of what to us is a *poem*, we should. She is sufficiently defined in the poem for the purposes of our response to the poetry—a child of nature, whether human or faery, her meat the primrose and the violet, her drink the chilled water of the well-spring.

The reference to a well-spring suggests the possibility that the song may originally have had some connexion with the 'well-wakes' —the worship of wells—which, there is abundant evidence, went on all through the Middle Ages. These well-wakes were particularly associated with St. John's Eve and so with the rites, ceremonies and practices of the great Midsummer festival as a whole.

We may guess from what is said in the song that the maiden, if she is human, has been undergoing some rite of initiation or purification. If she is a faery being—or the human impersonator of such in a dramatic dance—she may be the spirit of the well-spring. We know that the word 'maiden' was often used in a special sense as the title of a witch, the leader of a coven, one of the nuns of Diana, as it were.

This song also is evocative of a tranced mood. It has a kind of solemn gaiety, solemn like the gaiety of a child absorbed in what to it is a serious game. This quality would further suggest that this poem may in fact have been connected with rites and dances designed to promote fertility or in some other respect to influence the course of nature magically—in the spring or summer, as the flowers suggest. When we speak, as we well may, of this song's

† From John Speirs, *Medieval English Poetry: The Non-Chaucerian Tradition* (London: Faber & Faber Ltd.; New York: Hillary House Publishers, Ltd., 1957), pp. 63–64. Reprinted by permission of the publishers.

324 · *Peter Dronke*

enchanting innocence or magical lightness we may be nearer than
we perhaps think to the literal truth.

There are six English lines in a Latin Christian context in
another MS (Magdalen College, Oxford, MS 60, of the end of the
fourteenth century) which are about another maid beside a well.

> At a sprynge wel under a thorn
> Ther was bote of bale, a lytel here a-forn;
> Ther by-syde stant a mayde,
> fulle of love y-bounde.
> Ho-so wol seche trwe love
> yn hyr hyt schal be founde.

In this case the maid—judging by 'bote of bale' and 'trwe love'—is
Mary. She has, however, an unmistakable affinity with the maiden
by the well-spring, 'the spirit of the fountain'. The lines, though
they have lost the movement of the dance and are rhythmically
uncertain and even flat, illustrate how the imagery of the songs of
the earlier religion was being adapted to Christian meanings.

* * *

PETER DRONKE

[On "Maiden in the mor lay"]†

* * *

The anonymous English song of the moor-maiden (written
down, with some other snatches of lyric, on a scrap of parchment in
the early fourteenth century) must be understood in the light of
the popular beliefs to which it alludes.[1] This makes it rather less
enigmatic than has often been thought, though no less enchanting.

* * *

What is a moor-maiden? She is a kind of water-sprite living in
the moors; she appears in a number of German legends, especially
from Franconia.[2] It is appropriate that the English song should be
a dance-song, as one of the commonest legends associates the moor-

† From Peter Dronke, *The Medieval Lyric* (New York: Harper & Row, 1966), pp. 195–196. Reprinted by permission of the Hutchinson University Library and the author.
1. Some scholars have mistakenly proposed a Christian interpretation for the song, unaware that it was precisely the un-Christian, 'lewd, secular' nature of the words which led Bishop Richard de Ledrede, who held the see of Ossory in Ireland from 1317–60, to compose a sacred Latin text to replace them. (Cf. R. L. Greene, *Speculum* XXVII, 1952, 504–6).
2. Cf. H. Bächtold–Stäubli, *Handwörterbuch des deutschen Aberglaubens*, VI, 565, s.v. *Moorjungfern* (with principal references; further references in E. Fentsch, 'Volkssage und Volksglaube in Unterfranken', *Bavaria*, IV [1866], i, 203 ff.).

maiden with a dance. She tends to appear at village dances in the guise of a beautiful human girl, and to fascinate young men there, but she must always return into the moor at a fixed hour, or else she dies. Sometimes it is only for one hour in the week that she is allowed to leave the moor and mingle with human beings—this perhaps is also why in the song she waits in the moor 'sevenistes fulle ant a day'. Like other water-sprites, a moor-maiden may be linked with a particular well-spring; in two German folksongs such a well-maiden gives the children who come to the spring flowers 'to make them sleep' (whether sleep here implies death is not certain from the context). In the English song, however, the well and the flowers evoke the moor-maiden's more-than-earthly serenity and well-being: she has none of the cares and needs that mortals have. Is the lyric simply a meditation on this theme? I think it far more probable that the theme was made vivid for the dancers by a mime. Then at the start of the song a girl playing the moor-maiden would have lain as if asleep; the dancers approach her, admiring her beauty, and some of the young men try to wake her, at first in vain. Then, perhaps, a bell strikes: suddenly 'sevenistes fulle ant a day' are up, she comes of her own accord into the centre of the round, and is at once the acknowledged queen of the dance. An admirer offers her dainties to eat, which she refuses; he offers her primroses and violets, and these she pretends to eat. Another admirer offers her wine—again she makes a gesture of refusal; instead she goes to drink at her well. All the dancers make her a bed of flowers; she reclines on it; the bell sounds once more, and she falls back into sleep, again as out of reach as at the beginning. It is along these lines, I think, that we can picture the living reality that such a song may have been.

* * *

THOMAS JEMIELITY

[On "I sing of a maiden"]†

An apparently artless and conventional work, the medieval lyric "I Sing of a Maiden" is a highly imaginative poem, replete with liturgical symbols and allusions and very candid about the physical intimacies of Christ's conception in Mary. The poem celebrates the divine communion with man at the heart of the Christian myth, that paradoxically virginal yet fruitful intercourse with Mary which conceives the redemption that is Jesus. Yet, in the imagination of

† From Thomas Jemielity, " 'I Sing of a Maiden': God's Courting of Mary," *Concerning Poetry* (Western Washington State College, Bellingham, Wash.), 2 (1969), 53–71. [See p. 170, above.] Reprinted by permission of the publisher.

the medieval lyricist, it is Mary, not God, who commands the entire situation. The anxiety in this sexual approach is God's because the poem focusses on her willingness to be the mate and the mother of the divine. Approaching Mary as seed and as lover, Christ awaits her word like a knight awaiting his lady. Christ and Mary, the courtly ideals, are figured in this poem as knight and maiden. The sexual consummation desired in the courtly relationship is very clearly the object of Christ's desire: the incremental repetitions in the middle three stanzas speak of this union subtly but candidly, and then restate the manner of God's approach to Mary in images familiar to the medieval audience because of their use in the Advent liturgy. The language of the poem enhances the paradox it hymns because the poem must speak simultaneously of virginity and fruition, of God as lover and as seed. And Mary so clearly commands the moment of sexual and redemptive union that the poem is suffused throughout by the reverent, yet serenely confident tone of the voice celebrating the mystery, a voice so sure in its faith that it finds no unseemliness in its gentle punning about Mary's virginal conception of Jesus.

The first stanza of the poem makes evident that God is approaching the moment of redemptive intercourse with the tenderness and reverence of a lover seeking first of all a sign of his lady's favor. As the rhetorically and rhythmically emphasized last word of the stanza —*chees*—makes apparent, this poem celebrates not God's choice of Mary, but rather her willingness to accept the divine as mate and as son. The emphasis on *chees*, furthermore, quietly prepares for the sexual implications of place-restriction in the middle three stanzas, and suggests an almost knight-like courtesy as God seeks to consummate his love with the lady of his choice.

Mary appears first as the maiden, the young girl, in the strictest denotation of the term, but also, in its natural and extended sense, the virgin. She is the young girl, foretold by Isaiah, who is to bear Immanuel, that is, God with us. But the maiden is *makeless*: without a husband, first of all, for she and Joseph had not yet come together at the time she conceived Jesus, and, in her own phrase, did not "know man";[1] without a mate as well, the lyric puns, for

1. Although I would not disagree with David Halliburton's assertion that Mary and Joseph were married at the time she conceived Jesus, Mary was, in one sense, without a husband, for the passage in Matthew to which Mr. Halliburton refers (1:18–25) implies that Mary and Joseph had not yet come together at the time of Christ's conception. Furthermore, without allowing the poem or the critic to do violence to the traditions about Mary's divine motherhood, I would not look to the lyric for a definitive theological statement about an ambiguous and paradoxical marital relationship. See "The Myden Makeles," *Papers on Language and Literature*, 4 (1968), 115–120. Also, if the Christ-Mary relationship in this poem does suggest the knight-lady relationship of the courtly love triangle, then Joseph's status as Mary's husband completes the courtly love triangle in which the lady's lover is not her husband.

Mary is without equal, the note on which the poem concludes:

> Moder and maiden
> Was nevere noon but she . . . .

A soft and serene amusement underlies both the punning and the imaginative reversal that makes God dependent on Mary's choice.

The emphasis which *chees* places on Mary's willingness to be the mate and the mother of God is sustained throughout the next three stanzas. The word, in fact, determines the tone of the iterations, because Mary's decision demands a reverential approach from the God-lover. That tone is enhanced by the reiteration of *stille*, which qualifies the one literal predication in these three stanzas: *He cam*. *Stille* connotes God's respect for the virginity of Mary in its denotation as freedom from commotion or disturbance of any kind. God's approach is thus both physically and psychologically tender, and Mary's intercourse, unlike that of Yeats' Leda, is not violent. Mary's experience leaves her integral and virginal, albeit fruitful. In the words of the poem, Mary's intercourse with the divine leaves her *stille*. The qualification suggests as well the silence which tradition associates with Gabriel's announcement to Mary, recorded in Luke, and, looking forward to Christ's birth, to the silence of the manger. The Word of God quietly descends into Mary's womb in order to assume flesh. *Stille* suggests, thirdly, Mary's composure at this moment, traditionally at prayer when she receives the invitation to divine motherhood. Here again, the lyric reverses a convention, both theological and artistic, about the union of the divine and the human. In his classic commentary on the Christian liturgy, *The Church's Year of Grace*, Pius Parsch says that Mary is "startled by the angel," that she is "frightened and says not a word." And Yeats, who presents the classical annunciation as a violent and frightening experience for Leda, has Mary say, in "The Mother of God":

> Terror of all terrors that I bore
> The Heavens in my womb.[2]

But no such anxiety on Mary's part appears in this poem.

God, however, is also approaching Mary as a lover. And so the *stille* which captures the gentleness of Christ's coming as seed captures as well the tender anxiety and gentleness of God's coming as lover. For the threefold iteration of *stille*—itself significantly contributing to the tone of the poem—appears with an incremental repetition that restricts the place of God's coming first and generally to where Mary is, then to her bower, and finally to her bed.

2. Pius Parsch, *The Church's Year of Grace*, tr. William G. Heidt (Collegeville, Minn., 1957), I, III; "The Mother of God," in *The Collected Poems of W. B. Yeats* (New York, 1959), p. 244.

The sexual candor of the poem's celebration of the conception of Jesus is particularly apparent here. This restriction imaginatively dramatizes the God-lover's hesitant approach to Mary; it forcefully suggests his anxiety as he awaits her consent; and it unequivocally and candidly introduces the physical intimacies of the conception of Jesus. When God reaches Mary's bed and receives her acceptance, then the lyric almost immediately asserts the moment of consummation, the moment spoken of in the opening vesper antiphon of the New Year's Day liturgy: "O most wonderful intercourse, that has united heaven and earth!" Mary is now the divine mother as well as the divine maiden. God approaches only because Mary allows him; He approaches with the tenderness and anxiety of a love that has waited, in the biblical chronology, four thousand years to consummate with this woman His love for man. Although the reverence and hesitation of God's approach are perfectly consonant with the awesome dimensions of Mary's choice, the poem cannot conceal its secure amusement and delight at God's having to await his lady's consent to bear His son. The lyric effectively captures the human, intimate dimensions of the incarnation of Jesus.

Whatever the implications of the mystery celebrated in the poem, the lyric remains always conscious of God's reverentially intimate approach as lover and seed. A second incremental repetition figuratively restates the manner of God's approach as an April dew falling seminally on the grass, the flower, and the spray. Like the gradually restricted focus to Mary's bed, this incremental repetition moves from an image of general vitality to a metaphorically significant hint of fertility and reproduction in the spray. Prosodically emphasized in these three stanzas, the images of the dew, the flower, and the spray are important in the Advent liturgy as well.

According to Pius Parsch, Advent, the four-week season of preparation for Christmas, is of venerable antiquity, dating back to the early centuries of Christianity. During this time, Mary's role in the conception of Jesus receives special emphasis on the Wednesday of Ember Week, the third week of Advent, in a liturgy even older than that of the season in which it falls.[3] In the liturgy of these weeks, dew appears frequently as an image of the soon-to-be incarnated Christ. Its most common use is in the familiar Advent refrain that opens the Masses of Ember Wednesday and the fourth Sunday in Advent: "Send dew from above, you heavens, and let the skies pour down upon us the rain we long for, him, the Just One: may he, the Savior, spring from the closed womb of the earth" (Isaiah 45:8, tr. R. A. Knox). The seminal falling of the dew precedes the dawn, as Christ's conception in Mary precedes the visible dawning of redemption in the birth of Jesus. And as the dew comes but for a

3. Parsch, pp. 104, 106.

little while, Christ's visible incarnation is to be brief: the Greek of St. John's gospel says literally that the Word made flesh only pitched a tent among men. Suggesting, thus, the manner of God's approach to Mary in its gentleness, stillness, and fertility, the dew is fittingly an April dew. For the medieval liturgy, somewhat literal-minded, celebrated Christ's conception in Mary also on March 25, nine months before Christmas. That springtime feast, Lady Day, marked in the middle ages and well into the eighteenth century the beginning of the civil year, because the date marked as well the beginning of the new year of salvation in Mary's womb. The April dew of man's redemption restores the earth like Chaucer's *showres soote* physically reviving the company of pilgrims.

The grass, the flower, and the spray on which the dew falls refer both to Christ and to Mary's virginity. In each case the dew effects a salvific conception. The grass is a general symbol of vitality, a sign of the grassy earth, now brought to new life in Jesus, in the womb of Mary. The dew that falls on the grass transforms Mary into the earth's mother of salvation, for her son will revivify man. The dew falls on the flower, and the emphasis here is on the beauty of the blossom: the blossom of Mary's virginity, so lovely that God does not violate it even in intercourse; the blossom which is Jesus, resplendent like the flower of the familiar medieval carol *Flos de Radice Jesse*, the "Rose E'er Blooming." The medieval audience was not unfamiliar with the use of flower to mean virginity, although this usage is obsolete today. Climactically, the dew falls on the spray, on the slender, growing shoot which will grow into the tree of man's redemption on the tree of the cross. This spray is "the fresh root from Jesse's stem, the signal beckoning to all the peoples around" (Isaiah 11:10, tr. R. A. Knox).

Almost abruptly the lyric concludes with negative, absolute exclusions that correspond to the superlatives of the opening stanza. These hyperboles that open and close the poem state the delightful truth it celebrates: no other was ever maiden and mother; no other could be worthier to be the mother of God. The voice in the poem can scarcely conceal its satisfaction at the perfection of the God-knight's choice:

> Wel may swich a lady
> Godes moder be.

This celebration of Mary's intercourse with the divine is suffused with a serenity and confidence of tone that is, perhaps, the most remarkable achievement of this fine poem. God does not overpower Mary, as Zeus overwhelms Leda. Mary commands the moment, and God's reverential hesitation and anxiety appears throughout. For the plan He seeks to effect, after all, involves this woman in the

most physically intimate of relationships and He regards her willingness as indispensable to the consummation of His plan. With
obvious simplicity, but with delightful imagination, the poem casts
God as a knight approaching His maiden in what is to be a most
far-reaching love affair. The structure of the lyric, simple as it is,
parallels the hyperbolic statement of theme in the first stanza with
that of the last; and, in the body of the poem, parallels one incremental repetition that climaxes in a most fruitful intercourse, with a
second incremental repetition that restates this climactic fertility in
clear metaphorical terms. With wonder and a sense of the ineffable,
yet with delicacy and soft amusement, the poem emphasizes His
hesitation as He approaches the physically intimate moment of
intercourse and conception. In the seclusion of her bower, in the
stillness of her bed, Mary receives from her divine lover the seed
which He has waited four thousand years to implant in this most
efficaciously redemptive intercourse.

STEPHEN MANNING

[On "I sing of a maiden"]†

Although "I Syng of a Myden" has always been regarded as a
superlative lyric, and although it has received detailed discussion
by George Kane, John Speirs, and especially Leo Spitzer,[1] there are
many features of this extremely complex poem which need to be
pointed out: the richness of the imagery, the significance of the
puns, and the number symbolism, for example. Nor has anyone sin-
gled out the remarkable achievement of our poet in combining the
tone of wonder and exultation in Mary's dual role as maiden and
mother with an amazing wealth of the natural and theological
implications surrounding the event. A similar tone was often used
in speaking of the virgin-motherhood of Mary. * * * Although a
sense of the miracle involved is often part of this tone, there is
rarely any attempt at explanation. The general attitude is that of
the Middle English preacher toward the man of authority, knowledge, and holiness: "be not to be to inquisitiff how þat itt may be
þat þe virginite and þe moderhede be bothe in Oure Lady, for þe

† From Stephen Manning, " 'I Syng of a
Myden,' " *PMLA*, 75 (1960), 8–12. Reprinted by permission of the Modern
Language Association of America.
1. Kane, *Middle English Literature*
(London, 1951), pp. 161–165; Speirs,
Medieval English Poetry (London,
1957), pp. 67–69; Spitzer, *"Explication
de Texte* Applied to Three Great Middle

English Poems," *Archivum Linguisticum*,
III (1951), 152–163. Both Kane and
Spitzer discuss in detail the changes our
poet made in utilizing his 13th-century
source, "Nu þis fules singet," printed in
Carleton Brown, ed., *English Lyrics of
the XIIIth Century* (Oxford, 1932), p.
55.

cause her-of beþ not of common nature but of Goddes wurchynge
and is hiʒe myracle and abowen þe common cours of kynde."[2] Our
poet, on the other hand, while achieving a tone of exultation partly
by the incremental repetition in stanzas 2-4, is at the same time
explaining how it was possible for Mary to bear a child yet remain a
virgin. He explains in terms of what the preacher just quoted called
"Goddes wurchynge" and "hiʒe myracle"; he explains through his
imagery the theological and natural implications of the mystery of
Mary's virgin-maternity. Much of the tone of wonder and exultation arises, in fact, from our poet's realization of the factors
involved in this great mystery.

The poem is readily divided into three parts. The first part
(stanza 1) announces the theme: "I syng of a myden / þat is makeles." The second part (stanzas 2-4) proves the theme, but not by
the "naive tautology" of which Spitzer speaks (p. 154). The third
part (stanza 5) sums up the proof by the restatement of theme:
"moder and mayden / was neuer non but che," then extends this
restatement by echoing imagistic motifs found earlier in the poem.

The announcement of theme contains an important ambiguity.
Makeles means *matchless*, as editors usually gloss it, but this is a
secondary meaning derived from its primary meaning of *without
mate*, i.e., sexual mate.[3] The singularity of this maiden is emphasized by the rime-stress on the privative suffix. Our poet, then,
announces he is singing of a maiden who is without a mate and
thus calls immediate attention to her virginity. When we read the
last line of stanza 1 we find that this virgin has chosen a son, and
we are startled. Our poet has heightened his paradox by a shift in
tense from line 2 to line 4; the maiden *is* without a mate, yet she
chose a son. And it is precisely because this maiden had a son without benefit of sexual mate that she is matchless. This is an excellent
illustration of Walter J. Ong's comments on the use of the pun in
the medieval poetry of wit; puns are used, he says, "for serious
effects—that is, puns are used to another purpose than that of
giving a *prima facie* startling appearance to essentially drab fact.
Puns are used where semantic coincidence penetrates to startling
relations in the real order of things."[4] Apart from developing
Mary's matchlessness as derived from her matelessness, line 4 reinforces her supremacy by paraphrasing her *fiat* as "che ches." Under-

2. *Middle English Sermons*, ed. Wood-
burn O. Ross, EETS, CCIX (London,
1940), 221–222.
3. An exception is William Frost, ed.,
The Age of Chaucer, in *English Master-
pieces*, ed. Maynard Mack (New York,
1950), p. 336. Frost glosses it as "without a mate; also, 'matchless'." Speirs, p.
69, discusses the pun briefly; he would
extend it to include a pun on *maskelles*

(spotless) and *makeles*. Neither com-
mentator discusses the structural importance of the pun, however. The pun
could conceivably also appear in our
poet's 13th-century source, but the earlier poet does not utilize it structurally,
as does our poet.
4. "Wit and Mystery: a Revaluation in
Mediaeval Latin Hymnody," *Speculum*,
XXII (1947), 315.

scoring this matchlessness still further is the reference to Christ in
line 3 as the King of Kings, and the maiden would have to be
matchless indeed to choose him as her son.

In the first stanza, then, our poet has announced that he sings of
a maiden who is mateless and thereby matchless. Stánzas · 2-4
develop the theme of her matelessness and at the same time prove
her matchlessness. If Mary conceived without sexual intercourse,
the question is, how did she conceive, and our poet answers in three
parts.

> He cam also stylle
> þer his moder was
> as dew in aprille
> þat fallyt on þe gras

is the first part of his answer. Dew is, of course, a conventional
symbol of the Holy Spirit and his grace. This, then, is how Mary
conceived—through the grace of the Holy Spirit, recalling Gabriel's
words to Mary: "Spiritus sanctus superveniet in te" (Luke i.35).
Our poet uses the symbol of the dew three times, however.
Although threefold repetition is common in medieval poetry, the
particular context of our poem suggests an appropriateness not
found in other poems. Every well-informed Christian knew that
although a particular act was attributed to the Holy Spirit, that act
was the work of the entire Trinity, for the Trinity is indivisible.
Here, for example, are the comments of the author of the *Myroure
of Our Lady*: "For thoughe oure lord iesu cryste onely were made
man. yet the incarnacion of hym was wroughte by all thre persones.
for the outward dedes and warkes of the blyssed Trinitye ar vnde-
partable. and all that one dothe. all thre dothe. for they thre are
one."[5] The three-fold occurrence of the dew image in our poem,
then, has a doctrinal significance; Mary could conceive a child and
remain a virgin through the operation of the Trinity. She was therefore mateless and thereby matchless.

The dew image, however, has multiple connotations—connotations which the medieval exegetes and homilists were quick to
explore. These connotations further support our poet's theme. One
homilist sums up the properties of dew usually listed by sermon
writers and encyclopedists: "Ros refrigerat, fecundat, humectat,
penetrat, mundat, silenter intrat, calorem et serenitatem diei prae-
nuntiat. [Frost chills, fertilizes, moistens, penetrates, cleanses, enters
silently, augurs the warmth and serenity of the day.]"[6] All of these

5. Ed. John Henry Blunt, EETS ES, XIX
(London, 1905), 94. Among other references may be cited St. Augustine, *En-
chiridion*, I 38, *PL*, XL, 251; Aelfric,
"Annunciatio S. Mariae," *Sermones
Catholici*, ed. Benjamin Thorpe (London, 1844), I, 196.
6. Peter Cellensis, "In Annuntiatione
Dominica" VI, *PL*, CCII, 721. Discussions
of the dew image appear frequently in
commentaries upon, and in sermons
which allude to, Judges vi. 37-40 and

properties become connotations of the image in our poem. The fecund property of dew (i.e., God's grace) is seen in the progression from grass to flower to spray; thus our poet expresses much more subtly what St. Ambrose stated directly: "Alvus tumescit virginis. [The Virgin's womb swells.]"[7] When applied to the Virgin Mary, however, the quality of fecundity is modified by the corresponding quality of virginity; just as dew makes fecund and cleanses (mundat), so also the grace of God. * * * The silence with which the dew falls has also been identified with Mary's virginity. * * * Mary, in her miraculous conceiving,[8] was unlike other women in that there was not the slightest trace of concupiscence—one more aspect of her matchlessness.

But the dew image may also refer to Christ, since by the wording of the simile, *he* in line 5 may equal *dew* in line 7. This also is conventional. * * * All of the connotations of the dew image which refer to Christ are related to our poet's theme, for Mary's matchlessness is manifest in her choosing such a Son. Most of these connotations are related to Christ's act of redemption and, of course, to Mary's role in mankind's redemption. The most obvious connection between the dew image and Christ is the descent from heaven, of God becoming man, and Mary's consequent bearing the God-man. Christ's coming, moreover, was *still*, as our poet comments in line 5. In one sense the thought here is similar to a Scriptural passage often glossed with reference to the Incarnation. * * * We may see in this image of stillness a reference to Christ's humility in that he came in silence, not with any fanfare as would befit an earthly king. We may see further, prompted by St. Ambrose,[9] a reference to Christ's coming in silence so that the world would not know of his coming, so that the worldly would not confuse his spiritual mission with a temporal one. But the image may connote as well something of the awfulness of the act of Incarnation: the silence is reverence—both fear and ineffability. Perhaps, too, there may be a suggestion of the dual nature of God as viewed by some commentators: a paradox of tranquility and activity—"perfect stillness, perfect fecundity," according to John Ruysbroeck.[1]

Ps. lxxi. 6 (Vulgate). The qualities of dew mentioned in these passages are those mentioned also in, e.g., Hugh of St. Victor, *De Bestiis et Aliis Rebus,* IV, *PL,* CLXXVII, 158; Vincent of Beauvais, *Bibliotheca Mundi* (Duaci, 1624), I, 205. Another quality of dew is sweetness, which applies particularly to Jesus; several ME poems are on this subject.
7. *Analecta Hymnica* (abbreviated hereafter *AH*), ed. Guido Dreves and Clemens Blume (Leipzig, 1880–1922), LIV, viii, 13. Amedeus uses an image which is reminiscent of our poem: "uterus intumescat, gaudeat animus, *floreat alvus*" (italics mine), *De Maria Virginea Matri,*

III, *PL,* CLXXXVIII, 1318.
8. The doctrine of the virgin birth had been clearly defined for centuries; this doctrine is sometimes confused with the immaculate conception (Mary's preservation at conception from the least stain of sin), which was the cause of much controversy in the thirteenth and fourteenth centuries.
9. "De Natali Domini," III, *PL,* XVII, 634.
1. *De Vera Contemplatione,* XII, quoted by Evelyn Underhill, *Mysticism* (New York, 1955), p. 37, in a discussion of this point.

A further connotation of dew is that it pre-announces the warmth of the day, glossed as eternal life. Morning has definite connotations that fuse with the concept of redemption. It is allied to the image of Christ as sun, or light, Who drives away the darkness of sin. It has also the suggestion of a beginning, just as the Incarnation began the redemption of mankind. And as Spitzer comments upon another connotation: "The cool freshness of the morning dew is allowed to convey to us the idea of the moral *refrigerium*, or the rejuvenation, brought to humanity by the Redeemer" (p. 155). Similar connotations surround the image of April in line 7. April also has the sense of beginning, of rejuvenation, in contrast to the winter of "mankind's unredeemed age." These connotations, plus the fact that the feast of the Annunciation is celebrated the eighth Kalends of April, are noted by Adam in his *Mariale*.[2] * * * Thus April also has the connotation of fecundity, one of the properties of dew. These images, then, of April, morning, and dew, with their connotations of redemption, Mary's role in redemption, her purity, and her miraculous conceiving circle around the poet's theme of Mary's being *makeles.*

We have already noted the sequence from grass to flower to spray in connection with the fecund property of dew. Matching this progression is the spatial-temporal sequence in the second line of each of the middle stanzas; as Spitzer has pointed out: "the line 'there his mother was' . . . indicates a minimum of locality, merely the fact that there was a place where Mary was; the line 'to his mother's bower' provides an environment that befits a noblewoman (a 'lady'); and finally the line 'there his mother lay' delicately suggests the bed of child-birth" (p. 156). Matching these two progressions is a third, involving the connotations of the images of the grass, flower, and spray. Each is a simile for the Virgin, and the connotations of each reveal why Mary is matchless. The flower image has several related connotations. It is a term of general excellence: the flower is the choice part of the plant. More specifically, it is a symbol of beauty. In speaking of Mary, however, writers have associated physical and spiritual beauty, and the flower image is used most often in connection with Mary's chastity. Latin hymns speak of her as "flos virginitatis," "flos pudoris," "flos castitatis," "flos munditiae," and "flos pudicitiae" [flower of virginity, flower of decency, flower of chastity, flower of cleanness, flower of modesty]. The flower image is particularly apt in our poem because of Mary's virginity. The grass image I would interpret as a symbol of humility, although the usual medieval symbol is nard. Supporting this interpretation are the many medieval writers who have linked Mary's

2. *PL*, ccxi, 709.

chastity and humility; one especially apt parallel occurs in a Latin hymn.³ * * *

Although Mary's great humility is praised by medieval writers, the importance of this virtue in our poem is emphasized by a contemporary carol: "Thou art his moder for humylite." According to some commentators, it was chiefly because of Mary's humility that God chose her as His mother. As St. Bernard wrote: "Si igitur Maria humilis non esset, super eam Spiritus sanctus non requievisset; si super eam non requievisset, nec impraegnesset. [Therefore, had Mary not been humble, the Holy Ghost would not have rested upon her; had he not rested upon her, he would not have impregnated her.]"⁴ * * * This is exactly the point which the author of *Hali Meidenhad* stresses: "Nim ʒeme, meiden, ant understont herbi, þet mare for hir meokelec þen for hire meiðhad, ha lette bet ha ifont swuch grace ed ure lauerd. for al meiðhad, meokelec is muche wurð; ant meiðhad wiðuten hit is eðelich unwurð."⁵ This, then, explains the sequence in our poem from grass to flower: God took into account first Mary's humility and then her chastity. The image of the flower leads to the image of the spray, which completes the progression by referring symbolically to the actual birth of Christ. The image is a reference to Is. xi.1: "Et ingredietur virga de radice Jesse, et flos de radice ejus ascendat [And there shall come forth a rod out of the root of Jesse, and a flower shall rise up out of his root]," one of the most famous Messianic prophecies. *Spray*, in fact, seems to be an English translation of the Latin *virga*. The two virtues of humility and chastity were, then, in a sense, Mary's qualifications for bearing the Christ child. This is why she was matchless and therefore why God chose her to be mateless, which in turn increased her matchlessness.

In lines 17–18 the poet sums up the three middle stanzas by restating his theme. This restatement contains both meanings of *makeles*: Mary was a mother, but at the same time a maiden, and there has never been anyone else to whom this privilege has been given. The terms *moder* and *mayden* are brought together explicitly for the first time and thereby climax this motif. In the first stanza Mary is referred to as a maiden and mother separately; in the middle stanzas the poet has used the term *moder* and has implied Mary's virginity in the images of the dew and the flower and the spray. Now, having explained by his imagery how this virgin-maternity could be, our poet joins the two terms, "Moder and mayden" (line 17). In the last two lines he comments upon this uniqueness: "Well may swych a lady / Godes moder be!" The

3. *AH*, xxx, lviii, "Ad Nonam," 134.
4. "Super *Missus Est*" I, *PL*, CLXXXIII, 58.

5. Ed. F. J. Furnivall, rev. ed., EETS, XVIII (London, 1922), 62. I have normalized some of the spelling.

word *lady* sums up another motif running throughout the poem. It refers, first of all, to lines 3–4; anyone who can choose the King of Kings for her son obviously deserves such an epithet. It refers also to line 10; *bowr* is often connected with a lady. It refers also in a spiritual sense to Mary's virtues of humility and chastity, signified by the grass and flower images. And finally it refers to the connotation of the spray image; the branch in Is. xi.1 is to spring from the root of Jesse, the father of David, and therefore from a royal line. Our poet therefore refers to "*swych* a lady" for he has indicated all along her nobility. But our poet's phrasing very possibly refers to another reason for his choice; the etymology for *Maria* was believed to have been the Aramaic word for *lady*. This seems to have originated with St. Jerome and appears throughout the Middle Ages.[6] Thus when our poet exclaims about *swych* a lady, he is punning on the very name of that lady. These considerations indicate that the poet is not using the circular reasoning which Spitzer attributes to him; the "*Q.E.D.* quality of 'well may such a lady'" is not only poetic, as Spitzer says (p. 154), but also logical in view of her name and of her virtues and royal lineage.

"I Syng of a Myden," then, exhibits an amazing complexity in its puns, the multiple connotations and interactions of its images, and the profundity with which the poet has contemplated Mary's virgin-maternity. He has drawn freely upon traditional materials and upon his thirteenth-century source. But if this lyric is characterized by complexity and tradition, it is characterized also by freshness and simplicity. Herein lies its greatness. As a final example of the poet's artistry, we may notice that there are five stanzas to our poem, which, as we have seen, form a logical and poetic whole. We may see in this number a tribute to the Virgin, for the number five was often associated with her: there are five letters in her name and she had five joys.[7] This significance of the number of stanzas is interesting when we recall the source of our poem is an "Exemplum de beata virgine & gaudiis eius [Illustration of the Blessed Virgin and her joys]," according to the rubric, but the earlier poet composed six stanzas. This number symbolism is but one more reason why "I Syng of a Myden" represents the supreme achievement of the Middle English lyric.

6. *Liber de Nominibus Hebraicis, PL,* xxiii, 886.
7. For discussion of the five letters in *Maria,* see *AH,* xxx, lviii, 129; John Bromyard, *Summa Predicantium,* ed. Hieronymus Verdussus (Antwerp, 1614), pt. ii, p. 7–8. Number symbolism, it seems to me, may be divided into three kinds: structural (the three central stanzas of our poem), appropriate (our poem's five stanzas), and arbitrary (such as Walafrid Strabo's choice of 84 lines for one of his poems because that was the age of the prophetess Anna at Christ's birth). For the last example, and for further discussion of the latter two kinds, see Ernst R. Curtius, *European Literature and the Latin Middle Ages,* tr. Willard R. Trask (New York, 1953), pp. 504–509.

D. G. HALLIBURTON

[On "I sing of a maiden"]†

The popular Middle English lyric "I Syng of a Myden" is at once
more traditional and more readily comprehensible than its commentators have lately come to suppose. Indeed, it is precisely the reso-
nance of traditional associations which gives the poem its directness
and force.

> I syng of a myden
> þat is makeles;
> kyng of alle kynges
> to here sone che ches.[1]

"The announcement of theme," writes Stephen Manning, "contains an important ambiguity. *Makeles* means 'matchless,' as editors
usually gloss it, but this is a secondary meaning derived from its primary meaning of 'without mate,' i.e., sexual mate. . . . it is precisely
because this maiden had a son without benefit of sexual mate that
she is matchless."[2] John Speirs, although allowing the existence of
two meanings, similarly insists on the primacy of a sexual overtone.
" 'Makeles,' as of a bird without a mate, expresses Mary's compan-
ionless, maiden or virginal state. The meaning of the other word—
'without a flaw or blemish, immaculate'—is surely also present."[3]
Such drastic revision of the significance of the term *makeles*, revers-
ing as it does the virtually unanimous findings of earlier editors and
commentators,[4] requires the fullest kind of documentation; unfortunately, none has been forthcoming. On what basis, precisely, is one
to infer a *fundamentally* sexual implication in the poet's use of that
key word? Such a reading of *makeles* assumes, to begin with, an
unnecessarily narrow meaning of the root noun. Far from referring
to an individual with whom one has sexual relations, the first meaning is "equal, peer, match; one's like" (*OED*, s.v. *Make*, sb.[1], 1,
from *circa* A.D. 1000); the first meaning of *makeles* is, accordingly,
"Without an equal, matchless, peerless" (*OED*, a.1). The sense
connoting a mateless or wifeless state is not at all the primary
meaning, but a secondary one. One notes further that the *OED*

† From D. G. Halliburton, "The Myden
Makeles," *Papers on Language and Literature*, 4 (1968), 115–120. Reprinted by
permission of the publisher.
1. Citations are to the text in *Religious
Lyrics of the XVth Century*, ed. Carleton Brown (Oxford, 1939), p. 119.
2. *Wisdom and Number: Toward a Critical Appraisal of the Middle English Religious Lyric* (Lincoln, Neb., 1962), pp.
160–61.

3. *Medieval English Poetry* (London,
1957), pp. 68–69.
4. In addition to Speirs, Manning cites
only one other exponent of the proposed
reading (see *Wisdom and Number*, p.
168). Since the publication of Manning's
monograph, another editor has given the
notion of "matelessness" equal, though
not necessarily primary status. See R. T.
Davies, *Medieval English Lyrics, A Critical Anthology* (London, 1964), p. 155 n.

illustration for the narrower sense (from *The Seven Sages*, 1425) is far removed from a connection with the Blessed Virgin Mary: the fact is scarcely accidental, for neither the fifteenth nor any preceding century furnishes a poetic instance in which she is designated mateless in the sense of "without a sexual companion."

The critical method employed in the revisionist reading of the poem fails to bring out either the individual qualities of the work or its traditional richness. Speirs supports his interpretation with a supposedly analogous example of wordplay from *Pearl*. But the *annominatio* in the earlier poem is overt, and is made, in contrast with "I Syng of a Myden," a conspicuous aspect of structure. The designation "maskeless" as applied to "perle" is distinctly emphasized between lines 733 and 756 (three or four times, depending on one's view of the putative scribal error); again in line 768 as a conclusion to the stanza, and as a link to the opening line of the stanza following; while the sounds of both words (makeless-maskless) are exploited in the stanza-concluding line 780, "A makelez may and maskelez," where the paronomasia is clearly a calculated effect.[5] Where in "Myden" is there evidence of such wordplay? Manning pleads that the idea of matelessness is developed in the poem; but the argument again rests on the suspect reading of *makeles*. The traditional idea of peerlessness, by contrast, is developed in the clearest way. The lines

> moder & mayden
> was neuer non but che—
> wel may swych a lady
> godes moder be

are a pointed reiteration of that idea. That this statement is a natural elaboration of stanza 1 is apparent from the very structure of the poem. After characterizing the Lady as unequaled, the poet cites what is for the purpose of his lyric her most remarkable act, *viz.*, choosing the King of Kings as her son. In the middle three stanzas the result of that act (the coming of Christ as dew) is amplified:

> he cam also stylle
> þer his moder was
> as dew in aprille,
> þat fallyt on þe gras.
>
> he came also stylle
> to his moderes bowr
> as dew in aprille,
> þat fallyt on þe flour.
>
> he came also stylle
> þer his moder lay
> as dew in aprille,
> þat fallyt on þe spray.

5. Citations are to *Pearl*, ed. E. V. Gordon (Oxford, 1953).

Finally, the poet rounds out his praise: the Lady, he repeats, is unique; in view of this singularity she is well entitled to be the Mother of God: "well may swych a lady / godes moder be." That she is being viewed quite squarely in this capacity cannot be over-stressed. The contention that Mary's matchlessness depends primarily on her lack of a sexual partner is profoundly anachronistic: it is to make the miracle of the birth of Christ a merely natural phenomenon. Mary gave birth to a son without experiencing sexual relations, to be sure; but the paramount significance is His divinity: the wonder is that this son is the Son of God.

Comparison with the thirteenth-century lyric which served as a source for "Myden" suggests that the later poet has preserved as his central concept the idea of the maiden's peerlessness and singularity; "of on ic wille singen þat is makeles, / þe king of halle kinges to moder he hire ches," the first of the couplets from which the "Myden" lyricist borrowed, underlines the cause of the Lady's uniqueness—it was she and she alone whom the Son of God elected for His Nativity. The second source-couplet expands on the same idea: "Maiden and moder nas neuer non wimon boten he— / well mitte he berigge of godes sune be."[6] It is clearly not the oddity of her sexual state which is the basis of the mother's supremacy among women, but the fact of her having been chosen for the divine purpose. Since the "Myden" poet believed not only that the designation "makeles" warranted being used again, but that it warranted being used conspicuously, centrally, and in the identical context, it is likely that he meant to preserve the original and already time-honored sense. Indeed, the later poet has if anything intensified the singularity of the lady by changing her state from passive to active: while in the earlier poem it was the Son of God who chose, in the later work it is Mary herself who elects.[7] The view that the later poet is deliberately altering the sense of the original lines on the basis of an obscure sexual criterion needs, to be credible, far stronger external and internal support than it has so far received.

The notion that the poet is attempting in any important sense to break with tradition is arguable at best. The imagery of the work, as Barbara C. Raw has shown, is uniformly conventional,[8] while no feature in the innumerable poems on Mary is more familiar than the paradox of the mother who is at once a maiden.[9] When one encounters one of the rare poems in which Mary's sexual status is more or less explicitly discussed, we see all the more clearly how

6. Citations are to *English Lyrics of the XIIIth Century*, ed. Carleton Brown (Oxford, 1932), p. 55.
7. For an analysis of some of the artistic consequences of this change see Leo Spitzer, *Essays on English and American Literature*, ed. Anna Hatcher (Princeton, 1962), p. 244.
8. "As Dew in Aprille," *MLR*, LV (1960), 411–14.
9. See, for example, the group of songs and prayers to the Virgin in *Religious Lyrics of the XVth Century*.

very much the "Myden" poem belongs to the mainstream of Marian praise.

> Seolcudliche ure louerd hit diȝte
> þat þu, maide wið-ute wère,
> þat al þis world bicluppe ne miȝte,
> þu sscholdest of þin boseme bere.
> We ne stiȝte ne þe ne pritȝte
> in side in lende ne elles-where———[1]

After this explanation of Mary's sexual innocence the poet explains

> Wo godes sune aliȝte wolde
> on eórþe al for ure sake,
> herre teȝen he him nolde
> þene þat maide to beon his make.   (57-60.)

The distinction drawn by the poet in these two passages is especially revealing. The author elicits sexual associations only in the first, and then only to show their inappropriateness to the Virgin, who lacks all carnal knowledge. Is the maiden then without a "make"? What she lacks, on the contrary, is a "were." The poet is speaking of a man, a sexual companion, and accordingly uses one of the oldest and most unambiguous words signifying the human male. But in the final stanza, where the emphasis falls on the action of "godes sune" as regards the maid, the poet employs the term "make," shifting his attention from the problem of a carnal companion, to the idea of a spiritual consort who will assist Christ in His mission—He could have no "herre teȝen."

On the possible theological implications of their views the proponents of an "ambiguous" reading of our poem are silent. Yet the notion that Mary is without a mate raises large issues indeed, for assuredly she did not lack a companion, or even, for that matter, a husband. One need only go to the New Testament (Matthew, 1:18-25) to be reminded that the marriage of Joseph and Mary was a fact, while no less an authority than St. Thomas (*Sum. Theol.*, P.A. III, q.XXIX,a.2) explains that Mary's vow of chastity was no bar to the validity of her marriage (following St. Augustine, *De Cons. Evang.*, *P.L.*, XXXIV, col. 1071-72). To be sure, Mary herself says she did not "know" a man—"Dixit autem Maria ad angelum: quomodo fiet istud quoniam virum non cognosco?". ["Then said Mary unto the angel, How shall this be, seeing I know not a man?"] (Luke, 1:34); but this is in no way to deny the reality of her marital bond to Joseph. That bond was essential for the protection of Mary, for the perpetuation of the mystery of the Incarnation, and indeed for the preservation of Mary's very chastity.

---

1. *English Lyrics of the XIIIth Century*, pp. 117–18, ll. 49–54.

To declare Mary *without a mate* is perilously close to declaring her *without Joseph*.

On the subject of punning Manning invokes the authority of Walter J. Ong,[2] but a cautionary note is in order here, for Father Ong's revealing analysis concerns intentional Latin wordplay from a very special area, medieval hymnody, and should be called into service only with careful qualification. To be sure punning occurs in English medieval vernacular verse; but it is exceedingly rare in a poem of the type—if one will, the subgenre—to which "I Syng of a Myden" belongs. The possibilities for ambiguity inherent in a word like *makeles* are the sort that, as Beatrice White has pointed out,[3] a medieval poet would be interested to explore, not so much in his vernacular tongue, but in Latin. This is not to endorse the suggestion that the "Myden" poet "may also be punning on the Latin *sine macula*" [*without spot*].[4] The latter word is not unknown in connection with the virgin, occurring, for example, in the line "ffor macula, modur, was neuur in þe"; but the poem in which it appears is macaronic and quite straightforwardly pious, inviting no search for covert verbal nuances.[5] On the other hand, the overtone which a pun on "macula" introduces into "I Syng of a Myden," generating as it would still further tensions and ambiguities, is out of keeping with the dominant tone of the whole. If the pun is intended, it is unique, so far as I am aware, in English verse and prose. From a negative point of view the "solution" to the problem is to disallow the proposed new readings; positively, it is to see the poem as the mature fruit, if not the *terminus ad quem*, of a venerable tradition. The compression of form, the simplicity of diction, and the purity of tone all suggest an intense distillation of ingredients old but still remarkably vital. The center of the poem is not any single aspect of the paradox of mother and maid, but the paradox itself; its strength is not verbal but conceptual. From that moment when the maiden makes the decision through which she is to become the mother of Christ ("kyng of alle kyngs / to here sone che ches") to that moment when the miraculous duality of her status is articulated in so many words ("moder & myden / was neuer non but che"), it is precisely this paradox of which the reader is made aware. Whereas the earlier poem states the paradox flatly, "I Syng of a Myden" dramatizes, showing the entire wondrous progress of Christ's emergence. The result, for the reader, is the realization that the Lady is remarkable not merely for choosing but for being chosen: she is without equal for what she did *and* for

2. "Wit and Mystery: A Revaluation in Mediaeval Latin Hymnody," *Speculum*, XXII (1947), 310–41; reprinted in *The Barbarian Within, and Other Fugitive Essays and Studies* (New York, 1962), pp. 88–130.

3. "Medieval Mirth," *Anglia*, LXXVIII (1960), 284–301.
4. *Wisdom and Number*, p. 169.
5. *Religious Lyrics of the XVth Century*, p. 65.

what happened to her. To emphasize the traditional character of this paradox is not to imply that "I Syng of a Myden" is indistinguishable from other works of its type; it is clearly better, and may well be the best of its kind. But the real excellence of the poem is in the way it exfoliates, as it were, from the very root of tradition, persuading the reader anew of the uniqueness, the peerlessness of the Lady who is its subject. The poet, far from rejecting the possibilities open to him through tradition, has turned to it as to an inexhaustible source of imaginative nourishment.

LEO SPITZER

[On "I sing of a maiden"]†

* * *

The "immediate observation" with which we shall start is the introduction into the traditional story of Christ's birth from a virgin of the element of "poetic time", by which term I mean the relative time allotted by the poet to the enunciation of his themes in correspondence with their weight or nature, "time" used as a poetic device, as a means of expression. Within the framework offered by the first and the last stanza of our poem, the three central stanzas, with their parallelistic structure and their repetitions, have an inherent solemnity, a *rallentando* quality which forces us to linger on their content: on the poet's simple assertion that Christ came to earth as a *natural* phenomenon comparable to the dew in April.

The first and the last stanza, the *exordium* and the *conclusio*, as it were, are conceived in rigorous parallelism as befits the framework of the poem: in each the first two lines predicate the perfection of Mary, in each the third line offers a proud, triumphantly ringing title, first of Christ ("King of all Kings", the phrase generally used of the Old Testament God, appears here without article —as a title), then of Mary ("such a lady"—I take the word in the meaning of "sovereign", "ruler", "queen", parallel to that of "ledy of lealte" in our first poem); in each the last line establishes the relationship, the son-hood of Christ, the motherhood of Mary.[1]

† From Leo Spitzer, "*Explication de Texte* Applied to Three Great Middle English Poems," *Archivum Linguisticum*, 3 (1951), 1–22, 137–165. Reprinted by permission of the publisher.

1. Along with the parallelism just pointed out one may note a different, a chiastic parallelism of the tenses used in stanzas 1 and 5:

present: st. I: *is*   st. 5: *was*
preterite: *ches*   *be*

The poem opens and closes with a statement in the present tense, presenting Mary as a timeless being. With the preterite of st. I (*ches*) we begin to proceed in time (a choice has been made at a given moment) and are thereby prepared for the unfolding of the event in time, described in the *narratio* of the three central stanzas. And the preterite opening in the final stanza ("was") offers a similar fusion with the preceding narrative (throughout presented in the preterite), but is itself not narrative in character and rather represents a judgment which must lead immediately to the timelessness of the final prediction ("never *was* none but she" must become "she alone *is*").

Whereas the title of Christ is announced (like a trumpet blast) at the beginning of the poem immediately following the statement of Mary's perfection, the poet withholds Mary's title until the end—until the great, miraculous event has taken place, which justifies, as it were, the title of "lady". At the same time, however, this title is offered as justifying the event: it is because she is "such a lady" that she may be "God's mother". To the modern reader, the circularity of such reasoning is startling: he is tempted to smile at the naive tautology which indeed is perhaps always involved in any proof of religious beliefs—even though he must concede that this naive intellectualism (the *Q.E.D* quality of *"well* may such a lady") is poetic.

We have just spoken of circularity of reasoning—but, perhaps, we should rather think in terms of spiral movement: "spiral", for with the last stanza, we are on a higher plane, and "movement", since in the three central stanzas we are offered not static explanation, but the re-enactment of an event which is the result of a fact announced in the first stanza: there we are informed of Mary's choice; in the stanzas that follow, we *experience* the event which is Christ's response to that choice. She chose—He came. All that Mary did was to choose: *Ecce ancilla tua.* [Behold your handmaiden.] And thus she elicited the divine response, the miracle. Her passive act made possible the manifestation of divine power. How great then must be the implicit primary power of the gentle maiden—how great a "lady" must Mary be![2] "Well may such a lady Goddes mother be", the poet tells us in the quietly elated tone of one concluding a demonstration. Now that we have *experienced* the miracle, the factual concluding statement has become incontrovertible and the theorem-like proposition of the first stanza is vindicated.

What of the miracle itself as described in the *narratio* of the three central stanzas? "He came al so still—as dew in April", that is, the miracle is immediately described in terms of a regular phenomenon in nature which works quietly, with unassuming consistency. A miracle is generally defined as the extraordinary suspension (for the benefit of a human being) of the laws of nature—but has not Augustine said that the greatest miracles are those which seem natural to us, the daily rising and setting of the sun, etc.? The regular functioning of the laws of nature is indeed the greatest of miracles. In our poem, by a somewhat reverse procedure, the greatest miracle of Christianity and the most dramatic event in the Augustinian picture of the history of mankind, the descent of the deity to

2. The quiescent nature of the Lady Mary, whose inner being elicits outward response, is, of course, also in harmony with the picture of the lady, as seen in courtly poetry, according to which the beloved lady must be self-contained and passive, her power being that of eliciting powerful reaction. As Ortega has pointed out, in the culminating periods of civilization, woman has the prerogative of *being*, action remaining the province of man.

earth, is portrayed with the stillness and undramatic sweetness of a phenomenon in nature which can be expected to happen according to general laws, but when it happens is always wondrous as on the first day of creation. Christ comes with the *fascinans* quality of the Christian *numinosum*, gentle, but all-pervasive. Suddenly the spring dew is here, one April morning, after the winter of our discontent (the winter of mankind's unredeemed age) has gone. The scene in our poem is indeed not that of Christmas, as in the previous carol, but of spring, the Easter setting of Resurrection. "Still" as the miracle of resurrection comes about in nature, it is all-pervasive in its quiet power: once dew is on the grass, it is also on the flower, it is also on the bush. The three stanzas which move in slow gracefulness make us sense this divine ubiquity—in terms of nature (and nature, as is well known, is never brought into art in the Middle Ages for nature's sake, but for the purpose of the demonstration of the divine). The cool freshness of the morning dew is allowed to convey to us the idea of the moral *refrigerium*, or the rejuvenation, brought to humanity by the Redeemer. There may be sensed a climax in the extension of the dew from the grass to the flower to the bush, and parallel to this development runs another concerned with the presentation of the Virgin: the line "there his mother was" (the demonstrative "there" being equal to the relative "where") indicates a minimum of locality, merely the fact that there was a place where Mary was; the line "to his mother's bower" provides an environment that befits a noblewoman (a "lady"); and finally the line "there his mother lay" delicately suggests the bed of child-birth. Just as in the treatment of the dew, we feel the movement of extension in space (symbolizing the ubiquity of divine grace), here the development goes from the abstract to the concrete: a point postulated in space becomes a lady's chamber, and from the abstract predication of her presence ("where his mother was") we come to a slight indication of the physical attitude of a recumbent woman receiving her new-born son—who comes, we must believe, not from within her, but from without, from above, like the gentle dew that falls softly from the heavens.[3] The two parallel series ("on the grass—on the flour—on the spray" and "there his mother was—to his mother's bour—there his mother lay") suggest two different movements: extension and contraction: while the vista of dew-covered nature expands, our gaze is attracted more and more insistently toward the focal point of divine grace. Or rather, divine grace at the same time that it is unstintedly expended and everywhere visible, manifests itself in creative concentration. She-who-chose and He-who-came are only two aspects of the same divine act. And the solemnity of the three slow-cadenced stanzas

3. Cf. *New English Dictionary*, s.v. *dew:* "Formerly supposed to fall softly from the heavens."

that tell us thrice of the same event, holding our attention by the
two devices of extending and contracting movement (which fall
into one) has been achieved in order to give us that feeling of par-
ticipation in an event for which the consciousness of the passage of
time is necessary. For any inner event is characterized by the feeling
of *durée réelle* [*actual duration*], as Bergson has called it: con-
versely, in order to give us the feeling for the reality of the event,
the impression of the passage of time was created—by a poet pos-
sessed, like Dante, of the sense for "poetic time".

Up to this point we have treated the comparison of Christ with
the dew as an original invention of our poet which allowed him to
depict the coming of the Saviour in terms of a natural miracle. The
question whether there exists a dogmatic basis for this comparison,
so poetically convincing, has purposely not been raised because of
my (tacit) pledge to the reader to "stay within the poem". I con-
fess that only by chance did I indeed discover a general dogmatic
basis for the comparison in question: by looking up (in connection
with a problem quite different from our poem) the article *manna* in
the *Thesaurus linguae latinae*. As is well known, the story of the
manna appears in Exodus, chapter 16, after the mention (v. 13)
that "dew lay in the morning round about the host" of the Israel-
ites wandering in the desert: "after the dew that lay was gone up"
they saw the manna which is defined (v. 14) as "a small round
thing, as small as the hoarfrost on the ground". The patristic writers
seem to have identified the *manna*="hoarfrost" with the "dew"
that preceded it, for Antoninus Placentinus writes:[4] "*ros* de caelo
quem manna appellant" (obviously a blend of vv. 13 and 14).[5] Later
the equation "manna"="dew" must have been followed by the
other equation, of the well-known prefigurative type,
"manna=Christ" and this we find in Pelagius: *manna figura cor-
poris Christi fuit*[6] and Augustine: *manna Christus tamquam panis
vivus*[7]: the manna which in the Old Testament served as bread to
the Jews wandering in the desert foreshadows (is a prefiguration of)
the spiritual food given to the Christian who may derive sustenance
in the form of the sacrament in which Christ's living body is present (in the words of the previous poem: "Every day it schewit in
prystes hond"). Given the two equations:

$$manna = dew$$
$$manna = Christ,$$

it must follow (according to the principle: if two things are equal
to a third, they must be equal to each other) that a third equation
is possible:

$$dew = Christ.$$

4. See *Itinerarium*, PL, LXXII, 897–918.
5. "Dew from heaven, which they call manna."
6. "Manna was a prefiguration of the body of Christ."
7. "Manna, Christ, the living bread."

This is the one we find expressed in our poem, with the intermediary concept "manna" eliminated—a condensation highly poetic in which is presented the direct identification of natural phenomenon and deity, without the burden of Biblical lore.

Now that the basic conceit of our poem has been found to be based on a traditional idea, should we feel disappointed and tempted to blame indiscreet philology for the disenchantment it may produce to the reader? But, granted the traditional character of the idea that manna is dew and Christ is manna (and consequently dew), we should not lose sight of the fact that our poet has proceeded as if unaware of such tradition. Not only is there no mention of manna as such: there is actually no direct identification, the "third equation" is presented as a simile ("He came al so still *as* dew in April"), as a simile that suggests poetically the mysterious comparability of divine action with natural development. We may conclude then that the simile of the dew, even though inspired by dogmatic literature, has been relived by this extraordinary poet who was able to give the pristine beauty of nature to a venerable scriptural concept.

And our admiration for the poet must increase still more when we learn that our fifteenth-century carol is a reworking of a quite mediocre longer thirteenth-century version (published by W. Greg, *Mod. Phil.*, VII, 165, also printed in Carleton Brown's anthology, No. 31):

> Nu þis fules singet hand maket hure blisse
> and þat gres up þringet and leued þe ris;
> of on ic wille singen þat is makeles,
> þe king of halle kinges to moder he hire ches.
>
> Heo his wit-uten sunne and wit-uten hore,
> I-cumen of kinges cunne of gesses more;
> þe louerd of monkinne of hire was yboren
> to bringen us hut of Sunne, elles wue weren for-lore.
>
> Gabriel hire grette and saide hire, "aue
> Marie ful of grace, vre louer be uit þe,
> þe frut of þire wombe ibleset mot id be.
> þu sal go wit chide, for sout ic suget þe."
>
> and þare gretinke þat angle hauede ibrout,
> he gon to bi-þenchen and meinde hire þout;
> he saide to þen angle, "hu may tiden þis?
> of monnes y-mone nout y nout iuis."
>
> Mayden heo was uid childe & Maiden her biforen,
> & maiden ar sot-hent hire chid was iboren;
> Maiden and moder nas neuer non wimon boten he—
> wel mitte he berigge of godes sune be.

I-blessed beo þat suete chid & þe moder ec,
& þe suete broste þat hir son sec;
I-hered ibe þe time þat such chid uas iboren,
þat lesed al of pine þat arre was for-lore.

As the editors mentioned above have pointed out, it is obvious
that lines 3-4 and 19-20 of this older lyric form the opening and
concluding lines of our poem while the repetitional part (the part
dealing with Christ as Dew) is an addition of our poet. The "not
very remarkable" thirteenth-century version is a quite traditional
poem about the Annunciation, including a mention of the tree of
Jesse, a transcription of the *Ave Maria* and a prayer at the end.
Both commentators remark on the uniqueness of a verbatim appro-
priation of thirteenth-century poetic material by a fifteenth-century
poet. Professor Greg adds a quotation from Gummere's book on the
"Popular Ballads" (p. 116) to the effect that "incremental repetition", as known in the ballads, occurs exceptionally in our fifteenth-
century lyric "as if 'dancing for joy' ". The latter remark must be
taken together with Gummere's derivation of the ballad from a
dance-song (as the term "ballad" implies). I may offer a typical
instance of incremental repetition from the ballad "Sir Patrick
Spence":

> And mony was the feather bed
>   That flatter'd on the faem;
> And mony was the gude lord's son
>   That never mair cam hame.

> O lang, lang may the ladies sit,
>   Wi' their fans into their hand,
> Before they see Sir Patrick Spens
>   Come sailing to the strand!

> And lang, lang may the maidens sit
>   Wi' their gowd kames in their hair,
> A-waiting for their ain dear loves!
>   For them they'll see nae mair.

Gummere and Greg evidently assume that from the ballad, originally a dance-song, the incremental repetition was extended to our
carol where it should express the "dancing for joy" of the believer.
But the genre of the carol originates in a dance-song too (cf.
Margot Sahlin, *Étude sur la carole médiévale*, Uppsala, 1940).
Moreover, parallelistic structure with word variation is characteristic
of English religious poetry, cf. the first poem contained in Brown's
anthology:

> Nou goth sonne vnder wod,—
> me reweth, marie, þi faire Rode.

Nou goth sonne vnder tre—
me reweth, marie, þi sone and þe.

A student in Romance will immediately be reminded of Old Portuguese popular dance-songs, the *cantares de amigo* sung (and danced) by women, parallelistic in style:

Levad' amigo que dormides as manhanas frias,
toda' las aves do mundo d'amor diziam.
Levad' amigo que dormide las frias manhanas,
toda' las aves do mundo d'amor cantavam.

Even though we must assume for the incremental repetition in our fifteenth-century carol the source of a dance-song (whether derived directly from popular dance-songs or ballads retraceable thereto), the fact is undeniable that this dance-element was secondarily introduced into a carol which showed no repetitions or parallelisms. That this happened as late as the fifteenth century (a period when incremental repetition occurs also in the ballads), this fact must testify to a changed *Zeitgefühl*, a change in sensibility by which the inner evidence of a feeling is rendered dramatically in terms of the passage of time (as opposed to the indifference to poetic time of the high Middle Ages as evidenced in the thirteenth-century version of our carol): the "dancing for joy" occurs precisely in that section of the fifteenth-century carol in which the miracle of the Nativity is re-enacted. Moreover, the introduction of the incremental repetition, so essential for "poetic timing", must be seen in connection with another alteration which our commentators have failed to notice: l. 4 of the older version reads: *þe king of hall kinges to moder he hire ches* (notice *to moder*, not "to His mother"), ll. 3-4 of the more recent version: *King of all kings / To her son she ches.* If we take the former rendering together with l. 20 of the same version: *well mitte he berigge of godes sune be,* we must infer that in this version it was God the Father who chose Mary to be the mother of his son, whereas in the new version it is the Virgin who chooses her divine son (thereby deserving the title of a Lady). It was this all-important change that brought an inner dramatic movement (which was then explicited in the incremental repetition) into the poem. Mary is here not a purely passive instrument of the will of God, but active-passive: by her "choice" she unleashes the divine, or natural, forces which will bring about the miracle of His coming. The poet has cut off two significant couplets from the older version, those dealing with the beginning and the end of the development—to fill the gap not only by what our too technical-minded commentators call "incremental repetition" (a balladesque device), but precisely by the reenactment of the miracle. There is a threefold activity to be observed on the part of our poet: his changing of

Mary's inaction into dramatic action, his selection from a banal
sequence of lines of two climactic couplets producing a *rondo* effect
and his addition of a new *adagio* part which renders, by a musicality
all its own, an inner experience transcending all experience.

* * *

Select Bibliography

PRINCIPAL COLLECTIONS OF MIDDLE ENGLISH LYRICS

Brook, G. L., ed. *The Harley Lyrics.* Fourth ed. Manchester, 1968. [A facsimile edition of British Museum MS. Harley 2253 has been edited by N. R. Ker for the Early English Text Society, no. 255, London, 1964.]

Brown, Carleton, ed. *English Lyrics of the Thirteenth Century.* Oxford, 1932.

Brown, Carleton, ed. *Religious Lyrics of the Fifteenth Century.* Oxford, 1939.

Brown, Carleton, and G. V. Smithers, eds. *Religious Lyrics of the Fourteenth Century.* Second ed. (corrected). Oxford, 1957

Davies, R. T., ed. *Medieval English Lyrics. A Critical Anthology.* London, 1963.

Greene, R. L., ed. *The Early English Carols.* Oxford, 1935. [Greene has also issued a smaller *Selection of English Carols*, Oxford, 1962.]

Person, Henry, ed. *Cambridge Middle English Lyrics.* Seattle, 1953.

Robbins, R. H., ed. *Secular Lyrics of the Fourteenth and Fifteenth Centuries.* Second ed. Oxford, 1955.

Robbins, R. H., ed. *Historical Poems of the Fourteenth and Fifteenth Centuries.* New York, 1959.

Robbins, R. H., ed. *Early English Christmas Carols.* New York, 1961.

MUSIC

Stainer, J. F. R., and C. Stainer. *Early Bodleian Music.* 2 vols. London, 1901.

SCHOLARSHIP AND CRITICISM

Bowra, Sir Maurice. *Mediaeval Love-Song.* London, 1961. [A summary, informative survey of medieval European love lyric.]

Brown, Carleton, and R. H. Robbins. *The Index of Middle English Verse.* New York, 1943. See also R. H. Robbins and J. L. Cutler. *Supplement to the Index of Middle English Verse.* Lexington, Ky., 1965. [These volumes index poems by first lines and provide essential information about MSS and printed texts.]

Chambers, Sir E. K. "Some Aspects of Medieval Lyric," *Early English Lyrics,* ed. E.K. Chambers and F. Sidgwick. London, 1907; reprinted 1926, 1967.

Chambers, Sir E. K. "The Carol and Fifteenth-Century Lyric," *English Literature at the Close of the Middle Ages.* Oxford, 1945.

Dronke, Peter. *Medieval Latin and the Rise of European Love-Lyric.* 2 vols. Oxford, 1965–66. [A magisterial work. Vol. II contains many Latin texts with English translation.]

Dronke, Peter. *The Medieval Lyric.* New York, 1969. [An admirable introduction to the subject from a European perspective, with interpolated texts and translations from several languages, and extensive bibliographies.]

Kane, George. *Middle English Literature: A Critical Study of the Romances, the Religious Lyrics, Piers Plowman.* Part II. London, 1951.

Lever, J. W. *The Elizabethan Love Sonnet.* London, 1956. [Ch. I is a good discussion of Petrarch's love poetry and its background.]

Manning, Stephen. *Wisdom and Number: Toward a Critical Appraisal of the Middle English Religious Lyric.* Lincoln, Neb., 1962.

Moore, A. K. *The Secular Lyric in Middle English.* Lexington, Ky., 1951.

Oliver, Raymond. *Poems Without Names: The English Lyric 1200–1500.* Berkeley, Calif., 1970.

Reiss, Edmund. "A Critical Approach to the Middle English Lyric," *College English,* 27 (1965–66), 373–79.

Reiss, Edmund. *The Art of the Middle English Lyric.* Athens, Georgia, 1972.

Robbins, R. H. "Middle English Lyrics: Handlist of New Texts," *Anglia,* 83 (1965), 35–47.

352 · *Select Bibliography*

Speirs, John. *Medieval English Poetry: The Non-Chaucerian Tradition.* London, 1957.

Spitzer, Leo. *"Explication de Texte* Applied to Three Great Middle English Poems," *Archivum Linguisticum,* 3 (1951), 1–22, 137–65. Reprinted in Anna Hatcher, ed., *Essays on English and American Literature by Leo Spitzer.* Princeton, N.J., 1962. [Subtle and philologically sophisticated studies of "Ichot a burde in boure bright," "I sing of a maiden," and "Lestenyt, Lordynges, both elde and yinge."]

Stevick, R. D. "The Criticism of Middle English Lyrics," *Modern Philology,* 64 (1966), 103–17.

Weber, Sarah A. *Theology and Poetry in the Middle English Lyric.* Columbus, Ohio, 1969.

Wilhelm, J. J. *The Cruelest Month: Spring, Nature, and Love in Classical and Medieval Lyrics.* New Haven, Conn., 1965.

Woolf, Rosemary. *The English Religious Lyric in the Middle Ages.* Oxford, 1968. [The most distinguished book on the Middle English lyric.]

Index of First Lines

ANDERSON *Winesburg, Ohio* edited by Charles E. Modlin and Ray Lewis White
AQUINAS *St. Thomas Aquinas on Politics and Ethics* translated and edited by
Paul E. Sigmund
AUSTEN *Emma* edited by Stephen M. Parrish Second Edition
AUSTEN *Mansfield Park* edited by Claudia L. Johnson
AUSTEN *Persuasion* edited by Patricia Meyer Spacks
AUSTEN *Pride and Prejudice* edited by Donald Gray Second Edition
BEHN *Oroonoko* edited by Joanna Lipking
Beowulf (the Donaldson translation) edited by Joseph F. Tuso
BLAKE *Blake's Poetry and Designs* selected and edited by Mary Lynn Johnson and
John E. Grant
BOCCACCIO *The Decameron* selected, translated, and edited by Mark Musa and
Peter E. Bondanella
BRONTË, CHARLOTTE *Jane Eyre* edited by Richard J. Dunn Second Edition
BRONTË, EMILY *Wuthering Heights* edited by William M. Sale, Jr., and Richard Dunn
Third Edition
BROWNING, ELIZABETH BARRETT *Aurora Leigh* edited by Margaret Reynolds
BROWNING, ROBERT *Browning's Poetry* selected and edited by James F. Loucks
BURNEY *Evelina* edited by Stewart J. Cooke
BYRON *Byron's Poetry* selected and edited by Frank D. McConnell
CARROLL *Alice in Wonderland* edited by Donald J. Gray Second Edition
CERVANTES *Don Quixote* (the Ormsby translation, revised) edited by Joseph R. Jones and
Kenneth Douglas
CHAUCER *The Canterbury Tales: Nine Tales and the General Prologue* edited by
V. A. Kolve and Glending Olson
CHEKHOV *Anton Chekhov's Plays* translated and edited by Eugene K. Bristow
CHEKHOV *Anton Chekhov's Short Stories* selected and edited by Ralph E. Matlaw
CHOPIN *The Awakening* edited by Margo Culley Second Edition
CLEMENS *Adventures of Huckleberry Finn* edited by Sculley Bradley,
Richmond Croom Beatty, E. Hudson Long, and Thomas Cooley Second Edition
CLEMENS *A Connecticut Yankee in King Arthur's Court* edited by Allison R. Ensor
CLEMENS *Pudd'nhead Wilson and Those Extraordinary Twins* edited by Sidney E. Berger
CONRAD *Heart of Darkness* edited by Robert Kimbrough Third Edition
CONRAD *Lord Jim* edited by Thomas C. Moser Second Edition
CONRAD *The Nigger of the "Narcissus"* edited by Robert Kimbrough
CRANE *Maggie: A Girl of the Streets* edited by Thomas A. Gullason
CRANE *The Red Badge of Courage* edited by Donald Pizer Third Edition
DARWIN *Darwin* selected and edited by Philip Appleman Second Edition
DEFOE *A Journal of the Plague Year* edited by Paula R. Backscheider
DEFOE *Moll Flanders* edited by Edward Kelly
DEFOE *Robinson Crusoe* edited by Michael Shinagel Second Edition
DE BALZAC *Père Goriot* translated by Burton Raffel edited by Peter Brooks
DE PIZAN *The Selected Writings of Christine de Pizan* translated by Renate
Blumenfeld-Kosinski and Kevin Brownlee edited by Renate Blumenfeld-Kosinski
DICKENS *Bleak House* edited by George Ford and Sylvère Monod
DICKENS *David Copperfield* edited by Jerome H. Buckley
DICKENS *Hard Times* edited by George Ford and Sylvère Monod Second Edition
DICKENS *Oliver Twist* edited by Fred Kaplan
DONNE *John Donne's Poetry* selected and edited by Arthur L. Clements Second Edition
DOSTOEVSKY *The Brothers Karamazov* (the Garnett translation) edited by Ralph E. Matlaw
DOSTOEVSKY *Crime and Punishment* (the Coulson translation) edited by George Gibian
Third Edition
DOSTOEVSKY *Notes from Underground* translated and edited by Michael R. Katz

DOUGLASS *Narrative of the Life of Frederick Douglass, an American Slave, Written by Himself* edited by William L. Andrews and William S. McFeely
DREISER *Sister Carrie* edited by Donald Pizer Second Edition
Eight Modern Plays edited by Anthony Caputi
ELIOT *Middlemarch* edited by Bert G. Hornback
ELIOT *The Mill on the Floss* edited by Carol T. Christ
ERASMUS *The Praise of Folly and Other Writings* translated and edited by Robert M. Adams
FAULKNER *The Sound and the Fury* edited by David Minter Second Edition
FIELDING *Joseph Andrews with Shamela and Related Writings* edited by Homer Goldberg
FIELDING *Tom Jones* edited by Sheridan Baker Second Edition
FLAUBERT *Madame Bovary* edited with a substantially new translation by Paul de Man
FORD *The Good Soldier* edited by Martin Stannard
FORSTER *Howards End* edited by Paul B. Armstrong
FRANKLIN *Benjamin Franklin's Autobiography* edited by J. A. Leo Lemay and P. M. Zall
FULLER *Woman in the Nineteenth Century* edited by Larry J. Reynolds
GOETHE *Faust* translated by Walter Arndt, edited by Cyrus Hamlin
GOGOL *Dead Souls* (the Reavey translation) edited by George Gibian
HARDY *Far from the Madding Crowd* edited by Robert C. Schweik
HARDY *Jude the Obscure* edited by Norman Page
HARDY *The Mayor of Casterbridge* edited by James K. Robinson
HARDY *The Return of the Native* edited by James Gindin
HARDY *Tess of the d'Urbervilles* edited by Scott Elledge Third Edition
HAWTHORNE *The Blithedale Romance* edited by Seymour Gross and Rosalie Murphy
HAWTHORNE *The House of the Seven Gables* edited by Seymour Gross
HAWTHORNE *Nathaniel Hawthorne's Tales* edited by James McIntosh
HAWTHORNE *The Scarlet Letter* edited by Seymour Gross, Sculley Bradley, Richmond Croom Beatty, and E. Hudson Long Third Edition
HERBERT *George Herbert and the Seventeenth-Century Religious Poets* selected and edited by Mario A. DiCesare
HERODOTUS *The Histories* translated and selected by Walter E. Blanco, edited by Walter E. Blanco and Jennifer Roberts
HOBBES *Leviathan* edited by Richard E. Flathman and David Johnston
HOMER *The Odyssey* translated and edited by Albert Cook Second Edition
HOWELLS *The Rise of Silas Lapham* edited by Don L. Cook
IBSEN *The Wild Duck* translated and edited by Dounia B. Christiani
JAMES *The Ambassadors* edited by S. P. Rosenbaum Second Edition
JAMES *The American* edited by James W. Tuttleton
JAMES *The Portrait of a Lady* edited by Robert D. Bamberg Second Edition
JAMES *Tales of Henry James* edited by Christof Wegelin
JAMES *The Turn of the Screw* edited by Robert Kimbrough
JAMES *The Wings of the Dove* edited by J. Donald Crowley and Richard A. Hocks
JONSON *Ben Jonson and the Cavalier Poets* selected and edited by Hugh Maclean
JONSON *Ben Jonson's Plays and Masques* selected and edited by Robert M. Adams
KAFKA *The Metamorphosis* translated and edited by Stanley Corngold
LAFAYETTE *The Princess of Clèves* edited and with a revised translation by John D. Lyons
MACHIAVELLI *The Prince* translated and edited by Robert M. Adams Second Edition
MALTHUS *An Essay on the Principle of Population* edited by Philip Appleman
MANN *Death in Venice* translated and edited by Clayton Koelb
MARX *The Communist Manifesto* edited by Frederic L. Bender
MELVILLE *The Confidence-Man* edited by Hershel Parker
MELVILLE *Moby-Dick* edited by Harrison Hayford and Hershel Parker
MEREDITH *The Egoist* edited by Robert M. Adams
Middle English Lyrics selected and edited by Maxwell S. Luria and Richard L. Hoffman
Middle English Romances selected and edited by Stephen H. A. Shepherd
MILL *Mill* selected and edited by Alan Ryan

MILL *On Liberty* edited by David Spitz

MILTON *Paradise Lost* edited by Scott Elledge Second Edition

Modern Irish Drama edited by John P. Harrington

MORE *Utopia* translated and edited by Robert M. Adams Second Edition

NEWMAN *Apologia Pro Vita Sua* edited by David J. DeLaura

NEWTON *Newton* edited by I. Bernard Cohen and Richard S. Westfall

NORRIS *McTeague* edited by Donald Pizer Second Edition

Restoration and Eighteenth-Century Comedy edited by Scott McMillin Second Edition

RICH *Adrienne Rich's Poetry and Prose* edited by Barbara Charlesworth Gelpi and Albert Gelpi

ROUSSEAU *Rousseau's Political Writings* edited by Alan Ritter and translated by Julia Conaway Bondanella

ST. PAUL *The Writings of St. Paul* edited by Wayne A. Meeks

SHAKESPEARE *Hamlet* edited by Cyrus Hoy Second Edition

SHAKESPEARE *Henry IV, Part I* edited by James L. Sanderson Second Edition

SHAW *Bernard Shaw's Plays* edited by Warren Sylvester Smith

SHELLEY *Frankenstein* edited by Paul Hunter

SHELLEY *Shelley's Poetry and Prose* selected and edited by Donald H. Reiman and Sharon B. Powers

SMOLLETT *Humphry Clinker* edited by James L. Thorson

SOPHOCLES *Oedipus Tyrannus* translated and edited by Luci Berkowitz and Theodore F. Brunner

SPENSER *Edmund Spenser's Poetry* selected and edited by Hugh Maclean and Anne Lake Prescott Third Edition

STENDHAL *Red and Black* translated and edited by Robert M. Adams

STERNE *Tristram Shandy* edited by Howard Anderson

STOKER *Dracula* edited by Nina Auerbach and David Skal

STOWE *Uncle Tom's Cabin* edited by Elizabeth Ammons

SWIFT *Gulliver's Travels* edited by Robert A. Greenberg Second Edition

SWIFT *The Writings of Jonathan Swift* edited by Robert A. Greenberg and William B. Piper

TENNYSON *In Memoriam* edited by Robert H. Ross

TENNYSON *Tennyson's Poetry* selected and edited by Robert W. Hill, Jr.

THACKERAY *Vanity Fair* edited by Peter Shillingsburg

THOREAU *Walden and Resistance to Civil Government* edited by William Rossi Second Edition

THUCYDIDES *The Peloponnesian War* translated by Walter Blanco edited by Walter Blanco and Jennifer Tolbert Roberts

TOLSTOY *Anna Karenina* edited and with a revised translation by George Gibian Second Edition

TOLSTOY *Tolstoy's Short Fiction* edited and with revised translations by Michael R. Katz

TOLSTOY *War and Peace* (the Maude translation) edited by George Gibian Second Edition

TOOMER *Cane* edited by Darwin T. Turner

TURGENEV *Fathers and Sons* translated and edited by Michael R. Katz

VOLTAIRE *Candide* translated and edited by Robert M. Adams Second Edition

WASHINGTON *Up from Slavery* edited by William L. Andrews

WATSON *The Double Helix: A Personal Account of the Discovery of the Structure of DNA* edited by Gunther S. Stent

WHARTON *Ethan Frome* edited by Kristin O. Lauer and Cynthia Griffin Wolff

WHARTON *The House of Mirth* edited by Elizabeth Ammons

WHITMAN *Leaves of Grass* edited by Sculley Bradley and Harold W. Blodgett

WILDE *The Picture of Dorian Gray* edited by Donald L. Lawler

WOLLSTONECRAFT *A Vindication of the Rights of Woman* edited by Carol H. Poston Second Edition

WORDSWORTH *The Prelude: 1799, 1805, 1850* edited by Jonathan Wordsworth, M. H. Abrams, and Stephen Gill